THE WAR ON TERRORISM

A Collision of Values, Strategies, and Societies

THE WAR ON TERRORISM

A Collision of Values, Strategies, and Societies

Thomas A. Johnson

CRC Press
Taylor & Francis Group
Boca Raton London New York

CRC Press is an imprint of the
Taylor & Francis Group, an **informa** business

CRC Press
Taylor & Francis Group
6000 Broken Sound Parkway NW, Suite 300
Boca Raton, FL 33487-2742

Printed in the United States of America on acid-free paper
10 9 8 7 6 5 4 3 2 1

International Standard Book Number-13: 978-1-4200-7987-6 (Hardcover)

Visit the Taylor & Francis Web site at
http://www.taylorandfrancis.com

and the CRC Press Web site at
http://www.crcpress.com

Dedication

For our daughter Jacquelyn, her husband Jason Lee, and our two grandsons Collin Thomas and Sean Kenton.

Contents

Preface

As a result of the attacks on our nation on September 11, 2001, President George W. Bush declared a war on terrorism and in the process notified all nations that the United States would take action not only against terrorist organizations, but also any organization or nation-state that supported or provided assistance to terrorist groups, including and especially Al Qaeda. There has been a great deal of discussion as to how one launches a war against terrorism, how one measures and evaluates the programs of such a war, and if indeed a war is even the appropriate vehicle to use in attacking terrorist activities and terrorist groups. Some have suggested that terrorism is a "tool" that should be eradicated and that it is the ideology of the terrorist group that must be addressed and challenged and it is their ideology that must be defeated. To defeat ideological views that would encourage the use of terrorism as a tool, one needs more than a military, because it is the ideological philosophy that must be disputed and refuted. Clearly, there is a role and necessity for using military, intelligence, diplomatic, and national approaches to both contain and eliminate the use of terrorism as a weapon. However, this by itself is not sufficient, as the ideological grounding of the terrorist organization must be rejected and rejected by the societal groups it seeks to recruit as adherents.

This book discusses our war on terrorism and identifies the movement of globalization as the process most Islamic jihadist terrorist groups view as counter to their ideological beliefs and to the values they hold sacred to their very fundamentalist Islamic views. In essence, Al Qaeda and other Islamic jihadist terrorist groups view globalization by Western societies in general, and the United States in particular, as the perpetrator of a new form of "colonialism" that will continue to undermine their Islamic societies. Furthermore, this growing movement of Islamic jihadists also rejects the rulers of the Middle Eastern nations as corrupt and not practicing the more fundamentalist view of Islam. Therefore, we really do not have a clash of civilizations as much as a clash between a branch of very militant fundamentalist Muslims and more moderate Muslims. It is on this premise that ideology must be addressed and not solely by Western society and its armies, but by those moderate and progressive Muslims and their religious leaders who are capable of rebutting the medieval underpinnings of the Al Qaeda jihadist interpretation of Islam.

Because many terrorist groups, including Al Qaeda, are seeking weapons of mass destruction and have stated publicly they will use these weapons not only against our nation but other Western societies as well, we must be organized and continue to use our intelligence apparatus as well as our military to prevent this possibility. To do otherwise would be irresponsible and a dereliction of the executive responsibilities that our nation's leaders have to protect our national security. Therefore, this book discusses in Chapter 1, "Globalization, Ideology, and the Clash of Societies," the elements of the religious beliefs and environmental stress points that are attached to societies' abilities to grow and prosper.

Chapter 2, "Terrorism, Islamic Insurgency, or Religious War," discusses and characterizes what is entailed in a global war on terrorism. What are the tools that terrorist groups are using and how effective are counterterrorist instruments against the Islamic jihadist terrorist groups?

Chapter 3, "Targets of Terrorists," examines our nation's infrastructure targets most vulnerable to attack by terrorist organizations.

Chapter 4, "Weapons of Mass Destruction," explains our vulnerabilities to the five major categories of WMDs, namely chemical, biological, radiological, nuclear, and agricultural weaponization.

Chapter 5, "Our Intelligence Community," provides current descriptions of roles, responsibilities, and duties of each of our nation's 16 intelligence agencies, including our new Office of the Director of National Intelligence.

Chapter 6, "The Reform and Reorganization of our Intelligence Community," discusses the beginning of our nation's need for intelligence and describes activities from 1947 to 1993 in an era regarded as our "cold war" years. The intelligence agencies activities during two Gulf wars, the September 11, 2001 attack, and the Congressional reviews and assessments leading to a major intelligence reorganization are described. Three major transformational challenges are presented as important future issues requiring immediate action.

Chapter 7, "National Security and Counterterrorism Policy Formulation: Transformational Issues and Challenges," discusses the instruments of statecraft available to our nation for use as counterterrorism tools along with the Constitutional issues involved in their respective applications and uses. Major transformational issues and challenges are analyzed such as the role conflict between our National Security Council and the U.S. State Department. Also, the use of back-channel communications and negotiations with terrorist groups despite U.S. stated policy counter to this practice are discussed. Politically sensitive and counterintuitive policy formulation regarding national intelligence estimates, military options, and use of force with rules of engagement issues are also analyzed in terms of national and global values and challenges.

Chapter 8, "Future Trends in Global Terrorism: Mapping the Strategy to Defeat an Ideology," summarizes the challenge of globalization and how Islamic jihadist ideology is attempting to create terrorism to stop the movement of globalization. The trends in global terrorism are presented particularly in terms of linear and future estimates and forecasts through 2015 and 2020. Finally, 12 nation-states are discussed in terms of the issues and challenges they will present to the United States in the 21st century. These nation-states are:

India–Pakistan
Palestine–Israel
South Korea–North Korea
Syria
Saudi Arabia
Russia
China–Taiwan
Iran

In summary, our nation has many challenges to confront in the years that lie ahead, and it will require great resolve to combat the growing movement of terrorism throughout the Middle East. Given the continuing proliferation of nuclear weapons and the expanding availability of other weapons of mass destruction, we must be extraordinarily vigilant in protecting our nation. Our intelligence community is convinced that already some of these weapons of mass destruction are in the hands of terrorist organizations, and that the question is not "if" they will be used, but "when" and "where." This is not an acceptable state of affairs, and undoubtedly, resolution will require an intelligence community that has the full support, respect, and appreciation of our entire nation.

Acknowledgments

To my wife Colleen, whose patience, guidance, and editorial skills made this book possible through her steadfast support and enduring belief in my labor to produce this textbook. Susan Cusano's excellent support in the preparation of this manuscript was greatly appreciated. Jill Jurgensen and Carolyn Spence have both been vital to the preparation, completion, and publication of this manuscript, and we are grateful for their efforts on our behalf.

Author

Thomas A. Johnson, PhD, is co-founder and chairman of the board of directors of the California Sciences Institute, and also serves as a member of the board of directors of the SANS Technology Institute. Dr. Johnson is one of the founding partners of the Forensic Data Center, a company focused on computer forensics. He earned bachelor's and master's degrees from Michigan State University and a doctorate from the University of California—Berkeley.

Dr. Johnson founded the Center for Cybercrime and Forensic Computer Investigation and the Forensic Computer Investigation Graduate Program. Additionally, Dr. Johnson was responsible for developing the online program in Information Protection and Security and also founded the Graduate National Security Programs offered at two of our National Nuclear Security Administration Laboratories in California and New Mexico.

Currently, Dean Johnson serves as a member of the FBI Infraguard program and also is a member of the Electronic Crime Task Force, New York Field Office, U.S. Secret Service. The United States attorney general appointed him a member of the Information Technology Working Group, and he served as chair of the Task Force Group on Combating High Technology Crime for the National Institute of Justice. Dr. Johnson was also appointed an advisor to the Judicial Council of California on the Court Technology Task Force by the California Supreme Court.

Dr. Johnson has published five books, 13 refereed articles, holds copyrights on four software programs, and his chapter on "Infrastructure Warriors: A Threat to the U.S. Homeland by Organized Crime" was published by the Strategic Studies Institute of the U.S. Army War College. In addition to lecturing at the U.S. Army War College, he has also lectured at the Federal Law Enforcement Training Center and numerous universities.

Dr. Johnson has appeared in both state and federal courts as an expert witness and was a member of the Select Ad Hoc Presidential Investigative Committee and consultant to the American Academy of Forensic Sciences in the case of Sirhan B. Sirhan regarding evaluation of ballistics and physical evidence concerning the assassination of U.S. Senator Robert F. Kennedy.

1 Globalization, Ideology, and the Clash of Societies

Globalization entails a networked global economy based on the unrestricted flow of information, ideas, cultural values, financial instruments, trade, and commerce among nations throughout the world. Fundamental to the globalization of a world economy is the establishment of new international rules, treaties, and institutions such as the International Monetary Fund and the World Trade Organization. The impact of the movement of globalization has been the potential trade-off or loss of certain domestic and sovereign prerogatives, in favor of more of an international set of requirements and rules. Globalization has been sold to nations throughout the world as able to more effectively create a world economy that will benefit all participating nations by improving their economic structures and strengthening their political stability.

Many people have viewed globalization as an opportunity for improving their financial status and capabilities, but others fear this movement will result in their loss of power and the ability of small power elites with little or no accountability for their actions to rule over a majority with little recourse for policies. In fact, in both Europe and the United States, we have seen many outbreaks of protest and violence when meetings on globalization were held.

The Middle East does present a very different and unusual situation because most of the Middle Eastern nations are controlled by royal families or a monarch whose income is based on oil revenue and they see no reason to fully engage or participate in fear that they will experience a diminishment of their sovereignty. In addition to the ruling parties not fully embracing globalization within the Middle Eastern nations, we also see the birth of an ideology by Islamic militant fundamentalists who see globalization as a form of "colonialism" sponsored by the United States and other Western societies. This ideology has been premised on a form of religious extremism, and Islamic jihadist terrorist groups are creating great political instability in the Middle East accompanied by terrorist activities and attacks. In short, Osama bin Laden has positioned Al Qaeda as an alternative to the intrusion of what he terms United States "colonialism" in the form of globalization, and his message throughout the Middle East has been to reject the Western-dominated globalization, as well as those he believes in the Middle East to be corrupt royal ruling families and monarchs who are not practicing his form of militant fundamentalist Islam.

In his book, *The Pentagon's New Map: Blueprint for Action*, Thomas Barnett relates how globalization has spread to encompass two thirds of the world's population, defined as the "Global Economy's Functioning Core," and how one third of humanity remains trapped outside the connected global economy into what he terms the "Non-Integrating Gap."

> Since the end of the Cold War, all the wars and civil wars and genocide have occurred within the gap, and so my vision of ending war "as we know it" begins with shrinking this gap and ends with making globalization truly global and eradicating the disconnectedness that defines danger in the world today.[1]

The National Intelligence Council's *Global Trends 2015: A Dialogue about the Future with Non-Government Experts* states that those regions, countries, and groups feeling left behind in this globalization process will face deepening economic stagnation, political instability, and cultural alienation, and as a result they will foster political, ethnic, ideological, and religious extremism along with the violence that frequently accompanies it.[2] Resentment of globalization as a Western intrusion into their holy lands will be widespread, and Osama bin Laden's Islamic jihad will become a very attractive alternative to both the Western globalization and those ruling families and monarchs that permit this intrusion into Islamic nations. This brand of fundamental and militant Islam will become an option for millions of Muslims throughout the Middle East.

Samuel P. Huntington's essay on "the clash of civilizations" brings forward his hypothesis that the great divisions among humankind and the dominating source of conflict will be cultural. The clash of civilizations will dominate global politics and the fault lines between civilizations will be the battle lines of the future. In Huntington's view, the world will be shaped by the interaction of eight major civilizations: Western, Confucian, Japanese, Islamic, Hindu, Slavic-Orthodox, Latin-American, and African civilizations.[3]

Each civilization will be differentiated by its respective history, language, culture, traditions, and religion. Inasmuch as these differences are the product of centuries of values passed from one generation to another they are more fundamentally a part of these societies than even their political ideologies and political regimes. Accordingly, the clash of civilizations will occur over the struggle for territory and economic superiority as each civilization pursues its political and religious values.[4]

Conflict between Western and Islamic civilizations has a history of over 1300 years and Huntington states that the conflict is unlikely to decline and could even become more virulent. In fact, the jihadist militancy that uses a narrow view of Islamic religion is actually pursuing a political agenda to further efforts to destroy Western civilizations and rebuild their brand of fundamentalism on a new world order.

This chapter discusses how religion, moral certainty, and fundamentalism can on occasion yield to unreasonable positions. The fragile environment that permits some societies to succeed and causes others collapse is analyzed from a range of decision-making errors that involve government policymakers dating from past events in Cuba to current events in Iraq, and the implication these decisions have had on our contemporary presence in Iraq. Finally, the role of the university and research in the war on terrorism is filled with both opportunities and tension and must be more thoughtfully embraced by both our government authorities and our university community as well.

This chapter is organized around the following format.

1. The Clash of Societies
2. Religion, Moral Certainty, and Fundamentalism
3. Our Fragile Environment: How Societies Collapse
   - A. Decision-Making Errors in Policy
   - B. Decision-Making Errors in Structure
   - C. Policy Formulation Problems from Cuba to Iraq
   - D. Environmental Factors
4. The Management and Mitigation of Risk
   - A. Risk Assessment
   - B. Survivability of Societies
5. The Role of the University and Research in the War on Terrorism
   - A. World War II
   - B. The Cold War
   - C. Sputnik
   - D. End of the Cold War
   - E. Post-September 11, 2001 Attack
6. Summary

Endnotes

1. The Clash of Societies

All nations have in common an historical record and methods on which they have transferred their values, norms, and mores from one generation to another. Deeply embedded within each society are religious values and dogmas that have attached as a major part of the culturalization process of each new generation. The rules and laws each nation has adopted for its governance structure and for transmitting the deeply held values will vary from one nation to another. The arrival of new forms of technology that permit communication capabilities that instantly connect one nation to another, that permit individuals to anonymously interact with one another through the Internet, and to engage in business and commercial enterprise through new forms of globalizations have in effect reduced the cultural walls of isolation and separateness throughout the world. More important, the digital electronic revolution has seriously challenged, if not eroded, the abilities of societies to continue to transfer their cultural norms and mores. Consequently, the value systems of most nations are now in a process of reformulation in some and outright revolution in other nations.

We, in the 21st century, are witnessing a clash of societies that results from a collision of values brought about by deeply held religious dogma of the major religions of Christianity, Islam, Judaism, Hinduism, Confucianism, agnosticism, and Buddhism. The collision of religious dogma and values is also exacerbated by the collision of orthodox theology and religious liberalism. Further complicating this collision of values are the major Western philosophies of religion colliding with the major Eastern philosophies. The role of faith, the afterlife, and the definition of man as a sinner all have come to visit us in the 21st century, and more specifically, on September 11, 2001, a date we refer to as our 9–11 tragedy of unparalleled terrorism. This terrorist attack on the United States by Al Qaeda resulted in President George W. Bush declaring a war on terrorism, not only against terrorist organizations, but also against any state or nation that supports or gives comfort to such terrorist groups.

To conceive how someone would launch a war on terrorism is much more complex than one would imagine at first glance. The values of nations and societies that have been shaped by their historical heritage cannot in one day, or one event as horrendous as the 9–11 tragedy was, be reshaped to fully embrace and participate in a war on terrorism. The number of strategic and tactical questions and assumptions involved in defining, measuring, and evaluating such an effort are explored in greater detail later in this book, but first we must characterize the clash of societies before we assume consensus of purpose, goals, and effort.

2. Religion, Moral Certainty, and Fundamentalism

Robert M. MacIver speaks to the ending of an age of peace in his book on *Power Transformed*, in which he makes the following observation.

> No one who has grown up in the twentieth century knows what it means to enjoy the sense of peace on earth, to have the assurance that the sun of peace will rise tomorrow as certainly as it has risen today, to plan for the future without fear that some dark news will render the planning in vain. Growing up in such an age, the writer feels that he has left not only his youth far

> behind, but also the very world in which he lived. Its lineaments, its geography, its beliefs, its assumptions, its hopes are all consigned to the forever buried past.[5]

MacIver further observes that not only has the map of the earth been transformed, but also the minds of its inhabitants everywhere: their attitudes, their beliefs, their expectations, their credulities and fears. There is always a new age waiting to be born, but this new age did not come as the slow birth of time, but was midwifed by violence and disaster.[6] So it is that the war on terrorism will be viewed as a collision of values that will inevitably emerge from the clash of societies that the violence brought on by this 9–11 disaster created on a global scale in which a transformation of Western and Middle East values and moderate and fundamentalist militant religious practices and views have been put in motion.

To understand the attack of Al Qaeda on the United States, one must consider the jihadist view emerging from the Wahabi branch of Islam centered in Saudi Arabia. One must also understand the culture of the Arabian peoples, and in particular the tribal context of the Arab nations. To this equation, one must factor the age of science and technology and its impact on the values and mores of the Arab culture. Ultimately, the religions of Islam and Christianity will be called on to sort out the values and beliefs reflected in our hopes, our needs, and our fears.

Robert MacIver in discussing the primacy of knowledge as power comments on the reconciliation of religion and science and observes that as beliefs grow and proliferate, they become formalized and sanctified. The real danger begins when the creative process that initially produced them is atrophied by the taboos of orthodoxy, and the myths harden into dogmas, thus preventing the development of more enlightened beliefs.[7] This is the process on which militant fundamentalism is created within religious dogma.

To understand a war on terrorism presupposes a richness of the impacts religion, culture, science, technology, and values have on all nations involved, as allied nations may well be affected to the point that their support may be less than expected.

3. Our Fragile Environment: How Societies Collapse

One of the first major works on why societies destroy themselves through disastrous decisions was Joseph Tainter's *The Collapse of Complex Societies*. Tainter's view centered on the supposition that societies sit by and watch the encroaching disaster without taking appropriate action that would preclude the disaster. Tainter was skeptical of the impact of the depletion of environmental resources having a role in the collapse of societies. In fact, his view of complex societies centered on their inability to manage their environmental resources, and he focused on the failure of group decision making within the society that collapses.[8]

A. Decision-Making Errors in Policy

Barbara Tuchman's *The March of Folly: From Troy to Vietnam* reviews the disastrous decisions of complex societies and how provocation and power factors led to the collapse of these societies. It is clear that in all forms of collective human interaction there will always be a need for a decision-making process that will permit complex societies to function. The formulation of policies designed to guide these societies are premised on knowledgeable leaders who seek a wide range of advisory recommendations before committing their society to a course of action. Decision making is a result of the distribution of power, authority, and constitutional legitimacy and when improperly used the result can be both disruptive and potentially disastrous.

Jared Diamond's analysis incorporated the views of both group decision making and environmental depletion of resources as having a profound impact on the collapse of societies. His book, *Collapse, How Societies Choose to Fail or Succeed*, is rich in factual proof of how many societies have failed due to ineffective decision making by their leaders. He ties these past societal collapses based on environmental depletion of resources and mismanagement to defective group decision making and he charts out a course for how society must solve 12 major environmental problems or face collapse by 2050.

B. Decision-Making Errors in Structure

Irving Janis' excellent book, *Group Think*, describes the failure of group decision making and he analyzes the Bay of Pigs crisis during President John F. Kennedy's term of office, and also President Johnson's advisors' recommendation for the escalation of the Vietnam War. The critical errors that can arise in group decision making occur when "group think" creates a false sense of consensus. Janis suggests that "group think" happens when a group is attempting to reach a decision under stressful circumstances and the following elements lead to a disastrous decision:[9]

1. Stress
2. The need for mutual support
3. The need for approval
4. Suppression of doubts
5. Loss of critical thinking
6. A sharing of illusions
7. A premature consensus

With reference to our war on terrorism and events leading to the decision to invade Iraq it is incumbent on academicians, policymakers, and government officials to analyze whether these major decisions fell within the profile of a "group think" approach. Clearly, former Secretary of State Colin Powell endeavored on numerous occasions to provide critical, "out of the box" analysis of any decision to invade Iraq. Not only were his views not accepted, but eventually other members of President Bush's inner circle began to marginalize him and his contributions. Vice President Cheney, Secretary of Defense Rumsfeld, and Deputy Secretary of Defense Wolfowitz took positions many would find most strident to our secretary of state. To what degree a premature consensus may have led President Bush into making a decision to invade Iraq, only President Bush knows.

Another example of "group think" that resulted in a disastrous decision centered on Secretary Rumsfeld and Deputy Secretary Wolfowitz totally ignoring the professional advice of General Eric Shinseki, who maintained a force of 500,000 would be required to sustain the order and security in Iraq. Clearly, Secretary Rumsfeld's rationale for a lightning force invasion proved correct insofar as the initial invasion occurred, but General Shinseki was correct in his recommendation that many more troops were required on the ground to sustain peace and prevent looting and violence.

Again, an example of "group think" that neutralized the wise advice of Lt. General Jay Garner occurred when Ambassador Paul Bremer made the decision to exclude members of the Baath Party and exclude command officers of the Iraq army from participating in a role to restore order to the Iraq nation.

Ambassador Bremer's de-Baathification order was CPA Proclamation Number One and it was based on Under-Secretary of Defense Doug Feith's urging to prevent former Baath Party members from having a role in the new Iraq government. In fact, within four days of arriving in Iraq, Ambassador Bremer issued an order to extirpate Baathists and Baathism in Iraq forever. The fact that many of the Baathists were the type of skilled personnel that Iraq would need to rebuild its country was evidently of little significance to either Under-Secretary Feith or Ambassador Bremer. To further exacerbate this proclamation, Ambassador Bremer appointed Ahmed Chalabi to lead the de-Baathification Council. Chalabi was a known factor to the CIA, and was certainly opposed by the CIA for this position, and for that matter any influence in the Iraq reconstruction. Furthermore, it is interesting to note that Chalabi was passing highly sensitive, classified information to the Iranians, and the CIA learned this from very reliable information sources. Another major problem with Proclamation Number One was the simple fact that 40,000 school teachers who had joined the Baath Party simply to retain their jobs, as well as other Iraqi workers who had also been required to join the Baath Party to continue their employment were now all out of work due to Ambassador Bremer's de-Baathification order. The net effect of this order was to push skilled Iraqi personnel who would be useful in restarting the Iraqi government into unemployment and poverty. Therefore, the Proclamation Number One not only was destroying the institutional foundations of the country, but it was pushing those who lost their employment into insurgency.[10]

CPA Proclamation Number Two by Ambassador Bremer had even more profound negative results as it in effect dissolved the Iraqi Army, and more particularly, it made all of the officer corps unemployable and made the reconstruction effort Lt. General Jay Garner was to lead all but impossible. Not only did this order disallow any realistic effort of Iraqi participation in reconstruction and providing safety and security, but it also sent a great number of former Iraqi Army personnel into the insurgency camp. CIA personnel in the field consistently reported back the problems of both these proclamations and the negative impact they were having on maintaining stability. These reports were viewed by Ambassador Bremer as overly pessimistic, and Deputy Secretary of Defense Wolfowitz stated to one CIA Senior Officer, "You don't understand the policy of the U.S. government, and if you don't understand the policy, you are hardly in a position to collect the intelligence to help that policy succeed."[11] Aside from the arrogance of Secretary Wolfowitz' statement, the intelligence process is not designed to help government policies succeed, but to provide objective evidence on which government officials might establish policies. This fundamental misunderstanding by Secretary Wolfowitz is at the heart of the Bush administration's problems with formulating a policy for the war on terrorism.

As George Tenet, the former CIA Director correctly observed,

> [W]henever you decide to take the country to war, you have to know not only that you can defeat the enemy militarily, but that you have a very clear game plan that will allow you to keep the peace. There was never any doubt that we would defeat the Iraqi military, but what we did not have was an integrated and open process in Washington that was organized to keep the peace, nor did we have unity of purpose and resources on the ground. Quite simply, the National Security Council did not do its job.[12]

Perhaps most telling was Director Tenet's observation: "Our prewar analysis of postwar Iraq was prescient. The challenge for CIA analysts was not so much in predicting what the Iraqis would do. Where we ran into trouble was in our inability to foresee some of the actions of our own government."[13]

Policy formulation is a very complex process, particularly when the implementation of new or modified policies is at variance to the operational programs highly recommended by those professionals most closely responsible for the implementation and action stages. The disconnect between administrators removed from the actual operational programs and the inability of the operational professionals to convey the potential areas of policy dysfunctionalities can become a source of discouragement or even organization resistance and disruption.

C. Policy Formulation Problems from Cuba to Iraq

Individual leadership and decision-making skills of leaders may have a profound effect on the group decision-making process. An excellent example of this involved two major decisions made by the Kennedy administration in dealing with Cuba. The first invoked the Bay of Pigs invasion which was a colossal disaster, and the second major decision invoked the Cuban missile crisis and was a remarkable success and may well have prohibited a nuclear war between the Soviet Union and the United States. As Irving Janis observed in his book, *Group Think*,

> The Bay of Pigs deliberations exhibited numerous characteristics that tend to lead to bad decisions, such as a premature sense of ostensible unanimity, suppression of personal doubts and of expression of contrary views, and the group leader (Kennedy) guiding the discussion in such a way as to minimize disagreement. The subsequent Cuban Missile Crisis deliberations, again involving Kennedy and many of the same advisors, avoided those characteristics and instead proceeded along lines associated with productive decision-making, such as Kennedy ordering participants to think skeptically, allowing discussion to be freewheeling, having sub-groups meet separately, and occasionally leaving the room to avoid overly influencing the discussion himself.[14]

The important point is to observe how the directive of President Kennedy to his advisors regarding the 1961 Bay of Pigs invasion and its disastrous decision making was then reviewed and the revised decision-making process which was quite successful in defusing the Cuban missile crisis provided a model for future group decision processes. With reference to the war on terrorism in general, and more particularly the Iraq war, what decision-making process went through an "after-action" analysis? Can we be assured that future meetings of the National Security Council led by then Secretary of State Condoleezza Rice, will be any different when directed by Stephen Hadley, her Deputy National Security Advisor? Also, what decision-making processes that involve the Principal's Committee, a small group consisting of then, the attorney general, secretary of homeland security, director of the FBI, director of the CIA and chaired by the national security advisor were reviewed? Finally, what can be said for the inner circle of advisors for President Bush and Vice President Cheney, with reference to establishing a decision-making process that would ensure an opportunity for opposing points of view and "out of the box" thinking to be expressed and reviewed?

As our government leaders face continuing crises and challenges with Iran, Middle East instability, North Korea, and other areas, will the group decision-making and advising process provide for a more eclectic range of analysis than has been the case with the Iraq War and reconstruction effort?

These are examples of group decision making by our government officials that have all the earmarks of "group think" structural defects. So it is quite obvious that group decision making is an important aspect of any society's ability to survive and avoid making disastrous decisions.

Jared Diamond proposes a road map of factors contributing to the failures of group decision making, and he outlines four factors as follows.

1. A group may fail to anticipate a problem before the problem arrives.
2. When the problem does arrive, the group may fail to perceive it.
3. After they perceive it, they may fail even to try to solve it.
4. Finally, they may try to solve it, but may not succeed.[15]

The CIA consistently made Congress, President Clinton's administration, and the incoming Bush administration aware of the Al Qaeda terrorist organization and of Osama bin Laden. To what degree each administration fell into the four-factor analysis of group decision making and to what degree each should share in responsibility for ignoring the numerous comments of Director George Tenet regarding the potential danger of Al Qaeda, is yet to be assessed. In fact, George Tenet very clearly and professionally outlines the numerous calls he made to share our intelligence analysis with the policymakers in his illuminating book, *At the Center of the Storm: My Years at the CIA*.

> By 1996 we knew that bin Laden was more than a financier. An Al-Qa'ida defector told us that Usama Bin Laden was the head of a worldwide terrorist organization with a Board of Directors that would include the likes of Ayman al-Zawahiri and that he wanted to strike the United States on our soil. We learned that Al-Qa'ida had attempted to acquire material that could be used to develop chemical, biological, radiological, or nuclear weapons capability.[16]

The CIA's 1995 National Intelligence Estimate on the Foreign Terrorist Threat in the United States warned our government officials of the threat from radical Islamists and suggested the most likely targets of a terrorist attack would be national symbols, such as the White House and the Capitol and symbols of U.S. capitalism such as Wall Street. The report also stated that U.S. civil aviation was an especially vulnerable and attractive target.[17] In 1997, another National Intelligence Estimate with the coordinated judgments of the entire intelligence community identified civil aviation as an attractive target for terrorist attacks. Then in December of 1998 a Presidential Daily

Briefing for President Clinton was titled, "bin Laden Preparing to Hijack U.S. Aircraft and other attacks."[18]

Director Tenet made numerous trips to Capitol Hill informing the congressional oversight committees of the impending problem of Osama bin Laden and Al Qaeda. The director's reports began in 1995, a full six years prior to the September 11, 2001 attack on the World Trade Center and the Pentagon. Moreover, the approach and policy of addressing Osama bin Laden and Al Qaeda took two different forms, one under President Clinton which was to view this as a law enforcement problem and to build a legal case against Osama bin Laden and other Islamic militants. In June of 1998 bin Laden was indicted in the plan to murder U.S. soldiers in Yemen which occurred in 1992. Then in November of 1998, bin Laden was indicted for the East African Embassy bombings. The second approach, which was used by President George W. Bush, relied on a combination of overt military force and covert clandestine capabilities of the intelligence community.

All government officials, including Congress, were aware of the threat of Osama bin Laden and Al Qaeda; or were at minimum informed as such by the intelligence community. The intelligence community leaders did not feel they had sufficient resources to address this problem and also did not feel both government officials and Congress were properly focused on the intelligence estimates and reports presented to them. For example, despite the 1995 National Intelligence Estimate, and subsequent 1997 National Intelligence Estimate and the 1998 Presidential Daily Briefing to President Clinton, the major distraction to both the White House and Congress was the inordinate focus on the Monica Lewinsky scandal that took the focus off so many important domestic and international issues. As the Clinton administration was concluding its term in office, the new Bush administration was coming to power and Richard Clark, the former National Security Advisor to both Presidents, felt the new administration was not taking the bin Laden and Al Qaeda threat seriously.

In applying the four-factor analysis to explain a failure in group decision making regarding the September 11, 2001 tragedy we should view all of the parties to this governmental responsibility, and not solely the intelligence community. Of the four-factor analysis applied to two presidential administrations and their advisors; and to both congressional oversight committees of the intelligence community, and Congress itself, these four factors should be answered especially in light of the documented National Intelligence Estimates and the presidential daily briefings.

1. Did either or all of these groups fail to anticipate the Al Qaeda problem before the September 11, 2001 attacks?
2. When exactly did the respective groups become aware of Al Qaeda, and did they perceive it and properly organize in a coherent and strategic manner to address it?
3. With respect to each of the governmental entities, how specifically did they try to solve the Al Qaeda and bin Laden problems? Have after-action reports provided the focus to guide and ameliorate any further structural and organizational defects in addressing both bin Laden and Al Qaeda?
4. The fourth factor addressed the possibility that despite an attempt to solve the bin Laden and Al Qaeda problem, there is the possibility that we may not succeed.

Although clearly there are documented errors and problems in the manner our intelligence community addressed bin Laden and Al Qaeda, one must bear in mind the "authorities" delegated to address the capture or elimination of bin Laden are sourced by Presidential Executive Orders, especially 12333 previously issued by President Reagan. Furthermore, the total imbalance in focusing all responsibility and blame on the intelligence community, is most dysfunctional and not representative of the realities two presidential administrations and Congress played in this entire matter. The quality and effectiveness of a nation's leadership, policy formulation, decision making, and overall execution of both short-term and long-term policy actions can best be illustrated by examining the environmental factors that will affect their society. The leadership, decision-making, and policy formulation skills that are necessary for a society to address its environmental challenges are very similar to the processes that will be operationalized as our nation confronts terrorism.

D. Environmental Factors

Group decision making as applied by the government decision makers of any nation, along with the possible defects already outlined are but one element in how some societies may collapse. Another important element centers on environmental factors present within each society. Diamond observes the processes through which past societies have undermined themselves by damaging their environment which falls into 12 major threat areas:

1. Deforestation and habitat destruction
2. Soil problems (erosion, salinization, and soil fertility loss)
3. Water management problems
4. Overhunting

5. Overfishing
6. Effects of introduced species on native species
7. Human population growth
8. Increased per capita impact of people
9. Human-caused climate change
10. Buildup of toxic chemicals in the environment
11. Energy shortages
12. Full human utilization of earth's photosynthetic capacity[19]

Scientists are predicting that most of these environmental threats will have a worldwide effect within the next 25 years, and unless carefully addressed and resolved many nations will be vulnerable to collapsing when coupled with other contributing factors, such as the movement that has resulted in globalization and a greater interdependency on all nations to work and trade together. Another contributing factor is our destruction of national resources and the limited supply of readily accessible fossil fuels such as oil, natural gas, and coal which comprise the world's major energy sources. These factors associated with the population growth throughout the world mandate that more food, space, water, energy, and other resources be produced and shared among a growing population in excess of 6 billion people.[20]

In terms of demographics the current world's population of 6.1 billion people is estimated to grow to 7.2 billion people by 2015. Ninety-five percent of this increase in population will be in developing countries, and it is estimated that much of the Middle East population will be both significantly larger and poorer. Currently, in nearly all the Middle East nations more than 50 percent of their population is younger than 20 years of age. The Middle East nations will have a major problem of providing jobs, housing, and services to this new exploding young population.[21] Without vibrant educational institutions that will provide the necessary job skills for this young population, there exists the real possibility of substantial internal unrest within these nations.

The environmental stress points will affect all nations and third-world countries and their needs will draw all of the G-8 nations into addressing the realities of established nations providing the leadership, wisdom, and ability to cooperatively work within this new model of globalization. Thus, the maturity of governments, and the decision-making processes will require greater reliance on diplomacy and skills that assist in minimizing the impact of these environmental threats and stress points on even the least developed country.

Our community of nations is presently on a nonsustainable course of consuming the natural resources, and this point coupled with the 12 environmental threats, suggests that these environmental threats are analogous to time bombs with, as Jared Diamond observes, fuses shorter than 50 years.[22]

Clearly, all nations over the history of mankind have confronted environmental stress; and history has revealed that some nations were successful in addressing these environmental threats whereas other nations were more fragile and together with other contributing factors were not able to withstand the environmental stress points. The increased demands on our environment and its increasing degradation, along with the pressures of a population explosion, increased poverty, and political instability provide a fertile environment for the clash of societies.[23]

In terms of environmental stress points, the depletion of water tables in Africa, the Middle East, South Asia, and Northern China will present a major problem in most of these regions in less than a decade. The enormous population increase will create a concomitant demand for more water, yet it is estimated that every method to use water more efficiently as well as expanding the desalination programs will be insufficient to meet the water needs of these areas by 2015.[24] Water shortages in the Middle East combining with a young growing population in need of jobs, housing, and other services will create tension and very serious problems that ultimately will erode the political stability in these areas.

In searching for the predictors of nations that will fail, the environmental and population pressure produces:

1. High infant mortality
2. Rapid population growth
3. High percent of population in their late teens and early 20s
4. Large numbers of unemployed young men with few or no prospects for obtaining jobs and readily available for service in the militia

These factors produce the revolutions some nations experience, cause the collapse of authority, and result in violent regime changes.[25] These factors are clearly present when one observes the turmoil confronting many states of the Middle East and for that matter many states in Southeast Asia as well. Indeed, many of the early terrorist attacks following the 9–11 attack occurred in nations in Southeast Asia, including Malaysia, Indonesia, and the Philippines.

4. The Management and Mitigation of Risk

When confronted with the prospect of terrorism attacks or environmental degradation, before a nation's leaders develop policies to address these challenges it would benefit all concerned to analyze the risk that is presented by terrorists. The development of a risk management strategy that analyzes the risk at several levels such as the individual terrorist leader, the terrorist organization, and the nonstate or governmental entity is essential to the formulation of both policies and operational programs. The process of management and mitigation of risk involves risk recognition in which we describe the risk, measure the risk, and map and model the risk. The goal of risk resolution will focus on strategies to either prevent or mitigate the risk.

The quantification of the risk in terms of its potential harm adjusted by the probability or the likelihood of the harm occurring provides our leaders an opportunity to develop a policy to guide the operational personnel in delivering an effective response to minimize or control the consequences of the terrorist attacks. In our efforts to manage and mitigate risks our leaders must create policies that take into consideration that some actions will be deliberate, some may be accidental, and some unintentional, in which case we must have multiple strategies for initiating operational programs. So it becomes important to determine which risks can be reduced, which risks should be avoided, and finally which risks might be prevented. To enable our leaders to make these decisions we rely on probability theory and we reach back in time to Bayesian analysis for the necessary scientific tools.

Throughout the development of civilization, and especially during the Renaissance, mathematicians provided societies with the tools we now use to understand risk, to measure it, to understand its consequences, and to manage risk. Not only is the application of risk essential to the war on terrorism, but the entire emergence of science as we know it today would not be possible were it not for the richness of probability theory.

A. Risk Assessment

The ability to forecast future events and to select among alternative choices provides decision-making strategies that are based on probability theory that serve all segments of society by virtue of quantitative mathematics that permits the collection, organization, interpretation, and application of information to the formulation of decisions. The building of a society from its bridges to its medical systems, from its agriculture to its transportation systems, and throughout its entire business and financial systems could not occur without the richness of Bayesian theory and our ability to manage the risk in the decisions we are called on to make. In fact, as Peter Bernstein observes in his outstanding book, *Against the Gods*, "All the tools we use today in risk management and in the analysis of decision and choice, from the strict rationality of game theory to the challenges of chaos theory, stem from the developments that took place between 1654 and 1760, with only two exceptions."[26]

The ability of nations throughout the world to refine their decision-making processes, and to protect their environment from the pressures that forecast failure and collapse suggest that our reliance on science and its many applications is fundamental to our success. This of course presupposes a continuing commitment to the enhancement of our educational systems that generate the scientists of today and the future.

In his provocative book, *The World is Flat: A Brief History of the Twenty-First Century*, Thomas Friedman reports on a study by the Bank Boston Economics Department titled "MIT: The Impact of Innovation," and among its results was the founding of 4000 companies by MIT graduates that have created at least 1.1 million jobs worldwide and generated sales of $232 billion. Friedman observes that what makes our nation unique is not simply that we have an institution like MIT or that all the economic growth and innovations are occurring, but that the United States has 4000 colleges and universities and the rest of the world combined has 7768 institutions of higher education. California with its state support of higher education has more than 130 colleges and universities, and only 14 countries in the world have more colleges and universities than California alone.[27]

Despite our nation's heavy investment in higher education, federal and state funding for research in mathematics, science, and engineering has declined by 37 percent in a period between 1970 and 2004.[28] This decline of our nation's investment in the critical areas of physics, calculus, chemistry, and engineering is a serious mistake for our future. Our nation's economy and defense systems are totally dependent on our graduation of new scientists in these critical fields.

B. Survivability of Societies

Martin Rees observes in his book, *Our Final Hour*, that science is advancing at a faster rate than ever before, and on a broader front that includes biotechnology, cyber-technology, and nanotechnology—all offering extraordinary prospects for society. However, he does observe the potential for a "dark side" of science, one in which unintended consequences can empower individuals to perpetrate acts of megaterror; and even innocent errors could be catastrophic. In fact, Rees is concerned with our advances in biology and our capability to engineer new viruses, bacteria, and pathogens that either by bioerror or bioterror we could see a million people killed by the year 2020.[29]

Rees points out that in July 2002, researchers at the State University of New York assembled a polio virus using DNA and a genetic blueprint that could be downloaded from the Internet. Although this artificial virus posed little hazard as most people have been immunized against polio, the concern of creating infectious and lethal variants from a synthesis similar to this is quite possible. The genetic blueprint for the Ebola virus is already archived, and there are thousands of people able to assemble it using strands of DNA that are commercially available. This coupled with the creation of "designer viruses" is of great concern to scientists throughout the world.[30]

Historian Arthur Schlesinger, Jr., one of President John F. Kennedy's aides, reported that the 1962 Cuban missile crisis brought us closer to a premeditated nuclear exchange, and this was not only the most dangerous moment in the Cold War, it was by far the most dangerous moment in human history.[31] In Martin Rees' view, the advances made in science and technology which now make available powerful weapons of mass destruction in the realms of biology, chemistry, and radiology without the concomitant and necessary control systems suggest that our societies will become vulnerable to individuals who may acquire these materials for purposes of terrorism. In fact, Rees' view is that the odds are no better than 50 percent that our present civilization will survive to the end of the 21st century.[32]

It is apparent that the issue of terrorism has significant scientific dimensions. Science has a critical role to play in the war on terrorism. We need tools with which we can prevent, detect, and protect our society from terrorists. The prevention of future attacks and the management of current threats requires the involvement of our scientific community, as we must be prepared to address the challenges of chemical, biological, radiological, nuclear, and agricultural terrorism. Our universities have both a role and a responsibility to assist in the development of educational programs and research strategies to protect our nation from the threat of terrorist attacks.

Scientists from all nations have a responsibility to protect the incredible pace of innovation in technology and science from being used by terrorists. We must not only guard against misuse, but also human error of these new advances in science. Consequently, the role of educational institutions will be most important in providing the security our societies are entitled to receive.

5. The Role of the University and Research in the War on Terrorism

Our universities through their extraordinary research capabilities have a very important role to play in the efforts our nation must expend to protect our citizens from terrorism. The threats of chemical, biological, radiological, nuclear, and explosive devices are all areas in which our universities have some knowledge and capability to perform research and develop protective strategies. Our universities must also have an understanding of the requirements necessary for our critical infrastructure to operate efficiently and effectively. The protection of food supplies and agriculture is also a role universities are both researching and most intent on protecting. The challenge is to engage our universities with government in such a manner that a research agenda might be developed to offer greater protection for our nation.

Our nation has enjoyed a very robust research and development emphasis as a result of our federal government's allocation of fiscal resources to our research universities. M.R.C. Greenwood offers an excellent review of how universities and our government worked to develop a national security policy by reflecting on the linkage between national security and national science policy during five important eras.[33] The five eras are World War II, The Cold War, Sputnik, the end of the Cold War, and post-September 11.

A. World War II

World War II resulted in our government calling on our scientists, engineers, mathematicians, and language specialists to contribute their efforts in confronting the war. The government also mobilized the physics and technology community into a series of new national laboratories to develop the atomic bomb which ended the war.[34]

B. The Cold War

The Cold War brought many new difficulties, as the very weapons that ended World War II were now responsible for opening a new era of national security concerns focused on the proliferation of such weapons. Vannevar Bush's "Science—The Endless Frontier" defined nondefense R&D, and as he stated in that report, "Scientific progress is one essential key to our security as a nation, to our better health, to more jobs, to a higher standard of living, and to our cultural progress."

This pervasive viewpoint lay the foundation for the use of the American research university and the primacy of unfettered basic, or fundamental, research from the 1950s through the 1990s. This research was a driving force for innovation and growth in both civilian and defense R&D.[35]

C. Sputnik

The Sputnik launch in October 1957 caused a space race between the Soviet Union and the United States. The Soviet success with Sputnik sent shock waves throughout the educational systems of the United States, and resulted in numerous changes at the local, state, and national levels. Our nation geared up for a space race that culminated in our successful moon landing in 1969. The federal government's allocation of resources to our universities, particularly in the fields of engineering, mathematics, and the general sciences, was patterned after the creation of our national laboratory system.

D. End of the Cold War

The end of the Cold War which was marked by the fall of the Berlin Wall in November 1989 created a major shift in our national priorities. "In the face of perceived reduced risk our government leaders started to talk about 'peace dividend' resources that had been devoted to national security, which had been defined primarily in military terms, and would now be released for other uses."[36]

The implications of this "peace dividend" were profound, although they were not fully felt until after the September 11 tragedy. The congressional action to lower the funding levels to our military and our intelligence agencies had a devastating impact, particularly on our intelligence community. The result of the peace dividend decision to reduce funding for our intelligence community crippled our human intelligence capabilities and thwarted the ordinary development of intelligence personnel. As many intelligence agents were drawing to the ends of their careers, replacements were not authorized, and the five- to seven-year cycle required to develop case agents seriously eroded our nation's intelligence capabilities. In fairness to the new emerging national science policy during this era, the hope was to enhance research in health, economic, and environmental issues. It was the imbalance that handicapped our intelligence community, and this realization after 9–11 has resulted in an effort to rebuild our nation's intelligence community to assume a more defined role in the war on terrorism.

E. Post-September 11, 2001 Attack

Post-September 11 has resulted in new tensions and new opportunities for our universities and our government. Our government knows we need first-rate research, yet concerns exist as to the open publication of data and research methods in certain critical fields. On the other hand, universities have an expectation that research will be openly published in peer-reviewed journals to ensure controlling biases and offering replication of research studies to ensure validation and integrity of data and research methods.

Another new tension between our government and our universities centers on the issue of prohibiting certain international students from receiving education and training in sensitive areas that may have direct application to the development and use of weapons of mass destruction. These sensitive areas have been defined by the U.S. Department of State as follows.

Nuclear technology
Missile technology
Navigation and guidance control systems
Chemical and biotechnology engineering

Remote imaging and reconnaissance
Advanced computer and microelectronic technology
Materials technology
Information security
Lasers and directed energy systems
Sensors
Marine technology
Robotics
Advanced ceramics
High-performance metals and alloys[37]

A third level of tension between our government and our universities involves the number and tracking of international students studying within our universities. The revamping of our visa system to prevent abuse is very important to all parties. Equally important is the realization that a major issue confronting our nation centers on the fact that insufficient numbers of our native-born citizens are pursuing academic careers in the engineering and science fields, and we as a society can no longer afford to ignore this problem.

Eugene Skolnikoff reported that in 2002 the number of foreign scholars at American universities was close to 550,000 students which was an increase of 35 percent in a 15-year period. Sixty percent of these students were in the science, engineering, and health fields. More than 50 percent of the engineering doctorates and 25 percent of science doctorates were awarded to foreign nationals. In fact, in some departments and universities, there would be no educational or research function without foreign students.[38] Our nation must refocus its educational priorities within both our elementary and secondary school systems. We must also re-examine how we reward those students who pursue educational fields in the sciences and engineering. Our cultural expectations must also recognize we are moving on a pathway to a nation of scientific illiteracy. The fields of engineering, mathematics, chemistry, biology, and physics are the building blocks of a strong nation.

The war on terrorism will require extraordinary scientific progress by our university community so that we begin educating and preparing a new generation of graduates capable of meeting the enormous challenges that terrorists confront our society with, not only in the present day, but in the future years. Our national laboratory system, which is the crown jewel of our government-sponsored research in science and technology, will need a constant flow of new highly educated and skilled employees who will emerge from our university community.

6. Summary

The movement of globalization, which has created worldwide strains especially for those not participating in the benefits of enriched trade and resources, will require those societies Barnett defines as the global economy's functioning core to integrate the disconnected nations into fully active participating members within the global society. As this goal moves closer to achievement, there should be a corresponding reduction in the ideologies that enable the clashes of societies to occur.

The war on terrorism will have to more closely determine its objectives, which means we must not only identify our risks, but we must evaluate those risks and consider a range of alternative operational strategies to best confront terrorism. So as we assess our nation's assets and assess the threats posed by terrorists we must realistically determine our vulnerabilities and estimate the consequences we will confront. In this fashion, we can determine what countermeasures we might adopt and what their costs and benefits would be, especially in terms of evaluating the protection that would be gained by implementation of a terrorist strategy.

Finally and perhaps most important, we must make these decisions, not only in terms of our needs today, but we must also view the impact of our decisions to confront a war on terrorism on our future generations. We will look to our educational institutions and to the growing need for the science and technology that will flow from our universities to provide the tools and skilled educated professionals who will guide our nation in the daunting challenges that will confront us.

Endnotes

1. Thomas P. M. Barnett, *The Pentagon's New Map: Blueprint for Action: A Future Worth Creating*, Berkley, Penguin Group: New York, 2005, p. XII.
2. National Intelligence Council, *Global Trends 2015: A Dialogue About the Future with Non-Government Experts*, NIC-2000-02, Approved for Publication by the National Foreign Intelligence Board, Under the Authority of the Director of Central Intelligence, December 2000, p. 8.
3. Samuel P. Huntington, The clash of civilizations, *Foreign Affairs*, Council on Foreign Relations: Washington, DC, Volume 72, Number 3, Summer 1993, pp. 22, 25.
4. Ibid., p. 29.
5. Robert M. MacIver. *Power Transformed: The Age Slow Deliverance of the Folk and Now the Potential Deliverance of the Nations from the Rule of Force*. Macmillan, New York, 1964, p. 3.
6. Ibid., p. 4.
7. Ibid., pp. 115–116.

8. Jared Diamond, *Collapse: How Societies Choose to Fail or Succeed.* Penguin, New York, 2005, p. 420.
9. Ibid., p. 421.
10. George Tenet with Bill Harlow, *At the Center of the Storm: My Years at the CIA.* Harper Collins, New York, 2007, pp. 426, 446.
11. Ibid., p. 430.
12. Ibid., p. 447.
13. Ibid., p. 446.
14. Diamond, op. cit., p. 439.
15. Ibid., p. 421.
16. Tenet, op. cit., p. 102.
17. Tenet, op. cit., p. 104.
18. Tenet, op. cit., p. 105.
19. Diamond, op. cit., pp. 6–7.
20. Diamond, op. cit., pp. 7, 486–494.
21. National Intelligence Council, *Global Trends 2015*, op. cit., pp. 6, 56.
22. Diamond, op. cit., p. 498.
23. Diamond, op. cit., p. 498.
24. National Intelligence Council, *Global Trends* 2015, op. cit., p. 20.
25. Diamond, op. cit., p. 516.
26. Peter L. Bernstein, *Against the Gods: The Remarkable Story of Risk*, John Wiley, New York, 1998, pp. 3–6.
27. Thomas L. Friedman, *The World is Flat: A Brief History of the Twenty First Century*, Farrar, Straus and Giroux, New York, 2005, p. 244.
28. Ibid., p. 268.
29. Martin Rees, *Our Final Hour: A Scientist's Warning: How Terror, Error and Environmental Disaster Threaten Humankinds Future in this Century—On Earth and Beyond.* Basic, New York, 2003, pp. VII, 74.
30. Ibid., p. 55.
31. Ibid., p. 26.
32. Ibid., p. 8.
33. M.R.C. Greenwood, Research universities in the post-September 11 era, in the American Association for the Advancement of Science, *Science and Technology in a Vulnerable World*, Supplement to the AAAS Science and Technology Policy Yearbook 2003. Washington, DC, 2002, p. 7.
34. M.R.C. Greenwood, loc. cit., 2003.
35. Ibid., p. 8.
36. Ibid., p. 9.
37. Ibid., pp. 6, 13.
38. Eugene B. Skolnikoff, Research universities and national security, in the American Association for the Advancement of Science, *Science and Technology in a Vulnerable World*, Supplement to the AAAS Science and Technology Policy Yearbook 2003, Washington, DC, 2002, p. 71.

Terrorism, Islamic Insurgency, and Religious War

2

This chapter's focus on terrorism, Islamic insurgency, and religious warfare provides a framework for characterizing what has been termed the global war on terrorism. The uses of the Internet as an instrument to collect information, provide information, or even to function as an instrument of attack has provided terrorist organizations a transformational tool of enormous power and importance. Indeed, the organizational structures of terrorist groups, as well as the nature of the conflict itself have been forever altered as a result of the terrorist use of the World Wide Web and the electronic and digital environment now freely available in a totally unregulated worldwide capacity.

This chapter is organized around the following format.

1. The Global War on Terrorism—Instruments of Statecraft
2. Terrorism: Characteristics and Ideology
   A. Goals of the Terrorist Organization: Temporal or Transformational
3. Organizational Skills of the Terrorist Leader
   A Educational and Occupational Background of Jihadists
   B. Leadership Challenges in Religious-Based Terrorist Groups
   C. Religion, Political Activism, and Power
   D. Osama bin Laden's Role with Islamic Jihadism
4. The World Wide Web and Worldwide Terrorism
   A. The Internet as an Instrument of Change
   B. Islamic Jihadist Use of the Internet

Endnotes

What better way to begin this chapter, than to recall Paul Pillar's insightful observation:

> If there is a "war" against terrorism, it is a war that cannot be won. The metaphor of a war on terrorism must take cognizance of the fact that in terrorism we have no one set of fixed enemies, but as listed in the 2004 U.S. Department of State's official listing of designated terrorist organizations we have identified over 77 terrorist groups throughout the world. The impossibility of winning a war against so many diverse terrorist organizations ranging from the FARC to Al Qaeda; from religious motivated groups to state and substate motivated groups is simply not a realistic goal to set forth. One of the realities of our

efforts to apply counterterrorism programs and strategies has taught us that at best terrorism is a problem to be managed, not solved.[1]

1. The Global War on Terrorism—Instruments of Statecraft

Our nation has several instruments of statecraft to apply to the problem of terrorism, and over the years and many presidential administrations we have observed one or more selected from the following inventory of counterterrorist strategies.

Diplomacy
Law enforcement and the criminal justice system
Intelligence
Interdiction of financial assets and money laundering
Clandestine and covert operations and actions
Special operations, paramilitary, special forces
Military[2]

The instrument of statecraft that will be selected as the most appropriate counterterrorist strategy must be carefully tailored to the tactics and goals of the individual terrorist organization being confronted. Indeed, if a group such as Al Qaeda is addressed by counterterrorist strategies that are focused only within the domain of law enforcement or our criminal justice system, our nation's ability to defeat this terrorist group, let alone manage the terrorism it creates, would be substantially limited. In other words, if Al Qaeda has morphed into an insurgency or even a religious war as stated and declared by bin Laden then our selection of the statecraft tool must by definition be appropriate to the challenge presented by the terrorist organization.

If one defines terrorism as a criminal act, then the law enforcement or criminal justice system is the appropriate vehicle to address the terrorist group. On the other hand, if you define terrorism as war, then you must rely on military policies and capabilities as the appropriate vehicles to combat the terrorist group. Of course, there exist multiple strategies that can be applied simultaneously to the problem of terrorism. However, if the issue is to win a "war" or to manage a terrorist organization or conflict, then the application of appropriate power and resources must be applied and in full measure, without hesitancy or political compromise. Therefore, the definition of terrorism suggests the manner in which a particular policy will be articulated and conveyed to the world community in general, and to the terrorist organization in particular.

2. Terrorism: Characteristics and Ideology

Pillar offers a description used to define terrorism by the government as to include four fundamental characteristics.

1. The first, premeditation, means there must be an intent and prior decision to commit an act that would qualify as terrorism. . . . Terrorism is not a matter of mandatory rage or impulse. It is also not a matter of accident.
2. The second element, political motivation, excludes criminal violence motivated by monetary gain or personal vengeance. What all terrorists have in common and separates them from other violent criminals is that they claim they are serving some greater good.
3. The third element, that the targets are non-combatants means that terrorists attack people who cannot defend themselves with violence in return.
4. The fourth element, that the perpetrators are either sub-national groups or clandestine agents, is another difference between terrorism and normal military operations. An attack by government's uniformed or otherwise identifiable armed forces is not terrorism; it is war.[3]

Louise Richardson argues that "We should never have declared a global war on terrorism knowing that such a war can never be won. Our objective should not be the completely unattainable goal of obliterating terrorism; rather we should pursue the more modest and attainable goal of containing terrorist recruitment and constraining resort to the tactic of terrorism."[4] In fact, it may well be that the best way to manage terrorism is to understand its appeal and to then use this knowledge to develop and apply effective counterterrorist programs.

Richardson elaborates on Pillar's definition of terrorism and outlines seven important characteristics that provide a most enriching description of current terrorists.

1. First a terrorist act is politically inspired; if not it is simply a crime.
2. Second, if it does not involve violence or the threat of violence, it is not terrorism.
3. Third, the point of terrorism is not to defeat the enemy but to send a message.
4. Fourth, the act and the victim usually have symbolic significance.
5. Fifth, terrorism is the act of sub-state groups, not states, although many states such as Iran, Iraq, Syria and Libya have sponsored terrorism abroad because they did not want to incur the risk of overtly attacking more powerful countries. This, in essence becomes a strategy for engaging in proxy warfare. Iran's funding and use of Hezbollah is a perfect example of this proxy effect, claiming no responsibility for actions of Hezbollah, yet funding the terrorist organization.

6. A sixth characteristic is to select and use victims as a means of altering the behavior of the government.
7. The seventh and most defining characteristic of terrorism is the deliberate targeting of civilians. This factor distinguishes terrorism from other forms of political violence.[5]

A. Goals of the Terrorist Organization: Temporal or Transformational

In almost every decision of terrorism, inevitably someone points out the terrorist serving in the role of a "freedom fighter." This definitional problem was created by Yasser Arafat's 1974 speech to the United Nations in which he declared the difference between the revolutionary and the terrorist lies in the reason for which each fights. For whoever stands by a just cause and fights for the freedom and liberation of his land cannot be called a terrorist. In fact, Richardson's observation as to the anemic international cooperation in fighting terrorism is precisely a result of the power of the term of "freedom fighter" and the corresponding reluctance to label a group as "terrorists" when they are seen as fighting for legitimate goals.[6]

In the environment of violence and with the appearance of terrorist groups, we sometimes encounter guerrilla organizations as well. Terrorist groups generally focus all their violence against the regular forces of the state. Their goal is for the military defeat of the state, whereas the guerrilla group seeks to alter the behavior of the state through psychological intimidation, economic disruption, or political divisiveness. Richardson offers a most useful and theoretically sound matrix to view and analyze terrorist organizations. This matrix is designed to identify how the goals of terrorist organizations fall into either a category of temporal or transformational action.

1. Temporal terrorist groups are those whose political goals can be met without overthrowing the political system.
2. Transformational terrorist groups have goals which require the total destruction of a state system.

During the 1960s–1970s several terrorist groups with Marxist–Lenin-based philosophies sought the destruction of those nations or states that were defined as capitalists. This brand of terrorism has largely been replaced by groups that now are more motivated to use religious ideology to achieve their political goals, which in many cases are indeed quite transformational. In fact, Al Qaeda's entire philosophy and set of terrorist goals is for the total eradication of government states that do not totally and clearly embrace their religious views.[7]

The most contemporary formation of terrorist organizations is today based on an ideology, religious in nature, and capable of attracting a number of believers who are committed to a belief system of the terrorist group. The strength of the belief system holds the group together irrespective of geographical proximity. In one sense, the challenge for leadership is premised upon delegation of authority, decentralization of operations, and above all a common commitment to the greater religious tenets of a figurehead that all have reverence and deep belief in serving.

3. Organizational Skills of the Terrorist Leader

To become a successful terrorist leader then suggests a total commitment to the course and the goals of the terrorist group, forsaking all other material and economic aspirations. The ability to persuade others to join in the group's goals and beliefs, and quite important, to retain them as viable members, especially as the level of violence becomes practiced, is a unique and important charismatic skill. In short, the terrorist leader must provide clarity of the group's ideology, and must articulate such a clear and defined strategy that when members are faced with the decisions to operationalize violence they will not retreat from this responsibility no matter how horrendous it might otherwise appear.

In addition, the terrorist leader has to develop an infrastructure that will obtain the financial resources so that the equipment, weapons, and instruments of terror can not only be acquired but also be available for members' training and ultimate use. The leader of the terrorist group must then have certain organizational skills, and be capable of developing and implementing a "business plan" that will permit the enlistment of clearly trained and educated technical specialists who can not only implement the leader's "business plan," but also have the insight to provide additional innovative and creative enhancements to the "business plan."

Terrorist groups like other organizations have members who have to be fed, transported, trained, equipped, supervised, rewarded, disciplined, and prepared for action at the very moment a command or order is given. To keep members of the terrorist organization focused on the terrorist goals requires the identification of an opponent or enemy that is so large and compelling those members will not lose their commitment to the terrorist group. The challenge for a terrorist leader is to maintain this focal point of "enemy states" on a state or group so vigorously that the terrorist membership will commit to the goals of the organization not simply for a period of time but for the totality of the battle. Perhaps most important to the terrorist's leadership skills and abilities is the charismatic capability to convince all terrorist group members that what they are being called upon to perform is in reality a heroic task that will resound to the benefit of others, and will morally distinguish themselves as making a commitment few others could or would be able to achieve.

A. Educational and Occupational Background of Jihadists

If the leadership skills are so critical to the formation and sustaining of a terrorist organization, where and how are potential terrorist leaders sought and recruited to the terrorist group? In examining the background of Al Qaeda members, Marc Sageman has produced one of the first scholarly and well-researched books on this subject. His study, based on biographies of 172 terrorists obtained from open source material, provided data based on social, personal, and situational variables that challenged the conventional explanation of terrorism. He suggested this new form of terrorism is based on social networks, formed by alienated young men who become transformed into fanatics yearning for martyrdom and eager to kill.[8]

Sageman's analysis of the 172 Mujahedin reveals some interesting trends that distinguish this group of Al Qaeda terrorists from many other terrorist organizations.

Geographical Origins (A Sample Subset of Group)[9]

Saudi Arabia	–	31
Egypt	–	24
France	–	18
Algeria	–	15
Morocco	–	14
Indonesia	–	12

Education

In Sageman's sample of 137 terrorists only 123 or 17 percent had an Islamic religious primary and secondary education. All the rest attended secular schools. Thus, the data refutes the notion that madrassa religious training is brainwashing the Salafi terrorists. Sageman does note an exception with reference to the Indonesian network of terrorists.

Secular Education	Religious Education	Total
114	23	137

The level of educational attainment also suggests that the argument linking education and future terrorism to largely the uneducated or those brainwashed by the madrassa system is not accurate, as the data reveals over 60 percent of the sample had some college education which as a group makes them more educated than the average person worldwide.

Educational Level Achieved[10]

Less than High School	High School	College	B.A./B.S.	M.A.	Doctorate	Total
22	16	38	44	7	5	132

Socioeconomic Status

The traditional assumption that terrorists find their background in poverty, and this propels them in a struggle against the state, is certainly not the situation with the sample Sageman studied of 102 Salafi jihadist terrorists. In fact, there was an overrepresentation of upper and middle classes, with the leadership emerging principally from the upper and middle classes.

Socioeconomic Status of Family of Origin[11]

Upper Class	Middle Class	Lower Class	Total
18	56	28	102

Occupation

In many studies of terrorists, it is not unusual to have them described as largely disenfranchised from economic opportunity, or having little or no chance of obtaining a successful occupation or job. Sageman's study of 134 terrorists in his sample group found at the time they joined the jihad, that 42 percent were considered professionals (physician, architect, preacher, and teacher) and 33 percent were considered semi-skilled with occupations in the police, military, mechanics, civil service, small business, or students. Only 25 percent of the sample group was considered unskilled.

Occupation[12]

Professional	Semi-Skilled	Unskilled	Total
57	44	33	134

The analysis of Salafi jihadists by Sageman's study suggest that we are confronting a group of terrorists who benefit from leaders and other members who have above-average education, and have experienced stable employment in respected occupations. This coupled with their almost fanatical commitment to their religious ideology and goals suggest that our counterterrorist strategies will have to be measured to address the specifics that attract and permit them to forge their membership into this Salafi-based jihadist terrorist organization.

B. Leadership Challenges in Religious-Based Terrorist Groups

In analyzing religious-based terrorist groups, one of the first questions to probe centers on those issues that convince individuals to join these organizations Jessica Stern terms "holy war" organizations. Once they join such a terrorist group what provides them the rationale to stay with the group? Why do they risk their lives in support of their organization's purported public good? Ironically, their commitment to the religious ideology and goals of the terrorist group leads them to a position where they dehumanize their adversaries to the degree that they become capable of murdering their adversaries. Ironically, although they begin with the idea of purging the world of some evil, they become themselves agents of evil acts.[13]

The challenges confronting leaders of these terrorist organizations is to attract and sustain the members they feel best represent the group's ideologies and goals. The leaders of the Salafi jihadist movement rely on the alienation and humiliation many Arabs experienced after the Arab loss to Israel in the 1967 Six-Day War. Another aspect these leaders draw on is the dictatorial rule of Arab monarchs who have exploited the wealth for their own use, while ignoring the laws, customs, and mores as dictated by the Koran and Islamic law.

C. Religion, Political Activism, and Power

Religion has emerged as a powerful tool of dissent, simply because authoritarian Muslim rulers succeeded in silencing secular and nonreligious opposition. Therefore, it was the mosque that became the forum for a safe environment to voice dissatisfaction. Furthermore, because the Arab rulers have failed to provide jobs, social services, education, or defend their land against external threats they view as coming from Israel or the United States and Western society, many see Islamists coming to greater power. Islam is conferring legitimacy on those who challenge secular nationalism, which has already been discredited by decades of political oppression and military defeat. Although Muslims and "Islamists" disagree as to the role and function of Islam, it is nevertheless becoming clearer that Muslims are believers who may or may not be interested in politics, whereas Islamists are political activists whose fundamental goal is to seize power.[14] As Franz Gerges observes: "Militant Islamists share with Jihadists a willingness to use all means at their disposal, including terrorism, to overthrow the existing secular order and replace it with a theocratic one. . . . Thus the key to understanding the Jihadist and his journey lies in politics, not in religion."[15]

The emergence of radical Islamism began with the founding of the Muslim Brotherhood in 1920. The most influential of the leaders was an Egyptian Sayyid Qutb, who in the 1950s sparked the fever of jihadism not only in Egypt, but throughout the Muslim world. Qutb was the first to define "jihad" not in terms of a conflict focused on a specific target, or in a specific area, but as an "eternal revolution," against any and all enemies internal or external who had usurped God's sovereignty.[16]

Louise Richardson has observed that religion cannot be said to have caused terrorism, but Islamic fundamentalism has provided a justification for the use of terrorism in the belief of achieving a greater good. More specifically, the economic and social failures of so many Muslim countries have produced individuals willing to join terrorist organizations as a means of changing those humiliations. "In this way, religion interacts with social, economic and political factors and contributes to the creation of a culture of violence. . . . So while religion is a cause of terrorism only in combination with other social and political factors, religion does make terrorist groups more absolutist, more transnational and more dangerous."[17]

Ironically, as strident as many religious-based terrorist groups have been, it is important to note how singularly unsuccessful they have been in delivering the political change they seek. In fact, a striking aspect of most terrorist organizations is how little of their attention is devoted to the new world they seek to create. In short, most terrorist leaders are more interested in how they will destroy the existing system, and say precious little as to how they propose the new system will resolve the inequities and defects of the system they are so preoccupied with destroying. It is not so much their vision for a new world that motivates and moves them and their terrorist group, but rather what they perceive as the injustices of the present system that outrages them and their followers.[18]

D. Osama bin Laden's Role with Islamic Jihadism

Osama bin Laden's view of America, and for that matter Western civilization, was postulated on what he thought was a global crusade on the part of both Christians and Jews to crush Islam. He views the battle as not between Al Qaeda and the United States, but as a battle of Muslims against global crusaders from the Western civilization. In bin Laden's view, this is no less than a theological war and the redemption of humanity is at stake.[19]

The impact of the Egyptian Brotherhood and Sayyid Qutb's influence on restoring authentic Islam practices has had a profound effect on the Muslim world. Qutb's execution by the Egyptian government of Nasser, followed by the loss of the Six-Day War to Israel, the assassination of Anwar Sadat, the Iranian revolution, and the 2006 Hezbollah action against Israel all have moved militant Islamists closer to the views of jihadists. The Egyptian Islamic jihadist movement guided by Ayman Al-Zawahiri joining with Osama bin Laden's Al Qaeda has created a global Salafi jihad designed to re-establish traditional Muslim practices as set forth by the prophet Mohammed. However, under the interpretation as offered by both bin Laden and Al-Zawahiri this restoration of authentic Islam will take the form of a violent jihad, to eliminate any practices it regards as local political heresy or global interference with the establishment of what they define as a true Islamic state.

> Ajami, a distinguished Arab scholar has labeled the leaders of the Islamic movement as "angry sons of a failed generation" the ones who saw the secularist dream of Arab unity dissolve into corruption, poverty, and social chaos. For the most part, their anger has been incubated not in the deserts or small villages but in such major Islamic cities as Cairo, Jiddah, Karachi, or Kuwait.[20]

Joel Kotkin observes that as Muslim countries in the Middle East were developing many tried to adopt the Western models of city building, which had the effect of weakening the Muslim traditional bands of community and neighborhood. This exposure to the values of Western societies disrupted the shaping forces of the Muslim cultural identity, leaving a population alienated from both Western and Islamic value systems. From this reality, Islamic terrorism has emerged as a threat to the future of modern cities, because Islamic terrorists regard the West, particularly its great cities, as intrinsically evil, exploitative, and un-Islamic.[21]

A new cold war between the secular Western civilization and the religious Third World could well become the catalyst for the eruption of violence throughout the Middle East. The growing hostility of Islamists toward the West has been fueled by the seemingly unstoppable spread of Westernization, and this motivates the terrorists to commit more acts of violence to demonstrate their rage and the new power of militant radical Islamism.[22]

Osama bin Laden is the only terrorist leader to have formally declared a jihad, or holy war against the United States of America, and he has done so many times since 1996.[23] He views the presence of United States troops and personnel, as well as any corporate interest in the Middle East as the source of all crises afflicting the Muslim world. In his view, this Western presence precludes the establishment of the types of Islamic governments and rulers who would permit the practice of the Salafi form of Islamic religious practice.

In July of 1996 British newspapers were reporting that Osama bin Laden stated that the killing of American military at the Khobar Towers in Saudi Arabia was the beginning of a war between the Muslims and the United States. By August of 1996, bin Laden joined other radical Muslims in promulgating a *fatwa* or religious edict declaring war against all Western military targets on the Arab peninsula. By February of 1998, bin Laden issued another fatwa, this time stating that all Muslims had a religious duty to kill Americans and their allies, both civilian and military, anywhere in the world. To make matters worse the CIA learned that Al Qaeda was seriously attempting to acquire chemical, biological, radiological, and nuclear weapons capability and this effort began in 1996.[24] It is clear that bin Laden's declarations were to be taken seriously, and Al Qaeda's experimentation with bioweapons signaled that this declaration of war was to leave no doubt as to his intentions and those of his colleague Islamic jihadists.

In his book, *Imperial Hubris: Why the West is Losing the War on Terror*, Michael Scheuer maintains that we are fighting a worldwide Islamic insurgency and not simply criminal acts or terrorism. Although U.S. leaders will not say America is at war with Islam, some of Islam is waging war on the United States, and as bin Laden stated in 2001, the war is fundamentally religious. Scheuer further stated: "Let me stress that we are not choosing between war and peace. America has a war it cannot avoid and, at least for now, one that will grow more savage no matter what we do. . . . Simply put, the enemy wants war."[25]

The important policy point regarding our response to Al Qaeda and its terrorist activities is to decide whether this battle should be fought on the platform of criminal law, intelligence, special forces, or military resources. In short, we must determine whether our battle with Al Qaeda and the jihadists is terrorism, insurgency, or war. Although it is quite clear that the jihadists have chosen the war label, our policymakers have not so declared this as anything more than terrorism with occasional insurgency. In selecting the tools of statecraft we will use to confront Al Qaeda we must not over-rely on the criminal law option in dealing with Al Qaeda. The process of arrest and conviction is a superb tactical tool against Al Qaeda, but as Scheuer observes it is not a war winner. Therefore, the terrorist paradigm must be reassessed as Al Qaeda is so fundamentally different from other terrorist organizations we have dealt with, and we must recognize that Al Qaeda is leading a very popular, worldwide, and powerful Islamic insurgency. Insurgencies are fought in a different manner from terrorism, and on a much larger scale as well. Osama bin Laden and the Islamic jihadists are fighting an insurgency-based war against the United States, and we have no other option but to select those tools and instruments of statecraft that permit us to respond in a manner reflective of the challenge we currently are confronting.

In analyzing the Islamic jihad, Marc Sageman draws a most powerful conclusion by stating the following. "The global Salafi jihad is a threat to the world. Its theatre of operations spans the globe, and its apocalyptic vision melts away any barriers to its planned atrocities. It will not hesitate to use weapons of mass destruction to further its mission."[26]

4. The World Wide Web and World Wide Terrorism

Perhaps one of the most effective tools for terrorist organizations to use today is the World Wide Web, as it provides unparalled communications capability for the terrorist to use in any number of ways. The use of the Internet can be directed in such a manner that terrorists can use their computers as tools to achieve any of the following tasks.

1. Collecting Information
   Use as an intelligence-gathering device
   Collect information on selected target sites and infrastructure targets
   Plan attacks or target sites
   Data mining of websites in target country

2. Providing Information
   To recruit new terrorist members
   To justify the rationale for declaring a fatwa
   To provide information to remote sites and countries
   To request funding and donations to support the cause
   To circulate attack plans
   To provide new manifestos
   To share training materials

3. Acting as an Instrument of Attack
   Cyber-attack opponent's websites
   Cyber-attack electronic weapons systems
   Cyber-attack electronic transfer of funds
   Cyber-attack financial and stock exchanges
   Cyber-attack electronic grid sites

A. The Internet as an Instrument of Change

It is quite obvious that the operational significance of the Internet will change the organizational structures of terrorist groups, as well as the nature of the conflict. The Internet makes possible the virtual terrorist cell, and permits a level of decentralization of the terrorist group never before experienced. The Internet has accelerated the spread of radical Islamist ideology, and accompanied this message with a rationale for attacking the West, and has spread this message to every corner of the Muslim world.

E-mail along with a full panoply of electronic and digital communications has transformed the religious terrorist group by providing instantaneous ability to disseminate battle plans, tactics, training, and intelligence to terrorist members in the most remote areas. Even more alarming is the nature of material already available on the Web. People can download various computer viruses and Trojans and launch an attack with minimal computer skills necessary, as the attack script is already prepared and easily available for downloading and launching. "The distance learners of jihad have a wealth of material to choose from. If they visit the right websites, they can learn how to construct mines and hand grenades; build incendiary bombs; make RDX; rig a bomb for detonation by cell phone as was done in Madrid, Spain; mix chemical weapons; create botulism. . . ."[27]

Not only does there exist an enormous array of potentially damaging information stored in computer servers throughout the world and readily accessed by the Internet, but we have seen the number of websites related to terrorist groups grow from 12 in 1998 to over 4400 by 2005. As Gabriel Weiman reports there are countless other sites that espouse radical Islamist views without being associated with particular violent groups.[28]

Since the start of the invasion of Iraq in 2002, more than 200 suicide bombers have been recruited within Iraq and across the Muslim world. The use of the Internet to recruit these members and to display their message of accomplishment is most disturbing. Equally of concern is the use of the Internet to post videos of the beheadings of the numerous hostages. In the latter case, whether Arab or Western news organizations choose to broadcast these videos, the terrorist groups can use their computers to broadcast over the Internet directly into servers that anyone with a computer, anywhere in the world, can use to access the video. So the Internet can be an extraordinarily valuable tool for the terrorists to use to transmit their videos of terror, or their statements of propaganda because the vast audience that can be reached is incalculable.[29]

> The fact that terrorists themselves have direct control over the content of their websites offers further opportunities to shape how they are perceived by different target audiences, and to manipulate their image and the images of their enemies. Most terrorist sites do not celebrate their violent activities. Instead, regardless of their nature, motives or location—most emphasize two issues: the restrictions placed on freedom of expression, and the plight of their comrades who are new political prisoners. These issues resonate powerfully with their own supporters and are calculated to elicit sympathy from Western audiences.[30]

In addition to soliciting financial aid online, terrorists are using sophisticated website technologies of audio and digital video to present their most compelling message, and those visitors to the website are tracked, just as commercial organizations do, all in the hopes of better selling their message, recruiting new members, and hoping to attract additional money. Again, just as corporate and commercial firms engage in data mining so do some terrorist organizations. Their target of course is the valuable information stored in computer servers throughout the world. Access to over a billion pages of information provides a rich source for planning attacks against selected targets. An example of this point can be illustrated by

> a captured Al Qaeda computer which contained engineering and structural architecture features of a dam which had been downloaded from the internet. In other captured computers, investigators found evidence that Al Qaeda operatives spent time on Internet sites that offer software and programming instructions for the digital switches that run power, water, and transportation and communication grids.[31]

The Internet also has provided terrorist groups with an inexpensive and efficient way of networking, and this has enabled terrorist organizations to "outsource" their respective skills and to discuss strategies for collaboration.

Yusef Al-Ayeri was responsible for one of the websites that Al Qaeda relied on, Al-Neda, a website that carried both coded directives about Al Qaeda's plans and strategies. Two important documents that were posted on this website included, "The Future of Iraq and the Arabian Peninsula after the fall of Baghdad," designed to create support for Al Qaeda and criticize the United States. The second, "Crusaders War," outlined a tactical model for fighting American forces in Iraq, including assassination and poisoning the enemy's food and water, suicide bombings and remotely triggered explosives, and lighting strike ambushes.[32]

B. Islamic Jihadist Use of the Internet

Perhaps one of the most valuable tools for the Islamic jihadist movement in particular, and most terrorist organizations in general has been their use of the Internet. The electronic communications capability this has provided them truly has emerged as an asynchronous weapon that creates enormous problems and vulnerabilities for the strongest of nations, and particularly for the United States. Before the September 11, 2001 attacks on the United States Al Qaeda relied on the Internet to use as a mechanism to plan and collect information and have all arrangements in place for the attack. Since the 9–11 attack we have clear evidence as provided by captured computers that Al Qaeda operatives were fully involved in using the Internet to collect information to improve on their selection and use of weapons.

The proliferation of "Internet cafes" throughout the world provides easy access for terrorists and militant Muslims to use the Internet, and to meet and get to know each other, a familiarization and bonding process that in the 1980s and 1990s required a trip to Sudan, Yemen, or Afghanistan.[33]

The CIA discovered that Al Qaeda had been using two Internet websites, Al-Neda and Al-Ansar, since early 2002. Al-Neda which was known as the Center for Islamic Studies and Research, was recommended by a senior Al Qaeda commander Abu-Al-Layth to fellow Islamic jihad's online readers as a good website, and one run by reliable brothers. In fact the discovery went on to state the following:

> Al-Neda and Al-Ansar publish among other things, bi-weekly electronic journals containing analysis of the wars in Afghanistan and Iraq; evaluations and explanations by Islamic scholars and clerics of what Al Qaeda has done, is planning to do, and has urged others to do; and erudite, well-researched essays describing Al Qaeda's war aims and assessing how achieving these goals would benefit the Muslim Umanah by defeating the United States, and in their turn, Israel and the world's apostate Muslim governments.[34]

So much of the material posted on Arabic websites that describe Israel in the most derogatory terms permits Al Qaeda to justify its fight against not only Israel, but also Western culture sympathetic to Israel, including the United States. The impact of these websites and their repeated messages espousing a jihadist call for terrorism has made it most difficult for moderate Muslims to speak out against this very narrow jihad perspective. As a result, this narrow and bitter perspective has overwhelmed public discussion on Internet sites within the Muslim world and has contributed to a very militant and radical perspective that is unchallenged by more moderate Muslims.

One approach to counter some of the capabilities of Al-Neda was for U.S.-initiated website attacks to make it more difficult for Muslim readers to locate the site. In fact the Arabic daily *Al-Hayat* has reported that Al-Neda has been the target of over 20 U.S. attacks. These U.S.-based information-warfare attacks are then criticized by Islamists as evidence of the United States' fear of what Al Qaeda is saying, and that freedom of speech is not for Muslims, just as bin Laden has stated all along.[35] So there are strategic issues to weigh in the development of tactical plans that require careful thought and analysis. Another facet worthy of consideration centers on the intelligence data lost when you preclude intelligence analysts from having access to these websites, due to information warfare tactics.

In short, there are some occasions where it may be more beneficial to maintain a monitoring capability of the website, as opposed to taking action which burrows it deeper into areas more difficult to access and monitor. Clearly, the other side of this argument becomes evident when one realizes that Al Qaeda could use this medium to attract new members or those considering joining an Islamic jihadist movement. Of course, the question then pivots on freedom of speech, what we define as "balance," and who defines and makes these judgments.

Another consequence of not applying information warfare tactics to terrorist websites, or those websites which are not primarily terrorist, but in fact are Muslim or Islamist websites centers on the fact that as a communication medium Al Qaeda postings requesting assistance from all Muslims can still yield valuable information to Al Qaeda. For example, some Internet and chat room postings have been widely circulated throughout the entire Arabian peninsula asking all Muslims to report on the location of the offices and personnel of American corporations, the living quarters of American military personnel and their base locations, as well as much more definitive information on them. The difficulty in monitoring all these sites is not only one of sheer numbers, but also how easy it is to simply close down your site and reopen with a new URL. We also have fundamental language translation challenges as well.

Those militant Islamic and jihadist websites that provide training material to all corners of the world and make training videos and audio available in the use of weapon systems such as explosives, chemicals, or biological agents definitely have to be the targets of information warfare tactics and action.

Clearly, Al Qaeda has benefited from the use of the Internet as it has utilized this incredible instrumentality to collect information and intelligence on financial institutions in the United States. It has also been able to download photographs, maps, and structural architectural information on the sites selected as potential targets, thus providing a rich capability for planning the assault on the selected targeted site.

Ironically, just as terrorist organizations are using and relying on the Internet to access and data mine more websites throughout the Western world, we now find ourselves in the position of removing public access to so much of the valuable data which we once provided and traded so freely and openly, thus sacrificing important elements of knowledge building and economic advantage so as to provide greater data protection and security.

Therefore, the major benefit of the World Wide Web and the numerous new technologies available on or through the Internet, has enabled Al Qaeda and other Islamic jihadists the opportunity to improve both the effectiveness and the efficiency of their activities. The new digital environment we now live in has specifically facilitated terrorists in their control of operations over vast geographical areas and distances and minimized their need for a large physical presence.

> Lebanese Hezbollah now has cells on every continent except Antarctica. Several Sunni groups such as bin Laden's Al Qaeda organization, the Egyptian Al Gama' at Al Islamiyya and Palestinian Hamas have shown similar geographic growth in recent years . . . .Hezbollah's presence in South America... is anchored in a large cluster of mostly Shia Arabs who live in the area where

> the borders of Argentina, Brazil and Paraguay converge. The cells in such networks perform a variety of functions including recruitment, raising of money, procurement and movement of operatives and other support tasks such as the production of false documents.[36]

Our military has over the years been trained to look for what Clausewitz calls the enemy's "center of gravity" or to position attacks in such a manner that we will ultimately defeat them. In the case of Al Qaeda, we have assaulted bin Laden's safe havens, finances, leadership cadre, allied groups, and even the charitable donations and educational curricula believed to support him. However, bin Laden has turned Clausewitz on his head, because Al Qaeda has no "center of gravity" in the traditional sense, that is, no economy, no cities, no homeland, no power grids, and no regular military.[37] This is precisely why the Internet has proven to be such a valuable asset to Al Qaeda and it has, to a degree, leveled the field in a very asynchronous sense of the competition with a world superpower.

Endnotes

1. Paul R. Pillar, *Terrorism and U. S. Foreign Policy*, Brookings Institution Press: Washington, DC, 2001, pp. 217–218.
2. Ibid., p. 73.
3. Ibid., pp. 13–14.
4. Louise Richardson, *Understanding the Enemy: What Terrorists Want: Containing the Threat.* Random House: New York, 2006. p. XIX.
5. Ibid., pp. 4–6.
6. Ibid., p. 7.
7. Ibid., pp. 11–13.
8. Marc Sagemen, *Understanding Terror Networks.* University of Pennsylvania Press: Philadelphia, 2004, p. VII.
9. Ibid., p. 74.
10. Ibid., p. 75.
11. Ibid., pp. 73–74.
12. Ibid., p. 78.
13. Jessica Stern, *Terror in the Name of God: Why Religious Militants Kill*, Harper Collins, 2003, pp. XIX, XVIII.
14. Franz A. Gerges, *Journey of the Jihadist: Inside Muslim Militancy*, Harvest Book, Harcourt: Orlando, FL, 2007, pp. 9–10.
15. Ibid., pp. 11–13.
16. Ibid., p. 35.
17. Richardson, op. cit., pp. 68–69.
18. Richardson, op.cit., pp. 85–88.
19. Lawrence Wright, *The Looming Tower: Al Qaeda and the Road to 9/11*, Alfred A. Knopf, New York, 2006, pp. 208–209.

20. Joel Kotkin, *The City: A Global History*, Modern Library Chronicles, Random House: New York. 2005, p. 156.
21. Ibid., pp. 155–156.
22. Yossef Bodansky, *Bin Laden: The Man Who Declared War in America*, Forum, Prima: Roseville, CA, 2001, p. XVII.
23. Ibid., pp. IX–X.
24. George Tenet with Bill Harlow, *At the Center of the Storm: My Years at the CIA*, Harper Collins: New York, 2007, pp. 102–105.
25. Anonymous, *Imperial Hubris: Why the West is Losing the War on Terrorism*, Brassey's: Washington, DC, 2004, p. 253.
26. Sageman, op cit., p. 175.
27. Daniel Benjamin and Steven Simon, *The Next Attack: The Failure of the War on Terror and a Strategy for Getting it Right*, Times, Henry Holt: New York, 2005, p. 76.
28. Ibid., p. 60.
29. Thomas L. Friedman, *The World is Flat: A Brief History of the Twenty First Century*, Farrar, Straus and Giroux: New York, 2005, p. 432.
30. Ibid., p. 433.
31. Ibid., p. 434.
32. Ron Suskind, *The One Percent Doctrine: Deep Inside America's Pursuit of its Enemies Since 9/11*, Simon and Schuster: New York, 2006, p. 235.
33. Anonymous, ibid., p. 81.
34. Anonymous, ibid., p. 79.
35. Loc. cit.
36. Pillar, op. cit., p. 48.
37. Anonymous, op.cit., pp. 262–263.

Targets of Terrorists

3

As our nation moves forward in protecting its citizens from the actions of terrorists, we have had to identify the items we regard as targets that might well serve as the focus of terrorist actions. Some targets have intrinsic value beyond the measure of wealth; other targets represent symbolic icons that have considerable psychological and cultural value to our nation. The initial identification of our nation's targets was enumerated in Presidential Decision Directive (PDD) 63 by President Clinton and identified eight critical infrastructures that required our vigilance in protecting. After the attacks of September 11, 2001 an additional seven critical infrastructures and key assets were added by President George W. Bush. As a result of this action we have organized our federal government, as well as our 50 states, 4 territories, 87,000 local jurisdictions, and over 19,000 municipal police departments to all participate in a most demanding role of protecting our nations and its citizens.

Another outcome of the September 11, 2001 attack on America has been the creation of the Department of Homeland Security that resulted in the transfer of 20 federal agencies and over 190,000 personnel to this new federal department. Our nation's only other example of an effort this broad in scope was the creation of our Department of Defense in 1947. The reassignment of federal agencies and personnel to a new Department of Homeland Security is not without major political and personnel problems. In addition to the numerous organizational challenges, and in many cases conflicts surrounding goals and objectives of various organizational units, we have redefined the fundamental premises of homeland security from those of national security. *National security* is the responsibility of our federal government, and it is based on the collective and cooperative efforts of our Department of Defense, State Department, and our intelligence community in the defense of our nation as well as protection of our national interests overseas. *Homeland security* is now defined as protecting our critical infrastructure and key assets with the cooperation of our private sector organizations, and with coordinated assistance of our federal agencies. Ironically, the creation of a Department of Homeland Security to facilitate greater coordination and communication among all levels of government and their respective agencies, has propelled the classification system and our "need to know" into direct conflict with the sharing of information among and between agencies, as they go about their role of protecting our homeland from terrorists.

Although the targets as defined as our critical infrastructure and key assets are not in dispute, there is a growing school of thought that the strategy of focusing so much of our nation's resources on the task to neutralize the terrorists who seek to attack us has in effect weakened our critical infrastructure. Stephen Flynn, former U.S. Coast Guard Commander and Los Angeles Police Chief William Bratton speak eloquently to this point. So, local officials who feel most constrained regarding the maintenance of the critical infrastructure components in their respective governmental jurisdictions will also question the tactical versus strategic value of our national strategy to defeat terrorists.

The balance of this chapter is organized around the following topics.

1. The Challenge of Protecting Our Nation
2. Protecting Our Nation's Critical Infrastructure and Key Assets
   A. Agriculture and Food Production Systems
   B. Water
   C. Public Health
   D. Emergency Services
   E. Defense Industrial Base
   F. Telecommunications
   G. Energy
   H. Transportation
   I. Nuclear Power Plants
   J. Chemical Industry
3. Research and Development in Support of Critical Infrastructure
4. Focus on Targets, Not Terrorists

Endnotes

1. The Challenge of Protecting Our Nation

The critical infrastructures that have made America the strongest and wealthiest nation in the world are also our greatest weakness and our Achilles' heel. Consequently, it is incumbent on our nation's leaders to fashion both a strategy and appropriate tactical plans to protect the nation. The scope of the challenge can be measured by the number of infrastructure assets that require our protection. The inventory of assets requiring our vigilance is truly overwhelming, and the national strategy for the physical protection of critical infrastructure and key assets enumerates the challenges as follows.

The Protection Challenge

Agriculture and food	1,912,000 farms; 87,000 food-processing plants
Water	1800 federal reservoirs; 1600 municipal wastewater facilities
Public health	5800 registered hospitals
Emergency services	87,000 U.S. localities
Defense industrial base	250,000 firms in 215 distinct industries
Telecommunications	2 billion miles of cable
Energy	
Electricity	2800 power plants
Oil and natural gas	300,000 producing sites
Transportation	
Aviation	5000 public airports
Passenger rail and railroads	120,000 miles of major railroads
Highways, trucking, and busing	590,000 highway bridges
Pipelines	2 million miles of pipelines
Maritime	300 inland/coastal ports
Mass transit	500 major urban public transit operators
Banking and finance	26,600 FDIC insured institutions
Chemical industry and hazardous materials	66,000 chemical plants
Postal and shipping	137,000 million delivery sites
Key assets	
National monuments and icons	5800 historic buildings
Nuclear power plants	104 commercial nuclear power plants
Dams	80,000 dams
Government facilities	3000 government owned/operated facilities
Commercial assets	460 skyscrapers[1]

Each of the aforementioned sectors fulfills an important role within our nation's critical infrastructure that contributes to our success, economy, and strength. As a world superpower, our Department of Defense has no peer, and much to its credit no nation will confront it head to head, but more so in an asynchronous battle strategy. These sectors of our critical infrastructure are so vulnerable to asynchronous attack and their vulnerability to terrorist groups is quite pronounced. Because most of these sectors are not governmentally controlled, but in many cases under private ownership, the national strategy requires a rich interface involving federal, state, and local governments with private and corporate organizations, thus making the task of designing and managing a national strategy most difficult at best.

Our nation has organized its resources and federal agencies around the following structure.

Federal Government Organization to Protect Critical Infrastructure and Key Assets

President
↓
Secretary of Homeland Security
↓
Federal, State, Local, and Private Sector Coordination and Integration
↓
Comprehensive National Infrastructure Protection Plan
↓
Mapping Threats to Vulnerabilities and Issuing Warnings

Sector	Lead Agency
Agriculture	Department of Agriculture
Food:	
Meat and poultry	Department of Agriculture
All other food products	Department of Health & Human Services
Water	Environmental Protection Agency
Public Health	Department of Health & Human Services
Emergency Services	Department of Homeland Security
Government:	
Continuity of government	Department of Homeland Security
Continuity of operations	All departments and agencies
Defense Industrial Base	Department of Defense
Information and Telecommunications	Department of Homeland Security
Energy	Department of Energy
Transportation	Department of Homeland Security
Banking and Finance	Department of the Treasury
Chemical Industry and Hazardous Waste	Environmental Protection Agency
Postal and Shipping	Department of Homeland Security
National Monuments and Icons	Department of the Interior[2]

In analyzing our nation's critical infrastructure, one of the most inescapable conclusions is the extraordinary problem we as a society have created for ourselves, due to deferred maintenance. We simply have not maintained a coherent investment strategy to ensure the maintenance and modernization of the very sectors responsible for our success.

Stephen Flynn, reporting on the American Society of Engineers' 2005 study on 15 categories of our infrastructure, states that the narrative reads like a survey that might have been conducted on the eve of the collapse of the Roman Empire.

> Roads, dams, water purification facilities, the power grid, canal locks, roads, wastewater management systems have gone from bad to worse in the past four years. More than 3,500 dams around the country are unsafe and many pose a direct risk to human life should they fail. The nation's inland waterway system is literally falling apart. . . . Nearly one half of its 257 locks are functionally obsolete, and that number is projected to rise to 80% by 2020. The report also documents that while the U.S. power system is in urgent need of modernization, maintenance expenditures have been dropping by 1% per year since 1992.[3]

This problem is not simply a function of our national strategy for conducting the war on terrorism, nor is it solely a result of the tactical plans designed to pursue terrorists on foreign soil. Certainly, these are elements in the problem we face today, but we must also make note of a 40-year pattern of national, state, and local government leadership avoiding the investment of limited government resources in these important infrastructure sectors. Furthermore, because almost 85 percent of our critical infrastructure is under the direct control of private and corporate organizations, they have equally mismanaged their responsibilities for maintenance and modernization of our infrastructure sectors. As a result, today we must not only provide protection for these enormously important resources, but we must also encourage reinvestment of our limited resources for both deferred maintenance and modernization.

2. Protecting Critical Infrastructure and Key Assets

Now that we have identified our nation's critical infrastructures and the lead federal agencies responsible for coordinating federal, state, local, and private agencies' efforts to protect them, we briefly review the challenges in each of the infrastructure sectors.

A. Agriculture and Food Production Systems

Our nation's agriculture and food production systems are critical to our economy as they account for almost 20 percent of our gross domestic product. Furthermore, the National Research Council reported that the U.S. livestock industry with revenues of $150 billion annually, is extremely vulnerable to a host of highly infectious and often contagious biological agents (insects, viruses, and microbes) that have been eradicated from the United States, but if introduced from other countries, by terrorists into herds, could immediately halt export of U.S. livestock and livestock products.[4]

Simon Kenyon reports that our nation's wakeup call for the necessity of protecting our agriculture and food systems was not the terrorist attack on the World Trade Center on September 11, 2001, but was the foot-and-mouth disease outbreak in Great Britain in that same year. Kenyon further observes the importance of increasing our agriculture security measures, irrespective of the threat of terrorists as we have to protect our agricultural systems from the West Nile virus, mad cow disease, exotic Newcastle disease in poultry, and the possibility of a human pandemic caused by an avian influenza virus. The enhancement of agriculture security measures must also be accompanied by improved surveillance systems and improved diagnostic capabilities of our agriculture laboratories.

> Agroterrorism is a deliberate attack on agricultural production systems designed to cause economic injury, disruption of the production system, human disease or political change. Agroterrorism falls under the general rubric of agro security, which is the conceptual framework of a food system that is resistant to natural disasters, accidental introduction of disease agents or toxins, or deliberate mischief, and one that is economically self-sustaining. Preparation for, and mitigation of, terrorist attack is only one part of agro security.[5]

Deliberate introduction of animal or plant diseases by terrorists or criminal activity has been very rare, and Kenyon observes that the only documented case of casualties arising from an attack on the food system was from salmonella food poisoning among restaurant patrons in Oregon in 1984 by a religious cult. Ironically, although it is difficult to document terrorist attacks on our agricultural systems, we have examples of crop destruction and the propagation of disease by nation-states during the conduct of warfare. Attacks on commercial agricultural crops are capable of causing enormous economic distress on the U.S. system of agriculture, yet these types of attacks do not fit the profile of the terrorist selection of a symbolic event that will create massive public fear. Nevertheless, as the world's largest exporter of wheat accounting for 33 percent of total wheat exports worldwide, 40 percent of the world's maize, and over 40 percent of the world's soybean production, we must develop surveillance systems to protect our enormous agricultural resources.[6] The use of satellite surveillance systems can also be usefully directioned to monitor potential crop disease infestation caused by naturally occurring pathogens and microbes, totally independent of an attack by any terrorist organization.

Another vulnerability of our agricultural crops centers on the fact that the production of a substantial proportion of the seed used for growing U.S.

crops is produced in other countries, presenting a possible route for the introduction of dangerous plant pathogens as well as contaminated fertilizers and pesticides.[7] Consequently, agricultural crops are vulnerable to a potential terrorist use of biological weapons at the stage of acquisition of the seeds that will grow into a form of insect weaponization for which security monitoring may be low to nonexistent.

Although agricultural fields and crops may not represent the symbolic targets of value that terrorists might be inclined to attack, there is another agricultural target that could affect all cloven-hoofed animals and present both an enormously expensive economic hit on our agricultural system, while also providing a most alarming impact on the public in the shape of a terrorist target with symbolic value. The introduction of foot-and-mouth disease to an animal herd by a terrorist group could easily result in the destruction of millions of animals.

Stephen Flynn reports in his book, *America the Vulnerable*, that one California study estimated that an outbreak of foot-and-mouth disease would cost the state over $1 billion in lost business. Moreover, such an infectious disease could spread to 28 other states as determined by a simulation study by the Foreign Disease Laboratory at Plum Island, New York and result in the loss of America's $90 billion livestock industry. In fact, if foot-and-mouth disease occurred in the cattle herds around Amarillo, Texas, up to 1.5 million head of cattle located within a 100-mile radius would have to be destroyed.[8]

Foot-and-mouth disease is one of the most infectious viruses of humans and animals, and the General Accounting Office report in 2002 observed that the cost of eradicating a foot-and-mouth disease outbreak in the United States would be as much as $24 billion. To further aggravate the situation, the terrorists' symbolic target of value would be focused on the en masse pictures of domestic livestock slaughter, with carcasses lying in the fields and innumerable cattle and sheep being burned on funeral pyres or dredged into large ditches and buried.[9] The impact of an event such as this would cause enormous psychological distress to the American public and provide sufficient value to the terrorist organizations to make an attack such as this quite appealing. The National Research Council reports that mass burial and burning are the major means of disposal of diseased animals. Both methods are expensive and repugnant to many people. Novel methods for carcass disposal, for inactivation of the foot-and-mouth disease virus in and on carcasses, and alternatives to mass slaughter during disease outbreaks are needed.[10]

Kenyon summarized a number of agroterrorism agents that can be used in attacks against our agriculture and food systems.

1. Pathogens that affect animals only (e.g., rinderpest virus)
2. Pathogens that affect plants only (e.g., karnal bunt of wheat)

3. Zoonotic pathogens that affect animals and humans (e.g., anthrax, rabies, and brucella)
4. Pathogens spread by insect vectors to animals and humans (e.g., Venezuelan equine encephalomyelitis virus)
5. Animal and plant-related toxins (e.g., botulinum, ricin, aflatoxin, fumonisins, and tricocethenes)
6. Advanced biochemical agents such as genetically manipulated organisms with enhanced toxicity or pathogenicity[11]

Kenyon further suggests a classification scheme based on the agroterrorism agents that would directly affect our economic system, and erode public confidence in our food production and supply systems or result in zoonotic diseases. From a very large number of candidate pathogens, Kenyon observes that the following list could be considered to have a terrorism risk potential, which our Homeland Security System must be aware of and prepared to respond to, if necessary.

1. Economic Attack
   Animal Diseases
   - Foot-and-mouth disease
   - Exotic Newcastle disease
   - Classical swine fever
   - African swine fever

   Plant Diseases
   - Soybean rust
   - Corn seed blight
   - Karnal bunt
2. Public Confidence
   - Avian influenza
   - Anthrax
   - Brucellosis
3. Zoonotic Diseases
   - Rift Valley fever[12]

It is quite obvious that our nation's agricultural system is of extraordinary value, and deserving of the declaration by Homeland Security Presidential Directive #9 of our agriculture system as an official critical infrastructure of our nation. The U.S. Department of Agriculture has been designated as the lead federal agency in providing the policy directives and appropriate coordinating responsibilities with our Department of Homeland Security to assure the protection of agriculture and food systems. These responsibilities also include the network of food production facilities, product distribution systems, and food processing operations and facilities.

The potential damage to our nation, should a terrorist attack focus on our agriculture systems, could be one of the most devastating economic hits directed against us. The loss of our food production capabilities would have an immediate impact on all sectors of our society, and result in a level of psychological trauma to a degree we have never experienced. Our agriculture system is nothing less than the "crown jewel" of our critical infrastructure system.

B. Water

One of our nation's most important critical infrastructures is our vast water system which includes not only our fresh water supply, but also our wastewater collection and treatment systems. A fact which is of surprise to many people centers on the fact that most of our water systems are operated by private companies; roughly 85 percent of all our water systems are not government controlled and managed, but owned by the private sector. Our nation has over 170,000 public water systems, and as the National Strategy for the Physical Protection of Critical Infrastructure and Key Assets points out, these utilities are dependent on reservoirs, dams, wells, and aquifers, as well as treatment facilities that service the 19,500 municipal sanitary sewer systems, and their estimated 800,000 miles of sewer lines.[13]

In essence, our nation's water system consists of:

1. Supply
2. Treatment
3. Distribution
4. Sanitary removal

The manner in which our water utilities supply their customers with the water they use daily involves the use of water wells, aquifers, reservoirs, dams, aqueducts, and the transmission pipelines that provide the water to homes and workplaces. The treatment systems involve the use of filtration plants that remove water impurities and any biological contaminants and other harmful substances that would render our water unfit for human consumption. The distribution system relies on a vast network of reservoirs, pumps, and pipelines that deliver the water from the treatment facilities and plants to the final user. The sanitary and waste removal systems collect water which is already impure or contaminated and directs it to sanitary treatment facilities.[14]

To protect our nation's water infrastructure we look to the Department of Homeland Security and the Environmental Protection Agency (EPA) to assist the private sector in developing plans, policies, and programs to secure this critical resource. We focus on the following types of attacks.

1. Intentional release of toxic chemicals into our water system
2. Physical damage to or destruction of water system plants or pipelines
3. Physical damage to our wastewater filtration plants
4. Actual or threatened contamination of our water supply
5. Cyber attacks on the SCADA systems operating our water systems
6. Attacks on the chemicals we use to filter impurities from our water system particularly at our wastewater treatment facilities which use and consume large amounts of chlorine and sulfur dioxide
7. Attacks on our aqueduct systems which deliver water, and which in some cases are uncovered open channels such as the 400-mile long aqueduct carrying water from Sacramento to Southern California
8. Attacks that might involve the chemical, biological, or radiological contamination of our water supply
9. Attacks made possible due to unregulated access to water utilities, distribution systems, and wastewater and filtration plants which provide limited or no security systems
10. Attacks focused on other critical infrastructures that enable the successful operation of our water systems, namely, the electrical grid system, as our water system's dependence on both our energy infrastructure and our chemical industry infrastructure is paramount for its continued operation

In addition to the vigilance required to secure our water infrastructure from terrorist attack, we must also be aware of the problems created by deferred maintenance of our water systems, filtration plants, wastewater, and piping systems. Parts of our water infrastructure in some of our large East Coast cities date back to the 19th century. The National Research Council also calls to our attention the vulnerability to the 80,000 dams we have in the United States in the event of a dam failure creating massive problems for our water infrastructure. "As an example, should the Glen Canyon Dam on the Colorado River fail, the resulting flood would overtop Hoover, Davis and Parker Dams downstream, disrupt the power grid of the Southwest, destroy irrigation in Southern California, and flood the Imperial Valley."[15]

Therefore, in addition to natural disasters, deferred maintenance of critical systems, or simply inadequate protection of the boating facilities and lanes close to our dams could all result in a series of incidents that could have a cascading effect on our nation. Because most of our critical water infrastructure is in the private sector, our government agencies have a definite responsibility to encourage collaborative efforts to secure our water systems with the full cooperation of the private and corporate sector and address any vulnerabilities that may emerge.

C. Public Health

The principal functions and missions of most public health departments focus on managing infectious diseases, the investigation of epidemics and quarantine measures, and the preventive measures of prophylaxis and vaccination to protect the public from disease. However, the public health sector is quite vast and diverse, ranging from city departments of public health, county departments of public health, state departments of public health, and various federal agencies such as the Centers for Disease Control, the Surgeon General, and the Office of Emergency Preparedness of the Health and Human Services Department.

Terrorism is fundamentally different from infectious disease outbreaks because it is under the willful control of a malevolent individual, and the terrorist group that chooses to implement an attack using some pathogen or toxic chemical substance can select the target sites, repeat the attacks, and utilize a strategy of simultaneous attacks across wide geographical areas. Thus, the public health authorities realize they must have an established formal relationship with local first-responder teams as well as with the Federal Bureau of Investigation and the U.S. Department of Homeland Security.[16] In many jurisdictions very effective formal relationships have been established; however, in far too many jurisdictions the nature of the relationship between the medical community and the law enforcement community is informal, at best.

There are many challenges confronting the public health sector, but foremost are two very important ones. First, hospitals by their very nature are open facilities that provide an important array of vital medical services to the public, and are therefore vulnerable to attack. The difficulty in identifying potential threats or preventing someone with malicious intent from harming a hospital is a difficult but necessary requirement so as to protect this valuable community resource. The disruption of hospital services or physical damage could easily preclude the public health system from assuming its important role in the event of terrorist attack, thus preventing a full and effective response and even exacerbating an emergency situation. A second challenge relates to the maintenance and protection, and the distribution of stockpiles of critical emergency resources. Although the United States maintains a national strategic stockpile, it has limited resources for rotating and replenishing supplies of critical materials and medicines.[17] A simultaneous attack by an Al Qaeda terrorist cell could easily disrupt the national strategic stockpile allocation of critically needed medicines.

Stephen Flynn comments on additional challenges confronting our public health system by referencing the 2005 report by the Non-Profit Trust for America's Health which rated each state on ten key indicators of public health and emergency preparedness.

- Nearly half of the states do not use national standards to track disease outbreak information.
- Only seven states and two cities have been recognized by the U.S. Centers for Disease Control and Prevention as adequately prepared to administer and distribute vaccines and antidotes in the event of an emergency.
- Hospitals in nearly one third of states have not planned sufficiently for prioritizing distribution of vaccines or antiviral medications to hospital workers.
- Hospitals in more than 40 percent of states do not have sufficient backup supplies of medical equipment to meet surge capacity needs during a pandemic flu or other major infectious disease outbreak.[18]

Flynn reports that our public health profession is aging and with retirement rates expected to be as high as 45 percent over the next five years, our nation will lose many of its most experienced professionals.[19] With fewer graduates of our medical schools, nursing schools, and public health schools selecting careers within our public health sector, our nation will begin to experience personnel shortages in key discipline areas.

To prepare for the range of these challenges, the government's plan for implementing public health sector initiatives will entail the U.S. Department of Health and Human Services working more closely with the U.S. Department of Homeland Security. The challenge to each of these agencies is to pursue some of the following initiatives.

1. Review mission-critical operations, establish protection priorities, and ensure adequate security and redundancy for critical laboratory facilities and services.
2. Enhance surveillance and communication capabilities, and coordinate links between public health monitoring facilities and healthcare delivery systems.
3. Develop criteria to isolate infectious individuals and establish triage protocols, and develop isolation and quarantine standards to protect the unaffected population during a public health crisis.
4. Work with the health care sector to enable the protection of stockpiles of medical supplies and other critical materials, distribution systems, and the critical systems of medical institutions.
5. Identify providers of critical resources and ensure a ready stockpile of vital medicines for use in an emergency.[20]

The important role our public health agencies play in protecting our citizens in the event of a terrorist attack utilizing any chemical, biological, or radiological weapon has elevated this sector to act as an important national critical infrastructure. Prior to the 9–11 attack on our nation, public health organizations were poorly funded, equipment depleted, and not really recognized for the important role they enact in the protection of citizens. Fortunately, our national leaders have augmented the budgets and clarified the role of public health agencies, but much remains to be accomplished both at the local and state levels.

Clearly our public health agencies have become rich targets for terrorists, as any attack on our nation with a corresponding attempt to disrupt our hospitals and public health system would have devastating effects on our ability to recover from such a joint attack. For this reason, we must be prepared for such an occurrence, and we must be able to withstand joint attacks on our nation and its critical infrastructure system.

D. Emergency Services

The National Research Council reports that today more than 220 million Americans live in and around our major cities. Cities are by definition target-rich environments for terrorists. The fixed infrastructure components of our cities which include the public utility systems that provide the electricity, water, gas, and waste collection provide unique secondary target sites which, if attacked in conjunction with primary target sites, would complicate the responses of our emergency services personnel who rely on these infrastructure services to perform their jobs. The bridges, tunnels, and roads within our cities also are necessary to enable emergency service personnel to respond to calls for assistance and service, therefore, these components of our infrastructure must not only be monitored, but also be protected because they are clearly fixed assets.

Almost all major cities in the United States have emergency operations centers that provide the capability for the city and its first responders to address the problems caused by a natural disaster or even attacks by terrorists. These emergency operations centers have to coordinate the responses of police, fire, and emergency medical teams as calls for service originate from the community regarding hazards such as fires, floods, hurricane, or earthquake and tornado events. As a result of the attacks on 9–11, we now recognize that the placement of the emergency operations center is critical to the continuing function of protecting our citizens, because we lost a great deal of New York City's Emergency Operations Center when the World Trade Center buildings collapsed.

In a terrorist attack, first responders will be at the greatest risk due both to their responsibility for rushing to the scene of an attack, and the uncertainty as to the conditions they are liable to encounter. Another potential danger lies in the possibility of terrorists targeting first-responders so as to leave the remainder of the city and its population in a vulnerable position, and subject to secondary attacks.[21]

As a result of the attacks of 9–11 we realized that our fire, police, and emergency medical responders were not able to effectively communicate because their telecommunications and mobile radio systems were incompatible. In addition to providing modern communication systems, it is also imperative that we develop redundant communication networks.

Another very serious aspect that will affect our emergency services' response capability centers on what Stephen Flynn terms our "fraying" public health workforce and our shrinking emergency care system which are operating at the breaking point. More specifically, Flynn notes the following.

> On any given day in a major U.S. city, ambulance drivers are forced to search for an open emergency room that is accepting patients. When hospital emergency departments get overloaded they direct ambulances to go elsewhere, which usually involves driving longer distances and may mean taking patients to less appropriate facilities. . . . Forty-five percent of hospital emergency departments reported turning ambulances away at some point in 2003, resulting in 501,000 diversions nationally.[22]

Moreover, in 2005 over 50 percent of our nation's hospital emergency departments were routinely operating at or over capacity, thus complicating responses in the event of a terrorist attack.

Our nation's emergency response system is designed to protect our citizens in the event of natural disasters and routine calls for services. Perhaps the weakest link in our emergency service system centers on our health care, hospital, and emergency capabilities that are clearly overtaxed even without confronting a terrorist event. We have to increase our investment in our health care system, and until we do so we will not be able to take full advantage of our emergency response system.

E. Defense Industrial Base

Ever since World War II our nation's defense has rested on our superb military, but without our Department of Defense engaging our private sector defense industry we would not possess the extraordinary array of modern warfare equipment. Indeed, were it not for our very sophisticated private sector's contributions, the Department of Defense would not be able to execute its core defense mission, including the mobilization and deployment of our nation's military forces to any part of the world on a moment's notice. Also, the sophisticated electronic weapons systems, as well as our state-of-the-art aircraft and ships are all dependent on the incredible research and development performed by our nation's defense industrial base.

Despite former President Eisenhower's warning that the buildup of a military defense industrial complex would cause problems for our nation, it appears as though we can be fortunate that our private sector continues to compete for military contracts, while at the same time improving its capabilities to continue to develop systems that are pushing the envelope of the highest technology and sophistication. The challenges our private industrial defense base confronts center on market competition, consolidations, globalization, outsourcing, and very complex corporate mergers involving domestic and foreign corporations. This pressure is not only felt by our corporate partners, but also by the Department of Defense because it has fewer private sector suppliers on which to rely.

During times of war and military engagements short of war throughout the world in the form of peacekeeping activities, the Department of Defense requires a surge capacity reaction from the private defense base to supply products and services to the military. On the other hand, during times of peace, when Congress redirects the defense budget to so-called "peace dividends" we experience a severe crippling of research within our corporate defense industry base. Research and development must move forward in a continuous linear pathway, as any interruptions in the support of the R&D needed for new weapons systems and other needed military procurement systems cannot be deferred until a time of crisis, or we will lose the leadership edge our nation has enjoyed for so many years.

The Department of Defense is not the only federal agency that relies on our private corporate sector, as our nation's very impressive national laboratory system is equally dependent on long-range fiscal investments that Congress must continue if we are to enjoy scientific pre-eminence as a result of our national laboratory system. So, our Department of Energy also relies on private corporate investment along with our nation's universities to support the research and produce the next generation of scientists and researchers who work for the benefit of national defense and advancement of knowledge and science.

The defense industrial base requires a constant and sustained participation of leadership, first from Congress for continuous and uninterrupted fiscal support; second from the wisdom of our executive branch of government for the creation of policies that support a strong military in times of peace as well as war; and finally, for a fully committed university and research system to join in the important development of the next generation's scientists to work for the enhancement of defense.

F. Telecommunications

Our telecommunications industry has over the years consistently provided reliable, robust, and secure communications that have resulted in our economic prosperity and national security. The Department of Defense, as well as other federal, state, and local justice agencies is dependent on the communications capabilities provided by a number of telecommunications firms and companies. Moreover, our economic strength is built on a solid base provided by our telecommunications sector, as all businesses and commercial enterprises rely on the ability to communicate with their customers.

Our telecommunications infrastructure is similar to our energy and electrical grid infrastructure, in that any damage to it would create a cascading impact on other multiple infrastructures, as the requirement for fast secure communication channels and capabilities is implicit in all infrastructures. As a consequence, the government and the telecommunications industry must often work collaboratively to build and maintain a resilient and secure industry, capable of protecting its widely dispersed critical assets.

> The telecommunications sector provides voice and data service to public and private users through a complex and diverse public-network infrastructure encompassing the Public Switched Telecommunications Network (PSTN), the Internet, and private enterprise networks. The PSTN provides switched circuits for telephone, data, and leased point-to-point services. It consists of physical facilities, including over 20,000 switches, access tandems, and other equipment. These components are connected by nearly two billion miles of fiber and copper cable.[23]
>
> The advances in data network technology accompanied by the incredible demand for data services have resulted in the worldwide proliferation and use of the Internet. While the Public Switched Telecommunications Network remains the backbone of this important infrastructure, the cellular, microwave and satellite technologies all provide gateways into this very complex system. Due to the convergence of traditional circuit switched networks with the broadband packet-based IP networks the telecommunications infrastructure is undergoing a rather significant transformation, which will ultimately lead to the Next Generation Network (NGN). This convergence along with the growth of the Next Generation Network and the emergence of wireless capabilities continue to provide challenges to our telecommunications industry and to our government as well. The evolving new infrastructure must remain reliable, robust and secure.[24]

The telecommunications infrastructure is thus a very clear target of terrorist organizations and the government has a responsibility to work with the industry to help ensure its protection. At the same time the government depends on the cooperation of the industry to obtain electronic evidence of terrorist cell activity. The delicate nature of legally acquiring such evidence is of importance to the industry that seeks protection from lawsuits and liability and the government that seeks legal justification to continue electronic searching and use such material in subsequent litigation against terrorist members and organizations. Due to the realities of both cyber and physical threats to our nation and the telecommunications industry the government must work with the industry to determine our vulnerabilities, develop countermeasures, and establish policies, plans, and procedures that will result in the mitigation of these risks.

The attacks on our World Trade Center and the Pentagon on September 11, 2001 revealed the rather substantial threat that terrorism poses to our telecommunications infrastructure. While communication was not the object of direct attack by terrorists, it suffered significant collateral damage. The telecommunications infrastructure demonstrated great resiliency as damage to assets at the attack sites was offset by a diverse, redundant, and multifaceted communication capability. Moreover, it is apparent that a terrorist attack targeting our telecommunications infrastructure along with another infrastructure or target in a simultaneous manner would have an extremely profound impact. Accordingly, we can anticipate that our telecommunications infrastructure will be a more focused target of terrorists in future attempts to attack our nation.

G. Energy

Energy represents our nation's most critical infrastructure, as it is essential to every aspect of life. Our entire economy is dependent on the energy that is principally produced by our electric grid system and our oil and gas system. The very quality of life we enjoy is directly related to the efficient functioning of our energy system. Our health care systems, all aspects of employment, as well as our educational systems all rely on our production and use of energy. Our vital national security and defense systems are totally reliant on our energy infrastructure. The energy infrastructure is fundamentally organized around two principal sectors: electricity and oil and natural gas.

The first sector, which produces electricity, consists of three major components: generation, transmission, and distribution. The *generation* of electricity occurs through our use of hydroelectric dams, nuclear power plants, and fossil fuel plants. The *transmission* and *distribution* systems link into areas of our electrical grid system. The *distribution* systems manage, control, and distribute the produced electricity into our businesses, government organizations, and our individual homes.[25] Although electricity cannot be stored and can only be used when produced, it must be resilient to terrorist attack. The targeting of this sector can, therefore, focus on the three principal components of generation plants, transmission lines, and distribution centers and substations. An attack on any one of these three components can create massive problems. Contrary to popular belief, it is not only the vulnerability of our nuclear power plants and hydroelectric dams, but the transmission lines and substations most Americans are not even able to identify as to purpose, type, and function that are also vulnerable.

Most of the electricity produced in the United States is a result of fossil fuel coal-fired units which produce over 51 percent of the power generated, whereas our nuclear power plants produce 20 percent, oil and gas produce 18 percent, and hydropower and other renewable sources produce 11 percent. The *transmission* system includes high-voltage lines, towers, underground cables, and transformers, breakers, and relays, whereas the *distribution* system consists of lower-voltage distribution lines and cables as well as substations.

The most serious types of terrorist threat to our electric power system center around both physical attacks by terrorists or cyber and electromagnetic attacks. The physical attacks could focus on the generating stations or transmission and distribution components and could cause local disruption or, if used in a coordinated fashion with a cyber attack or an electromagnetic attack on our control systems, could result in a serious multistate blackout that could initiate a serious network destabilization outage to our integrated electric power grid. Theoretically, it is possible to cause our electric grid system to collapse, with cascading failures in equipment far removed from the point of the attack, thus leading to even longer and more serious blackouts.[26]

In protecting our electric grid system from cyber attack we must monitor and be aware of the new advances in cyber weapons. We must also better protect our supervisory control and data acquisition (SCADA) systems with improved security such as firewalls, use of encryption, and more refined measures for detecting cyber intrusion. Intelligent agent-based networks designed to monitor and respond to cyber threats will also be necessary if we hope to better protect our systems. Also, an area where additional research and development are required centers on ways to detect a cyber attack from internal sources such as disgruntled employees.[27]

Our national power grid is made up of these independent electric grids, the Eastern Interconnected System covering the eastern two thirds of the nation and the adjacent eastern Canadian provinces; the Western Interconnected system, consisting of our states west of the Rocky Mountains and including the western Canadian provinces; and our Texas Interconnected System covering Texas and part of Mexico. Within this decentralized system we have independent service operators (ISOs), more than 3000 local utilities, more than 15,000 generators of power to produce electricity, 10,000 power plants, and hundreds of thousands of miles of transmission lines and distribution networks all designed to meet our need for producing and distributing the electricity that we need to run almost every aspect of our society from our businesses, government, schools, and our homes.[28] This electricity cannot be stored but must be available on demand which means our interconnected system must be prepared to distribute electricity from any of the three interconnected systems to areas requesting electricity.

In 1992, the Energy Policy Act was introduced to deregulate the power industry under the assumption that power produced in the northwest and southeast at lower cost could be transmitted to those areas where the cost of power was more expensive. The deregulation also required the unbundling of generation transmission and distribution properties all previously controlled by local governments and local governmental public utilities. Another very critical aspect of this deregulation of the industry occurred when the legislative branch approved authorization permitting the industry to make campaign contributions to members of Congress. This created a perfect alignment of the mutual interests of the industry with members of Congress, all now in a new environment free of regulatory oversight.[29] Consequently, the potential for abuse was established in 1992 and needed only a few other events to occur in the ensuing years which paved the way for the Enron energy scandal. In June of 1996 the Financial Accounting Standard 125 permitted Enron to effectively book all the profit streams expected from a power plant purchase over the next several years in just one year. By buying up plants each quarter and declaring on its balance sheet the profits anticipated over the next several years, it could show quarterly profits, even if the plant failed to produce the profits or failed entirely."[30]

In March 2000, after four years of litigation the U.S. Supreme Court upheld the new regulations on transmission lines and the separation of production and distribution, thus requiring transmission lines to be open to all, and, in effect, to increase the value of long-distance sharing of our electric grid system. Electricity trading increased beyond belief, and wholesale dealers such as Enron were able to capitalize on purchasing electricity from the generators at the lowest cost, and selling to the distributor at the highest cost. Enron was actually performing in the role of an arbitrage wholesaler, in a totally unregulated market, and these three major conditions permitted it to cost the rate-payers of California over $30 billion and cause numerous blackouts and brownouts.[31]

Perhaps the irony of our efforts to deal with our most important infrastructure, namely our electric grid system, proved to be more vulnerable to those we entrusted this system to, than to the terrorists from whom we seek protection. In other words, our government officials who carelessly introduced the deregulation environment of our most critical resource, the corporations and executives that exploited this system to enrich their own profits and corporate bonus packages, all created an environment in which damages measured between $30 to $100 billion dollars to the citizen rate-payers. There is no recorded cost of any terrorist activity that has cost as much or has done as much damage as that caused by thoughtless Enron corporate executives and other government officials' careless performance of duties. Our critical infrastructures must be protected not only from terrorists also from the people entrusted to regulate and protect our valuable resources.

Our energy infrastructure is also dependent on our ability to manage our oil and natural gas sector. Our economy is dependent on a cost-effective system of oil production, refining, distribution, and transportation of this critical product. Our ability to transport crude oil is based on over 160,000 miles of pipelines, storage terminals, and a refinery system that includes more than 160 oil refineries producing between 5000 to 500,000 barrels per day. Although our nation has over 600,000 oil wells we must still import oil to manage the demands from our citizens and corporations. In fact, oil products provide 97 percent of the energy used in our transportation sector. As book is being prepared, the cost of oil is $107.58 per barrel with a 52-week high of $110.33 per barrel. One year earlier, the cost of oil per barrel ranged in the $40–$50 per barrel price structure. More ominous, is the fact that on November 16, 2007 some oil traders were already taking out oil future contracts based on $400 per barrel. So, in addition to our vulnerability to terrorists attacking any part of the oil production, refinement, or transportation systems, we also are vulnerable to the economic cost structure created by a complex international system of pricing.

The natural gas industry is a vast network of privately owned and operated facilities numbering in excess of 275,000 wells, 278,000 miles of natural gas pipelines, and more than 1,119,000 miles of natural gas distribution lines. This system was created to meet market demand and to maintain safety, and although vandalism was taken into account, the system like so many other parts of our infrastructure was not designed to withstand a terrorist attack.[32] Because natural gas provides over 25 percent of residential and industrial energy needs it is a critical portion of our energy infrastructure.

Our nation's electrical grid system and our oil and natural gas systems are all critical to the total functioning of almost every aspect of our economy and any disruption in these services for even a few days could have enormous consequences. The potential range of targets for these systems is enormous, both in terms of geographic issues, and the complex interdependencies that require coordinated system-to-system interface. Another important aspect to consider in protecting these systems from terrorist targeting opportunities is to acknowledge how totally dependent each of these industries is on computer systems. Because these industries have not yet experienced sophisticated cyber attacks, they have not fully integrated computer security and intrusion analysis programs to offset and protect themselves from this type of terrorist targeting.

H. Transportation

Our nation's multiple forms of transportation systems have provided great convenience to our citizens and also provided an important and indispensable service to our economic system. Virtually all infrastructure components rely on our transportation systems to provide delivery of the resources they require or the resources they produce.

Our highway system has been constructed in a pattern of interconnected state and local roads which include over 4 million miles of paved highway. These roads intersect with over 45,000 miles of interstate highway and toll ways, and included in this system are more than 590,000 bridges. In addition to our highway system, our nation also depends on our railroad network which extends for over 300,000 miles for freight traffic, and a commuter rail system which covers over 10,000 miles of rail. Another important feature of our transportation system is the existence of 500 commercial service airports, and 14,000 general aviation airports providing commercial service to the many components of our infrastructure system.[33]

Although our country has invested over $25 billion in protecting our aviation system since the 9–11 attacks, we have not been able to match this investment strategy in other important parts of our infrastructure. For example, Stephen Flynn reports on the 12,000 miles of our inland waterway system which includes such important rivers as the Mississippi and Ohio Rivers where barge traffic becomes a very cost-effective form of commercial transportation. A single barge can move the same amount of cargo as 58 trucks at one tenth the cost, resulting in more than a $7.8 billion annual transportation cost saving to shippers. Of the 257 locks along our inland waterway interstate navigation system, 30 were constructed in the 19th century, and another 92 locks are more than 60 years old despite an average planned life span of 50 years. We have over a $600 million backlog in maintenance projects and a need to invest over $5 billion just to keep the system operational.[34]

Our inland waterway system is also critical to the movement of hazardous chemicals, thus providing a safety factor to materials that would ordinarily travel on our highway system. Also, the nation's power generation plants to produce our electricity require coal and fossil fuel which can be transported in greater volume and at less cost on our waterway system, as opposed to highway traffic, thus reducing the cost of electrical power both to residential and commercial users.

Our railroad system which transports both freight and passengers also factors into public safety issues and concerns. The railroad freight system carries a large volume of chemicals such as chlorine gas and other materials that are extremely hazardous should an accident occur or should they become a terrorist target. Because trains carry more than 40 percent of all intercity freight they also remove most of these chemicals that would otherwise be transported over our highway system. When one factors the movement of 20 million intercity travelers using our railroad system annually, and the 45 million passengers who ride our trains and subways operated by local transit authorities, we experience a different type of vulnerability, because this volume of passenger traffic cannot be screened for potential weapons as we screen airline passengers. We thus allow a trade-off in safety for the necessity of managing a system that must move a large volume of passenger traffic at peak travel times, while minimizing disruption of boarding and disembarking of these rail and subway systems.

Our maritime shipping infrastructure which includes 361 seaports, as well as our coastal and inland waterway system and the numerous locks, dams, and canals constitutes a very complex system to protect, given both the range of cargo ships and the incredible volume of cargo that passes through our ports.

Port security is an especially vulnerable aspect of our infrastructure, because of modern container shipping practices. The speed at which containers are loaded and unloaded leaves little time for the inspection of the cargo loaded within each container. In fact, the number of containers that entered the United States in 2004 exceeded 9 million and 95 percent of these containers were not inspected. These 40-foot containers have the potential of becoming our 21st century Trojan horses as they could be loaded with WMDs or explosives that could easily sneak through our port inspection system without notice. The government's Container Security Initiative under which cargoes are to be inspected in foreign ports prior to departing for the United States is a wonderful plan but it does require a close and very cooperative program with foreign countries to ensure tamper-proof containers. It also will require that the shippers make the appropriate technical modifications so that their containers are tamperproof. The security requirements for providing safety assurance to U.S. ports will cost more than $7.3 billion over the next 10 years.[35]

It is obvious how important our transportation system really is to our economy and to our safety. The challenge in protecting our citizens and these transportation systems will require enormous effort both in research to develop new methods of protection such as passenger profiling systems that filter out lower-risk users and focus more on the anomalies and higher-risk users and sensor technologies for explosive detection such as x-ray diffraction which detects several types of explosives microwave/millimeter-wave scanners which penetrate denser substances, and nuclear quadrapole resonance which identifies the chemical compositions of selected materials.[36]

No single sensor technology can be expected to discover all threats; therefore, an array of multiple sensor technologies will have to be developed and networked in a manner to provide accurate information that will be free of false positive results. Preventing damage to our transportation system and harm to the citizens who use it or are geographically close to the vulnerable points of our system is a very challenging and complex endeavor. A great deal of research remains to be completed if we are to be successful in preventing harm to our citizens.

I. Nuclear Power Plants

The United States has 104 civilian nuclear power plants which include both commercial plants as well as research reactors at 25 universities and 11 research laboratories. These nuclear reactors are located within 31 states and are designed to withstand extreme events such as hurricanes, tornadoes, and earthquakes. The federal government has required these nuclear reactors to have in place robust security programs to withstand an attack of specified adversary strength and capability, and since the 9–11 attacks security has been enhanced. However, prior to the 9–11 attacks the security of our nuclear facilities did not anticipate an attack utilizing aircraft as occurred at the World Trade Center and the Pentagon. In addition to our improved security programs, the design of these nuclear facilities incorporates physically hardened structures.[37]

The current design of our nuclear power plants simply does not provide a defense against high-speed attacks using hijacked commercial aircraft or smaller aircraft loaded with high explosives. Currently, a great deal of classified research has been completed to model the impacts of aircraft collisions on steel-reinforced concrete structures, as well as the potential effect of aircraft fuel fire on a nuclear power plant. Although the main elements of this work remain very sensitive and classified, it is clear that such an attack on a nuclear power plant could have severe consequences.[38]

In addition to reactors, all nuclear civilian power plants contain storage facilities for spent nuclear fuel, and with few exceptions, all of the spent fuel produced by these reactors is stored where it was produced. Approximately 42,000 metric tons of spent fuel are currently stored under water for both cooling and shielding purposes. Some sites are storing their spent fuel outside the power plant in dry casks on concrete pods, and it is estimated that approximately 3000 metric tons are stored this way. The threat of a terrorist attack on the spent fuel storage facilities is dependent on the design features, but it is generally felt to be manageable with minimum radiation exposure.[39]

Research nuclear reactors at our universities are used to produce neutrons and gamma rays primarily for research and testing purposes, and because their thermal output is so low inasmuch as they produce such a minor amount of radiation, heat, and waste, they are not really considered a major problem in the event of a terrorist attack. Nevertheless, security at these university sites should be enhanced.

Since the 9–11 attacks, we have become conscious of our vulnerabilities, and our nuclear power plants provide a very inviting set of fixed targets for a terrorist attack utilizing aircraft as was the case in the World Trade Center attack. However, there are many equally inviting targets that could also result in devastating consequences, and these fixed targets include our petroleum refining plants and chemical plants. These targets are not as well protected, nor are they as well designed from a physical and structural point of view as our nuclear power plants.

J. Chemical Industry

Our chemical industries provide an incredible array of products that other parts of our nation's infrastructure depend upon for their continuing operation; an example is the chlorine that permits the purification of our water systems. The chemicals used in fertilizers that our agricultural industry relies on for crop production are also an important to our economic system. In fact, the chemical industry provides more than $97 billion of products that are directed to our health care system.[40] Also, our entire economy benefits from the creativity and productivity of our chemical industry that is the greatest exporter of its products thus contributing to our wealth in terms of our export–import and balance of payment reserve.

The chemical industry has plants of all types and sizes, in which their product mixes create a problem in terms of designing a security plan and system. There are more than 123 chemical facilities located in or near major metropolitan areas, and any one of these facilities could expose more than a million people to risk if a toxic release or terrorist attack occurred. In fact, one single plant located in New Jersey could threaten the safety of the 12 million people living in the New York metropolitan area.[41] The inherent danger to our population from a terrorist attack on chemical facilities would not only expose literally hundreds of thousands of citizens to toxic dangers, but it would also have a cascading effect on critical infrastructure components that rely on the products produced by this important industry. The consequences of any such terrorist attack would also be accompanied by a severe economic drawdown.

3. Research and Development in Support of Critical Infrastructure

Based on the government's identification of our critical infrastructure, the Executive Office of the President and the Office of Science and Technology Policy developed a research plan structured around nine science, engineering, and technology themes that would support the entire critical infrastructure sectors previously enumerated. The nine focused areas to encourage research and development for the critical infrastructure sectors are as follows.

- Detection and sensor systems
- Protection and prevention

- Entry and access portals
- Insider threats
- Analysis and decision-support systems
- Response, recovery, and reconstitution
- New and emerging threats and vulnerabilities
- Advanced infrastructure architectures and systems design
- Human and social issues[42]

By mapping the long-term overarching goals to the nine science, engineering, and technology themes the following research and development priorities were created.

1. Improve sensor performance.
    - Develop technology to detect unexploded ordinance.
    - Develop a real-time global positioning system synchronized for electric grid monitoring.
    - Improve sensor arrays and improved explosive and radiological detection.
    - Improve sensors for detection of tampering with water systems and building heating, ventilation, and air-conditioning (HVAC) systems.
    - Improve supervisory control and data acquisition (SCADA) security for water systems and HVAC systems.
2. Advance risk modeling, simulation, and analysis for decision support.
    - Standardize vulnerability analysis and risk analysis of critical infrastructure sectors.
    - Conduct quantitative risk assessments to better quantify terrorism risks to the critical infrastructure sectors.
3. Improve cyber-security.
    - Develop new methods for protection from automated detection of, response to, and recovery from. attacks on critical information infrastructure systems.
    - Foster migration to a more secure Internet infrastructure.
4. Improve prevention and protection.
    - Develop new, low-cost physical perimeter and area defense systems for critical infrastructure sectors, including systems to mitigate high explosive blast, projectile, and fire threats.
5. Better address the insider threat.
    - Improve technologies such as intent determination and anomalous behavior monitoring for insider threat detection, covering physical and cyber infrastructure.

6. Improve large-scale situational awareness for critical infrastructure.
    - Define the communication and computing system architecture needed to create a national common operating picture of the nation's critical infrastructures.
    - Develop links between real-time intelligence threat information with the identification of potentially threatened critical infrastructure.
7. Develop next-generation designs and architecture for devices and systems.
    - Development of such systems must become reliable, autonomic (self-repairing and self-sustaining), resilient, and survivable in order to continue to operate in diminished capacity, rather than failing in crisis conditions.
8. Develop a human–technology interface that allows better comprehension and decisions.
    - Provide an integrated view of societal risks from terrorist events, natural disasters, and other emergencies for incorporation in decision-support systems to anticipate and evaluate alternative risk reduction investments and emergency response decisions.[43]

To develop a more coherent national plan to protect our critical infrastructures, it is necessary to map this plan to other national research and development plans within the Department of Homeland Security, as well as other federal, state, and local agencies, and in some cases private industry plans. In fact, a large part of our critical infrastructure is not under government control, but operated in the private or corporate sector and this will mandate closer cooperation between government agencies and the private corporate world. In short, with over 85 percent of our critical infrastructure under the control of the private sector, we need to develop workable plans that engage both the government and the private sector in fostering programs to protect our nation and all its citizens.

4. Focus on Targets, Not Terrorists

Recognizing that it may not be possible to protect all aspects and components of our critical infrastructure, Benjamin and Simon suggest a strategic approach that would identify the most critical assets that could and should be shielded. Mathew Brzezinski's book, *Fortress in America*, comments on the top 100 targets within the United States as identified by the CIA, and our nation's governors have assembled their own list of 150 primary and 180 secondary targets.[44] The Department of Homeland Security has also surveyed and identified both primary and secondary targets at federal, state, and local levels and has designed plans to protect and respond to any terrorist assault on these targets.

Stephen Flynn provides a most provocative and stimulating approach by suggesting that when trying to protect the citizens of New Jersey, New York, or any other state from the hazards of a chemical plant or oil refinery that may be the target of a terrorist, the key should be focusing less on the terrorist and more on the prospective target. In this fashion one might be able to improve the protection to the citizens by making improvements of the prospective target that will minimize the exposure to toxic or hazardous chemicals. As Flynn observes:

> It is not the terrorists themselves that should be our top priority. Instead, we should be doing our best to improve our ability to weather the age of terrorism—and the age of disasters of a natural sort.[45] Or, as Admiral William Crowe stated, "the real danger lies not with what the terrorists can do to us, but what we can do to ourselves when we are spooked."[46]

In Flynn's opinion our top national priority must be to ensure that our society and our infrastructure are resilient enough not to break under the strain of natural disasters or terrorist attacks. Flynn recommends that our nation focus not only on developing plans to provide security for our critical infrastructure, but that we also make a very substantial investment in repairing and upgrading our crumbling industrial infrastructure, along with our deteriorating bridges and inland waterway systems. In general, our entire infrastructure needs such investment from years of deferred maintenance.[47] Flynn's view is to improve our critical infrastructure by making an investment not only in security, but also in upgrading through a modernization process of structure investment. This will result in improving our critical infrastructure and in the long run, it will strengthen our nation while improving its security elements. Perhaps Jessica Stern best captures the essence of our focus by her very cogent observation, "In the end, however, what counts is what we fight for, not what we oppose."[48]

To secure our infrastructure in a fashion that identifies critical vulnerabilities to only the most anticipated targets leaves other infrastructure vulnerable to attack. Therefore, our threat assessment has to assume a very balanced and objective analysis in which each critical infrastructure is carefully reviewed in terms of how we best can prevent attack, what measures are needed to protect it and should an attack be launched, how best to respond and assist in making a full operational recovery. Our focus turns upon our fight to protect and maintain our critical infrastructure. The investment we make to maintain modernization and security is more easily attained when our focus is premised on "fighting for a balanced nation's infrastructures" as opposed to simply focusing on strategies to apprehend or eliminate the terrorists alone. In short, our priority has to refocus our fight for the coherence of our critical infrastructure in a manner that more equitably allocates resources, so that we do not invest so much of our limited resources in one infrastructure such as the TSA and airline industry, at the expense of other vulnerable infrastructure.

Endnotes

1. The National Strategy for the Physical Protection of Critical Infrastructures and Key Assets, White House, Washington, DC, 2003, p. 9.
2. Ibid, p. 18.
3. Stephen Flynn, *The Edge of Disaster: Rebuilding a Resilient Nation*, Random House: New York, in cooperation with the Council on Foreign Relations, 2007, pp. 7–8.
4. Committee on Science and Technology for Countering Terrorism, National Research Council of the National Academies, *Making the Nation Safer: The Role of Science and Technology in Countering Terrorism*, National Academy Press: Washington, DC, 2002, p. 77.
5 Simon Kenyon, Agroterrorism, in Thomas A. Johnson (Ed.), *National Security Issues in Science Law and Technology*, Taylor & Francis: Boca Raton, FL, 2007, pp. 52–53.
6. Simon Kenyon, ibid., pp. 54, 57, 60.
7. National Research Council of the National Academies, op. cit., p. 78.
8. Stephen Flynn, *America the Vulnerable: How our Government is Failing to Protect us from Terrorism*, Harper Collins: New York, in cooperation with the Council on Foreign Relations, 2004, p. 114.
9 Simon Kenyon, ibid., pp. 54, 57, 60.
10. National Research Council of the National Academies, op. cit., p. 95.
11. Simon Kenyon, op. cit., p. 63.
12. Simon Kenyon, loc. cit., p. 63.
13. National Strategy for the Physical Protection of Critical Infrastructures and Key Assets, op. cit., p. 39.
14. National Research Council of the National Academies, op. cit., 245.
15. National Research Council of the National Academies, ibid., p. 246.
16. Michael P. Allswede, Medical response to chemical and biological terrorism, in Thomas A. Johnson (Ed.), *National Security Issues in Science, Law and Technology*, Taylor & Francis: Boca Raton, FL, 2007, pp. 25–26.
17. National Strategy for the Physical Protection of Critical Infrastructures and Key Assets, op cit., p. 41.
18. Stephen Flynn, *The Edge of Disaster: Rebuilding a Resilient Nation*, op cit., pp. 74–75.
19. Loc. Cit.
20. National Strategy for the Physical Protection of Critical Infrastructures and Key Assets, op. cit., p. 42.
21. National Research Council of the National Academies, ibid., p. 240.
22. Stephen Flynn, *The Edge of Disaster: Rebuilding a Resilient Nation*, op. cit., pp. 76–77.

23. National Strategy for the Physical Protection of Critical Infrastructures and Key Assets, op. cit., p. 47.
24. Ibid., p. 48.
25. Ibid., p. 50.
26. National Research Council of the National Academies, ibid., pp. 180–182.
27. Ibid., pp. 187–190.
28. Charles Perrow, *The Next Catastrophe: Reducing Our Vulnerabilities to Natural, Industrial and Terrorist Disasters*, Princeton University Press: Princeton, NJ, 2007, pp. 215–216.
29. Ibid., pp. 227–228.
30. Ibid., p. 236.
31. Ibid., pp. 232–233.
32. National Research Council of the National Academies, ibid., p. 196.
33. Ibid., p. 212.
34. Stephen Flynn, *The Edge of Disaster: Rebuilding a Resilient Nation*, op. cit., pp. 84–85.
35. Daniel Benjamin and Steven Simon, *The Next Attack: The Failure of the War on Terror and a Strategy for Getting It Right*, Henry Holt: New York, 2005, pp. 249–250.
36. National Research Council of the National Academies, op. cit., pp. 228–229.
37. National Strategy for the Physical Protection of Critical Infrastructure and Key Assets, op. cit., p. 74.
38. National Research Council of the National Academies, op. cit., pp. 42–43.
39. Ibid., pp. 46–47.
40. National Strategy for the Physical Protection of Critical Infrastructure and Key Assets, op. cit., p. 65.
41. Daniel Benjamin and Steven Simon, *The Next Attack: The Failure of the War on Terror and a Strategy for Getting It Right*, op. cit., pp. 130–131.
42. The Executive Office of the President; Office of Science and Technology Policy, The Department of Homeland Security, Science and Technology Directorate. *The National Plan for Research and Development in Support of Critical Infrastructure Protection*, White House, Washington, DC, 2004, p. VII.
43. Ibid., pp. VIII–XI.
44. Daniel Benjamin and Steven Simon, *The Next Attack: The Failure of the War on Terror and a Strategy for Getting It Right*, op. cit., p. 243.
45. Stephen Flynn, *The Edge of Disaster: Rebuilding a Resilient Nation*, op. cit., p. 93.
46. Loc. cit.
47. Ibid., p. 110.
48. Jessica Stern, *Terror in the Name of God: Why Religious Militants Kill*, Harper Collins: New York, 2003, p. 296.

Weapons of Mass Destruction

4

Advances in technology and science have created a range of opportunities for the improvement of societies throughout the world. However, at the same time, we must acknowledge the fact that some of these advancements have also made it possible for terrorists to develop and refine their weapons of mass destruction. The advancements made in molecular biology not only provide great discoveries and applications for all populations and nations, but unfortunately, they also have permitted the development of designer viruses and pathogens for which we have no existing antibodies and therapeutic interventions. The Internet has also provided incredible advances and opportunities for all societies, yet we observe once again, how terrorists have used this phenomenal advancement to achieve their own ends. Specifically, terrorists have been able to find very valuable information relating to the discovery and creation of cyber attack scripts, the creation of biological pathogens, and the formulas for chemical nerve agents, blood agents, and choking agents. Also, instructions for the design and construction of explosive bombs and materials are readily available on the Internet as well. In addition to the access of personal information on potential targets or victims, terrorists have also used the Internet to recruit new members, seek some sense of political legitimacy, or simply to communicate with their members or with allied cells and terrorist groups.

Another aspect of great concern to all counterterrorist organizations is the profound change in the breed of new terrorist groups. Not only are the motivations changing from socialistic terrorist groups, but the use of violence by groups motivated by religious conviction with apocalyptic, extremely violent beliefs draws them to seek out weapons of mass destruction.[1]

As terrorist groups, particularly Al Qaeda and other related jihadist cell groups seek out weapons of mass destruction, we are concerned that they will obtain nuclear bombs, radiological dispersal devices, bioterrorism weapons, or chemical weapons. These groups have expressed a clear willingness to use these WMDs. Prior to the September 11, 2001 attack on the United States by Al Qaeda, the CIA began receiving reports that in 1995 Sudanese leaders approved of bin Laden's request to begin production of chemical weapons for use against U.S. troops stationed in Saudi Arabia. There were also chemical weapon training programs at Al Qaeda camps in Afghanistan. In December 2000, Italian and German police arrested several Al Qaeda agents in Milan, Italy and Frankfurt, Germany for their activities and plans to bomb the European Parliament building in Strasbourg, France. Also in August 2002,

Russian authorities reported they had observed terrorist surveillance of a secret nuclear-weapons storage facility, and that they stopped an attempt to steal 18.5 kilograms of highly enriched uranium.

Even before these reported activities in Russia, the U.S. intelligence community was concerned about Al Qaeda's interest in acquiring nuclear weapons. In February 2001, Jamal Ahmad Al-Fadl arranged a deal in which Al Qaeda offered $1.5 million for some uranium from a Sudanese military officer, and U.S. officials believe the purchase of uranium from South Africa was successful. Furthermore, U.S. officials remain concerned regarding the meetings of two Pakistani nuclear scientists, Sultan Bashiruddin Mahmood and Abdul Majeed with Osama bin Laden and Ayman Al-Zawahiri, particularly because they were colleagues of Dr. Abdul Qadeer Khad, regarded as the father of the Islamic bomb who assisted Libya, North Korea, and Iran in their nuclear programs. Most alarming is Osama bin Laden's pronouncement made after the September 11, 2001 attacks on the United States that Al Qaeda already possesses both chemical and nuclear weapons.[2]

The format of this chapter is as follows.

1. Broken Borders and Illicit Trafficking in Nuclear Materials
2. Nuclear Terrorism
   - A. Nation-State Owned Nuclear Weapons
   - B. Improvised Nuclear Devices
   - C. Attacks on Nuclear Reactors
   - D. Nuclear Explosions in Outer Space
3. Biological Terrorism
   - A. Categorizing Biological Threats
     - a. Category A Biological Weapons
     - b. Category B Biological Weapons
     - c. Category C Biological Weapons
   - B. Size and Scope of Biological Weapons Laboratories
   - C. Genetically Engineered Biological Weapons
4. Chemical Terrorism
   - A. Chemical Plants as Targets of Terrorists
   - B. Categories of Chemical Weapons
     - Nerve Agents
     - Blister Agents
     - Choking Agents
     - Blood Agents
5. Agroterrorism
   - A. Agricultural Surveillance Programs
   - B. Livestock Vulnerabilities
   - C. Crop and Plant Vulnerabilities

1. Broken Borders and Illicit Trafficking in Nuclear Materials

One of our most pressing fears and concerns is that terrorists will acquire weapons of mass destruction, and will exploit the broken borders throughout the world to obtain and transfer these weapons. The former Soviet Union which held the world's largest arsenals of chemical, biological, and nuclear weapons has not been able to provide sufficient control of these weapons systems as a result of the fall of the old Soviet system. The economic desperation of so many unemployed Soviet weapons scientists coupled with the degraded system of command and control provides a window of opportunity for terrorists to acquire through purchase or theft materials that are easily converted into weapons of mass destruction. After the fall of the Soviet Union, 15 new countries were created with complex sets of borders and that many of these new countries had Soviet weapons laboratories and storage facilities.

> Organized crime is taking advantage of permeable borders between Russia and the Baltic states to smuggle stolen cars, weapons and metals, including radioactive materials. The borders of the southern tier – including Turkmenistan, Kazakhstan, Southern Russia and Azerbaijan – are completely unguarded in some areas; including points of entry into Iran.[3]

Clark Kent Ervin, the former Inspector General of the Department of Homeland Security observed that border protection is a major fear and a "nuke in a box" will find its way across the porous borders. In fact, there were over 650 confirmed cases of illicit trafficking in both radiological and nuclear materials across the globe between 1993 and 2004, as reported by the International Atomic Energy Agency.[4]

Technical documents discovered in Al Qaeda safe houses in Afghanistan after the fall of the Taliban revealed that Al Qaeda had focused attention on nuclear weapon design issues, and that two Pakistani nuclear scientists provided Al Qaeda with a blueprint for developing a nuclear bomb. This situation tied to estimates of 600 tons of poorly secured nuclear materials in the former Soviet Union caused great concern to U.S. counterterrorism officials.[5] In fact, one of the reasons our U.S. Department of Energy has dispatched skilled nuclear security officials from Sandia National Laboratory in Albuquerque, New Mexico to Russia is to provide Russian authorities with the science to better protect their existing nuclear weapons inventory.

The Nunn–Lugar Nuclear Threat Reduction Act was passed by Congress so that the United States could provide Russia with assistance in dismantling and safely storing the nuclear weapons that are now in the independent republics of Ukraine, Kazakhstan, and Belarus. In fact, the Russian nuclear black market has grown so rapidly since 1991, that it has become an international crisis. Numerous incidents of trafficking in nuclear weapons, weapons-grade material, triggers, weapons-related equipment, weapons schematics and blueprints, and scientists selling their expertise are so intense that the Director of the International Atomic Energy Agency termed the crisis a "nuclear Walmart [sic]."[6]

As the Soviet Union dissolved, one of the most formidable challenges President Putin would eventually confront was the newly emerged Republic of Chechnya. In fact, one of the first cases of a radiological dispersal device or a dirty bomb was by Dzokhar Dudayev, the Chechen Mafia leader who placed several canisters of cesium-137 in Izmailovsky Park in Moscow and demanded concessions from the Russian government. No concessions were made. In 1995, Dudayev offered to sell his stockpile of nuclear weapons to the United States, if the United States would recognize Chechnya as an independent state. The United States refused to do so, and it is reported that Dudayev sold an estimated 20 nuclear suitcase bombs to Al Qaeda for $30 million and two tons of Grade 4 heroin.[7]

Did, in fact, Dudayev have control of 20 suitcase bombs, and did Al Qaeda really acquire those nuclear suitcase bombs? We find no firm evidence to either prove or disprove this concern. However, in 1997, General Alexander Lebed, who at the time was President Boris Yeltsin's assistant for National Security Affairs reported that 84 of an estimated 132 special KGB "suitcase" nuclear weapons were not accounted for in Russia.[8] General Lebed also informed a visiting U.S. congressional delegation in May of 1997 that of the 132 "suitcase bombs" that the Soviet arsenal had, they'd only been able to locate 48, leaving 84 of these small nuclear weapons, called atomic demolition munitions, missing from their nuclear weapons arsenal. General Lebed later retracted his claim, but then in November of 1997 repeated it on the BBC, this time describing the devices as RA-115s, their weight as 30 kilograms, and their yield as 2 kilotons.[9]

Even more alarming was the statement made by Stanislav Lunev, the highest-ranking Soviet military intelligence officer to defect, that during the cold war Russian Spetsnaz (Russian Special Forces) were forward deployed with some of these atomic demolition munitions inside the United States. In the event of a United States–Soviet war, the Spetsnaz would detonate ADMs in strategic locations throughout the United States. According to several sources, Soviet-made ADMs have found their way into the Russian black market and into the hands of terrorists. Interrogations of captured Al Qaeda leaders, uncovered a plan that was termed the "American Hiroshima," and based upon multiple detonations of nuclear weapons in major U.S. cities, using weapons already smuggled into the United States.[10]

In late 2001, when U.S. Special Forces and CIA operatives toppled the Taliban, thousands of pages of documents, videos, computers, and computer disks were captured. This material provided firm proof that Al Qaeda was acquiring chemical and biological weapons as well as plans for a "super bomb." In fact, the 25-page essay on the "super bomb" included information on the types of nuclear weapons, the physics and effects of nuclear explosions. Our nuclear experts who reviewed this document concluded that "the author of the document understood shortcuts to making crude nuclear explosives."[11]

In March of 2004, Hamid Mir, Osama bin Laden's biographer, told the Australian Broadcasting Corporation that in 2001, Ayman Al-Zawahiri claimed that Al Qaeda already possessed nuclear weapons. Al-Zawahiri told him, "If you have $30 million go to the black market in Central Asia, contact any disgruntled Soviet scientist and . . . dozens of smart briefcase bombs are available." Furthermore, the Arabic language magazine *Al Watan Al Arabi* reported that bin Laden's representatives had purchased 20 nuclear warheads from Chechen mobsters in exchange for $30 million in cash and two tons of opium.[12]

The dilemma for our intelligence community is trying to firmly establish whether Al Qaeda does possess weapons of mass destruction. There is clear agreement that Al Qaeda has experimented with chemical weapons including nerve gas, biological weapons including anthrax, and nuclear radiological dispersal devices, commonly known as "dirty bombs." However, does Al Qaeda actually possess "suitcase" nuclear weapons? Also, has Al Qaeda managed to acquire highly enriched uranium or plutonium? In short, does Al Qaeda have a nuclear bomb or other weapons of mass destruction? Some intelligence analysts simply are not certain, whereas others maintain that, in fact, Al Qaeda does have nuclear weapons and is simply waiting for the appropriate time to launch a sophisticated multiple site attack within major U.S. cities.

To further complicate this situation, all one has to do is recall the abject terror created one month after the September 11, 2001 attack when George Tenet, then director of the CIA informed the president that "Dragon Fire," a code-named CIA agent, reported that Al Qaeda terrorists possessed a ten-kiloton nuclear bomb stolen from the Russian arsenal and this nuclear weapon was now in New York City. Although the CIA had no independent confirmation of this report, neither did it have any basis on which to dismiss it.

> Did Russia's arsenal include a ten-kiloton weapon? Yes. Could the Russian government account for all the nuclear weapons the Soviet Union had built during the cold war? No. Could Al Qaeda have acquired one or more of the weapons? Yes. Could it have smuggled a nuclear weapon through American border controls into New York City without anyone's knowledge? Yes.[13]

Fortunately, in this case, the report was eventually disproved, but this incident resulted in President Bush ordering Vice President Cheney to leave Washington, DC for an undisclosed location to provide assurance for continuity of governmental succession and operation in the event of a disaster of this type, revealing the complexity of decision making in events of this nature. In short, one has to arrive at a basis for confirming events such as these, or discounting them, but without factual proof to establish verification, one must also possess a sound basis on which to reject certain hypotheses and assumptions.

2. Nuclear Terrorism

Nuclear and radiological threats fall within three major categories:

Nation-state owned nuclear weapons
Improvised nuclear devices
Attacks on nuclear reactors

A. Nation-State Owned Nuclear Weapons

Nation-state owned nuclear weapons are owned by the following nations.

China
France
Great Britain
India
Israel
Pakistan
Russia
United States

Other nations that are believed to have active nuclear weapons development programs or nuclear weapons are as follows.

South Africa
Iran
North Korea

The fundamental key to these nations' nuclear weapons programs is how seriously they guard and secure their nuclear weapons arsenals, since the threat to terrorists obtaining these weapons is dependent on the security programs or the weaknesses of the nuclear weapons security programs. The United States

> has the most secure and well guarded nuclear arsenal, and our tactical weapons have integrated permissive action links to prevent unauthorized use. The nuclear weapons of Britain, China, France and Israel are well protected. The nuclear weapons of India and especially Pakistan are under secure control of the military, but in the case of Pakistan, we see a very unstable political situation. Russia has the most troubling inventory control system for their extensive and very large nuclear weapons arsenal.[14]

B. Improvised Nuclear Devices

The second category of improvised nuclear devices focuses on any stolen or diverted nuclear material such as highly enriched uranium or plutonium that could be fabricated into a weapon. Improvised nuclear devices can be fabricated by terrorists because the basic technical information needed to construct an operable nuclear device is readily available in the open literature. Terrorists can acquire the nuclear material by theft from existing stockpiles of highly enriched uranium, or reactor-grade plutonium contained in commercial spent fuel rods. There are an estimated 150 metric tons of separated plutonium and 1200 metric tons of highly enriched uranium in Russia, and with this amount it is imperative that both inventory controls and security systems permit much better accountability of this enormous nuclear weapons materials inventory.[15]

> Al Qaeda's meeting with two Pakistani nuclear scientists, Sultan Bashiruddin Mahmood and Abdul Majeed occurred because the two Pakistani nuclear scientists were told that Al Qaeda had succeeded in acquiring nuclear material for a bomb from the Islamic movement of Uzbekistan. Al Qaeda was told the nuclear material that they secured could not produce an explosion but could be used in creating a "dirty bomb." U.S. intelligence agencies concluded that the two Pakistani nuclear scientists Mahmood and Majeed had provided bin Laden and Al Qaeda with the blueprint for constructing nuclear weapons.[16] These two Pakistani nuclear scientists worked in Pakistan's Atomic Energy Commission and were colleagues of Dr. A.Q. Khan, the developer of the nuclear bomb for Pakistan.

The catalog of products offered by Khan's network included the following.

- A comprehensive "starter" kit for Iraq's uranium enrichment program
- Rudimentary P-1 centrifuge blueprints
- More sophisticated P-2 centrifuge designs
- Necessary components to build P-2 centrifuges
- State-of-the-art P-3 centrifuges
- Blueprints of Chinese-designed nuclear warheads

- Nearly two tons of uranium hexafluoride, enough for one nuclear bomb if sufficiently enriched
- Contact information for consulting services in assembly and repair[17]

C. Attacks on Nuclear Reactors

The potential terrorist threats in this category include attacks on our nuclear power plants as well as those national laboratories and universities that maintain nuclear research reactors. Of these three types of nuclear facilities, the commercial nuclear power plant is the most vulnerable simply because the design phases of these commercial nuclear power plants never anticipated the threat of terrorists attempting to destroy their facilities. The United States currently has 103 operating civilian nuclear power reactors at 65 sites which are responsible for generating 20 percent of our nation' s electrical power supply. Present-day concerns of an attack on one of our nuclear power plants are focused on an airline being hijacked or flying directly into the containment core, causing the steel-reinforced concrete structure to crack and permit radioactive materials to escape. Also, the impact of aircraft fuel fire encapsulating the commercial nuclear power plant as a byproduct of the crash is also a vulnerability to be assessed.

Another factor in the vulnerability of commercial nuclear power plants over research reactors located at our universities and government laboratories is visibility. A commercial nuclear power plant can be identified quite easily due to its isolated location as well as the smoke exhaust plumes visible for miles. In comparison, the 36 operating nuclear research reactors located in 23 states are clearly not apparent to most people as their visibility within a university community or a government laboratory, is substantially more removed from public awareness. For one reason, their thermal output only produces .01 to 20 megawatts, and consequently much less radiation, heat, and waste in the form of spent fuel rods than the much larger commercial nuclear power plants which have thermal outputs of 2000 to 3000 megawatts. In fact, the large thermal output of our commercial nuclear power plants also requires rather extensive cooling pools to contain the nuclear fuel rods. This requirement introduces another security vulnerability as it presents a target-rich environment. Should the nuclear reactor containment core fail, the large spent fuel storage pools for cooling and shielding purposes located adjacent to the nuclear reactor containment buildings (currently containing over 42,000 metric tons of spent fuel throughout our entire system) may well be vulnerable to ground attacks. It should also be noted that not all spent nuclear fuel is contained in large cooling ponds, as approximately 3000 metric tons of spent fuel are stored outside the commercial power plant buildings in dry casks on concrete pads above ground. The threat of terrorist attacks on spent fuel storage facilities, similar to the reactors is totally dependent upon design characteristic, and since the September 11, 2001 attack, we have been reviewing all aspects of our nuclear power plant and nuclear reactor inventory.[18]

Khalid Sheikh Mohammed, the person responsible for planning the September 11, 2001 attack utilizing aircraft to attack the World Trade Center, the Pentagon, and the plane thought to be directed to either our Capital or the White House stated in an interview he gave to the Al Jazeera television station in April 2002, just before he was captured by U.S. officials, that they "first thought of striking a couple of nuclear facilities," but with regret he stated, "It was eventually decided to leave out the nuclear targets — for now." When the interviewer asked, "What do you mean for now?" Mohammed replied, "For now means for now."[19] Clearly Al Qaeda senior leadership, despite Mohammed's capture, has not given up consideration of our nuclear power plants as rich targets of opportunity.

Although there have to date been no attacks on nuclear power plants, the two major incidents that have occurred date back to March 28, 1979 when a combination of both human and technical error at the Three Mile Island Power Plant in Pennsylvania came within an hour of a total meltdown simply because failure of a valve that drained water from the reactor core went unnoticed by the technicians on duty who by mistake turned off the emergency cooling pump which caused the reactor to overheat. If the meltdown occurred, it would have resulted in the release of massive amounts of radiation to the two million people living in the area. In contrast to the Three Mile Island accident, the meltdown of the Chernobyl Nuclear Power Plant in the Ukraine on April 26, 1986 was a full disaster, as the 1000-ton steel and concrete roof containment structure exploded as a result of temperatures inside the core exceeding 3632 degrees Fahrenheit. This resulted in excess of 50 tons of radioactive material spewing into the air and the environment, killing over 6000 people. Deaths from cancer as a result of the radiation exposure continue to occur and the 18 square miles around the Chernobyl power plant have been designated as an "exclusion zone" from which all were evacuated and no one has been permitted to return.[20]

With reference to commercial nuclear power plants in the United States, Graham Allison reports the following.

> Power plants are designed to withstand earthquakes, tornadoes and other natural disasters, but according to the Nuclear Regulatory Commission, none of the 103 operating U.S. nuclear reactors was designed to withstand the impact of a Boeing 767 jetliner. Twenty-one of these reactors are located within five miles of an airport. . . . The pools of water where spent nuclear fuel is stored present an even softer target than the thick containment domes. Simply draining the water from the pools can lead to combustion of the spent fuel.[21]

Perhaps we have underestimated the damage that may be caused by attacking the cooling ponds that store the spent fuel rods, because of focus on the nuclear reactor containment core. Of course, both deserve our attention, but a report released from the Brookhaven National Laboratory reports that a severe release from a cooling pool containing spent fuel rods could cause as many as 28,000 cancer fatalities and render about 188 square miles of land unfit for human habitation.[22]

The terrorist's potential use of a radiological dispersion device, more commonly referred to as a "dirty bomb," also presents serious problems. This attack is brought about by the use of conventional explosives coupled with radioactive material designed to be scattered by the explosion of the weapons or bomb. Any nuclear material including medical isotopes can be used, and such radioactive material can come from hospitals, dental offices, universities, laboratories, and so on. Radioactive materials that terrorists may seek to acquire for their dirty bombs include the following sources and materials.

Source	Material	Isotope
Hospital Radiation Therapy	Iodine	125
	Cobalt	60
	Cesium	137
Pharmaceuticals	Iodine	131
	Iodine	123
	Technetium	99
	Thallium	201
	Xenon	133
Nuclear Power Plant Fuel Rods	Uranium	235
Universities, Laboratories, Radiography	Cobalt	60
	Cesium	137
	Iridium	92
	Radium	226

A weapon fashioned from the above-enumerated materials would not produce a nuclear yield, but would spread contamination. The volume of radioactive materials used would determine the lethality of the release.[23] Whether first responders would be vulnerable to radiation exposure, and whether the area in which the radiological device was exploded had sufficient quantity of radioactive material to preclude human habitation would be dependent on the device used, the quantity of radioactive material acquired, and the general sophistication of the terrorist group planning such an attack.

D. Nuclear Explosions in Outer Space

The potential damage to nations throughout the world who aspire to use or are presently using satellites in low-orbit flight patterns to provide a number of commercial or military services may find these services disrupted or eliminated if a thermonuclear weapon is discharged in outer space. The U.S. discovered the extremely strong disruptive electromagnetic pulse effect in July 1962 during research using a Thor ballistic missile and a 1.4-megaton orbital burst. As a result of the orbital explosion, local radio stations and telephone service failed for a time due to the electromagnetic forces created by the orbital detonation. During the following months, seven low earth-orbit satellites were crippled; this was a third of all existing satellites at the time. Today, more than 250 commercial and military satellites orbit the earth in the lowest altitudes and these satellites are defenseless against the radiation that could be released by a high-altitude atomic explosion. Satellites that would be affected most would be those providing such services as navigation, communication, earth imaging, weather forecasting, and broadcast and cable television. Satellites that were damaged could cost over $100 billion in replacement costs.[24]

In addition to the economic costs to the commercial satellites, the potential for a terrorist group or a nation-state supporting such a space-based strategy using a low-yield 10-kiloton bomb could seriously blind the U.S. military electronic warfare capabilities. China recently shot down one of its weather satellites thus demonstrating that research is moving forward in this orbital domain, and we have to devise plans and programs to protect both our commercial and military assets.

In February 2008, the United States had the U.S.S. Lake Erie shoot down a disabled U.S. spy satellite carrying over 1000 pounds of toxic fuel and not responding to ground control signals. The Navy used a SM-3 missile which is designed to take out incoming enemy missiles, not orbiting satellites. The successful endeavor occurred at a low altitude and hit a target that traveled in a polar orbit at more than 17,000 mph. Because the satellite was in a relatively low-altitude orbit at the time it was hit, the debris re-entered the earth's atmosphere where it burned up on re-entry, with no fragment larger than a football re-entering the earth's atmosphere. If the military did not shoot this 5000-pound satellite down, it would eventually have hit earth during the first week of March 2008, and the United States was worried that the fuel supply of hydrazine might injure or kill people if they were to come into contact with the downed spy satellite. Also, the U.S. government did not want to chance any possibility of China or Russia re-engineering the intelligence collection apparatus aboard the satellite in the event it did not fully burn up on re-entry into the earth's atmosphere.

3. Biological Terrorism

Regarding biological terrorism issues, there are two basic types of threats. The first and perhaps most disturbing is the release of a communicable infectious agent such as smallpox, Ebola, or a foot-and-mouth disease that would be targeted primarily against livestock. The second type of threat consists of biological agents that may cause disease or death in individuals, but typically are not communicable or transmitted from one individual to another, and the best example of this biological agent is *Bacillus anthracis* or anthrax.[25]

A. Categorizing Biological Threats

Biological weapons can be directed at humans, animals, or agricultural crops, and because there is such a wide range of biological agents, they constitute excellent terror weapons as they induce both physiological consequences as well as psychological fear. These weapons can be categorized in five main categories.

Bacterial Agents	Anthrax
	Plague
	Brucellosis
	Typhoid fever
Rickettsial Agents	Typhus
	Rocky Mountain spotted fever
	Q fever
Viral Agents	Smallpox
	Influenza
	Yellow fever
	Encephalitis
	Dengue fever
	Chikunguna
	Rift Valley fever
	Hemorrhagic fevers
	Ebola
	Marburg
	Lassa
Toxins	Botulinum
	Staphylococcus enterotoxin
	Aflatoxin
Fungal	Coccidioidomycosis[26]

The Centers for Disease Control (CDC) categorize biological weapons according to their lethality, and it designates these weapons into three major categories A, B, and C. The category A biological weapons are considered the most lethal and the most dangerous because they can easily be transmitted from one person to another with high mortality rates.

Category A Biological Weapons[27]

Variola major (smallpox)
Bacillus anthracis (anthrax)
Yersina pestis (plague)
Clostridium botulinum toxin (botulism)
Francisella tularensis (tularemia)
Filoviruses
- Ebola hemorrhagic fever
- Marburg hemorrhagic fever

Arenaviruses
- Lassa (Lassa fever)
- Junin (Argentine hemorrhagic fever) and related viruses

Category B agents include biological weapons that are moderately easy to disseminate, cause low mortality, but require enhanced disease surveillance.

Category B Biological Weapons[28]

Coxiella burnetti (Q fever)
Brucella species (brucellosis)
Burkholderia mallei (glanders)
Alpha viruses
- Venezuelan encephalomyelitis
- Eastern and Western equine encephalomyelitis

Ricin toxin from *Ricinus communis* (castor beans)
Epsilon toxin of *Clostridium perfringens*
Staphylococcus enterotoxin B

A subset of category B agents includes pathogens that are food- or waterborne. These pathogens include:

Salmonella species
Shigella dysenteriae
Escherichia coli
Vibrio cholerae
Cryptosporidium parvum

Category C agents include emerging pathogens that could be engineered for mass dissemination with a potential for high morbidity and mortality as well as a major health impact.

Category C Biological Weapons[29]
- Mipah virus
- Hantaviruses
- Tick-borne hemorrhagic fever viruses
- Tick-borne encephalitis viruses
- Yellow fever
- Multidrug-resistant tuberculosis

These biological weapons offer a means of attack that is potentially lethal, but a great deal also depends on wind patterns, temperature, and the life of the agent.

B. Size and Scope of Biological Weapons Laboratories

The range of both size and scope of biological weapons laboratories can vary from a sophisticated nation-state laboratory to a lone individual with some knowledge of microbiology and $10,000 worth of laboratory equipment which would include glassware, centrifuges, growth media, and typical laboratory chemicals and equipment and access to the Internet where information on the reproduction and growth of biological agents is plentiful. Terrorists who have access to both money and experts with knowledge of molecular biology or microbiology may present a very serious challenge because they conceivably could create designer biological agents, pathogens, or toxins. The creation of new biological agents in which no knowledge or research exists as to their effects would make biodefense strategies significantly vulnerable and create a substantial threat to the targeted population. The incredible advances made in molecular biology, plus the knowledge that is openly available to even the most elementary biology students provides terrorist organizations a new resource for planning terrorist attacks. Also, the opportunities for recruitment of individuals with skills and a background in biology who may be of assistance to the terrorist organization's plans are easily accessible at virtually no cost to the terrorist organization.

However, many nation-states over the years have made incredible investments in this field. They typically have unlimited capacity for establishing biological weapons laboratories, staffing their laboratories with very skilled microbiologists and other scientists. Also, rarely is financing a barrier to their pursuit of both research and weaponization programs. Perhaps the former Soviet Union represented the most extreme case of any nation seeking to build biological weapons. The Soviet Biopreparat at its height employed more than 25,000 very skilled scientists and stationed them at many laboratories and research and development sites. The Biopreparat specialized in growing biological agents in antibiotics to make them resistant and ensure that victims could not be cured.[30]

In a fascinating chart comparing the production of dry agents between the United States and the Soviet Union, it is quite apparent as to the enormous stockpiling of weaponized biological weapons the Soviet Union was maintaining. The chart describes the following.

Comparison of Dry Agent Production[31]

	Metric Tons per Year	
Agent	**United States**	**Soviet Union**
Staphylococcal enterotoxin B	1.9	0
Francisella tularensis (tularemia)	1.6	1500
Coxiella burnetti (Q fever)	1.1	0
Bacillus anthracis (anthrax)	0.9	4500
Venezuelan equine encephalitis virus	0.8	150
Botulinum	0.2	0
Yersinia pestis (bubonic plague)	0	1500
Variola virus (smallpox)	0	100
Actinobacillus mallei (glanders)	0	2000
Marburg virus	0	250

Why the Soviet Union would even envision it would need 4500 metric tons of anthrax or 100 metric tons of variola (smallpox) was consistent with its intent to mate these biological weapons to ICBM missiles with the intention of destroying cities in the United States should a war occur; but its strategy was far more sinister: attacking entire continents with their biological weapons.

Fortunately President Nixon ordered our biological weapons program to be closed in 1969, and with the fall of the Soviet Union we now have programs in which our nation tries to employ or provide research grants to former Soviet scientists so that they can develop peaceful commercial applications to assist their economy while transitioning from biological weapons production.

Today, fewer than 10,000 individuals with experience in government programs have the capability to produce military quality biological weapons. However, the number of people who have basic scientific skills in microbiology who can culture pathogens and perform some of the new cutting-edge genetic engineering now make it possible to produce more dangerous biological agents and to increase their numbers into the hundreds of thousands.

The revolution in biotechnology makes this possible, and also diminishes our ability for genuine global oversight of this very dangerous area. Therefore, our challenge in the area of counterterrorism is not only to better secure the former Soviet Union's bioweapons inventory, but also to limit the spread of the Al Qaeda jihadist ideology before the terrorist groups turn to the manufacture of genetically engineered biological weapons that have never been previously seen or identified.[32]

C. Genetically Engineered Biological Weapons

The ease with which biological weapons can now be produced through new molecular, biological, and genetic engineering techniques provides new and incredible challenges against which we must guard. These new genetically engineered pathogens can be designed to have any or all of the following attributes.

- Safer handling and deployment
- Easier propagation or distribution
- Improved ability to target the host
- Greater transmissivity and affectivity, such as engineering a disease like Ebola to be as communicable as measles
- New weapons
- Increased problems in detection
- Greater toxicity, more difficult to treat
- Combinations of some or all of the above

Scientists suggest that the following new types of biological weapons are now deployable.

- Binary biological weapons
- Designer genes, DNA shuffling, and life forms
- Gene therapy weapons to transform viruses and DNA vectors carrying Trojan horse genes
- Stealth viruses
- Host swapping diseases
- Designer diseases[33]

In short, our nation will have to increase its abilities and develop a comprehensive approach to addressing the bioterrorism challenges that lie ahead. This implies a continuing improvement in our intelligence collection and analysis capabilities in this important biological weapons area. We must also improve on our capabilities of detecting covert biological weapons programs and devise viable strategies for neutralizing bioweapons programs when discovered.

4. Chemical Terrorism

Clearly chemical agents do not have the same potential for producing widespread casualties and destruction as do the previously described biological weapons or nuclear weapons. Nevertheless, it may well be that the most plausible use of chemicals is in attacking aggregations of people in enclosed spaces such as subways, airports, or other such locations.[34]

A. Chemical Plants as Targets of Terrorists

One of our vulnerabilities centers on the 123 chemical facilities located in or near major metropolitan areas, and a terrorist attack on any one of these chemical plants could put more than 1 million people at risk. One plant in New Jersey, if successfully attacked, could threaten the safety of several million people living in the New York metropolitan area.[35] In short, industrial chemicals if improperly released into an unprepared urban environment could be devastating to the local population. Because chemical plants are vulnerable to trucks filled with ammonia nitrate and parked adjacent to transport vehicles carrying supplies into the plant or products out of the plant, an attack similar to the Oklahoma City federal building attack could be devastating.

B. Categories of Chemical Weapons

Chemical weapons fall within the following categories: nerve agents, blister agents, choking agents, and blood agents.

1. Nerve agents incapacitate a person and disrupt the nervous system by binding to enzymes critical to nerve functions and causing convulsions and paralysis. Death from lethal doses can occur within minutes. The following is a listing of common nerve agents.
   Tabun
   Sarin
   Soman
   VX[36]
2. Blister agents destroy the skin and tissue, cause blindness on contact with the eyes, and can also result in fatal respiratory damage. Blistering appears from hours to days, but the effect on the eyes is much more rapid. Examples of blister agents are the following.

Sulfur mustard (H or HD)
Distilled mustard (DM)
Nitrogen mustard (HN)
Lewisite (L)
Phosgene oxime (CX)
Mustard lewisite (HL)[37]

3. Choking agents cause the blood vessels in the lungs to hemorrhage, and fluid to build up, until the victim chokes or drowns in his or her own fluids; this is pulmonary edema. The only treatment is inhalation of oxygen and rest. Examples of choking agents are the following.
   Phosgene (CG)
   Diphosgene (DP)
   Chloropicrin (PS)
   Chlorine gas[38]
4. Blood agents kill through inhalation, and they provide little warning except for nausea, headache, and vertigo. These are very rapid action agents killing within seconds to minutes of exposure. Examples of blood agents are the following.
   Hydrogen cyanide (AC)
   Cyanogen chloride (CK)[39]

One of the key problems in responding to a chemical attack is to coordinate the efforts of local law enforcement with emergency services and fire personnel. Pre-existing plans developed in conjunction with hospital and public health authorities are also critical. Decontaminating victims before transporting to a hospital is a mandatory feature of a well thought out response plan to a chemical attack.

5. Agroterrorism

Our vulnerabilities to a terrorist attack on our agriculture system are enormous and serious. Our livestock, crops, and food production systems are among the best in the world and over the years, we have taken the security and safety of these systems for granted, and have been far too permissive of unrestricted and unsupervised visits to farms and ranches. Our nation is dependent on our ability not only to feed our own people, but from an economic point of view, our agriculture systems are among the foremost economic drivers to our GNP and economy. As we discuss our vulnerabilities to acts of terrorism against our crop or animal agriculture systems, we must realize that we are not simply talking about the impact of a terrorist act on our agricultural economy, but also on the entire security of our food supply and food production systems.

Livestock, like people, can be exposed to biological pathogens such as anthrax or smallpox, or to toxins such as botulinuum or staphylococcus enterotoxin, or simply ingest contaminated food or water. Our crops can also be exposed to biological weapons at the seed stage, in the field, or after harvest.[40] We must plan to establish programs to protect our livestock and our agricultural crops, and this will imply the establishment of agriculture surveillance systems that consider both domestic and international issues.

A. Agricultural Surveillance Programs

The need to establish agricultural surveillance programs similar to programs that exist to monitor human interests that our Centers for Disease Control have in operation would be a worthwhile and long-needed effort. The U.S. livestock industry has revenues of $150 billion annually and is vulnerable to a number of highly infectious and contagious biological agents, viruses, and microbes that we have eradicated but which exist in other nations. This suggests we should establish surveillance programs to monitor international import of animals, livestock, crops, and seed.

The United States Department of Agriculture, Animal and Plant Health Inspection Service (APHIS) has been effective in diagnosing and responding to naturally occurring disease, but it will require more staff and funding to address those problems that might occur through the intentional introduction of diseases and biological agents. In short, we need to develop a set of research and surveillance programs for both plant and animal diseases similar to how the Centers for Disease Control oversee and monitor human diseases.[41] Because highly infectious naturally occurring plant and animal pathogens exist outside U.S. borders and are readily transported, either intentionally or inadvertently with little risk of detection, it seems only logical that we would begin to provide the U.S. Department of Agriculture with the resources to directly establish these needed surveillance programs.

B. Livestock Vulnerabilities

One of the results of the recent market trend in the concentration and specialization in the livestock industry is that we now see fewer feedlots and those that remain concentrate several thousand animals in tight quarters, thus opening potential problems. For example, if a highly contagious agent such as a virus from the picornavirus family, namely foot-and-mouth disease (FMD), is introduced into these tight quarters the aerosol transmission has a high likelihood that all of the confined animals will be infected. Also, we now see that animals are moved across large geographic and international borders to smaller centralized feedlots. In 2001, the state of Iowa received a million swine from 24 states and Canada. Therefore, in situations such as these, we need to be able to recognize an infected animal immediately, which means we need rapid field diagnostic assays for the pathogens likely to infect our livestock. Also needed is an integrated national reporting system that can electronically notify the U.S. Department of Agriculture of any found disease and infestation.[42]

Our livestock are also vulnerable to anthrax, Q fever, brucellosis, foot-and-mouth disease, Venezuelan equine encephalitis, hog cholera, African swine fever, avian influenza, Newcastle disease, Rift Valley fever, and rinderpest. Foot-and-mouth disease could cost the nation as much as $20 billion during restricted trade of our livestock due to international embargos. As documentation to this issue of foot-and-mouth disease, the 1997 outbreak of FMD in Taiwan required the destruction of 1.6 million animals at a cost of over $1 billion per year until all embargos were removed.[43] Simon Kenyon reported that the 2001 animal disease epidemic in Great Britain resulted in substantial collateral damage to the tourism industry. The Cumbria region of Britain lost 31 percent of its tourist revenue and the gross domestic product in Britain fell by 2.5 billion pounds, of which 1.93 billion was accounted for by the reduction in tourism expenditures.[44]

A recent California study estimated that an outbreak of foot-and-mouth disease could cost the state over $1 billion in lost trade. Also, a training simulation by the Agricultural Foreign Disease Laboratory on Plum Island, New York, estimated that by the time it confirmed the first case of foot-and-mouth disease that it would likely spread to 28 states at which point most of the $90 billion livestock industry would be decimated. Another highly infectious hazard is "mad cow disease," and on December 23, 2003 an infected cow was found in the state of Washington which immediately led to a ban by 30 nations on all U.S. beef exports. If a contagious foot-and-mouth disease occurred in one of the Amarillo, Texas feedlots, up to 1.5 million head of cattle within a hundred mile radius would have to be slaughtered.[45]

C. Crop and Plant Vulnerabilities

Just as livestock has vulnerabilities to agroterrorism, so does our crop and plant system. They intersect with threats to our livestock because they provide animal feed to our livestock. Also, crops have virtually no surveillance and monitoring, and one reason is the enormous size of most of our crop fields. We need to be vigilant in the monitoring and detecting of any pathogen entering our crop fields. Remote satellite monitoring of our crops focused on identifying any disease outbreak would be useful. However, it is surprising that a substantial proportion of the seed used for growing our crops is actually produced in other countries, thus presenting a possible route for the introduction of dangerous plant pathogens. Any crop may contain several pathogens that are not yet found in the United States, although they cause major issues in other countries; therefore, we either should produce more seed or be more vigilant on the seed stock we import. Recently, a report from the National Research Council observed the following.

> For animal disease, USDA operates several laboratories—Plum Island and Ames among them—that perform diagnoses, carry out research and provide training for veterinarians. CDC is the central agency for the control and prevention of communicable human disease, but no center currently exists to serve the same function for plant disease. Such a center is desperately needed. . . . A major research, development, and training center is called for that would address fungal, bacterial, and viral diseases of plants. Programs would focus on genomics and proteomics, data basing and informatics, forensics, pathogenesis, host–parasite interactions, diagnostics, sensors, food safety, analytical methods, epidemiology, modeling of disease outbreaks, intervention and management.[46]

The challenges that confront us will require that our land grant universities and colleges of agriculture play a more formidable role in these important areas.

D. Risk of Animal and Plant Disease

The recent history of foot-and-mouth and other diseases in Europe and the United States make it clear that the risk of unintentional spread of animal and plant diseases is at least as great as the risk of deliberate attacks on agriculture and the food supply. The wake-up call for our agriculture and food system was not the terrorist attack on the World Trade Center in 2001, but the foot-and-mouth disease outbreak in Britain earlier in the same year.[47] The important point when discussing risk is to realize that we have both unintentional and deliberate measures to consider as we plan on protecting our agriculture system. Although many professionals within the agriculture community are more focused on the natural evolution of disease in both the livestock and crop and plant systems, the threat of terrorism directed at our livestock and crops has actually focused our collective attention on the areas in which more focused research parallel to the Center for Disease Control efforts would be beneficial.

We must be realistic and realize how easy an attack on our livestock or crop systems could be, should a terrorist organization such as Al Qaeda decide to launch such an attack. Although Al Qaeda generally takes responsibility for its activities and attacks, during the cold war we were confronted with the Soviet Union and its approach was to use "plausible deniability" in adversarial activities focused upon us. After the fall of the Soviet Union we discovered it had plans to target our agriculture and livestock as one element of a larger disruptive process and they developed a range of biological agents that would have been effective in this capacity.[48]

When discussing agriculture terrorism, we should be clear as to our understanding of unintentional and deliberate pathways to disease so that we maintain a balance in perspective, funding, and research into these areas. Simon Kenyon's approach to viewing agroterrorism as a subset of agriculture security is a most constructive and useful framework to apply to this important subject area.

E. Research Challenges

Since World War II, the United States agriculture system has undergone some significant changes, in which we now recognize our increased vulnerability to livestock and crop diseases. There has been a very profound reshaping of competition in which giant corporate farms have replaced the small individual farmer. Today, four companies in the United States now slaughter and process 85 percent of the domestically produced meat. Livestock is now raised in very large centralized feeding operations, and fewer and larger feedlots now provide an opportunity for corporate financial savings, yet they have also introduced an enormous risk in the event of a contagious disease outbreak. Also, we now have vast amounts of land devoted to one or two crops such as corn or soybeans; so our agriculture is now absent the diversification necessary should a major crop failure occur either from a pathogen as an unintentional event or a deliberate event or act.

As one reviews government support for agricultural research, it has remained flat in constant dollars for the past 25 years. The private sector supports more agriculture research than the states and federal government combined; however, these industry initiatives are focused on the development of biotechnology products, pesticides, and other items related to agricultural production and sales.[49] The states and federal government must revisit their funding strategies as our agriculture system has not had the funding and support to make the advancement necessary to maintain its worldwide leadership position. Our research needs are vast and should include substantial monies devoted to pure research. We also need to plan more joint research activities involving our agriculture colleges and the Defense Threat Reduction Agency, U.S. Joint Forces Command, and U.S. Department of Homeland Security.

Endnotes

1. Jessica Stern, *The Ultimate Terrorists*, Harvard University Press: Cambridge, MA, 1999, pp. 8–10.

2. Jessica Stern, *Terror in the Name of God: Why Religious Militants Kill*, Harper Collins: New York, 2003, pp. 255–258.
3. Jessica Stern, *The Ultimate Terrorists*, op.cit., pp. 88, 91, 102.
4. Clark Kent Ervin, *Open Target: Where America is Vulnerable to Attack*, MacMillan: New York, 2006, p. 118.
5. Daniel Benjamin and Steven Simon, *The Next Attack: The Failure of the War on Terror and a Strategy for Getting it Right*, Henry Holt, 2005, pp. 132–133.
6. David York, Illicit trafficking in nuclear and radiological materials, in Thomas A. Johnson (Ed.), *National Security Issues in Science, Law and Technology*, Taylor & Francis: Boca Raton, FL, 2007, p. 76.
7. David York, Illicit trafficking in nuclear and radiological materials, loc. cit.
8. Graham Allison, *Nuclear Terrorism: The Ultimate Preventable Catastrophe*, Henry Holt: New York, 2004, p. 10.
9. Jessica Stern, *The Ultimate Terrorists*, op. cit., p. 90.
10. David York, Illicit trafficking in nuclear and radiological materials, op. cit., p. 77.
11. Graham Allison, op. cit., p. 26.
12. Graham Allison, op. cit., p. 27.
13. Graham Allison, op. cit., pp.1–2.
14. National Research Council, *Making the Nation Safer: The Role of Science and Technology in Countering Terrorism*, The National Academy Press: Washington, DC, 2002, pp. 39, 42.
15. National Research Council, *Making the Nation Safer: The Role of Science and Technology in Countering Terrorism*, ibid., p. 40.
16. Graham Allison, op. cit., pp. 21–24.
17. Graham Allison, op. cit., pp. 61–62.
18. National Research Council, *Making the Nation Safer: The Role of Science and Technology in Countering Terrorism*, op. cit., pp. 44–46.
19. Graham Allison, op. cit., pp. 19–20.
20. Graham Allison, op. cit., pp.54–55.
21. Graham Allison, op. cit., p. 55.
22. Graham Allison, op. cit., p. 56
23. Anthony E. Cordesman, *Terrorism, Asymmetric Warfare, and Weapons of Mass Destruction: Defending the U.S. Homeland*, Praeger: Westport, CT, 2002, pp. 194–196.
24. Daniel G. Dupont, Nuclear explosions in orbit, *Scientific American*, 290: 6, June, 2004, pp. 100–103.
25. National Research Council, *Making the Nation Safer: The Role of Science and Technology in Countering Terrorism*, op. cit., pp. 65–66.
26. Anthony E. Cordesman, op. cit., p. 135.
27. Anthony E. Cordesman, op. cit., p. 135.
28. Anthony E. Cordesman, op. cit., p. 138.
29. Anthony E. Cordesman, loc. cit.
30. Jessica Stern, *The Ultimate Terrorists*, op. cit., p. 101.
31. Judith Miller, Stephen Engelberg, and William Broad, *Germs: Biological Weapons and America's Secret War*, Simon & Schuster: New York, p. 254.
32. Daniel Benjamin and Steven Simon, op. cit., p. 134.
33. Anthony E. Cordesman, op. cit., pp. 168–170.

34. National Research Council, *Making the Nation Safer: The Role of Science and Technology in Countering Terrorism*, op. cit., p. 108.
35. Daniel Benjamin and Steven Simon, op. cit., pp. 130–131.
36. Anthony E. Cordesman, op. cit., p. 115.
37. Anthony E. Cordesman, loc. cit.
38. Anthony E. Cordesman, op. cit., p. 116.
39. Anthony E. Cordesman, loc. cit.
40. National Research Council, *Making the Nation Safer: The Role of Science and Technology in Countering Terrorism*, op. cit., p. 65.
41. National Research Council, *Making the Nation Safer: The Role of Science and Technology in Countering Terrorism*, op. cit., p. 77.
42. National Research Council, *Making the Nation Safer: The Role of Science and Technology in Countering Terrorism*, loc. cit., 2002.
43. Anthony E. Cordesman, op. cit., pp. 175–176.
44. Simon Kenyon, Agroterrorism, in Thomas A. Johnson (Ed.), *National Security Issues in Science, Law and Technology*, Taylor & Francis: Boca Raton, FL, 2007, p. 58.
45. Stephen Flynn, *America The Vulnerable: How our Government is Failing to Protect us from Terrorism*, Harper Collins: New York, 2004, p. 114.
46. National Research Council, *Making the Nation Safer: The Role of Science and Technology in Countering Terrorism*, op. cit., pp. 78–79.
47. Simon Kenyon, op. cit., p. 52.
48. Anthony E. Cordesman, op. cit., p. 174.
49. National Research Council, *Making the Nation Safer: The Role of Science and Technology in Countering Terrorism*, op. cit., p. 93.

Our Intelligence Community

5

Our nation has created 16 major intelligence agencies operating under the direction of the Director of National Intelligence. There are numerous other governmental agencies that also have a relationship with the Office of the Director of National Intelligence. This chapter discusses the manner in which we have organized our intelligence community and the roles, responsibilities, and functions expected of each of our 16 intelligence organizations. The intelligence process is discussed in terms of the collection, processing, and exploitation of data leading to the analysis and production of intelligence for the purposes of providing our policymakers with processed intelligence for their use in formulating our nation's policies.

This chapter is organized around the following format.

1. Office of the Director of National Intelligence
   A. Mission and Authorities of the Director of National Intelligence
   B. Mission Managers
2. National Intelligence Program Agencies
   A. Central Intelligence Agency
      1. The National Clandestine Service (NCS)
      2. The Directorate of Intelligence (DI)
      3. The Directorate of Science and Technology (DS&T)
      4. The Directorate of Support (DS)
   B. Federal Bureau of Investigation
      1. Counterterrorism Division
      2. Counterintelligence Division
      3. Directorate of Intelligence
   C. Department of the Treasury
   D. Department of Energy
   E. Department of State
   F. Department of Homeland Security
   G. United States Coast Guard
   H. Drug Enforcement Administration
3. Military Intelligence Program Agencies
   A Defense Intelligence Agency
   B. National Security Agency
   C. National Reconnaissance Office
   D. National Geospatial Intelligence Agency
   E. United States Air Force

- F. United States Army
- G. United States Navy
- H. United States Marine Corps

4. Congressional Oversight Committees
   Senate Select Committee on Intelligence
   House of Representatives Permanent Select Committee on Intelligence
5. The Intelligence Process
   - A. Planning and Direction: Customer Requirements
   - B. Collection
     - Signals Intelligence
     - Imagery Intelligence
     - Measurement and Signature Intelligence
     - Human-Source Intelligence
     - Open-Source Intelligence
     - Geospatial Intelligence
   - C. Processing and Exploitation
   - D. Analysis and Production
   - E. Dissemination of Intelligence Products
6. Summary

Endnotes

Our intelligence community prepares and routes its studies and analytical reports to the National Security Council which recommends action or establishes policy regarding national security matters. The National Security Council was established in 1947 by President Harry Truman and over the years each president has utilized this body in various fashions depending on the nature of the crisis.

The National Security Council has only four statutory members: the president, the vice president, secretary of state, and secretary of defense. In addition it has statutory advisors; the chairman of the Joint Chiefs of Staff and now the director of the Office of National Intelligence, as well as the national security advisor to the president who has an executive role. In effect, the National Security Council has become one of our nation's most important organizations for establishing foreign, military, and national security policy.[1]

Since the formation of the council in 1947, we have resolved a number of crises that have involved other nation-states and which have each created unique circumstances for both our National Security Council and our intelligence community, as well. Today, for the first time, we are at war on terrorism, with an enemy that has no infrastructure to attack, and no geographic boundaries. As Robert Baer astutely observes, "The only way to defeat such an enemy is by intelligence, by knowing what they plan to do next, and where they might launch their next attack from."[2] An enemy such as Al Qaeda with cells throughout the world, with no formal organizational structure along the lines of most nation-state forces, creates a unique problem as it can retreat into an anonymous underground. Mobilizing a force to counter this type of an enemy requires patience, international cooperation, and above all, extraordinary intelligence.

Since the attack on our nation, September 11, 2001, we have made substantial, and in many cases, enormous changes and improvements in our intelligence community. Two agencies were totally refocused with mission priorities: the Central Intelligence Agency and the Federal Bureau of Investigation and both now operate with different goals, objectives, and congressional demands far more intrusive than ever before. Congress provided both the legislation and the budgetary authorization for a new Office of the Director of National Intelligence with the expectation of more focused and improved coordination within the entire intelligence community. To appreciate the scope of managing such a large intelligence community, it is imperative to understand the roles and responsibilities of each of these 16 individual intelligence agencies.

We begin first with a description of the Office of the Director of National Intelligence, the newly created office charged with the responsibility for managing the entire intelligence community, and with presenting intelligence reports to the National Security Council and the president of the United States.

1. Office of the Director of National Intelligence

A. Mission and Authorities of the Director of National Intelligence

The Director of National Intelligence (DNI) serves as the head of the Intelligence Community (IC), overseeing and directing the implementation of the National Intelligence Program (NIP) and acting as the principal advisor to the president, the National Security Council, and the Homeland Security Council for intelligence matters. Working with the Principal Deputy of National Intelligence (PDNI), and with the assistance of mission managers and four deputy directors, the Office of the Director of National Intelligence's goal is to protect and defend American lives and interests through effective intelligence.

With this goal in mind, Congress provided the DNI with a number of authorities and duties, as outlined in the Intelligence Reform and Terrorism Prevention Act (IRTPA) of 2004. These charge the DNI to:

- Ensure that timely and objective national intelligence is provided to the president, the heads of departments and agencies of the executive branch, the chairman of the Joint Chiefs of Staff and senior military commanders, and the Congress.

- Establish objectives and priorities for collection, analysis, production, and dissemination of national intelligence.
- Ensure maximum availability of and access to intelligence information within the intelligence community.
- Develop and ensure the execution of an annual budget for the National Intelligence Program based on budget proposals provided by IC component organizations.
- Oversee coordination of relationships with the intelligence or security services of foreign governments and international organizations.
- Ensure the most accurate analysis of intelligence is derived from all sources to support national security needs.
- Develop personnel policies and programs to enhance the capacity for joint operations and to facilitate staffing of community management functions.
- Oversee the development and implementation of a program management plan for acquisition of major systems, doing so jointly with the secretary of defense for the Department of Defense (DoD) programs, that includes cost, schedule, and performance goals and program milestone criteria.

The Office of the Director of National Intelligence has four principal directorates and they are as follows.

1. Policy Plans and Requirements
2. Collection
3. Analysis
4. Acquisition

Each of these directorates works in concert with the others so that a more cohesive community-wide intelligence product is developed.

The Office of the Deputy Director of National Intelligence for Collection was established to coordinate collection throughout the intelligence community under the authorities of the DNI and ensure that the National Intelligence Strategy (NIS) priorities are appropriately reflected in future planning and systems acquisition decisions.

Intelligence is driven by requirements, and the Office of the Deputy Director of National Intelligence for Requirements is responsible for ensuring decision makers receive timely and actionable information that allows them to fulfill their respective national security missions by articulating, advocating, and coordinating requirements within the IC. The deputy director for requirements interfaces with the variety of intelligence customers at the national, state, and local levels in order to act as an advocate for them. The deputy director for requirements provides organizations not traditionally associated with national intelligence a link to information, products, and avenues for sharing, anticipates customer requirements, and evaluates and reports on how effective and timely the IC is in meeting the needs of senior decision makers.

To meet the requirements of senior policymakers, intelligence must be synthesized by analysts throughout the IC. It is the responsibility of the Office of the Deputy Director of National Intelligence for Analysis to manage and establish common policies and standards to ensure the highest quality, timeliness, and utility of analytic resources. To achieve this goal, the DNI for analysis works to increase expertise and improve analytic tradecraft at individual, agency, and community levels through specialization, training, collaboration, and crossfertilization. Some of the most important functions of the DDNI for analysis include establishing analytic priorities, ensuring timely and effective analysis and dissemination of analysis, tasking of analytic products, and encouraging sound analytic methods, all-source analysis, competitive analysis, and resource recommendations regarding the need to balance collection and analytic capabilities. These key functions can only be accomplished in close coordination with the deputy directors for collection and requirements. Finally, the deputy director for analysis manages the production of the president's daily brief and serves concurrently as the chairman of the National Intelligence Council (NIC).

B. Mission Managers

The director of national intelligence also created six mission managers to serve as the principal intelligence community officials responsible for overseeing all aspects of intelligence relative to their focused target areas.

Iran: Led by the mission manager for Iran
North Korea: Led by the mission manager for North Korea
Cuba and Venezuela: Led by the mission manager for Cuba and Venezuela
Counterterrorism: Led by the director of the National Counterterrorism Center (NCTC)
Counterproliferation: Led by the director of the National Counter Proliferation Center (NCPC)
Counterintelligence: Led by the director of the National Counterintelligence Executive (NCIX)

In each area, mission managers are responsible for understanding the requirements of intelligence consumers, providing consistent overall guidance on collection priorities, integration and gaps, assessing analytic quality capabilities and gaps, sharing of intelligence information on the target, and recommending funding, investment, and R&D resource allocations.

Three important organizations were codified by Congress and placed in the Office of Director of National Intelligence. First, the National Counterterrorism Center is the primary organization for incorporating and analyzing all intelligence pertaining to terrorism and counterterrorism and conducting strategic operational planning by including all instruments of national power.

Second, the National Counter Proliferation Center coordinates strategic planning within the intelligence community to enhance intelligence support for U.S. efforts to stem the proliferation of weapons of mass destruction and related delivery systems. It works with the intelligence community to identify critical intelligence gaps or shortfalls in collection, analysis, or exploitation, and develop solutions to ameliorate or close those gaps. It also works with the intelligence community to identify long-term proliferation threats and requirements and develop strategies to ensure the IC is positioned to address those threats and issues. NCPC will reach out to elements both inside the intelligence community and outside the IC and the U.S. government to identify new methods or technologies that can enhance the capabilities of the IC to detect and defeat future proliferation threats.

The third new organization, the National Counterintelligence Executive, is placed within the Office of the Director of National Intelligence to coordinate our nation's counterintelligence efforts and to provide strategic direction to secure our nation against foreign espionage. Also, the protection of the integrity of our intelligence system must be guaranteed by a vigorous counterintelligence effort designed to detect attempts to penetrate our intelligence organizations. In collaboration with other agencies within the intelligence community, the NCIX office will protect our economic and trade secrets and other vital national assets.[3]

Prior to the passage of the Intelligence Reform Act of 2004 by Congress, most of the budget for intelligence activities was sent to the Department of Defense, and although the director of the CIA (DCI) was the executive head of the intelligence community, there existed no real authority to allocate budget, resources, or plans to intelligence agencies under the direction of the Department of Defense.

With the passage of the Intelligence Reform Act in 2004, the Director of National Intelligence has extensive statutory authorities for developing and determining the National Intelligence Program (NIP), and for presenting it to the president for approval. The president then forwards the NIP to Congress as part of the annual budget submission in January or February of each year. The Office of the DNI (ODNI) serves as the DNI's staff for annual budget preparation and submission. The DNI participates in the development of the Military Intelligence Program (MIP) by the secretary of defense. The under secretary of defense for intelligence (USDI) has the responsibility to oversee all defense intelligence budgetary matters to ensure compliance with the budget policies issued by the DNI for the NIP. The USDI also serves as program executive for the MIP and supervises coordination during the programming, budgeting, and execution cycles.

Thus, in the development of both the NIP and the MIP essential roles are fulfilled by the Office of the DNI and the Office of the USDI. The two offices have overlapping responsibilities and close coordination is required. In fact, the intelligence budget as authorized by Congress is now divided into two parts, the National Intelligence Program and the Military Intelligence Program. NIP programs (formerly categorized as the National Foreign Intelligence Program (NFIP) are those undertaken in support of national level decision making and are conducted by the CIA, DIA, NSA, NRO, National Geospatial Agency (NGA), and other Washington area agencies. MIP programs are undertaken by DoD agencies in support of defense policy making and of military commanders throughout the world.

Until September 2005, there were two sets of programs within DoD: the Joint Military Intelligence Program (JMIP) and Tactical Intelligence and Related Activities (TIARA). JMIP programs, established as a separate category in 1994, supported DoD-wide activities. TIARA programs were defined as

> a diverse array of reconnaissance and target acquisition programs which are a functional part of the basic military force structure and provide direct support to military operations. In recent years, the overlap among intelligence and intelligence-related activities has grown—satellite photography, for instance, can now be made immediately available to tactical commanders and intelligence acquired at the tactical level is frequently transmitted to national-level agencies. As a result, JMIP and TIARA were combined by the Defense Department into the MIP in September 2005.[4]

Although the director of national intelligence is designated as the position in charge of all our nation's intelligence community, it is clear that by bifurcating our intelligence community into a National Intelligence Program, and a Military Intelligence Program, a very careful coordinated role between the DNI and the under secretary of defense for intelligence will be required. In fact, the specific responsibilities and functions of the under secretary of defense for intelligence are as follows.

Providing oversight and policy guidance for all DoD intelligence activities and establishing priorities to ensure conformance with Secretary and, as appropriate, Director of Central Intelligence (DCI) policy guidance.

Advising the Secretary, the Secretaries of the Military Departments, the Chairman of the Joint Chiefs of Staff (CJCS), and the combatant Commanders on the performance of national and defense intelligence capabilities.

Providing policy oversight of all the intelligence organizations within the DoD, to include ensuring these organizations are manned, trained, equipped and structured to support the missions of the Department and fully satisfy the needs of the DCI.

Providing assessments of and advising the Secretary and the CJCS on the adequacy of military intelligence performance.

Advising the Secretary concerning the Department's responsibilities regarding the national intelligence community and supporting the Secretary's role in the Intelligence Community Executive Committee.

Exercising management and oversight of all DoD counterintelligence and security activities, including personnel security and industrial security.

Overseeing intelligence support to critical infrastructure protection, departmental information assurance programs and homeland defense.

Coordinating DoD intelligence and intelligence-related policy, plans, programs, requirements and resource allocations. This includes responsibility for the DoD components within the National Foreign Intelligence Program, the Joint Military Intelligence Program, the Foreign Counterintelligence Program, and the Tactical Intelligence and Related Activities account.

Ensuring the execution of DoD intelligence policy and resource decisions are fully responsive and complementary to the direction of the DCI.

Exercising overall supervision and policy oversight of the DoD intelligence infrastructure and civilian intelligence personnel management systems. This will include policy regarding the Defense Civilian Intelligence Personnel Systems (DCIPS).

Overseeing provision of intelligence support and involvement in information operations, focused on assessments in support of operations.

Ensuring that intelligence activities of DoD are conducted jointly, as appropriate. In this capacity, the USD(I) shall:

Serve, in conjunction with the CJCS, as the Secretary's intelligence interface in his appointed duties with other government agencies, including the State Department, the Justice Department, foreign governments, international organizations, state agencies, and the Intelligence Community, as well as the Congress.

Lead departmental activities in programmatic processes related to intelligence and intelligence-related programs, including, but not limited to, program change proposals, program evaluations, assessments, and recommendations. Coordinate with the DCI's staff on joint activities related to intelligence and associated programs. Chair, as appropriate, groups established to address programmatic issues.

Provide support to the OSD PSA's, as necessary, regarding certain requirements associated with resource management, analysis, budget-preparation matters, reporting activities, congressional material, and architectural design related to those areas under the USD(I)'s responsibility.

Coordinate with the Assistant to the Secretary of Defense for Intelligence Oversight and the Inspector General of the Department of Defense to ensure that intelligence components and activities of the Department are in compliance with regulatory guidance and departmental and national policies and directives.

Coordinate civilian intelligence personnel policy, in particular regarding DCIPS, with the Under Secretary of Defense for Personnel and Readiness.

Advise the Under Secretary of Defense for Acquisition, Technology and Logistics on intelligence and intelligence-related programs and exercise authorities, as delegated, for acquisition, technology, and logistics regarding intelligence and intelligence-related programs reassigned to the USD(I).

Participate as a member of the Defense Acquisition Board for systems of which intelligence, intelligence-related support or intelligence inputs or products are involved.

Maintain close coordination with the DCI and consult with the DCI on the development, design, acquisition and operation of intelligence programs and systems of the DoD.

Exercise authority, direction, and control over the Defense Intelligence Agency (DIA), the National Imagery and Mapping Agency (NIMA), the National Reconnaissance Organization (NRO), the National Security Agency (NSA), the Defense Security Service (DSS), and the DoD Counterintelligence Field Activity (CIFA). Ensure that these organizations, as appropriate, have adequate acquisition management structures and processes in place to deliver intelligence programs on time and within budget.[5]

The intelligence agencies that fall within the National Intelligence Program are described and as are by those intelligence agencies that have membership in the Military Intelligence Program.

2. National Intelligence Program Agencies

A. Central Intelligence Agency

The Central Intelligence Agency (CIA), established by the National Security Act of 1947, is responsible to the president through the director of national intelligence and accountable to the American people through the intelligence oversight committees of the Congress. The director of the CIA (DCIA) also serves as the national human intelligence (HUMINT) manager.

The core mission of the CIA is to support the president, the National Security Council, and all officials who make and execute U.S. national security policy by:

- Providing accurate, comprehensive, and timely foreign intelligence and analysis on national security topics

- Conducting counterintelligence activities, special activities, and other functions related to foreign intelligence and national security as directed by the president

To accomplish the mission, the CIA works closely with the rest of the intelligence community and other government agencies to ensure that intelligence consumers—whether administration policymakers, diplomats, or military commanders—receive the best intelligence possible.

The CIA is organized into four mission components called directorates, which together carry out "the intelligence process," the cycle of collecting, analyzing, and disseminating intelligence:

1. *National Clandestine Service (NCS)*

The *NCS* is the clandestine arm of the CIA. Its core mission is to support security and foreign policy interests by conducting clandestine activities to collect information that is not obtainable through other means. The information the NCS collects is reviewed for reliability before its dissemination to policymakers. Although the primary focus of the NCS is the collection and dissemination of foreign intelligence, it also conducts counterintelligence activities abroad and special activities as authorized by the president. The Director of the National Clandestine Service (DNCS) serves as the national authority for the integration, coordination, deconfliction, and evaluation of clandestine HUMINT operations across the intelligence community, under the authorities delegated to the director of the CIA as the national HUMINT manager. As part of its community responsibilities, the NCS develops common standards for all aspects of clandestine human intelligence operations, including human-enabled technical operations, across the IC. The DNCS also oversees the Central Intelligence Agency's clandestine operations.

2. *Directorate of Intelligence (DI)*

The DI supports the president, administration policymakers, the Congress, Pentagon planners and war fighters, law enforcement agencies, and negotiators with timely, comprehensive all-source intelligence analysis about a wide range of national security issues. The DI integrates, analyzes, and evaluates information collected through clandestine and other means, including open sources, to generate value-added insights. The substantive scope of the DI is worldwide and covers functional, as well as regional, issues.

3. *Directorate of Science and Technology (DS&T)*

The DS&T works closely with the National Clandestine Service and Directorate of Intelligence to access, collect, and exploit critical intelligence by applying innovative scientific, engineering, and technical solutions.

4. *Directorate of Support (DS)*

The DS provides integrated, mission-critical support to the National Clandestine Service, the Directorate of Intelligence, the Directorate of Science and Technology, and across the intelligence community.[6]

B. Federal Bureau of Investigation

National Security Branch (NSB)

Since the attacks of September 11, 2001, the overriding priority of the Federal Bureau of Investigation (FBI) has been protecting the U.S. by preventing future attacks. The FBI has refocused its priorities to better accomplish its mission and is making comprehensive changes in its overall structure, organization, and business practices. Even as it evolves, the FBI continues to meet its traditional responsibilities to uphold and enforce federal criminal laws and to provide leadership and criminal justice services to federal, state, municipal, tribal, and international agencies and partners. The FBI remains committed to performing these responsibilities in a manner that is responsive to the needs of the public and is faithful to the Constitution and the laws of the United States.

The FBI's top three priorities are: (1) protecting the United States from terrorist attack, (2) protecting the United States against foreign intelligence operations and espionage, and (3) protecting the United States against cyber-based attacks and high technology crimes. In addition, the FBI continues to combat public corruption at all levels, protect civil rights, and combat major white-collar crime and significant violent crime.

The National Security Branch (NSB) consists of the Counterterrorism Division, the Counterintelligence Division, and the Directorate of Intelligence. The NSB promotes the development of a national security workforce with the skills, training, and experience necessary to carry out our national security investigative and intelligence programs. It also coordinates our national security efforts with the rest of the intelligence community under the leadership of the director of national intelligence.

1. Counterterrorism Division—The Joint Terrorism Task Forces (JTTFs), located in every FBI field office and many resident agencies, play a central role in virtually every terrorism investigation, prevention, or interdiction within the United States. Analysts in the Counterterrorism Division and in the Field Intelligence Groups (FIGs) produce assessments of the composition, activities, tradecraft, ideology, and linkages of terrorist groups to guide and further FBI investigations, assist FBI management in deploying resources against the terrorist target, and to assist in the war on terrorism.

2. Counterintelligence Division—As the lead counterintelligence agency in the United States, the FBI is responsible for identifying and neutralizing ongoing national security threats. The Counterintelligence Division provides centralized management and oversight for all foreign counterintelligence investigations.

3. Directorate of Intelligence—The mission of the intelligence program is to optimally position the FBI to meet current and emerging national security and criminal threats by: (1) aiming core investigative work proactively against threats to U.S. interests, (2) building and sustaining enterprise-wide intelligence policies and capabilities, and (3) providing useful, appropriate, and timely information and analysis to the national security, homeland security, and law enforcement communities.[7]

C. Department of the Treasury

Office of Intelligence and Analysis

The Office of Intelligence and Analysis (OIA) was established by the Intelligence Authorization Act in 2004. The Act specifies that OIA shall be responsible for the receipt, analysis, collation, and dissemination of foreign intelligence and foreign counterintelligence information related to the operation and responsibilities of the Department of the Treasury. The Act established the assistant secretary for intelligence and analysis as the head of OIA and placed the office within the Office of Terrorism and Financial Intelligence (TFI). OIA is a member of the intelligence community.

Strategic Goals:

- Support the formulation of policy and execution of Treasury authorities by providing expert analysis and intelligence production on financial and other support networks for terrorist groups, proliferators, and other key national security threats.
- Provide timely, accurate, and focused intelligence support to the department on the full range of economic, political, and security issues.
- Establish Treasury as a fully integrated member of the IC.
- Coordinate and oversee intelligence throughout the department, including OFACs and Fin-CENs intelligence analysis.
- Invest in personnel and information technology.

Strategic Priorities:

- *Terrorist Financing:* OIA will continue to develop its analytic expertise and expand its analytic coverage on the financial and other support networks of the various terrorist groups and networks bent on attacking the United States and its allies.

- *Insurgency Financing:* OIA will continue to improve its understanding of the insurgency financing, primarily through the Baghdad-based Iraq Threat Finance Cell (ITFC) for which Treasury serves as the co-lead with Department of Defense. ITFC was established to enhance the collection, analysis, and dissemination of intelligence to combat the Iraqi insurgency. Such intelligence is critical to support and strengthen U.S., Iraqi, and coalition efforts to disrupt and eliminate financial and other material support to the insurgency.
- *Rogue Regimes/Proliferation Financing:* OIA has assumed an increasingly important role in Treasury's effort to combat other national security threats, including rogue regimes involved in WMD proliferation, such as Iran, Syria, and North Korea. OIA will continue to build on its efforts in these critical areas.[8]

D. Department of Energy

Office of Intelligence and Counterintelligence (IN)

The Department of Energy's Office of Intelligence and Counterintelligence (IN) brings the access and expertise of the DOE and its nationwide complex of laboratories and other facilities to bear on the most daunting challenges facing U.S. intelligence and national security. IN's core mission is to

- Defend the DOE complex from foreign penetration.
- Gauge the worldwide threat of nuclear terrorism.
- Help counter the spread of nuclear technologies, materials, and expertise.
- Enrich intelligence community access to information in DOE core areas, particularly with respect to energy.
- Evaluate emerging foreign technology threats to U.S. economic and military interests.

The DOE's intelligence program is distinguished by a strategic long-term focus and a unique ability to leverage and represent the technological excellence of the department's workforce. Challenging analytic conventions, taking on the most intractable intelligence problems, and anticipating the obstacles and opportunities of the future are at the heart of DOE's approach.[9]

E. Department of State

Bureau of Intelligence and Research (INR)

The Bureau of Intelligence and Research (INR) provides the secretary of state with timely, objective analysis of global developments as well as real-time insights from all-source intelligence. It serves as the focal point within the

Department of State for all policy issues and activities involving the intelligence community. The INR assistant secretary reports directly to the secretary of state and serves as the secretary's principal advisor on all intelligence matters.

INR's expert, independent foreign affairs analysts draw on all-source intelligence, diplomatic reporting, INR's public opinion polling, and interaction with U.S. and foreign scholars. Their strong regional and functional backgrounds allow them to respond rapidly to changing policy priorities and to provide early warning and in-depth analysis of events and trends that affect U.S. foreign policy and national security interests. INR analysts—a combination of foreign service officers often with extensive in-country experience and civil service specialists with in-depth expertise—cover all countries and regional or transnational issues.

The bureau provides daily briefings, reports, and memoranda to the secretary and other department principals. INR also briefs members of Congress and their staffs on request. INR products cover the globe on foreign relations issues such as political and military developments, terrorism, narcotics, and trade. INR contributes to the community's national intelligence estimates, the presidential daily brief, and other analyses, offering its particular focus on relevance to policy. Many of INR's analyses are disseminated on the intelligence community's Intelink system, to which members and staff of the congressional intelligence committees have access. In support of the statutory authority of the secretary of state and chiefs of mission for the conduct of foreign policy and oversight of U.S. government activities overseas, INR coordinates on behalf of the department on issues concerning intelligence, counterintelligence, and special operations. INR participates in a wide variety of intelligence community working groups and policymaking committees, including those involving visa denial, intelligence sharing, analytic production, requirements, and evaluation for collection in all intelligence disciplines. INR develops intelligence policy for the Department of State and works to harmonize all agencies' intelligence activities abroad with U.S. policy.[10]

F. Department of Homeland Security

Office of Intelligence and Analysis (I&A)

Intelligence in the Department of Homeland Security (DHS) consists of the Office of Intelligence and Analysis (I&A) and intelligence offices located within DHS' operational components. An assistant secretary for intelligence and analysis, who also serves as chief intelligence officer, oversees DHS intelligence, providing direction, oversight, and evaluation of the intelligence activities of the department.

DHS intelligence focuses on five principal areas: (1) improving the quality and quantity of its analysis, (2) integrating the intelligence elements of the department, (3) sharing threat information and assessments with state and local governments and the private sector, (4) ensuring DHS is an effective member of the national intelligence community, and (5) strengthening relations with Congress.

DHS intelligence analysts not only track terrorists and their networks, but also assess threats to U.S. critical infrastructures, bio- and nuclear terrorism, pandemic diseases, threats to our borders (air, land, and sea), and radicalization within U.S. society.

To integrate DHS intelligence, the chief intelligence officer has established the Homeland Security Intelligence Council (HSIC), comprising intelligence principals from the department's operating components. The HSIC establishes common standards across the department on such diverse issues as recruiting and training of intelligence officers and production and sharing of information. The HSIC also is the mechanism by which DHS intelligence program goals are established and the adequacy of resources is evaluated. To secure our borders, DHS I&A is working with Customs and Border Protection (CBP), and Immigration and Customs Enforcement (ICE) to ensure the full capabilities of the national intelligence community are used to increase intelligence collection along our borders.[11]

G. United States Coast Guard

The United States Coast Guard is a military, multimission, maritime service within the Department of Homeland Security. The Coast Guard is one of the nation's five armed services, with maritime security and core roles of protecting the public, the environment, and guarding U.S. economic and security interests. It performs those missions in any maritime region in which those interests may be at risk, including international waters, and America's coasts, ports, and inland waterways. To assist in accomplishing its diverse missions, senior leadership, and operational commanders rely on the Coast Guard Intelligence and Criminal Investigations Program (CGICIP).

Because the Coast Guard employs unique expertise and capabilities in the maritime environment—in domestic ports, coastal waters, offshore regions, and even in foreign ports—where other U.S. government agencies typically are not present, it has the opportunity to collect intelligence that supports its missions and other national security objectives, as well.

The Coast Guard's Intelligence and Criminal Investigations Program includes its National Intelligence Element, the Criminal Investigations Service, the Counterintelligence Service, and the Cryptologic Service. Its mission is to direct, coordinate, and oversee intelligence and investigative operations and activities that support all Coast Guard objectives by providing actionable (timely, accurate, and relevant) intelligence, to strategic decision makers, as well as operational and tactical commanders. The CGICIP also supports the National Strategy for Homeland Security and applicable national security objectives.

The Coast Guard became a member of the intelligence community on December 28, 2001. In the post-9/11 environment, the program has increased its capability by the creation of:

- Maritime intelligence fusion centers
- Field intelligence support teams
- Intelligence Coordination Center's COASTWATCH and targeting programs
- Counterintelligence Service
- Attaché positions in coordination with the DoD HUMINT
- Global maritime intelligence integration capability (partnering with the U.S. Navy and other key IC members)
- Permanent presence on the FBI National Joint Terrorism Task Force and ad hoc JTTFs providing a maritime nexus and expertise
- A service cryptologic element, as part of the NSA Central Security Service

H. Drug Enforcement Administration

Office of National Security Intelligence (NN)

The DEA's Office of National Security Intelligence (NN), a part of the DEA Intelligence Division, is a member of the intelligence community (IC). DEA/NN personnel are assigned to analysis, liaison, and central tasking management functions. The designation of DEA/NN as a member of the IC does not grant DEA new authority, but does formalize the long-standing relationship between the DEA and IC and gives the DEA and other members of the IC the ability to work on issues of national security interest in an integrated fashion.

DEA/NN's Contribution to Intelligence

The Office of National Security Intelligence is responsible for providing drug-related information responsive to IC requirements. DEA/NN establishes and manages centralized tasking of requests for and analysis of national security information obtained during the course of DEA's drug enforcement. The office also centrally manages requests from the IC for information deposited with DEA pursuant to the authority the administration derives from Title 21 USC or obtained for the IC through existing assets operating pursuant to DEA's law enforcement mission.[12]

3. Military Intelligence Program Agencies

The intelligence programs that are directly under the supervision of the under secretary of defense for intelligence, but still report to and through the (USD(I) to the office of the director of national intelligence are described below.

A. Defense Intelligence Agency

DIA is a major producer and manager of foreign military intelligence for the Department of Defense and is a principal member of the U.S. intelligence community. Established on October 1, 1961, and designated a combat support agency in 1986, the DIA's mission is to provide timely, objective, all-source military intelligence to policymakers, to U.S. armed forces around the world, and to the U.S. acquisition community and force planners to counter a variety of threats and challenges across the spectrum of conflict.

The director of the DIA is a three-star military officer who serves as the principal advisor on substantive military intelligence matters to the secretary of defense and the chairman of the Joint Chiefs of Staff. Additionally, the director of the DIA is the program manager for the General Defense Intelligence Program, which funds a variety of military intelligence programs at and above the corps level, and is the chairman of the Military Intelligence Board which examines key intelligence issues such as information technology architectures, program and budget issues, and defense intelligence inputs to national intelligence estimates.

With headquarters in the Pentagon, DIA's 8000 highly skilled civilian and military personnel are located around the world with major activities at the Defense Intelligence Analysis Center on Bolling Air Force Base in Washington, DC; the Missile and Space Intelligence Center at Redstone Arsenal in Huntsville, Alabama; and the Armed Forces Medical Intelligence Center at Fort Detrick, Maryland. DIA also deploys military and civilian personnel worldwide during crises or conflicts to better support military forces.

In April 2006, DIA established the Defense Joint Intelligence Operations Center (DJIOC) to seamlessly integrate all defense intelligence resources on the transnational threats to U.S. national security and to enhance defense intelligence collaboration. The DJIOC collaborates with the DoD and national intelligence resources to manage risk and resource requirements. It integrates and synchronizes all-source military and national level intelligence capabilities in support of the war fighters.

DIA employs extensive analytic expertise in a number of areas such as foreign military forces, their intentions and capabilities, foreign military leadership analysis, proliferation of weapons of mass destruction, defense-related political and economic developments, advanced military technologies and materiel production, information warfare, missile and space developments, and defense-related medical and health issues.

To support all-source analytical efforts, DIA directs and manages Department of Defense intelligence collection requirements for the various disciplines such as human intelligence (HUMINT), measurement and signature intelligence (MASINT), imagery intelligence (IMINT), and signals intelligence (SIGINT).

DIA's Directorate for Human Intelligence (DH) conducts human intelligence operations worldwide to obtain critical intelligence often not available from technical collection means. DH operations provide in-depth and actionable intelligence to policymakers and military forces in the field. DH manages the Defense Attaché System, which assigns military attachés to more than 135 U.S. embassies. These attachés are an integral part of the U.S. diplomatic presence abroad and help develop working relationships with foreign military forces. They represent the secretary of defense and other senior DoD officials to their overseas military counterparts.

DIA manages various national and DoD activities related to MASINT, which is technically derived information that measures, detects, tracks, and identifies unique characteristics of fixed and dynamic targets. To further MASINT's usefulness, DIA spearheads significant advances in this complex collection technology, such as unattended sensors for chemical and biological programs. MASINT technologies allow the DoD to confidently monitor arms control agreements, to make "smart" weapons even smarter, and to effectively support force protection and missile defense efforts.

To support DoD efforts in the global war on terrorism, DIA established the Joint Intelligence Task Force for Combating Terrorism (JITF-CT) to consolidate and produce all-source terrorism-related intelligence. JITF-CT leads and manages the DoD counterterrorism intelligence effort and exploits all sources of intelligence to warn U.S. forces and to support offensive counterterrorism operations. It collects, analyzes, and shares intelligence with military commanders, government officials, and other intelligence agencies.[13]

B. National Security Agency/Central Security Service

The National Security Agency (NSA) is the nation's cryptologic organization that coordinates, directs, and performs highly specialized tasks to produce foreign intelligence and to protect U.S. information systems. A high technology organization, NSA is at the forefront of communications and information technology. NSA is also one of the most important centers of foreign language analysis and research within the U.S. government.

Founded in 1952, the NSA is part of the Department of Defense and a member of the U.S. intelligence community. The agency supports military customers, national policymakers, and the counterterrorism and counterintelligence communities, as well as key international allies. The National Security Agency performs two vital functions:

- Signals intelligence (SIGINT) is the exploitation of foreign signals for national foreign intelligence and counterintelligence purposes.
- Information assurance is the protection of the intelligence community and allied information through technical solutions, products, and services, and defensive information operations.[14]

C. National Reconnaissance Office

The National Reconnaissance Office (NRO) was established in September 1961 as a classified agency of the Department of Defense. The existence of the NRO and its mission of overhead reconnaissance were declassified in September 1992. The NRO is the "nation's eyes and ears in space." Headquartered in Chantilly, Virginia, the NRO develops and operates unique and innovative overhead reconnaissance systems and conducts intelligence-related activities essential for national security.

The NRO collaborates closely with its mission partners, NSA, NGA, CIA, U.S. Strategic Forces Command, U.S. Air Force, U.S. Army, and the Department of the Navy as well as other intelligence and defense organizations. NRO receives its budget, known as the National Reconnaissance Program (NRP), via the National Intelligence Program (NIP) and the Military Intelligence Program (MIP).[15]

D. National Geospatial Intelligence Agency

The National Geospatial Intelligence Agency (NGA) provides timely, relevant, and accurate geospatial intelligence in support of national security objectives. Geospatial intelligence is the exploitation and analysis of imagery and geospatial information to describe, assess, and visually depict physical features and geographically referenced activities on the Earth.

Information collected and processed by NGA is tailored for customer-specific solutions. By giving customers ready access to geospatial intelligence, NGA provides support to civilian and military leaders and contributes to the state of readiness of U.S. military forces. NGA also contributes to humanitarian efforts such as tracking floods and fires, and in peacekeeping.

NGA is a member of the U.S. intelligence community and a Department of Defense combat support agency. Headquartered in Bethesda, Maryland, the NGA operates major facilities in the St. Louis, Missouri and Washington, DC areas. The agency also fields support teams worldwide.

The national system for geospatial intelligence provides accurate, up-to-date geospatial intelligence to support our senior national decision makers as well as to help plan and prosecute military objectives. NGA's strategy supports operational readiness through a set of geospatial foundation data including controlled imagery, digital elevation data, and selected feature information that can be readily augmented and fused with other spatially referenced information such as intelligence, weather, and logistics data. The result is an integrated digital view of the mission space.[16]

The four branches of our military services provide intelligence services that are designed to provide commanders with mission-essential intelligence for assistance in the operational planning of combat activities. Also, the intelligence is acquired to better facilitate force protection strategies. The U.S. Navy, Army, and Marine Corps are particularly strong in these areas. The U.S. Air Force intelligence role is broader than the roles of the other branches due to its unique aerial intelligence collection capabilities which provide intelligence information to the benefit of the entire intelligence community.

E. United States Air Force

Air Force intelligence plays a critical role in the defense of our nation, providing aerial reconnaissance and surveillance. The Air Force has added unmanned aerial vehicles such as the Global Hawk and Predator as intelligence platforms. Additionally, the Air Force is a key to the development and use of intelligence gathered from space platforms.

Air Force Intelligence, Surveillance Reconnaissance (ISR)

The Air Force harnesses the integration of manned and unmanned aeronautical vehicles, and space-based systems to provide persistent situational awareness and executable decision-quality information to the joint warfighters and national decision makers. Air Force ISR collection assets and analysis contribute to the overall defense intelligence goal of increasing the nation's ability to gather and analyze intelligence on our adversaries. This includes increasing our understanding of the full spectrum of adversaries and threats, enhancing our ability to anticipate adversary courses of action, developing capabilities that enhance deterrence and provide greater lead time for our armed services, and providing predictive battle space awareness to start and stay ahead of our adversaries, all while protecting our own technology, assets, and personnel. We carry out these missions in an increasingly dynamic environment, amid rapid proliferation of information technologies, and against adversaries that have no geopolitical boundaries.

Air Force ISR resources are embedded in each unified command's air component, down to the wing and squadron levels. Air Force ISR professionals work at every level of command and across the entire national intelligence community, continuously preparing for and conducting operations from full-scale conflict to peacekeeping, counterdrug, counterterrorism, and humanitarian/disaster relief.

Current Contributions to Intelligence

Air Force ISR is fully engaged in worldwide operations engaging in the global war on terror. Air Force ISR assets including the U-2, RC-135, Global Hawk, Predator, Senior Scout, Theater Airborne Reconnaissance System (TARS), Scathe View, and the AF Distributed Common Ground System (AF DCGS) are providing continuous support to the U.S. Central Command and other combatant commands as they execute their GWOT operations. The key role played by the Air Force ISR is integral to the success of these operations and responds directly to the most pressing needs of the combatant commanders. Air Force intelligence also provides the nation with technical collection against foreign ballistic missile development, using a global network of airborne, ship-borne, and ground-based collectors.

Furthermore, through the National Air and Space Intelligence Center (NASIC), the Air Force is the executive agent for the technical analysis of adversary aircraft, long-range ballistic missiles, and space-based technologies.[17]

F. United States Army

The U.S. Army is adapting to face a changed paradigm of warfare. Ongoing counterterrorism and counterinsurgency operations in Iraq, Afghanistan, and elsewhere reflect enduring challenges inherent in countering extremist enemies in highly complex environments. The Army Intelligence Campaign Plan drives military intelligence (MI) transformation efforts to increase full-spectrum operational capacity at the brigade combat team (BCT) level, and provides fused, all-source actionable intelligence along tactically useful timelines, to soldiers and commanders at all levels. Four key components are:

- Increasing MI capacity and skills balance
- Enabling distributed access to an all-source “flat” integrated network
- Revitalizing Army human intelligence (HUMINT)
- Increasing intelligence readiness[18]

G. United States Navy

The naval intelligence primary production organization, the Office of Naval Intelligence (ONI), located at the National Maritime Intelligence Center (NMIC) in Suitland, Maryland, is the lead Department of Defense production center for maritime intelligence. ONI supports a variety of missions including U.S. military acquisition and development, counterterrorism, counterproliferation, counternarcotics, customs enforcement through partnerships and information-sharing agreements with the U.S. Coast Guard and U.S. Northern Command, Homeland Security and Homeland Defense. Although ONI is the largest naval intelligence organization, with the largest concentration of naval intelligence civilians, most of naval intelligence is comprised of active duty military personnel, serving in joint intelligence centers, cryptologic elements, and afloat units, supporting strike warfare, SPECWAR, collections, HUMINT, and Operational Intelligence (OPINTEL).

The breadth of naval intelligence experience and technical expertise, applied to the analysis of foreign naval weapons, systems, and activities, combined with the operational expertise of its assigned operators and warfare specialists, provide joint and operational commanders worldwide, and U.S. decision makers, with fully integrated maritime intelligence support on demand.[19]

H. United States Marine Corps

The Marine Corps intelligence mission is to provide commanders at every level with seamless, tailored, timely, and mission-essential intelligence and to ensure this intelligence is integrated into the operational planning process. Because Marine forces are employed primarily at the tactical level, Marine Corps intelligence activities are oriented toward tactical support. Accordingly, two-thirds of all intelligence Marines serve in the Fleet Marine Force (FMF), with the majority assigned to the staffs and units of tactical commands.

The service allocates resource and manpower to develop and maintain specific expertise in the areas of human and technical reconnaissance and surveillance, general military and naval intelligence duties, human-source intelligence, counterintelligence, imagery intelligence, signals intelligence, and tactical exploitation of national capabilities.

Marine Corps resources allocated to the Military Intelligence Program (MIP) provide for tactical capabilities necessary to support the operational forces with the U.S. fleet or as otherwise assigned to the combatant commands.

The Marine Corps participates in three components of the National Intelligence Program (NIP): (1) the Consolidated Cryptologic Program (CCP), (2) the Foreign Counterintelligence Program (FCIP), and (3) the General Defense Intelligence Program (GDIP).[20]

The entire array of intelligence agencies comprise the intelligence community which reports to the Office of the Director of National Intelligence who has the responsibility of reporting to the National Security Council and ultimately to the president of the United States. There are, however, very important relationships with other governmental bodies and organizations that must also be fulfilled; foremost among these are the U.S.Senate Select Committee on Intelligence and the U.S. House of Representatives Permanent Select Committee on Intelligence.

4. Congressional Oversight Committees

The curious fact regarding congressional oversight committees centers on how their responsibilities overlap and become somewhat duplicative. For example, the Senate Select Committee on Intelligence has a membership of 13 to 17 members who serve terms of eight years. The committee membership has the responsibility of authorizing appropriations for intelligence activities as well as authorizing significant intelligence activities. The Senate must confirm presidential appointments of the director of national intelligence, the principal deputy director of intelligence, the director of the Central Intelligence Agency, and the inspector general of the Central Intelligence Agency. One additional role of the Senate Select Investigations Committee pertains to approving treaties, and in this case the Senate Select Committee on Intelligence reviews the ability of the Intelligence Committee to verify the provisions of a treaty under consideration for ratification. However, the role of the Senate has focused more specifically upon the review of intelligence activities that have created legal, moral or sensitive problems for our nation.

The House of Representatives Permanent Select Committee on Intelligence members also serve terms of eight years on this committee. There are 19 members on this committee and they also have the responsibility for authorizing intelligence activities as well as requested appropriations. Their role in reviewing intelligence covert activities and programs is parallel to the role Senate Select Committee on Intelligence.

The president, by law, has the responsibility for notifying each oversight committee of all covert action programs within our intelligence community that have received presidential approval. Furthermore, the president is required to inform both committees as to any significant intelligence failures. In short, the president is legally bound to keep both oversight committees "fully and currently" informed of the activities of the intelligence community.

There are other congressional committees that have jurisdiction over the Department of Defense and the Justice Department, and because we have intelligence agencies within the Justice Department and the Department of Defense, there may occasionally exist reasons for concurrent jurisdiction.

Two other organizations that merit discussion because they report to the president of the United States are the President's Foreign Intelligence Advisory Board and the President's Intelligence Oversight Board. The President's Foreign Intelligence Advisory Board focuses on assessing the quality of intelligence collected, analysis, and the counterintelligence activities of our intelligence community. This 16-member board appointed by the president can also work with the director of national intelligence. The President's Intelligence Oversight Board conducts independent oversight investigations and reviews the oversight practices and procedures of the inspector general and the general councils of the intelligence agencies.

It is apparent that our intelligence community perhaps more than most other organizations, receives extensive oversight and review. Its activities are critical to security and defense, and for these reasons, we must have confidence that the intelligence activities and products reflect the highest quality standards.

Now that we have identified these agencies within our intelligence community both in terms of our National Intelligence Program and our Military Intelligence Program, we describe the process of creating foreign intelligence and the major elements in this important process.

5. The Intelligence Process

Intelligence consists of essentially five major steps designed to assist our nation's policymakers in selecting a course of action which will result in effective results. The five major steps to the intelligence process are as follows.

A. Planning and direction: customer requirements
B. Collection
C. Processing and exploitation
D. Analysis and production
E. Dissemination and productivity

A. Planning and Direction: Customer Requirements

This is a critical phase in the intelligence process because there must be a clear understanding of what an intelligence problem is before one can begin the collection and analysis stages. Therefore, customer "needs," particularly if they are complex and time-sensitive require a careful assessment before they are expressed as intelligence requirements. Defined intelligence requirements translate the customer needs into a well-reasoned intelligence action plan, which in turn, guides the collection strategy and the final intelligence product.[21] It is the responsibility of the National Security Council, the president, or his top aides to clarify their intelligence requirements so that an orderly process of planning and direction will define their needs and requirements. In fact, any government agency or official who initiates requests for an intelligence product should be prepared for a probing dialogue that will permit clarification and identification of the problem, so that a statement of the problem can permit an orderly and sound methodological approach to the collection of the data required for assessment and analysis.

B. Collection

Once the process for translating the customer's intelligence needs into a set of intelligence requirements with senior officials establishing an intelligence action plan has been completed, the selection of collection methodologies can begin. The intelligence need defines the collection requirement and ultimately the selection of one of the six collection sources or disciplines.[22]

There are six basic intelligence sources or collection disciplines:

1. Signals intelligence (SIGINT)
2. Imagery intelligence (IMINT)
3. Measurement and signature intelligence (MASINT)
4. Human source intelligence (HUMINT)
5. Open source intelligence (OSINT)
6. Geospatial intelligence

SIGINT*—Signals intelligence* is derived from signal intercepts comprising—individually or in combination:

- All communications intelligence (COMINT)
- Electronic intelligence (ELINT)
- Foreign instrumentation signals intelligence (FISINT)

The NSA is responsible for collecting, processing, and reporting SIGINT. The National SIGINT Committee within the NSA advises the director, NSA, and DNI on SIGINT policy issues and manages the SIGINT requirements system.

IMINT*—Imagery intelligence* includes representations of objects reproduced electronically or by optical means on film, electronic display devices, or other media. Imagery can be derived from visual photography, radar sensors, infrared sensors, lasers, and electro-optics. NGA is the manager for all imagery intelligence activities, both classified and unclassified, within the government, including requirements, collection, processing, exploitation, dissemination, archiving, and retrieval.

MASINT*—Measurement and signature intelligence* is technically derived intelligence data other than imagery and SIGINT. The intelligence locates, identifies, or describes distinctive characteristics of targets. It employs a broad group of disciplines including nuclear, optical, radio frequency, acoustic, seismic, and materials sciences. Examples are the distinctive radar signatures of specific aircraft systems or the chemical compositions of air and water samples. The Central MASINT Organization, a component of the DIA, is the focus for all national and DoD MASINT matters.

HUMINT*—Human intelligence* is derived from human sources. To the public, HUMINT remains synonymous with espionage and clandestine activities, but most work is performed by overt collectors such as diplomats and military attachés. HUMINT is used mainly by the CIA, the Department of State, the DoD, and the FBI. Collection includes clandestine acquisition of photography, documents, and other material; overt collection by personnel in diplomatic and consular posts; debriefing of foreign nationals and U.S. citizens who travel abroad; and official contacts with foreign governments.

To improve HUMINT throughout the IC in response to the recommendations made by the WMD Commission, the CIA, working closely with the Office of the Director of National Intelligence (ODNI) established the National Clandestine Service (NCS). The NCS serves as the national authority for coordination, deconfliction, and evaluation of clandestine HUMINT operations across the intelligence community, both abroad and inside the United States, consistent with existing laws, executive orders, and interagency agreement. Although the ODNI establishes policy related to clandestine HUMINT, the NCS executes and implements that policy across the IC.

OSINT*—Open source intelligence* is publicly available information appearing in print or electronic form including radio, television, newspapers, journals, the Internet, commercial databases, and videos, graphics, and drawings. Although open source collection responsibilities are broadly distributed through the IC, the major collectors are the Foreign Broadcast Information Service (FBIS) and the National Air and Space Intelligence Center (NASIC).

Geospatial Intelligence—This is the analysis and visual representation of security-related activities produced through an integration of imagery, imagery intelligence, and geospatial information.

C. Processing and Exploitation

It is important to remember Mark M. Lowenthal's instructive admonition, that "collection produces information, not intelligence." The information must undergo processing and exploitation before it can be regarded as intelligence, and ultimately given to an analyst.[23] The processing of collected data or material will depend on what form it is collected in, for example, reducing telemetry to meaningful measures or exploiting imagery will be necessary before an analyst can even begin to work and process this information into a comprehensible intelligence report. This is also the case for encrypted computer information that must first be decrypted. Also, foreign languages must be translated if an analyst is expected to work with the information.

D. Analysis and Production

This important phase of the intelligence process is dependent on well trained intelligence analysts. Analysis is not simply reorganizing data and information into a new format. The intelligence analyst's responsibility is to fully describe and provide as much usable and explanatory information about the intelligence target as possible. Intelligence assessments are based on the data and information captured by the collection disciplines and are refined by research methodologies used by the intelligence analyst. If the analysis of the data can reach beyond the descriptive and explanatory levels to a synthesis, which then results in an estimation, the intelligence will be of value and may be produced as an intelligence report or other intelligence product.

Most intelligence organizations assign analysts to a particular geographic or functional specialty. Analysts obtain information from all sources pertinent to their areas of responsibility through the collection, forwarding, and processing systems. Analysts absorb incoming information, evaluate it, produce an assessment of the current state of affairs within an assigned field or substantive area, and then forecast future trends or outcomes. Analysts are encouraged to include alternative futures in their assessments and to look for opportunities to warn about possible developments abroad that could either threaten or provide opportunities for U.S. security and policy interests. The analyst also develops requirements for collection of new information.

The intelligence analyst has the responsibility of reviewing the collected information and going beyond the descriptive and explanatory levels of analysis to synthesize the facts by verification of information. The findings must be presented to the policymaker in such a fashion that the analyst forecast reduces the uncertainty that confronts decision makers and policymakers.

To effectively produce intelligence forecasts, estimates, warnings, or trends, the intelligence analyst must be able to apply the rigors of the scientific method to the intelligence analysis. To minimize error and institute proper controls, the intelligence analyst must clearly employ a research methodology and, where possible, statistical tests to provide for validated levels of statistical confidence. When decision makers are confronted with a range of difficult choices, they will demand as much confidence in the intelligence assessment or report as possible.

There are a number of analytical methods that intelligence analysts may employ in assessing a body of collected information that is presented to them for their review. Several of these methods of analysis have been designed and implemented because of past failures of intelligence estimates and reports. Some of the methods of analysis that intelligence analysts will use are as follows.

- Scientific method including induction, deduction, and abduction
- Linchpin analysis
- Opportunity analysis
- Competitive versus cooperative analysis
- Alternative analysis
- Red cell analysis
- Contingency analysis
- High impact/low probability analysis
- Scenario development
- Indications and warning
- Computer and database analysis
- Data mining analysis
- Numerous other classified analytical bases[24]

E. Dissemination of Intelligence Products

The intelligence community has the responsibility of preparing and transmitting intelligence reports to the customer. The defined intelligence problem targeted by the appropriate collection disciplines and processed by the analysis and production phase of the process will result in an intelligence product moving from the intelligence producer to the consumer. The traditional intelligence products include the following reports.

- *The President's Daily Brief* prepared daily by the CIA, but now delivered by the new DNI. It provides information as to any event that has national security ramifications and has occurred within the past 24 hours, anywhere in the world.
- *The Senior Executive Intelligence Brief* is prepared by the CIA in coordination with other intelligence agencies and provides a briefing of national security issues to senior executives and members of the Senate and House Intelligence Oversight Committees.
- *The National Intelligence Estimates* are the responsibility of national intelligence officers, who are members of the National Intelligence Council, which is now under the DNI. National intelligence estimates represent the opinion of the entire intelligence community and are presented to the president and the National Security Council by the DNI. National intelligence estimates are long-term intelligence products that estimate the likely events or direction an issue will take in the future. These are important products that have the ability to shape the views of our policymakers, however, as with any intelligence product, the

recipient may choose to follow its parameters, ignore it, or accept only certain portions.

Intelligence products or reports can also be presented in briefings to the president or senior officials. Intelligence reports can be transmitted via secure video conferencing methods, secure telephone calls, and secure and encrypted computer messages to senior government officials and to other intelligence agencies.

There are five categories of finished intelligence, and the three agencies responsible for producing all-source intelligence are the CIA's Directorate of Intelligence, the DIA's Directorate of Intelligence, and the State Department's Bureau of Intelligence and Research. Within the Department of Defense, there are four service agencies (Navy, Marine, Army, and Air Force) that also produce finished intelligence.

The five categories of finished intelligence available are as follows.

1. *Current intelligence* addresses day-to-day events, seeking to apprise consumers of new developments and background, to assess their significance, to warn of their near-term consequences, and to signal potential dangerous situations in the near future.
2. *Estimative intelligence* deals with what may happen. Its main purpose is to provide informed assessments of the range and likelihood of possible outcomes.
3. *Warning intelligence* sounds an alarm or gives notice to policymakers. This includes identifying or forecasting events that could cause the engagement of U.S. military forces. Warning intelligence also identifies events that could affect U.S. foreign policy.
4. *Research intelligence* consists of in-depth studies that underpin both current and estimative intelligence. Two categories of research are (a) basic intelligence that consists primarily of the structured compilation of geographic, demographic, social, military, and political data on foreign countries; and (b) intelligence for operational support incorporating all types of intelligence production tailored, focused, and produced for planners and operators.
5. *Scientific and technical intelligence* includes information on technical developments and characteristics, performance, and capabilities of foreign technologies. It covers the entire spectrum of sciences, technologies, weapon systems, and integrated operations.

The dissemination of intelligence reports is an important phase of this entire process; however, one of the difficulties of this phase centers on the protection of sources and methods. Frequently, the recipient of such intelligence reports wants the assurance of the factual and objective veracity of the intelligence report, while at the same time, the intelligence-producing agency must be vigilant to protect sources and methods and may be limited in providing a full suite of information.

The entire intelligence process exists to provide the policymaker carefully analyzed and informed judgments on the particular problem under review so as to assist the policymaker in the decision-making process. It is imperative that the intelligence officer and intelligence process maintain objectivity and not push for specific outcomes or choices. The intelligence process has a supporting role and should not cross over into advocacy of policies or positions. In short, the goal of the entire intelligence process is to put the policymaker in the best position available to make the best informed decision possible.[25]

6. Summary

This chapter has focused attention on how our intelligence process works to protect our nation from national security threats and vulnerabilities. As earlier observed, the manner in which we have organized our intelligence system to confront the challenges posed by large nation-states is not as fully applicable and useful to the challenges we now confront from terrorist organizations. We must continue to improve on our collection disciplines, especially engaging them in more "jointness" with the human intelligence discipline. This chapter has provided a framework and described our nation's intelligence processing capability. It is hoped that it will provide insight as to how we can continue to gather information to protect our nation from the threats we will encounter from terrorist organizations in the future.

Endnotes

1. Karl F. Inderfurth and Lock K. Johnson, *Fateful Decisions: Inside the National Security Council*, Oxford University Press: New York, 2004, pp. XIII–XIV.
2. Robert Baer, *See No Evil: The True Story of a Ground Soldier in the CIA's War on Terrorism*, Random House, 2002, p. 271.
3. Office of the Director of National Intelligence, *An Overview of the United States Intelligence Community: A Report*, U.S. Government, January, 2007, pp 1–4.
4. Richard A. Best and Elizabeth Bazan, *Intelligence Spending: Public Disclosure Issues*, CRS Report for Congress, Congressional Research Service; The Library of Congress: Washington, DC, February 15, 2007, pp. 3–4.
5. United States Intelligence Community, Deputy Secretary of Defense Memorandum on Implementation Guidance on Restructuring Defense Intelligence and Related Matters (Excerpt), May 8, 2003.
6. Office of the Director of National Intelligence, *An Overview of the United States Intelligence Community*: A Report, op.cit., pp. 5–6.

7. Office of the Director of National Intelligence, ibid., pp. 15–16.
8. Office of the Director of National Intelligence, ibid., p. 8.
9. Office of the Director of National Intelligence, ibid., p. 10.
10. Office of the Director of National Intelligence, ibid., p. 12.
11. Office of the Director of National Intelligence ibid., p.11.
12. Office of the Director of National Intelligence, ibid., p. 14.
13. Office of the Director of National Intelligence, ibid., pp. 7–8.
14. Office of the Director of National Intelligence, ibid., p. 20.
15. Office of the Director of National Intelligence, ibid., p. 19.
16. Office of the Director of National Intelligence, ibid., p 17.
17. Office of the Director of National Intelligence, ibid., pp. 22–23.
18. Office of the Director of National Intelligence, ibid., p. 24.
19. Office of the Director of National Intelligence, ibid., p. 30.
20. Office of the Director of National Intelligence, ibid., p. 28.
21. Thomas A. Johnson, An introduction to the intelligence process for addressing national security threats and vulnerabilities, in *National Security Issues in Science, Law and Technology*, CRC Press: Boca Raton, FL, 2007, p. 6.
22. Ibid., p. 7.
23. Mark M. Lowenthal, *Intelligence: From Secrets to Policy*, third ed., Congressional Quarterly Press: Washington, DC, 2006, p. 54.
24. Thomas A. Johnson, *An Introduction to the Intelligence Process for Addressing National Security Threats and Vulnerabilities*, op.cit., pp. 12–13.
25. Ibid., pp. 17–19.

The Reform and Reorganization of Our Intelligence Community

6

This chapter is organized around the following format which traces the historical emergence of our intelligence agencies, the Cold War years leading to two Gulf wars, and the September 11, 2001 attack, the impacts of two major national commission reports culminating in the Intelligence Reform and Terrorism Prevention Act of 2004, and resulting transformation of our intelligence community.

1. Historical Emergence of Intelligence Organizations
2. The Cold War Years: 1947–1989
   A. 1950 – Korea
   B. 1953 – Iran
   C. 1954 – Guatemala
   D. 1961 – Cuba: The Bay of Pigs
   E. 1962 – Cuba: The Cuban Missile Crisis
   F. 1972 – ABM Treaty and SALT I Accord
   G. 1979 – Iran: Seizure of U.S. Embassy
   H. 1986 – Iran: Contra Affair
   I. 1989 to 1991 – The Collapse of the Soviet Union
3. Two Gulf Wars and Middle East Terrorist Activity
   A. Intelligence Evaluation in Two Gulf Wars
   B. Middle East Terrorist Activities
4. September 11, 2001 Attacks and Five Categories of Failure
   A. National Commission on Terrorist Attacks upon the United States
   B. The Commission on the Intelligence Capabilities of the United States Regarding Weapons of Mass Destruction
   C. Review of Intelligence on Weapons of Mass Destruction: Report of a Committee of Privy Counselors: Lord Butler, House of Commons, British Report
   D. Intelligence Reform and Reorganization
   E. Theories of Intelligence
5. Transforming the Intelligence Community
   A. Three Major Transformational Challenges
6. Summary

Endnotes

1. Historical Emergence of Intelligence Organizations

To appreciate the task of reforming and reorganizing our intelligence community, one must first realize that we are dealing with an institution that is roughly 60 years old. There have been episodic events in our nation's use of intelligence, dating back to our first president, who used agents to spy on the British forces to collect information during the Revolutionary War. Those experts were followed by intelligence activities and failures during the War of 1812, and again during our Civil War with both Union and Confederate intelligence activities experiencing both success and failure.

President Theodore Roosevelt used intelligence to incite a revolution in Panama which permitted him to justify annexing the Panama Canal, and historians noted that he supported the most active use of intelligence for foreign policy purposes by any president until he took office in 1907. With the advent of World War I, President Woodrow Wilson who was most reluctant to use intelligence services until the British government provided him with decrypted German diplomatic naval traffic that revealed Germany's attempt to entice Mexico to join Germany in the war against the United States, then appreciated the use of intelligence and this played a major role in his 1917 address to Congress urging a Declaration of War against Germany. Four years later in 1921, President Hoover decided that the interception of diplomatic cables should not be tolerated.

The next major intelligence activity occurred under President Franklin Roosevelt during World War II. In 1941, he appointed William Donovan as coordinator to collect and analyze all information and data that would have been relevant to national security. Again the British Government, under the urging of Prime Minister Winston Churchill, provided assistance and training in this new intelligence effort, the most formidable our nation was to embark upon in its history. The surprise attack on Pearl Harbor by the Japanese forces removed all doubt that our nation should never again be vulnerable to such an attack. In fact, it was this very point that eventually led to the establishment of the Office of Strategic Services (OSS) which in 1946 became the Central Intelligence Group (CIG) and then with the passage of the National Security Act of 1947 became the Central Intelligence Agency.

President Harry Truman's signing of the National Security Act also created our National Security Council to coordinate national security policy, while also creating the position of secretary of defense as well as unified and separate military Departments of the Army, Navy, and Air Force. This Act also created the Joint Chiefs of Staff to serve as principal military advisors to the president. The Central Intelligence Agency was authorized to perform "services of common concern" to other intelligence agencies as may be determined by the National Security Council and to perform "such other functions and duties" related to intelligence affecting national security as the National Security Council may from time to time direct. Although this language in the statute was vague, there was no wording in the statute that mentioned "espionage" or "spying," nor was there any wording to suggest covert actions as part of the new agency's charter, nor was any language present that precluded these activities.[1]

The sketchy beginnings of what has now become our nation's intelligence community clearly reveal that our national leaders saw a need to create an intelligence capability principally for times of war. Therefore, we must recognize that our presidents have had a major role in shaping how our intelligence community will discharge its duties. Clearly, Presidents Wilson and Hoover had the greatest reservation about the use and existence of the intelligence process, and the attitude within the Hoover administration was quite simply "Gentlemen do not read other peoples' letters, cables, and diplomatic documents." This attitude gradually dissipated with two major world wars and the emergence of the cold war.

Today even greater questions of both moral and constitutional issues are raised regarding the appropriateness of an intelligence operation within our democracy. In fact, a major dilemma facing our nation centers on how our intelligence community can retain the trust and confidence of citizens who are concerned about the protection of civil liberties, privacy, and the freedom they enjoy as a result of our constitutional form of governance. So, although every president has the responsibility for protecting our nation's national security, our intelligence community is used to gather the information and provide the warning as to impeding danger.

Thus, the president and the National Security Council set the stage for the protection of constitutional freedom as they directly order the intelligence community to engage in various operations. Accordingly, the role of the president and the National Security Council cannot be excised from the entire focus of reform and reorganization of the intelligence community, because their roles are so paramount to the actions ordered to be operationalized. Our president and all our national leadership confront a difficult dilemma which pivots on their responsibility to protect the nation, yet to do so they engage our sophisticated intelligence system which involves world class technology methods for the collection of data along with covert programs, clandestine efforts, deception, and secret operations that become classified and limited from public scrutiny. In our effort to protect our nation, we must carefully balance the intelligence methods and operations we select and authorize for use, because many citizens feel that a too-aggressive intelligence apparatus may well threaten the fabric of our society.

As we look to the reform and reorganization of our intelligence community, it is appropriate also to ask our national leaders generally, and Congress specifically, to determine whether our 16 intelligence organizations can productively coexist as they work within our democracy to serve and protect. In short, what are the acceptable parameters that our citizens will accept, as those in the intelligence community work throughout the world to protect them? Is it acceptable to penetrate terrorist organizations to collect actionable intelligence? Is it acceptable to engage in covert action programs? Is it acceptable for intelligence officers to use cover? Is it acceptable to use espionage tactics that may require clandestine activities that in other countries may be deemed illegal and violations of their legal system? How much deception is permissive, and under what conditions are there to be limitations? Who is to define these conditions?

Some of the most difficult questions a democracy must deal with emerge from our efforts to protect our national security through the intelligence community "whether, when, and how the government may consort with criminals, influence elections, listen in on private conversations, eliminate adversaries, withhold information from the public, or alternatively release it at some cost to the sources and methods used to collect it."[2] These actions will precipitate a collision of values which our society currently is experiencing.

In our war on terrorism, the government has created three new national organizations to protect our homeland. These new organizations are the U.S. Department of Homeland Security, the Northern Command as a new element in our Department of Defense strategy, and the National Counter Terrorism Center. These new agencies will have a responsibility for digesting an enormous amount of intelligence collected by our 16 intelligence agencies, and they will have to utilize this and other domestic information and intelligence to protect our homeland. So, the new strategies will also be viewed by some as a collision path to the privacy and civil liberties that many feel will be threatened by too aggressive an intelligence apparatus.

On the other hand, a legitimate question that national security officials can ask of our citizens, "So you want us to protect you from terrorists, but what specifically is it that you will permit us to do to protect you?" Also, "What specifically will you not allow us to do, as we seek to protect you?" In essence, what are the conditions and expectations that will be placed on us to protect our society from terrorists? Identification of the acceptable and unacceptable practices is extraordinarily difficult and to begin a dialogue on the efforts to bring them within collective expectations and consensus is more difficult than the appointment of special legislative commissions which seek to offer blue ribbon structural modifications of our intelligence agencies.

2. The Cold War Years: 1947–1989

The emergence of our intelligence agencies during the first two world wars had a great deal to do with the effort to collect information to determine how best to anticipate enemy action against our military forces. At the end of World War II, we saw the beginning of the Cold War in 1947 which ended in 1991 and resulted in a transition of more operations for our intelligence agencies. Several of these intelligence operations met with abject failure and some with success; the important point when reviewing these major activities is to note that most were under the direction of the National Security Council and the president of the United States. Nevertheless, some of the operations were clearly failures of the intelligence analysis process and could only be attributable to analysis errors by the intelligence analysts.

The major intelligence activities for purposes of our review include the following.

A. 1950: Korea and the intelligence failure in predicting the invasion of North Korean troops into South Korea.
B. 1953: Iran and the U.S.-sponsored coup that overthrew Premier Mossadegh and restored the rule of the Shah. This covert action became a model that would be repeated by U.S. clandestine intelligence operations during the 1950s in other parts of the world.
C. 1954: Guatemala coup to overthrow President Guzman due to U.S. concern that he was more inclined to support the Soviet Union. The United States provided a clandestine operation to effect this operation.
D. 1961: The Bay of Pigs operation to use Cuban exiles trained by the CIA to invade Cuba and overthrow Fidel Castro was an intelligence disaster for the Kennedy administration.
E. 1962: The Cuban missile crisis was both a failure and success. The failure centered on the intelligence analysis to predict the Soviet plans for deployment of missiles in Cuba. The success was in the intelligence community's ability to provide proof of the location of the Soviet missiles within Cuba.
F. 1972: ABM Treaty and SALT I Accord during the Nixon administration antiballistic missile negotiation found the intelligence community playing a critical role in verification and monitoring through satellite and other technology.
G. 1979: Iran, the revolution created by Ayatollah Khomeini's return to depose the Shah, and to take over the U.S. Embassy and hold hostage U.S. citizens was another incident in which the intelligence community failed to provide warnings to our nation's policymakers.
H. 1986–1987: Iran–Contra affair in which a member of the National Security Council formulated a plan to sell missiles to Iran and provide the proceeds to sustain the Contras in Nicaragua in their fight against the Sandinista government. This incident clearly violated U.S. law and really was more of a National Security Council program than any program within our intelligence community.

I. 1989–1991: The fall of the Soviet Union and its formal dissolution in 1991 culminated in the end of the Cold War. The intelligence community was criticized for not seeing the end of the Soviet Union or the timeframe of its dissolution. On the other hand, a great deal of material suggests that the intelligence community was providing President Reagan with the necessary information needed for him to keep pressure on Premier Gorbachov.[3]

Accompanying the fall of the Soviet Union and the general realization that our 44-year Cold War had now concluded was the congressional realization that the financial resources provided to Department of Defense and to the intelligence community could now be reallocated to other congressional interests. The decade between 1991 (the fall of the Soviet Union) and 2001 (the attack of 9–11 on the World Trade Center and the Pentagon) was a period of substantial terrorist activity. During this period, and immediately after the fall of the Soviet Union in 1991, Congress bears a large responsibility for the many inadequacies within our intelligence community. Many in Congress even questioned whether the nation needed an intelligence community, and those that did not participated in approving deep financial budgetary cuts to our intelligence agencies. The term "peace dividend" was coined and became a major lever to reallocate monies for other congressional matters and priorities.

However, another factor contributing to a growing disdain toward the intelligence community resulted from congressional inquiries and reviews principally of the Central Intelligence Agency. The three major commission reviews were for actions taken by intelligence agencies during the Cold War years. The Rockefeller Commission Report in 1975 confirmed the existence of a CIA domestic mail opening operation, and also found that in the late 1960s and early 1970s the CIA kept files on 300,000 U.S. citizens and organizations related to domestic dissident activities. The Senate impaneled the Church Committee and reviewed both CIA domestic activities and covert activity in foreign countries, including alleged assassinations of foreign leaders. The Pike Committee which was the House of Representatives' counterpart to the Senate's Church Committee also made inquiries into allegations of improper activities of federal intelligence agencies, and although the House voted down the Pike Committee report and refused to accept it, a copy was leaked to the New York newspaper called the *Village Voice*.

Perhaps the three major events that were to hamper our intelligence community's capabilities in confronting our nation's next major crisis of terrorist activities were the following.

1. The impaneling of congressional committees to review the improper activities of intelligence agencies, especially the major committee hearings during the mid-1970s.
2. The illegal activities created by the National Security Council in allocating Iran Contra money for missiles to trade for hostages and fund an operation Congress disapproved.
3. The potential reallocation of funding of intelligence agencies under the peace dividend, as a result of the ending of the Cold War.

In short, Congress was tired of dealing with the problems created by the intelligence community and with few friends and many critics, the intelligence community was in a weakened position. These were the realities and factors that were present as we embarked on two Gulf wars and suffered the 9–11 terrorist attack.

3. Two Gulf Wars and Middle East Terrorist Activity

A. Intelligence Evaluation in Two Gulf Wars

Our intelligence community's involvement in the two Gulf wars can be evaluated on the information and recommendations offered to two distinct groups.

1. The president and the National Security Council
2. The Joint Chiefs of Staff, theatre generals, and battlefield commanders

In the first Gulf War, the results of the information provided to both groups by the intelligence community were regarded as most favorable and effective. General Schwarzkopf placed enormous demands on the abilities of the Defense Intelligence Agency, the National Geospatial Intelligence Agency, and the National Reconnaissance Office for live data feeds directly to his battlefield commanders, as opposed to the former practice of material data centered in Washington, DC. This direction was extremely useful in placing the information where most needed by the decision makers in the field. Directing data for decision making at the battlefield commander level is one of the major reasons our military is so strong and so different from any other military force in the world. The data required for decision making at the theatre and battlefield level must be provided on a continuous live feed basis by our intelligence community. The intelligence provided to the National Security Council and to the president in the first Gulf war was also rated as superb on most accounts.

However, based on the second Gulf war in Iraq, the intelligence community has been severely taken to task for its failure to predict the lack of weapons of mass destruction in Iraq. Although this criticism focused on the intelligence provided to the National Security Council and to the president, on the other hand, intelligence provided to the military for the initial invasion was regarded as excellent. Criticism continues to be raised as to our inability to address the insurgency actions, and the delayed response of military counterinsurgency programs and activities.

Because both Gulf wars were preceded by a sustained rate of Middle East terrorist activity, we must also examine the performance of our intelligence community with relationship to Middle East terrorist groups. A brief review of the Middle East terrorist patterns reveals the following groups and timelines of their activities.

B. Middle East Terrorist Activities

1970–1975: Sudan and Lebanon: several American diplomats were murdered and others were kidnapped by agents of the Palestine Liberation Organization (PLO).

1973: Khartoum: the Saudi Arabian Embassy was attacked by the Black September Organization (BSO), the U.S. Ambassador was wounded, and several diplomats were taken hostage. Negotiations for the diplomatic hostages were not successful and Fatah headquarters in Beirut ordered the killing of two United States officials and the Belgian chargé.

1979: Iranian students attacked the U.S. Embassy and took 52 American hostages and held them for 444 days.

April 1983: The American Embassy in Beirut, Lebanon was attacked by a suicide bomber, killing the CIA station chief and wounding 120 other people. This attack was delivered by Hezbollah, an Islamic terrorist organization created by Iran and Syria.

October 1983: Another Hezbollah suicide bomber blew up the U.S. Marine barracks at the Beirut airport killing 241 marines and wounding 81 marines.

December 1983: American Embassy in Kuwait was bombed.

September 1984: The U.S. Embassy Annex near Beirut was attacked by a truck bomb, again by Hezbollah.

December 1984: A Kuwaiti airplane was hijacked and two American passengers employed by the U.S. Agency for International Development were murdered by Hezbollah agents.

June 1985: TWA flight 847 was hijacked by Hezbollah agents and a U.S. naval officer was killed and hurled to the tarmac.

October 1985: The *Achille Lauro*, an Italian cruise ship, was hijacked by the PLO's Abu Abbas working with Libyan agents and they murdered Leon Klinghoffer, a U.S. citizen who was thrown overboard.

December 1985: Five Americans were among 20 people killed when the Rome and Vienna airports were bombed.

April 1986: West Berlin, Germany was the site of Libyan bomb attacks against a discotheque where U.S. soldiers met.

1986: Three U.S. citizens who worked at American University in Beirut, Lebanon were killed by Palestinian terrorist Abu Nidal.

December 1988: The bomb placed inside Pan American Flight 103 exploded over Lockerbie, Scotland killing 270 people; this operation was performed by three Libyan agents.

February 1993: The first attack on our World Trade Center in New York City by Omar Abdel Rahman and Ramzi Yousef and ten other radical Islamic terrorists killed 6 people and injured over 1000.

April 1993: Former President George H. W. Bush was the target of an assassination attempt by Iraqi Intelligence agents during his visit to Kuwait.

March 1995: Two American diplomats were killed in Karachi, Pakistan, and a third was wounded.

November 1995: Five Americans died when a car bomb exploded in Riyadh, Saudi Arabia.

June 1996: The bombing of Khobar Towers in Dhahran, Saudi Arabia killed 19 and wounded 240 military personnel stationed in Saudi Arabia.

June 1998: The U.S. Embassy in Beirut was attacked by individuals throwing grenades at the facility.

August 1998: Our embassies in Kenya and Tanzania were attacked on the same day by Al Qaeda.

October 2000: The *U.S.S. Cole* which was refueling in Yeman was attacked by Al Qaeda terrorists who killed 17 sailors and wounded 39 other personnel.[4]

The pattern of attacks by terrorist organizations, some which have been state-supported and the current nonstate terrorist activities of Al Qaeda points to many problems the intelligence community has in attempting to gather information on these groups. Despite terrorist activities for more than 40 years in this region, we have made little headway in forecasting attacks and new terrorist movements. In part, the reason centers on language difficulties, the absence of a long-term human intelligence presence in the area, and numerous other geopolitical factors. By most accounts, our intelligence community requires additional human intelligence and collection of data, but also more rigorous analytical assessment of data to better forecast trends and identify patterns that will permit our policymakers to make the decisions that will protect our citizens and allies.

4. September 11, 2001 Attacks and Five Categories of Failure

A. National Commission on Terrorist Attacks upon the United States

The National Commission on the Terrorist Attacks upon the United States was formed by Congress and the president on November 27, 2002 as a result of Public Law 107-306. The mandate was to investigate facts and circumstances relating to the terrorist attacks of September 11, 2001, including those related to intelligence agencies, law enforcement agencies, diplomacy, immigration issues and border control, the flow of assets to terrorist organizations, commercial aviation, the role of congressional oversight and resource allocation, and other areas determined relevant by the commission. In the process of inquiry, the commission interviewed more than 1200 individuals in 10 countries, reviewed more than 2.5 million pages of documents, and interviewed all senior officials from the current Bush administration and previous administrations who had responsibility for topical areas under the commission's mandate. The commission also held 19 days of public hearings and took testimony from 160 witnesses. The commission also held "closed" hearings to process material that was sensitive and classified.[5]

The commission reviewed materials related to the rise of Al Qaeda as a terrorist organization and bin Laden's appeal in the Islamic world, along with bin Laden's declaration of war against the United States. The commission also reviewed our responses to Al Qaeda's attacks against Americans in foreign countries. The planning of the attack upon the United States and the strategies and tactics of Al Qaeda were also reviewed. The commission also reflected on the development of a global strategy and how we should organize our government to better protect the United States during these terrorist attacks. Finally, with reference to both our past governmental efforts and how we should prepare with greater foresight, the commission focused an assessment which found four specific areas in need of greater improvement, especially in regard to our intelligence community. These four areas are (1) imagination, (2) policy, (3) capabilities, and (4) management of both operational and institutional personnel and programs.

B. The Commission on the Intelligence Capabilities of the United States Regarding Weapons of Mass Destruction

These four areas of failure of our intelligence community were further expanded by the 2005 Report of the Commission on the Intelligence Capabilities of the United States Regarding Weapons of Mass Destruction. This report was commissioned as a direct result of not finding any weapons of mass destruction in Iraq. The report presented to the president stated the following in the most emphatic terms.

> We conclude that the Intelligence Community was dead wrong in almost all of its pre-war judgments about Iraq's weapons of mass destruction. This was a major intelligence failure. Its principal causes were the Intelligence Community's inability to collect good information about Iraq's WMD programs, serious errors in analyzing what information it could gather and a failure to make clear just how much of its analysis was based on assumptions, rather than good evidence. On a matter of this importance, we simply cannot afford failures of this magnitude.[6]

It is equally important to note that the commission found no indication that the intelligence community distorted the evidence regarding Iraq's weapons of mass destruction; what it reported it sincerely believed, but the community was simply wrong.

The commission's 601-page report is derived from a 692-page classified report to the president. The report prepared for the public reviewed the intelligence community's prewar assessments on Iraq's nuclear weapons, biological warfare, and chemical warfare programs and delivery systems. The postwar findings of the Iraq Survey Group and a review of the collection, analysis, and information-sharing systems that caused the intelligence community inaccurate prewar assessments were also presented. The report also reviewed and compared intelligence assessments with Libya and Al Qaeda activities in Afghanistan. The classified version focused on monitoring the development of nuclear capabilities in Iran and North Korea.

The report discussed how to build an integrated intelligence community under a new organization which included the director of national intelligence. A focus on creating "jointness" and greater organizational coordination similar to what the Goldwater–Nichols Act did in creating a more unified military as an example that would be recommended for the intelligence community. The improvement of individual collection disciplines and creating an integrated collection enterprise were also recommended. A rigorous focus on improving analysis and improving our counterintelligence capabilities was also recommended by the commission to the president.

Perhaps the most important consequence of the commission report on our intelligence capabilities regarding weapons of mass destruction was the impact it had on both Congress and the White House. This report was directly responsible for Public Law 108-458 which is the Intelligence Reform and Terrorism Prevention Act of 2004. This 221-page Act was responsible for the creation of the Office of Director of National Intelligence and the inclusion of many of the commission's recommendations. In short, this Act has been the most formidable change in the intelligence community since its inception in the National Security Act of 1947.

C. Review of Intelligence on Weapons of Mass Destruction: Report of a Committee of Privy Counsellors: Lord Butler, House of Commons, British Report

Just as the United States was reviewing the intelligence capabilities of its forces regarding weapons of mass destruction, a parallel inquiry was ordered by the House of Commons in England to review the British intelligence on weapons of mass destruction. The British report emerged from committees appointed by the prime minister and charged to investigate the intelligence available in respect to WMD programs in countries of concern and with reference to global trade in WMD. Also, the prime minister asked the committee to investigate the accuracy of intelligence on Iraqi WMD, and to examine any discrepancies between the intelligence gathered, evaluated, and used by the government before the conflict, and between that intelligence and what had been discovered by the Iraq Survey Group.

The committee was also asked to make recommendations to the prime minister for the future gathering, evaluation, and use of intelligence on WMD in light of the difficulties of operating in countries of concern. The Committee of Privy Counselors met 36 times and traveled to Washington, DC where they met with members of the President's Commission on the Intelligence Capabilities of the United States Regarding Weapons of Mass Destruction, and other officials. The committee also met with the British Joint Intelligence Committee to obtain intelligence assessments, and then to obtain from the intelligence agencies a full list of the underlying intelligence, both accepted and rejected, that was available to inform those assessments. The Privy Committee also obtained policy papers from all relevant government departments to determine the use made of the intelligence.[7]

The British report also focused on the nature and use of intelligence, its collection, and validation and analysis. The limitations of intelligence, the risks of good assessment, and the use of intelligence were also probed. Similar to the U.S. Commission Report, the British study also reviewed countries of concern other than Iraq, namely, Libya, Iran, and North Korea. A review of terrorism from 1995 to 2001, as well as intelligence on Al Qaeda capabilities in the nuclear, chemical, and biological areas was also analyzed. The capabilities of Iraq in the nuclear, biological, chemical, and ballistic missile programs were reviewed, especially in terms of the government's dossier and the intelligence behind the dossier. The report offered conclusions as to Iraqi capabilities and deception and concealment programs, and what has been found in Iraq since the war.

The British report reviewed specific issues in Iraq such as links between Al Qaeda and the Iraqi regime, the uranium from Africa, mobile biological weapons laboratories, and aluminum tubes, and also offered conclusions on specific and broader issues as well.

D. Intelligence Reform and Reorganization

Commission reports such as the three major ones just reviewed tend to offer recommendations related to the reorganization of the intelligence structure and to the process that can be improved. However, there have been numerous studies of our intelligence community functions over the years, and one very notable study by Richard A. Best, Jr., "The Intelligence Community in the 21st Century," examined 19 major studies, reviews, and proposals from 1949 to 1996. Thus, efforts to improve, alter, or reorganize the intelligence community have been frequent and have endeavored to refocus the intelligence community on managerial improvements, or on efforts to prevent the recurrence of abuses of authority or illegal acts, which was the case in the Church Committee Report.[8]

The cumulative impact of so many scathing reviews and congressional reports, inquiries, and monitoring by both the Senate Select Committee on Intelligence and the House Permanent Select Committee on Intelligence was to make intelligence agencies that should be risk-prone actually risk-aversive. Not only have we observed professionals within all segments of our intelligence community become more pronouncedly risk-aversive, but administrators and officials who are the recipients of intelligence reports are also becoming risk aversive.

E. Theories of Intelligence

One fundamental premise is that intelligence cannot be usefully reformed without a good sense of the theory behind what intelligence is or should be about. As Jennifer Sims observes, intelligence theory is in its infancy and that at best, most understand intelligence as the collection, analysis, and dissemination of the information to national security decision makers. However, in reality, the "most immediate measure of success for any intelligence service is not the number of secrets it collects or the truth of the analysis it generates, but rather the timeliness, efficiency and accuracy with which it supports National Security decision making."[9] In essence, the national security decision makers at the top level of our government, military leaders, and battlefield commanders all look to the intelligence product as providing them "decision advantage" with reference to the action they will be required to implement.

Another defect with many commission reports and recommendations that strive to improve our intelligence community is their failure to recognize that organizations outside the sphere of our formal intelligence agencies may in actuality impede our intelligence community by underfunding research in areas that become important to collection and analysis programs. An example of this centers on our excellent national laboratory system, and if the Department of Energy transfers funding or reduces funding or projects in the nanotechnology area, it can have a very profound impact upon our intelligence community.

Also, if decision makers are untrained in the intelligence process, there is a learning curve in which they will have to gain expertise and skill sets in terms of how to best utilize the intelligence reports in their decision making responsibilities. Therefore, commission reports and studies should provide awareness of their important role as active participants in the intelligence process, and not simply as uninvolved recipients with decision making responsibilities. In other words, there are consequences for the intelligence process if a decision maker assumes an adversarial role to the intelligence process. We want decision makers to be critical (constructively speaking) of our intelligence reports and products. We also recognize that they can take action or decide not to take action, or defer action to a more appropriate time.

Judge Richard Posner offers an interesting critique of both the September 11 Commission report and the WMP report by suggesting that each suffers from an absence of academic, historical, and comparative perspectives. Also, as is the case with most official investigatory commissions, these two commissions have the structural problem of selected members who are chosen more on a basis of prominence and political diversity as opposed to expertise, especially academic expertise. In fact, Posner suggests the absence of academic input is illustrated by the failure of both the 9/11 Commission and the WMD Commission to utilize historical, social–scientific, and comparative perspectives on intelligence. Posner further comments on the shallowness of the 9/11 Commission's analysis and criticizes its indifference to the relevant scholarly literature, as it relates to foreign experience and history.[10]

It is instructive to contrast the British Report generally referred to as the Butler Privy Committee Report to our WMD Report. The Butler Report notes the limitations of intelligence in terms of its collection, analysis, and validation, and although the Butler Report is critical of the British intelligence service, it lacks the condemnatory tone of both the 9/11 Commission and WMD Commission reports. Moreover, it does not call for an overhaul of the British intelligence service on the basis of a mistake.[11]

5. Transforming the Intelligence Community

The 9/11 Commission report clearly set the stage for coming to terms with an improved method of organizing our intelligence agencies. The WMD Commission provided the major rationale for Congress approving the Intelligence Reform and Terrorism Act of 1974 that has, among its many features, created an Office of Director of National Intelligence, but it has also created opportunities for congressional micromanagement of intelligence agencies that are exclusively in the executive branch of government and not within the purview of the legislative branch.

A. Three Major Transformational Challenges

For an effective transformation of our intelligence community to occur, three major issues must be confronted in order to achieve major improvement in both purpose and function. These three issues are as follows.

1. Guide, coordinate, and provide the forces for the integration of our nation's 16 intelligence agencies from individual agency missions to a coherent, well-organized intelligence community mission through the Office of the Director of National Intelligence.
2. Address the issue of congressional oversight of our intelligence community and restructure its current dysfunctional approach of House and Senate committee oversight to a new model of joint committee oversight, balancing the constitutional requirements of the legislative and executive branches to avoid congressional intrusion and micromanagement of executive branch agencies.
3. Improve our intelligence analysis capabilities, training, and education, and introduce a more coherent management structure for the intelligence analysis segment of our intelligence community.

The first challenge of integrating our 16 individual intelligence agency missions requires us to capture the benefits of collaboration without destroying the unique perspectives and capabilities of the individual intelligence agencies and to forge their collective strengths into a more coherent entity. The new director, Admiral Mike McConnell clearly sees a path to accomplish this by following the model provided by the Goldwater–Nichols Act which created a mandate for the U.S. to move to a "joint" military. This provided not only great improvements in joint operations, but also training, and it created incentives for interservice collaboration and fundamentally changed the nature of our military.[12] Fortunately, Admiral McConnell's military background will permit him the experience, insight, and sensitivity to use the "jointness" model as he transforms our 16 separate intelligence agencies into a true intelligence community.

The second major challenge required for an effective transformation of our intelligence community centers on the question of congressional oversight. In fact, the 9/11 Commission report stated that, of all our recommendations, strengthening congressional oversight may be among the most difficult and important. Congress should create a Joint Committee for Intelligence, modeled after the former Joint Atomic Energy Committee, or should create House and Senate Committees with combined authorized and appropriations powers.[13]

What the 9/11 report did not say about congressional oversight, but was reported by the *Washington Post* was the issue of the Senate Select Committee on Intelligence holding only one hearing devoted to Al Qaeda and Osama bin Laden in the months prior to the September 11, 2001 attack, despite the fact that the Senate Committee had access to intelligence suggesting that an attack against U.S. interests somewhere in the world could well be in the offing. The fact is, that both the Senate and House Committees on Intelligence Oversight had received voluminous intelligence concerning bin Laden and Al Qaeda for years prior to the September 11 attack and did relatively little to alert their colleagues or to raise issues of concern the general public should have been aware of regarding Al Qaeda. For these and other failings of the oversight committee, the 9/11 Commission report described the congressional oversight as dysfunctional.[14]

An important and worthwhile document that provides great insight into how Congress might wish to reorganize its oversight responsibility of our intelligence community is provided by Frederick M. Kaiser's paper "Congressional Oversight of Intelligence: Current Structure and Alternatives."[15] Kaiser describes the Joint Committee on Atomic Energy as a model and proceeds to describe the methods of establishment of a proposed Joint Committee on Intelligence describing jurisdiction and authority, as well as staffing, budget, and funding responsibilities. The pros and cons are clearly listed as an alternative to creating a joint committee.

If Congress is to take seriously its role in oversight of our intelligence community, it can begin by thoroughly restructuring its role and providing greater support for our intelligence agencies. However, as Congress considers how to improve its oversight role, it would be well advised to take note of several comments offered by Judge Richard A. Posner of the U.S. Court of Appeals relative to constitutional issues that should be respected by both the executive and legislative branches of government.

Judge Posner has raised some concerns regarding the Intelligence Reform and Terrorism Prevention Act of 1974 as passed by Congress with rather specific restrictions on the role of the Director of National Intelligence. The Act limits the authority of the Director of National Intelligence to transfer personnel between existing agencies or new intelligence entities such as the Counter Proliferation Center, and only permits the transfer of 100 employees to a new center; and the transfer cannot exceed 2 years.[16] This level of intrusion into what should be an executive agency decision amounts to congressional micromanagement at best and constitutional intrusion into the executive branch of government at worst. Clearly, Congress has an important role to play in the oversight of our intelligence community, but greater care must be exhibited than the recent history of both the House and Senate Select Committees on Intelligence.

The third major transformational challenge centers on substantial improvement in the analysis capabilities of our entire intelligence community. Not only do we require much improved training for new intelligence analysts, but also for their continuous development. We need much more than in-service training and agency-based termed university programs. As Jeffrey Cooper correctly observes, the intelligence community currently lacks many of the scientific community's self-correcting features. Among the most significant features are the creative tension between evidence-based experimentalists and hypothesis-based theoreticians in which a strong tradition of investigator-initiated research with real horizontal peer review and proof by independent replication exists. Experience-based analysis is essentially inductive reasoning, whereas hypothesis-based analysis is deductive reasoning. The two should be viewed as complementary approaches, not competitors for ownership of the analytic process.[17]

Intelligence analysis remains a "craft culture" operating within a guild structure and relying on an apprenticeship model that it cannot sustain, and its use of the terminology of "tradecraft" and agency universities are parts of the culture that will require change.[18] In many respects, the fault for this situation lies with our university community that has assiduously ignored developing educational programs that would provide a sufficient number of graduates trained for the challenges of an intelligence analyst. Not only have our nation's universities ignored this important academic role and responsibility, they have performed little research that would advance knowledge in this field.

The model of "jointness" which so effectively moved the military forward offers great promise as we more fully integrate our military and civilian intelligence agencies to meet these new challenges. Our next challenge in this will center on how well we integrate our national intelligence with our law enforcement agencies. This effort in peacetime and also in maintaining the respect for our citizens' civil rights and liberties will require much sensitivity and skill. However, the simple fact remains that our intelligence community must conform to the legal requirements of our Constitution, and fully respect the rights of all citizens. As we move more intelligence demands into our domestic arena to protect our citizens from terrorists, we also have the obligation of protecting our citizens and their constitutional rights and liberties.

6. Summary

As our nation continues to invest great resources in our intelligence community, there is an expectation that our intelligence agencies will now focus their missions in a much more pronounced manner, so that a more coherent and integrated intelligence community will emerge. A transformation of the magnitude expected by our citizens will require an effective Office of the Director of National Intelligence that will coordinate our military intelligence capabilities with our national intelligence agencies, and also be able to more effectively coordinate the collected intelligence with our domestic law enforcement agencies and to develop appropriate methodologies for sharing this information so as to elevate the security of our nation. The transformation, if successful, will also mandate very substantial structural changes in the congressional oversight of our intelligence community. Congress should clearly review the role it played in all the activities leading up to the September 11, 2001 attack and should make the necessary modifications. Our nation deserves much more than the past ineffectual congressional oversight.

Endnotes

1. The Evaluation of the U.S. Intelligence Community — An Historical Overview, pp. 1–6, July 2004, http:www.gpo.gov/int/int022.html.
2. Jennifer E. Sims and Burton Gerber (Eds.), *Transforming U.S. Intelligence*, Georgetown University Press: Washington, DC, 2005, p. XII.
3. Mark M. Lowenthal, *Intelligence: From Secrets to Policy*, third ed., Congressional Quarterly Press: Washington, DC, 2006, pp. 21–25.
4. Norman Podhoretz, *World War IV: The Long Struggle Against Islamic Fascism*, Doubleday: New York, 2007, pp. 27–35.
5. National Commission on Terrorist Attacks upon the United States, *The 9/11 Commission Report: Authorized Edition*, W. W. Norton: New York, 2004, p. XV.
6. The Commission on the Intelligence Capabilities of the United States Regarding Weapons of Mass Destruction, Report to the President of the United States, Letter of March 31, 2005.
7. Report of a Committee of Privy Counsellors, Lord Butler, Chairman, *Review of Intelligence on Weapons of Mass Destruction*, House of Commons, London: The Stationery Office, 2004, p. 1.
8. Lowenthal, op.cit., pp. 274–276.

9. Jennifer E. Sims, Understanding friends and enemies: The context for American intelligence reform, in Jennifer E. Sims and Burton Gerber (Eds.), *Transforming U.S. Intelligence*, Georgetown University Press: Washington, DC, 2005, p. 15.
10. Richard A. Posner, *Uncertain Shield: The U.S. Intelligence System in the Throes of Reform*, Rowman and Littlefield, in cooperation with the Hoover Institution, Stanford University: New York, 2006, pp. XIV, 4–7.
11 Posner, op cit., pp. 38–39.
12. Mike McConnell, Overhauling intelligence, *Foreign Affairs*, 86: 4, July–August, 2007, pp. 50–53.
13. National Commission on Terrorist Attacks upon the United States, op.cit., pp. 419–420.
14. L. Britt Snider, Congressional oversight of intelligence after September 11, in Jennifer E. Sims and Burton Gerber (Eds.), *Transforming U.S. Intelligence*, Georgetown University Press: Washington, DC, 2005, pp. 246–247.
15. For detailed information see Frederick M. Kaiser, Congressional Oversight of Intelligence: Current Structure and Alternatives, CRS Report for Congress, Congressional Research Service, February 15, 2007, Order Code RL32525.
16. Posner, op. cit., pp. 172–173.
17. Jeffrey R. Cooper. *Curing Analytic Pathologies: Pathways to Improved Intelligence*, Center for the Study of Intelligence, Central Intelligence Agency, Government Printing Office: Pittsburgh, PA, December 2005, p. 50.
18. Cooper, ibid., p. 6.

7 National Security and Counterterrorism Policy Formulation: Transformational Issues and Challenges

One of the difficulties a nation has in establishing policies to confront terrorist activities centers upon obtaining consensus on a policy that will embrace the political will of the state and the citizens. In a democracy such as ours, the formulation of national security policies on counterterrorism must meet the standards as set forth by our U.S. Constitution and its Bill of Rights. This chapter discusses the instruments of statecraft that permit both policy formulation and executive action and sets forth five major transformational issues and challenges that we must be prepared to address in the coming years. The format of this chapter is as follows.

1. Instruments of Statecraft
   Intelligence: Covert Action Programs, Clandestine Activities
   Diplomacy: Criminal Justice and Legal System
   Interdiction of Financial Assets; Military Force
   A. Executive Options
   B. Constitutional Law
2. Transformational Issues and Challenges
   A. Role Conflict between National Security Council and U.S. Department of State
   B. Politically Sensitive and Counterintuitive Decisions in the Use of National Intelligence Estimates
      1. Unclassified Portions of the National Intelligence Estimate on Iran: Nuclear Intentions and Capabilities
      2. Declassified Material from the 1962 Cuban Missile Crisis: National Intelligence Estimate
   C. Back-Channel Communications and Negotiating with Terrorists
   D. Military Options: Use of Force
   E. Global Values
3. Summary

Endnotes

The formulation and approval of counterterrorist policies are difficult under any circumstances and particularly when creating policies that are focused around state-supported terrorism. The creation of national security counterterrorist policies becomes much more difficult as we now confront nonstate ethnoreligious organizations such as Al Qaeda. As we formulate policies to protect our domestic and foreign interests, these counter-terrorist policies must engender the understanding, support, and respect of our citizens as well as of the citizens and governments of other nations.

Osama bin Laden has organized Al Qaeda around the belief that its battle against the United States and western civilization is on the basis of a religious war. Indeed, bin Laden views the United States as the vanguard of a global crusade on the part of Christians and Jews to stop his movement toward an Islamic resurgence. As Lawrence Wright observes, bin Laden may not have read Samuel P. Huntington's 1993 treatise on the "clash of civilizations," but he clearly has seized on the idea and in many of his statements acknowledged that it was his duty to promote such a clash. Bin Laden has further stated that this is a battle of Muslims against the global crusaders, and that it is a theological war, and the redemption of humanity is at stake.[1]

Clearly, central to bin Laden's belief system and the marshalling of Al Qaeda supporters is a set of values that we must carefully understand, so that our policies, programs, and actions against such a narrow-minded and mistaken assessment of our values does not become a dysfunctional counterforce to confronting Al Qaeda's brand of terrorism. We face numerous avenues for misunderstanding when the counterterrorist policy has to be framed around a terrorist organization that is claiming a "religious war" as its fundamental premise and cause for action. Our government has a number of instruments of statecraft that can be used to frame and develop counterterrorism policies.

1. Instruments of Statecraft

The U.S. government has available several instruments of statecraft that it can use as executive options or instruments to implement or enforce counterterrorist policy. The selection of the particular instrument of statecraft will depend on numerous variables, but the recommendation for its use will be made by the National Security Council to the president. The instruments of statecraft are as follows.

1. Intelligence
2. Covert action

3. Clandestine programs
4. Diplomacy
5. Criminal justice and legal system
6. Interdiction of financial assets
7. Military force

A. Executive Options

Each of these instruments of executive power is carefully evaluated and could be tailored for use with a complementary counterterrorist policy. The National Security Council, which is our government's most important formal institution for making foreign and national security policy, plays the major advisory role to the president on the integration of the domestic, foreign, and military policies related to the appropriate selection of which instrument of statecraft to employ.

The instruments of statecraft which include intelligence covert action and clandestine programs are all designed with the expectation that they will detect terrorist plans in time for appropriate measures to be taken to eliminate such threats of terrorism.

Diplomacy is important as an instrument of statecraft, particularly in working with allied nations to develop and coordinate plans and programs to eliminate or contain the terrorist threat. Also, through the use of diplomacy, it is possible to transfer apprehended terrorists from one state to another nation-state where arrest warrants may exist for terrorist activity. Recently, the use of "rendition" programs where a terrorist may be transferred to a country that uses extrajudicial techniques of interrogation has raised substantial concerns within the United States, and also within many of our allied nations. The diplomatic community also feels somewhat betrayed by various intelligence programs that were responsible for initiating this "shuttle airplane" transfer of prisoners from countries known to have used extraordinary pressures to obtain information from terrorists.

Our criminal justice/law enforcement system has been used since the Comprehensive Crime Control Act of 1984 authorized federal prosecution of hostage-taking overseas that involves American citizens or the United States as a target. The second important development in this area was the Omnibus Diplomatic Security Anti-Terrorism Act of 1986, which extends extraterritorial jurisdiction to any terrorist act against U.S. citizens or interests, anywhere in the world.[2] These two important congressional Acts were critical in the successful investigation and indictment of Osama bin Laden for the attacks on the two U.S. embassies in Nairobi, Kenya and Dar es Salaam, Tanzania. Additional investigation in Kenya and Tanzania also revealed excellent working relationships again through a combination of diplomatic and law enforcement efforts. On the other hand, the reverse occurred in the

Khobar Tower bombing of our military barracks in which Saudi officials refused cooperation with both our law enforcement and diplomatic requests even to interview the suspects they apprehended.

The interdiction of financial assets is a very important and critical method of containing terrorist activity. The freezing of financial assets belonging to terrorist groups or those that support terrorist groups is accomplished by the U.S. Secretary of Treasury designating such action. The U.S. issued orders to freeze the financial assets of or related to Al Qaeda, the Taliban, Iraq, Libya, and members of Hammas, Hezbollah, and the Palestine Islamic Jihad. Because many Middle Eastern countries and groups transfer money around the world, we have by necessity, had to improve our methods of financial investigations into money laundering and related financial transfer techniques.

Military force against terrorism is used in rescuing hostages or to preemptively strike against terrorist camps to impair their capabilities and disrupt their operations. Another reason for use of a military option is to retain the implicit threat of further retaliation with the goal of deterring a terrorist group from any further attack.[3]

B. Constitutional Law

Our current experience in confronting Al Qaeda has raised several serious legal and constitutional issues ranging from prisoners held in Guantanamo Bay, Cuba as enemy combatants and not as prisoners of war. Also, the detention of over 1200 foreign nationals living in the United States in the immediate aftermath of the September 11, 2001 attack in which they were arrested and detained in considerable secrecy has raised concerns of civil liberty activists. The detention and confining of two American citizens without judicial review and restricting access to counsel has been raised in two major cases: the first case involved Yasser Esam Hamdi who held dual U.S. and Saudi Arabia citizenship and was finally deported to Saudi Arabia. The second case involved Abdullah Al Muhajir, born as José Padilla, who was recently convicted in Federal Court after years of litigation in which his case reached to the U.S. Supreme Court.

Additional and more recent constitutional-based concerns emerged from the Foreign Intelligence Surveillance Act in which intercepts were made without first obtaining a judicial warrant from the Foreign Intelligence Surveillance Court (FISC). We are now confronting the issue of "waterboarding" by the CIA as a form of interrogation tactic and the destruction of videotapes of this process used on an individual who sought judicial relief for certain aspects of his incarceration.[4]

We must be guided by our Constitution; issues such as habeas corpus are fundamental to our entire democracy. The habeas corpus application of law permits a person to have the courts test the constitutionality of his custodial status. The issue for the future will be whether this right will be offered to foreign nationals and those who do not presently have U.S. citizenship.

Other constitutional rights that will be placed in question by our instruments of statecraft as we confront our war on terrorism are the right to a trial, the right to be represented by counsel, due process of law, the right to confront our accusers, and the right of appeal. All are fundamental rights guaranteed to U.S. citizens under the Bill of Rights to our Constitution. The issue is whether we will tolerate noncitizens being deprived of the rights that U.S. citizens enjoy. Also, will our Congress and judiciary continue to stand by and observe these situations or will they begin to take action that will expand noncitizen rights to these legal remedies, or take action to curtail or further restrict the executive branch's use of instruments of statecraft.

2. Transformational Issues and Challenges

Although many issues and challenges will confront our nation as we face the prospect of continuing terrorist attacks, our government will have to confront five major transformational challenges to formulate our counterterrorist policies. These transformational challenges are as follows.

A. Role conflict between the National Security Council and the U.S. Department of State
B. Politically sensitive and counterintuitive decisions in the use of our intelligence community's national intelligence estimate
C. Back-channel communications and negotiation with terrorists
D. Military options and use of force
E. Global values

These, by no means, are the only transformational issues and challenges that will confront our national security decision makers, but they are of such significance that both our congressional and judicial branches of government will eventually become involved in the approval or review process.

A. Role Conflict between National Security Council and U.S. Department of State

Despite serving as one of the four statutory members of the National Security Council, the secretary of state and the U.S. Department of State have recently become marginalized by the increased role of the National Security Council on the formulation of national security policies. The other three statutory members of the National Security Council are the president, the vice president, and the secretary of defense. The two statutory advisors are the chairman of the Joint Chiefs of Staff and the director of the Office of National Intelligence.

The president's national security advisor serves as the executive officer of the National Security Council. One can quickly surmise that the balance of President Bush's National Security Council is heavily positioned by individuals whose role responsibilities are "defense-based," as opposed to the responsibilities of the secretary of state. The structure of the National Security Council can create role conflict between the National Security Council and the Department of State, particularly if the president's national security advisor uses his access to the president to influence the national security policy-formulated process over that of the Department of State. Perhaps, the two best examples of this role conflict occurred during President Carter's and President Nixon's terms in office and their use of the National Security Council.

Zbigniew Brzezinski and Secretary of State Cyrus Vance had substantial disagreements over the U.S. policy with reference to the Soviet Union. Brzezinski's hard-line approach was in conflict with the policy of détente that Secretary Vance and the State Department were interested in pursuing. It is thought that President Carter's inexperience in foreign affairs, and his reliance upon Brzezinski permitted this to occur.[5]

In stark contrast to any other national security advisor, Henry Kissinger had more power and control over national security policies and all foreign policies. In fact, his role so overwhelmed Secretary of State William Rogers that Rogers eventually resigned in protest and was immediately replaced by Henry Kissinger. This occurred under President Nixon's administration, and principally as a result of his reorganization and use of the National Security Council as a command and control center for his foreign policy formulation. In both the Kissinger and Brzezinski roles as national security advisor to the president, their access provided enormous authority and power, even to the point that confusion was created domestically and in foreign capitals as to who really spoke for the United States; was it the national security advisor or the secretary of state?[6]

Under President Reagan's administration, the role of the National Security Council did not create overwhelming conflict for Secretary of State George Schultz, because National Security Advisor Robert McFarlane authorized members of the national security staff led by Oliver North to engage in secret covert operations. These secret operations included the sale of arms to Iran in exchange for U.S. hostages, followed by siphoning of these profits through a secret Swiss bank account to support the Contras in their battle in Nicaragua. These unheard-of covert events by National Security Council staff occurred without the knowledge of the secretary of state and the president, and without the knowledge of congressional oversight committees that were required by statute to have advance knowledge before covert plans were to be implemented.[7] Never before or since this Iran Contra affair has the National Security Council engaged in such activities that were so antithetical to its official statutory mandate of advising the president and coordinating national security policy. This venture of National Security Council staff into covert operations almost destroyed the utilility of the council.

Critics of how the National Security Council has been used by every president since President Kennedy have complained about the central and largely secret role which is often at odds with other governmental departments and agencies that are responsible for foreign and defense policies and especially the Department of State. In point of fact, the institutional tension between the National Security Council and the Department of State has reduced the Department of State to a "Department of Routine Affairs."[8]

Great concern has been expressed in President George W. Bush's administration, especially during his first term in office when his National Security Advisor Condoleezza Rice was often at odds with Secretary of State Colin Powell. In fact, the Bush policies emanating from the National Security Council so discouraged Secretary Powell, that he decided to remain as Secretary of State for only Bush's first term of office.

Each president chooses how to use his National Security Council and his actions can both create role conflict and tension with other governmental officials and agencies and confuse foreign nations as well. As our nation formulates counterterrorist policies, it is important that all segments of tension and confusion are minimized if not eliminated.

B. Politically Sensitive and Counterintuitive Decisions in the Use of Our National Intelligence Estimates

One of the most important instruments of statecraft from the intelligence community is the national intelligence estimate, considered the most important and well-researched intelligence products we provide our national leaders as they consider policy options to be selected with reference to the given situation or country. Preparation of the national estimate is a project of considerable work and analysis and entails all intelligence agencies within our intelligence community. Although these documents are exceedingly well researched and prepared, the government leaders who are called to review them and formulate policies may have experiences that are counterintuitive to an estimate, and having to make decisions regarding our nation's national security in very politically sensitive areas can be most difficult.

An example of this is the recent national intelligence estimate on Iran's nuclear intentions and capabilities which was prepared in November 2007. Part of the political sensitivity of this National Intelligence Estimate is that its conclusions are contrary to the public statements and pronouncements of both President Bush and Vice President Cheney. Another politically sensitive aspect to this National Intelligence Estimate is that prior to our war in Iraq, the American public was informed that Iraq had weapons of mass destruction, and because none have been located at this point in time, there is skepticism regarding accepting any pronouncements from our senior government leaders regarding Iran. Even more to the point, several Democratic congressional leaders have indicated and charged that both President Bush and Vice President Cheney are planning a war with Iran.

The reality confronting President Bush is that first and foremost his responsibility is to protect our nation and all our citizens. A second reality he no doubt observes is that Hezbollah, an armed group that started as a terrorist organization, has blossomed into a small army totally supported by Iran, and is the group responsible for killing more Americans throughout the world in terrorist attacks than any other group. A third reality confronting President Bush is that Iran's President Mahmoud Ahmadinejad has publicly called for the annihilation of Israel, and on many occasions, has called for Israel to be wiped off the map. A fourth reality is that Iran has for more than 20 years deceived inspectors from the International Atomic Energy Agency about its uranium enrichment programs and its efforts to produce plutonium. Given these realities, the president requested a new national intelligence estimate on Iran's nuclear intentions and capabilities.

1. *Unclassified Portions of the National Intelligence Estimate on Iran's Nuclear Intentions and Capabilities*

The national intelligence estimate and assessment noted with high confidence that in the Fall of 2003, Iran had halted its nuclear weapons program. The following provides a portion of the material our president assessed in determining a national security policy regarding Iran's nuclear intentions and capabilities.[9]

National Intelligence Estimates and the NIE Process

National Intelligence Estimates (NIEs) are the Intelligence Community's (IC) most authoritative written judgment on national security issues and are designed to help U.S. civilian and military leaders develop policies to protect U.S. national security interests. NIEs usually provide information on the current state of play, but are primarily "estimates," that is, they make judgments about the likely course of future events and identify the implications for U.S. policy.

The NIEs are typically requested by senior civilian and military policymakers, Congressional leaders and at times are initiated by the National Intelligence Council (NIC). Before a NIE is drafted, the relevant National Intelligence Officer is responsible for producing a concept paper or terms of reference (TOR) and circulates it throughout the Intelligence Community for comment. The TOR defines the key estimative questions, determines drafting responsibilities, and sets the drafting and publication schedule. One or more IC analysts are usually assigned to produce the initial text. The NIC then meets to critique the draft before it is circulated to the broader IC. Representatives from the relevant IC agencies meet to hone and coordinate line-by-line the full text of the NIE. Working with their Agencies, representatives also assign the level of confidence they have in each key judgment. IC representatives discuss the quality of sources with collectors, and the National Clandestine Service vets the sources used to ensure the draft does not include any that have been recalled or otherwise seriously questioned.

All NIEs are reviewed by a National Intelligence Board, which is chaired by the Director of National Intelligence and is composed of the heads of relevant IC agencies. Once approved by the National Intelligence Board, NIEs are briefed to the President and senior policymakers. The whole process of producing NIEs normally takes at least several months.

The NIC has undertaken a number of steps to improve the NIE process under the DNI. These steps are in accordance with the goals and recommendations set out in the Senate Select Committee on Intelligence and WMD Commission reports and the 2004 Intelligence Reform and Prevention of Terrorism Act. Most notably, over the last year and a half, the IC has:

Created new procedures to integrate formal reviews of source reporting and technical judgments.

The Directors of the National Clandestine Service, National Security Agency, National Geospatial Agency, and Defense Intelligence Agency and the Assistant Secretary/INR are now required to submit formal assessments that highlight the strengths, weaknesses, and overall credibility of their sources used in developing the critical judgments of the NIE.

Applied more rigorous standards.

A textbox is incorporated into all NIEs that explains what is meant by such terms as "we judge" and that clarifies the difference between judgments of likelihood and confidence levels. There has been a concerted effort to not only highlight differences among agencies but to explain the reasons for such differences and to prominently display them in the Key Judgments.

This National Intelligence Estimate (NIE) assesses the status of Iran's nuclear program, and the program's outlook over the next 10 years. This time frame is more appropriate for estimating capabilities than intentions and foreign reactions, which are more difficult to estimate over a decade. In presenting the Intelligence Community's assessment of Iranian nuclear intentions and capabilities, the NIE thoroughly reviews all available information on these questions, examines the range of reasonable scenarios consistent with this information, and describes the key factors we judge would drive or impede nuclear progress in Iran. This NIE is an extensive reexamination of the issues in the May 2005 assessment.

This Estimate focuses on the following key questions:

What are Iran's intentions towards developing nuclear weapons?
What domestic factors affect Iran's decision making on whether to develop nuclear weapons?
What external factors affect Iran's decision making on whether to develop nuclear weapons?
What is the range of potential Iranian actions concerning the development of nuclear weapons, and the decisive factors that would lead Iran to choose one course of action over another?
What is Iran's current and projected capability to develop nuclear weapons? What are our key assumptions, and Iran's key chokepoints/vulnerabilities?

This NIE does *not* assume that Iran intends to acquire nuclear weapons. Rather, it examines the intelligence to assess Iran's capability and intent (or lack thereof) to acquire nuclear weapons, taking full account of Iran's dual-use uranium fuel cycle and those nuclear activities that are at least partly civil in nature.

This Estimate does assume that the strategic goals and basic structure of Iran's senior leadership and government will remain similar to those that have endured since the death of Ayatollah Khomeini in 1989. We acknowledge the potential for these to change during the time frame of the Estimate, but are unable to confidently predict such changes or their implications. This Estimate does not assess how Iran may conduct future negotiations with the West on the nuclear issue.

This Estimate incorporates intelligence reporting available as of October 31, 2007.

Key Judgments

A. We judge with high confidence that in fall 2003, Tehran halted its nuclear weapons program; we also assess with moderate-to-high confidence that Tehran at a minimum is keeping open the option to develop nuclear weapons. We judge with high confidence that the halt, and Tehran's announcement of its decision to suspend its declared uranium enrichment program and sign an Additional Protocol to its Nuclear Non-Proliferation Treaty Safeguards Agreement, was directed primarily in response to increasing international scrutiny and pressure resulting from exposure of Iran's previously undeclared nuclear work.

We assess with high confidence that until fall 2003, Iranian military entities were working under government direction to develop nuclear weapons.

We judge with high confidence that the halt lasted at least several years. (Because of intelligence gaps discussed elsewhere in this Estimate, however, DOE and the NIC assess with only moderate confidence that the halt to those activities represents a halt to Iran's entire nuclear weapons program.)

We assess with moderate confidence Tehran had not restarted its nuclear weapons program as of mid 2007, but we do not know whether it currently intends to develop nuclear weapons.

We continue to assess with moderate-to-high confidence that Iran does not currently have a nuclear weapon.

Tehran's decision to halt its nuclear weapons program suggests it is less determined to develop nuclear weapons than we have been judging since 2005. Our assessment that the program probably was halted primarily in response to international pressure suggests Iran may be more vulnerable to influence on the issue than we judged previously.

B. We continue to assess with low confidence that Iran probably has imported at least some weapons-usable fissile material, but still judge with moderate-to-high confidence it has not obtained enough for a nuclear weapon. We cannot rule out that Iran has acquired from abroad—or will acquire in the future—a nuclear weapon or enough fissile material for a weapon. Barring such acquisitions, if Iran wants to have nuclear weapons it would need to produce sufficient amounts of fissile material indigenously—which we judge with high confidence it has not yet done.

C. We assess centrifuge enrichment is how Iran probably could first produce enough fissile material for a weapon, if it decides to do so. Iran resumed its declared centrifuge enrichment activities in January 2006, despite the continued halt in the nuclear weapons program. Iran made significant progress in 2007 installing centrifuges at Natanz, but we judge with moderate confidence it still faces significant technical problems operating them.

We judge with moderate confidence that the earliest possible date Iran would be technically capable of producing enough HEU for a weapon is late 2009, but that this is very unlikely.

We judge with moderate confidence Iran probably would be technically capable of producing enough HEU for a weapon sometime during the 2010–2015 time frame. (INR judges Iran is unlikely to achieve this capability before 2013 because of foreseeable technical and programmatic problems.) All agencies recognize the possibility that this capability may not be attained until after 2015.

D. Iranian entities are continuing to develop a range of technical capabilities that could be applied to producing nuclear weapons, if a decision is made to do so. For example, Iran's civilian uranium enrichment program is continuing. We also assess with high confidence that since fall 2003, Iran has been conducting research and development projects with commercial and conventional military applications—some of which would also be of limited use for nuclear weapons.

E We do not have sufficient intelligence to judge confidently whether Tehran is willing to maintain the halt of its nuclear weapons program indefinitely while it weighs its options or whether it will or already has set specific deadlines or criteria that will prompt it to restart the program.

Our assessment that Iran halted the program in 2003 primarily in response to international pressure indicates Tehran's decisions are guided by a cost–benefit approach rather than a rush to a weapon irrespective of the political, economic, and military costs. This, in turn, suggests that some combination of threats of intensified international scrutiny and pressures, along with opportunities for Iran to achieve its security, prestige, and goals for regional influence in other ways, might—if perceived by Iran's leaders as credible—prompt Tehran to extend the current halt to its nuclear weapons program. It is difficult to specify what such a combination might be.

We assess with moderate confidence that convincing the Iranian leadership to forgo the eventual development of nuclear weapons will be difficult given the linkage many within the leadership probably see between nuclear weapons development and Iran's key national security and foreign policy objectives, and given Iran's considerable effort from at least the late 1980s to 2003 to develop such weapons. In our judgment, only an Iranian political decision to abandon a nuclear weapons objective would plausibly keep Iran from eventually producing nuclear weapons—and such a decision is inherently reversible.

F. We assess with moderate confidence that Iran probably would use covert facilities—rather than its declared nuclear sites—for the production of highly enriched uranium for a weapon. A growing amount of intelligence indicates Iran was engaged in covert uranium conversion and uranium enrichment activity, but we judge that these efforts probably had not been restarted through at least mid-2007.

G. We judge with high confidence that Iran will not be technically capable of producing and reprocessing enough plutonium for a weapon before about 2015.

H. We assess with high confidence that Iran has the scientific, technical and industrial capacity eventually to produce nuclear weapons if it decides to do so.

To place into perspective the dilemma President Bush confronts with a national intelligence estimate that runs almost 180 degrees counter to his fears, concerns, and possible expectations, one should examine the situation that President Kennedy experienced on his receipt of a national intelligence estimate in 1962 regarding Cuba.

Key Differences between Key Judgments of Estimate of Iran's Nuclear Program and the May 2005 Assessment

2005 IC Estimate	2007 National Intelligence Estimate
Assess with high confidence that Iran currently is determined to develop nuclear weapons despite its international obligations and international pressure, but we do not assess that Iran is immovable.	Judge with high confidence that in fall 2003, Tehran halted its nuclear weapons program. Judge with high confidence that the halt lasted at least several years. (DOE and the NIC have moderate confidence that the halt to those activities represents a halt to Iran's entire nuclear weapons program.) Assess with moderate confidence Tehran had not restarted its nuclear weapons program as of mid-2007, but we do not know whether it currently intends to develop nuclear weapons. Judge with high confidence that the halt was directed primarily in response to increasing international scrutiny and pressure resulting from exposure of Iran's previously undeclared nuclear work. Assess with moderate-to-high confidence that Tehran at a minimum is keeping open the option to develop nuclear weapons.
We have moderate confidence in projecting when Iran is likely to make a nuclear weapon; we assess that it is unlikely before early-to-mid next decade.	We judge with moderate confidence that the earliest possible date Iran would be technically capable of producing enough highly enriched uranium (HEU) for a weapon is late 2009, but that this is very unlikely. We judge with moderate confidence Iran probably would be technically capable of producing enough (HEU) for a weapon sometime during the 2010–2015 time frame. (INR) judges that Iran is unlikely to achieve this capability before 2013 because of foreseeable technical and programmatic problems.
Iran could produce enough fissile material for a weapon by the end of this decade if it were to make more rapid and successful progress than we have seen to date.	We judge with moderate confidence that the earliest possible date Iran would be technically capable of producing enough highly enriched uranium (HEU) for a weapon is late 2009, but that this is very unlikely.

2. *Declassified Material from the 1962 Cuban Missile Crisis: National Intelligence Estimate*

President John F. Kennedy received a national intelligence estimate on the *Situation and Prospects in Cuba*, Number 85-2-62, on August 1, 1962.[10] Portions of this now declassified document are presented below, and it is clear that the intelligence assessment did not provide any warning to President Kennedy about the then ongoing development and shipment of nuclear ballistic missiles to Cuba.

NATIONAL INTELLIGENCE ESTIMATE
Number 85-2-62
The Situation and Prospects in Cuba
August 1, 1962

The Problem

To analyze the situation in Cuba and to estimate the prospects over the next year or so, with particular reference to Castro's relations with the Communists and to the potential for resistance to his regime.

Conclusions

A. Fidel Castro has asserted his primacy in Cuban communism; the "old" Communists have had to accommodate themselves to this fact, as has the USSR. Further strains may develop in these relationships, but they are unlikely to break the ties of mutual interest between Castro and the "old" Communists and between Cuba and the USSR.
B. By force of circumstances, the USSR is becoming ever more deeply committed to preserve and strengthen the Castro regime. The USSR, however, has avoided any formal commitment to protect and defend the regime in all contingencies.
C. The Cuban armed forces are loyal to the personal leadership of the Castro brothers. Their capabilities have been and are being greatly enhanced by the Soviet Bloc's provision of military equipment and instruction. Cuban military capabilities; however, are essentially defensive. We believe it unlikely that the Bloc will provide Cuba with the capability to undertake major independent military operations overseas. We also believe it unlikely that the Bloc will station in Cuba Bloc combat units of any description, at least for the period of this estimate.

Events building up in Cuba called for a new special intelligence estimate which was titled *The Military Build up in Cuba* Number 85-3-62, issued on September 19, 1962. The two major paragraphs in their conclusion listed as A and B were regarded as the intelligence best analysis of the situation at the time.[11]

SPECIAL
NATIONAL INTELLIGENCE ESTIMATE
Number 85-3-62
The Military Buildup in Cuba
September 19, 1962

The Problem

To assess the strategic and political significance of the recent military buildup in Cuba and of the possible future development of additional military capabilities there.

Conclusions

A. We believe that the USSR values its position in Cuba primarily for the political advantages to be derived from it, and consequently that the main purpose of the present military buildup in Cuba is to strengthen the Communist regime there against what the Cubans and the Soviets conceive to be a danger that the U.S. may attempt by one means or another to overthrow it. The Soviets evidently hope to deter any such attempt by enhancing Castro's defensive capabilities and by threatening Soviet military retaliation. At the same time, they evidently recognize that the development of an offensive military base in Cuba might provoke U.S. military intervention and thus defeat their present purpose.

B. In terms of military significance, the current Soviet deliveries are substantially improving air defense and coastal defense capabilities in Cuba. Their political significance is that, in conjunction with the Soviet statement of September 11, they are likely to be regarded as ensuring the continuation of the Castro regime in power, with consequent discouragement to the opposition at home and in exile. The threat inherent in these developments is that, to the extent that the Castro regime thereby gains a sense of security at home, it will be emboldened to become more aggressive in fomenting revolutionary activity in Latin America.

C. As the build up continues, the USSR may be tempted to establish in Cuba other weapons represented to be defensive in purpose, but of a more "offensive" character: e.g., light bombers, submarines, and additional types of short-range surface-to-surface missiles (SSMs). A decision to provide such weapons will continue to depend heavily on the Soviet estimate as to whether they could be introduced without provoking a U.S. military reaction.

D. The USSR could derive considerable military advantage from the establishment of Soviet medium and intermediate range ballistic missiles in Cuba, or from the establishment of a soviet submarine base there. As between these two, the establishment of a submarine base would be the more likely. Either development, however, would be incompatible with Soviet practice to date and with Soviet policy as we presently estimate it. It would indicate a far greater willingness to increase the level of risk in U.S.–Soviet relations than the USSR has displayed thus far and consequently would have important policy implications with respect to other areas and other problems in East–West relations.

E. The Latin American reaction will be to the evidence of an increased Soviet commitment to Cuba, rather than to the technical implications of the military buildup. Many Latin Americans will fear and resent a Soviet military intrusion into the Hemisphere, but will regard the problem as one to be met by the U.S. and not their responsibility. We estimate the chances are better now than they were at Punta del Este to obtain the necessary two-thirds OAS majority for sanctions and other steps short of direct military action aimed at Cuba. If it became clear that the USSR was establishing an "offensive" base in Cuba, most Latin American governments would expect the U.S. to eliminate it, by whatever means were necessary, but many of them would still seek to avoid direct involvement.

The continuing acceleration of Soviet delivery to Cuba created a great concern to our national security leaders. Discussion was revolving around the accuracy of the national intelligence estimate and plans were discussed for U-2 overflights of Cuba; however, there were certain political sensitivities that accompanied this option. We had one U-2 shot down in May of 1960 over the Soviet Union, lost another U-2 over mainland China and another U-2 strayed over Sakhalin Oblast, Russia; and our secretary of state was expressing that caution be used as the international community would be focused on another event of this type.

U-2 overflights were authorized by the president and by October 14, 1962 through mission 3101 we acquired photographic evidence that strategic offensive missiles and weapons were being introduced to Cuba.[12] In fact, the Joint Evaluation of the Soviet missile threat in Cuba was prepared on October 19, 1962 and what it revealed clearly demonstrated that the previous two national intelligence estimates were absolutely incorrect in their assessment that the Soviet Union was unlikely to introduce strategic offensive weapons into Cuba.

JOINT EVALUATION
OF
SOVIET MISSILE THREAT IN CUBA
Prepared By
Guided Missile and Astronautics Intelligence Committee
Joint Atomic Energy Intelligence Committee
National Photographic Interpretation Center
2000 Hours
October 19, 1962
This report is based on relatively complete photo interpretation
of U-2 photography made on:
October 14, 1962, Mission 3101
October 15, 1962, Missions 3102 & 3103
October 17, 1962, Missions 3104, 3105, 3106, 3109 and part
of 3107 and 3108

Offensive Missile Deployment

1. At least one Soviet regiment of 1020-nm (SS-4) medium range ballistic missiles is now deployed in western Cuba at two launch sites near San Cristobal. Each of these sites presently contains eight missiles and four unrivetted, field-type launchers which rely on mobile erection, check-out, and support equipment. These missiles are probably those reported moving into this area during September. Although there is continuing improvement of these sites, this regiment must be considered operational now. The presence of eight missiles at each site indicates a refire capability from each of the four launchers. Refire could be accomplished in 4 to 6 hours after the initial firing. A third facility in this area, previously identified as Launch Site 3, could be either a technical support area for this regime or a third launch site; however, the early stage of development precludes a positive identification of this activity.
2. An additional regiment of Soviet 1020-nm (SS-4) missiles is now deployed at two sites east of Havana in the Sagua La Grande area, nine miles apart. These sites closely resemble the sites of San Cristobal but appear to be more permanent in nature. Terrain features have dictated considerable clearing and grading for deployment of the system. Also, there are permanent structures at the launch pad areas which are not found at the San Cristobal sites. There are four launch positions at each site and we estimate an operational capability for each site within one week. The sizes of the missiles, associated equipment, and buildings found at the San Cristobal and Sagua La Grande sites are almost identical and are compatible with the 1020-nm MRBM system.
3. Two fixed sites are under construction in the Guanajay area near Havana. Four launchers, two blockhouses, and underground propellant storage are being built at each site. We believe that the 2200-nm (SS-5) IRBM is probably intended for these sites because they closely resemble Soviet sites

believed to be associated with testing and deployment of this missile system. Site 1 is considered to be in a mid-to-late-stage of construction and should be operational within six weeks. Site 2 is in an earlier stage of construction and could be operational between December 15 and December 30, 1962. There are no missiles or support equipment detectable within the Guanajay Area at the present time.

Command and Control

4. All of the offensive missile systems in Cuba are Soviet manned and controlled. We believe that offensive action by these systems would be commanded from the Soviet Union, but have not yet identified the communication link.

Nuclear Warheads for Offensive Missiles

5. We believe that a nuclear warhead storage site is under construction adjacent to the most complete of the fixed missile launch sites near Guanajay. . . . This site could become operational at about the same time as the associated Launch Site 1. Construction of similar facilities has not yet been identified at other sites.
6. An especially secure port facility located at Punta Gerardo may be used for nuclear weapons offloading.
7. There is still no evidence of currently operational nuclear storage facilities in Cuba. Nevertheless, one must assume that nuclear weapons could now be in Cuba to support the operational missile capability as it becomes available.
8. The 1020-nm missiles would probably be equipped with nuclear warheads yielding 2 to 3 megatons. The 2200-nm IRBMs could have 3 to 5 megaton warheads, if our planning estimate for the payload weight is correct.

Offensive Force Levels

9. We believe that there are now at least two regiments equipped with 1020-nm MRBMs in Cuba. One is located in the San Cristobal area and the other in the Sagua La Grande area. In addition, we believe a regiment equipped with 2200-nm IRBM's is being deployed to the Guanajay area. When operational, present MRBM and IRBM units will have an aggregate total of 24 launchers. Each launcher will have a refire capability. A summary of the MRBM and IRBM threat, including the projected number of operational ready missiles for each site. . . . The corresponding nuclear yield deliverable from each site . . . the technical characteristics of the two offensive missile weapons systems are summarized

Support and Supply

10. Offensive missile systems are being introduced into Cuba, probably through the Port of Mariel. A new Soviet ship, the Poltava, possibly designed as a ballistic missile transport, has been noted making frequent trips between the USSR and Cuba. This ship has made two trips to Cuba since July 17, and is next estimated to arrive in Cuba on or about November 2, 1962.
11. Possible central missile checkout, storage, and repair bases have been located at Soroa, between the two eastern deployment areas, and at Managua, south of Havana.
12. It is significant that three of the Soviet missiles now being deployed in Cuba (SS-4, SS-5, SA-2) probably use red fuming nitric acid as the oxidizer, permitting exploitation of a common system for propellant supply and storage.

Coastal Defense Missiles

13. Three coastal defense missile sites have now been identified in Cuba, two of which must now be considered operational (Banes and Santa Cruz del Norte). These cruise missiles have a range of 35 to 40 miles and are probably derived from the AS-1. They can be fired in about 10 minutes in an alert status, with subsequent firings from each launcher at 5 minute intervals.

Air Defense Missiles

14. There are now 26 surface-to-air missile (SA-2) sites located in Cuba, two of which appear to be alternate sites. Of these, 16 are believed to be individually operational at the present time. The remaining SA-2 sites could be operational in two to three weeks. The list of sites considered to be operational is presented.
15. Such SA-2 sites provide for six launchers with missiles, and an additional six missiles in an adjacent hold area. The initial firing can take place anytime after an alert, providing the site has reached readiness status. Reload and refire from a single launcher will take approximately 3 to 5 minutes.
16. Still Classified.

Tactical Missiles

17. There are several refugee reports indicating the presence of tactical (FROG) missiles in Cuba, although there is no photographic confirmation thus far.

Significance

18. The magnitude of the total Soviet missile force being deployed indicates that the USSR intends to develop Cuba into a prime strategic base, rather than as a token show of strength. Some of the deployment characteristics include permanent elements which suggest that provision is being made for a Soviet presence of long duration.
19. The rate of deployment to date, as well as the speed and variety of construction indicates that the Soviet military build up in Cuba is being carried out on an urgent basis. This buildup has proceeded by deploying defensive weapons first, followed by deployment of offensive weapons. The pattern of missile deployment appears calculated to achieve quick operational status and then to complete site construction.
20. A mixed force of 1020- and 2200-nm missiles would give the USSR a significant strategic strike capability against almost all targets in the U.S. by deploying stockpiled MRBM IRBMs at overseas bases, the Soviet Union will supplement its ICBM home force in a significant way.
21. This same offensive force also poses a common threat to the U.S. and a large portion of Latin America for the first time.
22. The USSR is making a major military investment in Cuba with some of their most effective guided missile systems. The planning for this operation must have started at least one year ago and the operation itself begun last spring.

After the Soviet Union withdrew its offensive weapons from Cuba, there were a number of past crisis reviews and assessments, and the February 4, 1963 now-declassified top secret document from the president's Foreign Intelligence Advisory Board commented directly on the quality of items ranging from clandestine agent coverage, photographic surveillance, U-2 overflights, and the intelligence assessment function. Their comments regarding our intelligence analysis and the preparation of the national intelligence estimates were most striking.

Intelligence Analysis

We find the need for improvements of the processes used in making national intelligence estimates and the processes used in making current intelligence analyses, and also in the techniques for relating these two functions.

The President and policy-advisory officials were ill served by the Special National Intelligence Estimate issued by the Intelligence Community on September 19, on "The Military Buildup in Cuba." This estimate concluded that the establishment of Soviet medium and intermediate range ballistic missiles in Cuba would be inconsistent with Soviet practice to date and with Soviet policy as the community then assessed it. This mistaken judgment, made at the very time when the Soviets were installing MRBMs and IRBMs in Cuba, we attribute to (1) the lack of adequate intelligence coverage of Cuba, (2) the

> rigor with which the view was held that the Soviet Union would not assume the risks entailed in establishing nuclear striking forces on Cuban soil, and (3) the absence of an imaginative appraisal of the intelligence indicators which, although limited in number, were contained in reports disseminated by our intelligence agencies. (We reach this conclusion even though we recognize the absence at the time of any conclusive photographic intelligence.)
>
> The Estimates of September 19 pointed away from the likelihood of the establishment of Soviet nuclear missile systems in Cuba. An important cautionary statement appeared in a discussion paragraph; namely, that the contingency of such a development should be examined carefully, even though it would run counter to current Soviet policy. This cautionary statement; however, was not carried forward into the conclusions of the Estimate. We believe that since this statement was of momentous significance and was in direct contradiction to the Estimate's principal finding, it should have been highlighted so as to alert policy makers and intensify the intelligence collection efforts of the agencies involved.
>
> Turning to another important aspect of the intelligence assessment function, we find that in the analysis of the intelligence indicators and in the production of current intelligence reports, the Intelligence Community failed to get across to key government officials the most accurate possible picture of what the Soviets might be up to in Cuba, during the months preceding October 14. The importance of this conclusion is not diminished by the fact that hindsight is easier to apply than foresight in determining the significance of particular indicators included in the mass of reports available for intelligence analysis.
>
> We believe that the near-total intelligence surprise experienced by the United States with respect to the introduction and deployment of Soviet strategic missiles in Cuba resulted in large part from a malfunction of the analytic process by which intelligence indicators are assessed and reported. This malfunction diminished the effectiveness of policy advisers, national intelligence estimators, and civilian and military officers having command responsibilities.[13]

The concern that the incorrect national intelligence estimates provided President John F. Kennedy in the 1962 Cuban Missile Crisis, might be presented to President George W. Bush with reference to the Iranian attempt to build its nuclear capabilities cannot be overlooked.

C. Back-Channel Communications and Negotiating with Terrorists

The official United States position as expressed in a counterterrorist policy is that the United States will not negotiate with terrorists, nor will it make concessions to terrorists, and this has been the policy of virtually every president's administration. Although this has been the officially expressed policy of the United States, we must realize that we have participated in creating back-channel communication with terrorist groups. Indeed, the Oslo Accord came about between Israel and the Palestine Liberation Organization as a result of the U.S.-led back-channel communication approaches to establish opportunities for American corporations to negotiate with terrorist groups that have captured and held hostage their American employees. Another instance of the United States negotiating with terrorists occurred in the covert National Security staff-led Iran Contra operation. In that case, perhaps the worst experience the United States has ever had in this area, negotiations were held with Iran which at the time was holding American hostages, and weapons were shipped through Israel to Iran, with cash going to aid the Contras in their battle with the Sandinista guerilla movement. Although we as a nation have an official policy against negotiating with terrorists, one can see that there have been several instances in which our government has seen fit to ignore this policy.

The argument against negotiating with terrorists is simple. Democracies must never give in to violence, and terrorists must never be rewarded for using violence. Moreover, negotiations with terrorists give legitimacy to their methods, and it is generally thought that negotiating with terrorist groups weakens the resolve of international efforts to outlaw terrorism. Nevertheless, there have been instances of other nations negotiating with terrorist organizations; perhaps the most successful example is that of the British government creating a back-channel to the IRA and this ultimately led to a very successful truce.[14]

If a government decides to negotiate with terrorists, it should establish a precondition that the violence must end, and this precondition would have to be met before any serious talks could commence. Also, the goals of the terrorist group should be assessed as to their rationality; for example, a terrorist organization that has absolute or apocalyptic goals which are oftentimes religiously inspired or based on the use of violence may make it almost impossible to negotiate. The question is whether it would be possible to negotiate with a terrorist group such as Al Qaeda, which has to be assessed in terms of goals stated to include re-creating an Islamic empire based on a philosophy of fundamentalism representative of seventh-century thinking. Also, Al Qaeda has not renounced its use of violence, which has had great utility. The chance of any successful negotiation with Al Qaeda seems impossible. The additional problem in negotiating with Al Qaeda or other terrorist organizations is that negotiation confers upon them a sense of political legitimacy, while undermining both moderates across the Muslim world and the negotiating governments as well.[15]

One of our nation's largest standing policies in dealing with terrorists is to make absolutely no concession to them. The principle is simple: not rewarding terrorism will remove the incentive for terrorists to continue to take hostages or to apply their violent strategies against us.[16]

One of the transformational challenges we will have to confront is whether we wish to continue to declare our policy as "no negotiations with terrorist organizations." And, if so, are we leaving the door open to back-channel contact to begin communication with terrorist groups, so as to retain some flexibility should the situation present opportunities for possible success. What do other governments think and expect that we will do, and how do we minimize confusion about this policy both domestically and within the international community?

D. Military Options: Use of Force

In discussing the legitimacy of U.S.foreign policy since the launching of the second Iraq war and our battle with Al Qaeda, Robert Tucker and Donald Hendrickson present a most critical view of the Bush administration and observe that the United States has gone down a road in which the use of force has become a chronic feature of our foreign policy and because of this, our security has been weakened.[17]

U.S. Senator Chuck Hagel maintains the opposite view in which he states that although the world's problems will not be solved by the military alone, force remains the first and last line of defense of U.S. freedom and security. Hagel also notes that in taking military action against Al Qaeda and the Taliban, President Bush understood that the war on terrorism must be more than a rightful use of military force. There must be a purpose commensurate with our use of power. President Bush told a joint session of Congress that "we have a greater objective than eliminating threats and containing resentment. We seek a just and peaceful world beyond the war on terror."[18]

A wise foreign policy is determined as much by our commitment to principle as by our exercise of power. Our ability to rely on our military to secure our peace and security is fundamental to securing freedom and democracy. We have always been reluctant to engage our military, and only with the approval of Congress. Even then, we have consistently selected those military options that use as little force as necessary, as we realize the awesome power of our military.

A foreign policy that includes as one of its instruments of statecraft a military with a use of force under civilized control and responsible to our Congress and president provides a bridge to freedom between the United States and the community of nations. Although our ability to use force, when and only when required, provides our nation the ability to shape a foreign policy, it also guarantees all the freedoms our citizens expect and desire.

E. Global Values

Former Prime Minister of Great Britain, Tony Blair, commenting on our response to the September 11 attacks observed that the event has proven even more momentous than it seemed at the time, because we could have chosen security as the battleground, but instead we chose values.

> We know that you cannot defeat a fanatical ideology just by imprisoning or killing its leaders; you have to defeat its ideas. . . . We will not win the battle against global extremism unless we win it at the level of values as much as that of force. We can win only by showing that our values are stronger, better, and more just than the alternative.[19]

Just as the Cold War between 1947 and 1991 ended when the Soviet Union and East Germany gave up on a bankrupt ideology, so will the battle against Al Qaeda and Islamic fascism be won when the seventh-century ideology that underpins it loses its appeal. Without U.S. forces occupying the Kremlin, it was evident to the people of the Soviet bloc countries that their sacrifices were meaningless. That caused them more suffering and little to show for their years of belief. The war on terror will also end with the collapse of the violent ideology that caused it, that is, when bin Laden and Al Qaeda's cause comes to be seen by its followers as a failure. Their ideology will not be destroyed by military power, but ultimately extremist Islamism is not an ideology that will garner enduring support. As terrorism is not a strategy with which Muslims will want to be associated, eventually it will create a backlash within Muslim countries. Philip Gordon observes:

> If the United States and its allies make the right choices, Muslims themselves will turn against the extremists in their midst. Somewhere in the Muslim world, at some point possibly sooner than many realize, new Lech Walesas, Vaclav Havels, and Andrei Sakharevs will emerge to reclaim their people's future from those who have hijacked it. . . . If the United States is strong, smart, and patient, they will come. And they, not the West, will transform their world and ours.[20]

As former Prime Minister Blair stated, this is a battle of values and for progress, and therefore it is one that must be won. If we want to secure our way of life, there is no alternative but to fight for it. That means standing up for values, not just in our own country but the world over. We need to construct a global alliance for these global values and the message we send should convey:

> Islamist extremism's whole strategy is based on a presumed sense of grievance that divides peoples against one another. Our answer has to be a set of values strong enough to unite people with one another. This is not just about security or military tactics. It is about hearts and minds, about inspiring people, persuading them, showing them what our values stand for at their best...We have to show that our values are not Western, still less American or Anglo-Saxon,

> but values in the common ownership of humanity, universal values that should be the right of the global citizen.[21]

In short, it is not as Samuel P. Harrington observed in his treatise on a "clash of civilization," it is more to Prime Minister Tony Blair's observation that this is not a clash *between* civilization; it is a clash *about* civilization.

3. Summary

The formulation of our counterterrorism policy has many issues and challenges to confront, especially in view of the instruments of statecraft that we use to protect ourselves. There are many constitutional challenges that lie ahead of us as we fight this war on terrorism. There will continue to be great congressional scrutiny of the actions our national leaders implement. Also, the prospect of greater judicial review of our national security operations will certainly occur. Finally, as our nation confronts this global war on terrorism, we will have to become more fully engaged with our allies and the entire international community on a level that establishes global values of truth, honesty, and freedom. Terrorism is simply a tool used by Al Qaeda to promote its ideology which is no more than a form of religious totalitarianism. Therefore, our challenge is to go beyond tactical measures of stopping terrorists, which must be accomplished. Additionally, we must formulate strategic measures that engage the international community with us in a message of global values that refute this jihadist intolerance and extremism. We must also involve moderate Islamic nations and people, and help them recapture their religion from the fundamentalist Islamic jihadists who promise a return to a seventh-century form of religious intolerance and extremism.

Endnotes

1. Lawrence Wright, *The Looming Tower: Al Qaeda and the Road to 9/11*, Alfred A. Knopf: New York, 2006, pp. 208–209.
2. Paul R. Pillar, *Terrorism and U.S. Foreign Policy*, Brookings Institution Press: Washington, DC, 2001, p. 80.
3. Paul R. Pillar, ibid., pp. 97, 102.
4. For further and more detailed information, see Gregory F. Treverton, Balancing security and liberty in the war on terror, in Campbell Public Affairs Institute and the Institute for National Security and Counterterrorism, *Information Sharing and Homeland Security*, Syracuse University: New York, 2004, pp. 9–10.
5. Karl F. Inderfurth and Loch K. Johnson (Eds.), *Fateful Decisions: Inside the National Security Council*, Oxford University Press: New York, 2004, p. IV.

6. John P. Leacacos, Kissinger's apparat, in Karl F. Inderfurth and Loch K. Johnson (Eds.), *Fateful Decisions: Inside the National Security Council*, Oxford University Press: New York, 2004, pp. XV and 85.
7.. Inderfurth and Johnson, op.cit., p. XV.
8. Inderfurth and Johnson, op.cit., p. XVIII.
9. National Intelligence Council, *National Intelligence Estimate on Iran: Nuclear Intentions and Capabilities*, unclassified portions of report, November, 2007.
10. Mary S. McAuliffe (Ed.), *CIA Documents on the Cuban Missile Crisis 1962*. These documents have been declassified and approved for release through the Historical Review Program of the Central Intelligence Agency, September 16, 1992, HRP: 92-9; *National Intelligence Estimate Number 85-2-62, The Situation and Prospects in Cuba*, August 1, 1962, excerpts pp. 9–12, Central Intelligence Agency, 1992.
11. McAuliffe, op. cit., *National Intelligence Estimate 85-3-62, The Military Buildup in Cuba*, September 19, 1962, excerpts pp. 91–93, Central Intelligence Agency, 1992.
12. McAuliffe, op. cit., Joint Evaluation of Soviet Missile Threat in Cuba, October 19, 1962, excerpts pp. 203–208, Central Intelligence Agency, 1992.
13. McAuliffe, op. cit., President's Foreign Intelligence Advisory Board, Memorandum for the President and Report, February 4, 1963, excerpts pp. 366–367, Central Intelligence Agency, 1992.
14. Peter R. Neuman, Negotiating with Terrorists, *Foreign Affairs*, 86: 1, January–February 2007, p. 128.
15. Neuman, ibid. pp. 129, 136.
16. Paul R. Pillar, *Terrorism and U.S. Foreign Policy*, Brookings Institution Press: Washington, DC, 2001, p. 35.
17. Robert W. Tucker and David C. Hendrickson, The sources of American legitimacy, *Foreign Affairs*, 83: 6, November–December, 2004, p. 32.
18. Chuck Hagel, A Republican foreign policy, *Foreign Affairs*, 83: 4, July–August 2004, pp. 64–65.
19. Tony Blair, A battle for global values, *Foreign Affairs*, 86: 1, January–February 2007, p. 79.
20. Philip H. Gordon, Can the war on terror be won?: How to fight the right war, *Foreign Affairs*, 86: 6, November–December 2007, pp. 55, 60, 66.
21. Tony Blair, op. cit., p. 87.

8 Future Trends in Global Terrorism: Mapping the Strategy to Defeat an Ideology

This concluding chapter discusses transformational challenges and issues that will be incumbent upon the development of a strategy to come to terms with the ideology that has motivated Al Qaeda. In addition to mapping a new strategy, we also discuss some of the projected key drivers that will be moving trends through the year 2020. We conclude with the 21st century conflicts and challenges that will confront our nation in dealing with 12 other nations.

This chapter is organized around the following format.

1. Globalization, Ideology, and Security
2. Trends in Global Terrorism
3. Global Trends—2015 and Mapping the Global Future—2020
   - A. Seven Key Drivers
     1. Demographics
     2. Natural Resources and Environment
     3. Science and Technology
     4. Global Economy and Globalization
     5. National and International Governance
     6. Future Conflict
     7. The Role of the United States
   - B. World Community Challenges
   - C. Implications for Terrorism in 2020
     1. Transmitting International Terrorism
     2. Weapons, Tactics, and Targets
4. 21st Century Nation-State Issues and Challenges
   - A. India–Pakistan
   - B. Palestine–Israel
   - C. South Korea–North Korea
   - D. Syria
   - E. Saudi Arabia
   - F. Russia
   - G. China–Taiwan
   - H. Iran
5. Summary

Endnotes

1. Globalization, Ideology, and Security

If September 11, 2001 was the beginning of our war on terrorism, we have to understand what this war is about. We are not fighting to eradicate terrorism, as terrorism is just a tool. We are fighting to defeat an ideology which in this case is a form of religious totalitarianism. Religious totalitarianism cannot be fought by armies alone, but must be fought in schools, mosques, churches, and synagogues, and as Thomas Friedman observes, can only be defeated with the help of imams, rabbis, priests, and ministers. This is not a clash of civilizations in which the Islamic world contronts the Western world, but is a clash between those Muslims with a modern and progressive outlook and those with a medieval belief.[1] Therefore, this is a clash within a civilization, and this clash has been going on since Sayyid Qutb and the Egyptian Brotherhood Movement took root in Egypt. Other Middle Eastern nations that have been experiencing this clash with the fundamentalists of these various sects have been Algeria, Saudi Arabia, Jordan, and Pakistan. And as Daniel Piper reports, "If Militant Islam is the problem, moderate Islam is the solution."

Samuel P. Huntington's *The Clash of Civilization* maintained that the future of global conflict would be defined by where the world's major civilizations collide with one another, and it does not matter as to who is good or bad at globalization, as it is the reality that different cultures value globalizations resulting in connectivity in very different ways. Osama bin Laden and his followers view globalization as a form of colonialism that the United States is visiting upon the Islamic culture and nations. Thomas Barnett's book on *The Pentagon's New Map: War and Peace in the Twenty First Century* discusses globalization at length and suggests that whether we realize it or not, America serves as the ideological wellspring for globalization. "We are the only country in the world purposely built around the ideals that animate globalization advance: freedom of choice, freedom of movement, freedom of expression. . . . Globalization is this country's gift to history."[2]

To Barnett, globalization is a strategy to connect nations together so that all may participate in the trade, economics, and well-being that we all desire. He envisions the creation of rule sets that provide equal rules for all nations to participate successfully and equally in globalization. He states, "You want a future worth creating; it is called globalization." He also frames two questions for the future of globalization. The first question is, "What will constitute the great dividing line between who's in and who's out of globalization[']s functioning core?" Another way of saying this is, "How big will the non-integrating gap end up being?" The answer is critical because the size and composition of the gap, or those not participating in the globalization movement will, in essence, determine the nature of warfare in the 21st century.[3]

Barnett, in discussing the attack of September 11, 2001, observed the following.

> On 9/11, America got a real dose of what asymmetrical warfare is going to be in the twenty first century. . . . The real asymmetrical challenge we will face will come from globalization disenfranchised, or the losers largely left behind in the states most disconnected from globalization's advance. The main thrust of this challenge will be led by educated elites, like Osama bin Laden, who dreams of disconnecting societies from globalization's grasp and—by extension—from America's "empire."[4]

In Thomas Friedman's view, the September 11, 2001 attack happened because America lost its deterrent capability and lost it because we failed to take action against those terrorists who murdered Americans. We never retaliated against them or brought them to justice. From the first suicide bombing of the U.S. Embassy in Beirut, to the bombings of the Marine barracks at the Beirut airport, the TWA hijacking, the attacks on our military troops at Khobar Towers in Saudi Arabia, and to numerous other hostage-taking incidents, our nation did absolutely nothing.[5]

Norman Podhoretz discusses how presidential inaction to these and other terrorist incidents really emboldened the terrorists to take action against us. This record of U.S. Presidents Nixon, Ford, Carter, Reagan, and Clinton during which so many terrorist attacks went without response certainly created an attitude among terrorists that we would do nothing to avenge their acts of terrorism.[6] Osama bin Laden was encouraged by his followers that the United States was too fearful of losing life and public opinion and did not have the courage to fight.

It is in this context, that the leadership provided by President George W. Bush in responding to the September 11, 2001 attack and taking forceful action against the terrorists deserves praise. In fact, his administration has finally thrown down the gauntlet in the Middle East and has made it quite clear the United States will not stand on the sidelines any longer. Those who state he has "staked his entire presidency" on Iraq do not see that he has done much more than that; he has engaged our nation into the Middle East and has had us stand up for our values, and has refused to retreat from his presidential responsibilities and obligations.[7]

Another aspect to the Bush administration entry and policies in the Middle East, as a result of our role in Iraq, was the very clear message that was sent to other Middle East nations such as Iran that may well have curtailed their nuclear weapon intentions in 2003, as some intelligence reports are now stating. Also, Saudi Arabia has been given a very clear message that its exporting of fundamentalists, particularly terrorists outside of the kingdom would only last so long before it was turned inward toward the House of Saud, and indeed this is what Osama bin Laden did, in fact, do. The Saudi practice of funding madrassa schools in an attempt to buy the good will of the fundamentalists was also criticized at the highest diplomatic levels. It was also made clear to the Saudi royal family that any future incidents like the Khobar Towers bombing would not be met with U.S. government indifference as was the case in past administrations.

We have been far too permissive in allowing the double standards of our Middle East allies and other nations to go on, and as Thomas Friedman states, this must stop. A country like Syria has to decide whether it wants a Hezbollah embassy in Damascus or an American embassy. If it wants a U.S. embassy, then our government should make it clear Syria cannot play host to the terrorist groups permitted to operate in their country.[8]

If we, as a nation, wish to map a strategy to defeat the ideology of the Islamic jihadists, it will require greater consensus of our political leaders. Also, we should develop a clear Middle East policy that will withstand the change of presidential administrations, and be clearly understood by all nations. The policy we develop should embrace the confidence of the community of nations that will be observing our new strategic directions. Consensus building should become a critical part of our Middle East policy that our diplomatic corps and state department will have to work with other nations to refine. We must enhance the consultative process with other nations, especially because they are fully aware of our intentions on bringing a total halt to the operations of terrorist organizations such as Al Qaeda. We must also realize that the ideology which Al Qaeda is based on is replete with a value structure that is so anomalous to the values most Muslims wish to embrace.

Just as the cold war was ended by an ideology that crumbled from within, we will also see in time that the Islamic culture will not support and will reject the message and plans of Osama bin Laden and Al Qaeda. A strong Middle East policy must represent strong political consensus within Congress and our executive branch. Also, we must be committed to a vibrant role for our diplomatic community focused upon the explanation of the value structure to which the community of nations must adhere. Equally important will be the presence of our military to demonstrate our commitment to establishing a secure environment where peace can and will prevail.

> . . . deep down I truly believe that not only is the United States Government the greatest force for good the world has ever known, but the U.S. Military is the single greatest instrument of that good as well. Show me a part of the world that is secure in its peace and I will show you strong or growing ties between local militaries and the U.S. Military. Show me regions where major war is inconceivable and I will show you permanent U.S. Military bases and long term security alliances.[9]

Our nation has the capacity to export security to all parts of the world, all within our democratic principles of freedom and our values which will withstand the closest scrutiny and will outlive those values of the Al Qaeda terrorist organizations.

2. Trends in Global Terrorism

As our government maps out a new strategy to defeat the ideology that Al Qaeda has embraced, it will be necessary to utilize the national intelligence estimates prepared by our intelligence community. Selected declassified key judgments from the April 2006 national intelligence estimate on *Trends in Global Terrorism: Implications for the United States* provides insight into the issues our policymakers will have to assess as they construct our nation's policies. It is clear that our intelligence community sees the global jihadist movement which includes Al Qaeda and other affiliated and independent terrorist groups, as well as emerging networks and cells as spreading and adapting to our counterterrorism efforts. The following are segments of this report as released by our National Intelligence Council.

> Although we cannot measure the extent of the spread with precision, a large body of all-source reporting indicates that activists identifying themselves as Jihadists, although a small percentage of Muslims, are increasing in both number and geographic dispersion.
>
> If this trend continues, threats to U.S. interests at home and abroad will become more diverse, leading to increasing attacks worldwide.
>
> Greater pluralism and more responsible political systems in Muslim majority nations would alleviate some of the grievances Jihadists exploit. Over time, such progress, together with sustained, multifaceted programs targeting the vulnerabilities of the Jihadist movement and continued pressure on Al Qaeda, could erode support for the Jihadists.
>
> We assess that the operational threat from self-radicalized cells will grow in importance to U.S. counterterrorism efforts, particularly abroad but also in the homeland.
>
> The Jihadists regard Europe as an important venue for attacking Western interests. Extremist networks inside the extensive Muslim diasporas in Europe facilitate recruitment and staging for urban attacks, as illustrated by the 2004 Madrid and 2005 London bombings.
>
> The Iraq conflict has become the *cause celebre* for Jihadists, breeding a deep resentment of U.S. involvement in the Muslim world and cultivating supporters for the global Jihadist movement. Should Jihadists leaving Iraq perceive themselves, and be perceived, to have failed, we judge fewer fighters will be inspired to carry on the fight.
>
> Four underlying factors are fueling the spread of the Jihadist movement: (1) [e]ntrenched grievances, such as corruption, injustice, and fear of

> Western domination, leading to anger, humiliation, and a sense of powerlessness; (2) the Iraq "Jihad;" (3) slow pace of real and sustained economic, social, and political reforms in many Muslim majority nations; and (4) pervasive anti-U.S. sentiment among most Muslims—all of which Jihadists exploit.

Concomitant vulnerabilities in the Jihadist movement have emerged that, if fully exposed and exploited, could begin to slow the spread of the movement. They include dependence on the continuation of Muslim-related conflicts, the limited appeal of the Jihadists' radical ideology, the emergence of respected voices of moderation, and criticism of the violent tactics employed against mostly Muslim citizens.

> The Jihadists' greatest vulnerability is that their ultimate political solution—an ultra-conservative interpretation of shari'a-based governance spanning the Muslim world—is unpopular with the vast majority of Muslims. Exposing the religious and political straitjacket that is implied by the Jihadists' propaganda would help to divide them from the audiences they seek to persuade.
>
> Recent condemnations of violence and extremist religious interpretations by a few notable Muslim clerics signal a trend that could facilitate the growth of a constructive alternative to Jihadist ideology: peaceful political activism. This also could lead to the consistent and dynamic participation of broader Muslim communities in rejecting violence, reducing the ability of radicals to capitalize on passive community support. In this way, the Muslim mainstream emerges as the most powerful weapon in the War on Terror.
>
> Countering the spread of the Jihadist movement will require coordinated multilateral efforts that go well beyond operations to capture or kill terrorist leaders.

Other affiliated Sunni extremist organizations, such as Jemaah Islamiya, Ansar al-Sunnah, and several North African groups, unless countered, are likely to expand their reach and become more capable of multiple or mass-casualty attacks outside their traditional areas of operation.

> We assess that such groups pose less of a danger to the homeland than does Al Qaeda but will pose varying degrees of threat to our allies and to U.S. interests abroad. The focus of their attacks is likely to ebb and flow between local regime targets and regional or global ones.

We judge that most Jihadists groups— both well-known and newly formed —will use improvised explosive devices and suicide attacks focused primarily on soft targets to implement their asymmetric warfare strategy, and that they will attempt to conduct sustained terrorist attacks in urban environments. Fighters with experience in Iraq are a potential source of leadership for Jihadists pursuing these tactics.

> Chemical, biological, radiological and nuclear (CBRN) capabilities will continue to be sought by Jihadist groups.

Although Iran, and to a lesser extent Syria, remain the most active state sponsors of terrorism, many other states will be unable to prevent territory or resources from being exploited by terrorists.

> Anti-U.S. and antiglobalization sentiment is on the rise and fueling other radical ideologies. This could prompt some leftists, nationalist, or separatist groups to adopt terrorist methods to attack U.S. interests. The radicalization process is occurring more quickly, more widely, and more anonymously in the Internet age, raising the likelihood of surprise attacks by unknown groups whose members and supporters may be difficult to pinpoint.
> We judge that groups of all stripes will increasingly use the Internet to communicate, propagandize, recruit, train, and obtain logistical and financial support.[10]

As our national security policymakers review national intelligence estimates such as the *Patterns of Global Terrorism: Implications for the United States*, they must think in terms of creating a foreign policy that will have ramification for other nations as well as ours. It is also clear that these jihadist groups are taking advantage of the Internet to spread their message, and this implies that additional thought must be given to how our counterterrorism strategies and tactical plans will address this issue. Will we choose to monitor this Internet traffic or stop it, or even use a combination of both approaches, after first reviewing the Internet traffic flow and pattern?

3. Global Trends—2015 and Mapping the Global Future—2020

Two very significant studies released by the National Intelligence Council dealing with global trends by 2015 and the mapping of the global future by 2020 are each designed to examine how the world might be changed. Studies such as these are rich opportunities for national security policymakers to refine the existing national security policies or create new policies. The first of these two important studies identified the seven major key drivers that will shape important trends by the year 2015. The seven key drivers are as follows.

1. Demographics
2. Natural resources and environment
3. Science and technology
4. The global economy and globalization
5. National and international governance
6. Future conflict
7. The role of the United States

A. Seven Key Drivers

1. *Demographics*

World population in 2015 will be 7.2 billion, up from 6.1 billion in the year 2000, and in most countries, people will live longer. Ninety-five percent of the increase will be in developing countries, nearly all in rapidly expanding urban areas. Where political systems are brittle, the combination of population growth and urbanization will foster instability. Increasing life spans will have significantly divergent impacts.

- In the advanced economies—and a growing number of emerging market countries—declining birthrates and aging will combine to increase healthcare and pension costs while reducing the relative size of the working population, straining the social contract, and leaving significant shortfalls in the size and capacity of the workforce.
- In some developing countries, these same trends will combine to expand the size of the working population and reduce the youth bulge, increasing the potential for economic growth and political stability.

2. *Natural Resources and Environment*

Overall food production will be adequate to feed the world's growing population, but poor infrastructure and distribution, political instability, and chronic poverty will lead to malnourishment in parts of sub-Saharan Africa. The potential for famine will persist in countries with repressive government policies or internal conflicts. Despite a 50 percent increase in global energy demand, energy resources will be sufficient to meet demand; the latest estimates suggest that 80 percent of the world's available oil and 95 percent of its gas remain underground.

- Although the Persian Gulf region will remain the world's largest single source of oil, the global energy market is likely to encompass two relatively distinct patterns of regional distribution: one serving consumers (including the United States) from Atlantic Basin reserves, and the other meeting the needs of primarily Asian customers (increasingly

China and India) from Persian Gulf supplies and, to a lesser extent, the Caspian region and Central Asia.

- In contrast to food and energy, water scarcities and allocation will pose significant challenges to governments in the Middle East, sub-Saharan Africa, South Asia, and northern China. Regional tensions over water will be heightened by 2015.

3. *Science and Technology*

Fifteen years ago, few predicted the profound impact of the revolution in information technology. Looking ahead another 15 years, the world will encounter more quantum leaps in information technology (IT) and in other areas of science and technology. The continuing diffusion of information technology and new applications of biotechnology will be at the crest of the wave. IT will be the major building block for international commerce and for empowering nonstate actors. Most experts agree that the IT revolution represents the most significant global transformation since the Industrial Revolution beginning in the mid-eighteenth century.

- The integration or fusion of continuing revolutions in information technology, biotechnology, materials science, and nanotechnology will generate a dramatic increase in investment in technology, which will further stimulate innovation within the more advanced countries.
- Older technologies will continue lateral development into new markets and applications through 2015, benefiting U.S. allies and adversaries around the world who are interested in acquiring early-generation ballistic missile and weapons of mass destruction (WMD) technologies.
- Biotechnology will drive medical breakthroughs that will enable the world's wealthiest people to improve their health and increase their longevity dramatically. At the same time, genetically modified crops will offer the potential to improve nutrition among the world's one billion malnourished people.
- Breakthroughs in materials technology will generate widely available products that are multifunctional, environmentally safe, longer lasting, and easily adapted to particular consumer requirements.
- Disaffected states, terrorists, proliferators, narcotic traffickers, and organized criminals will take advantage of the new high-speed information environment and other advances in technology to integrate their illegal activities and compound their threats to stability and security around the world.

4. *Global Economy and Globalization*

The networked global economy will be driven by rapid and largely unrestricted flows of information, ideas, cultural values, capital, goods and services, and people, that is, globalization. This globalized economy will be a net contributor to increased political stability in the world in 2015, although its reach and benefits will not be universal. In contrast to the Industrial Revolution, the process of globalization is more compressed. Its evolution will be rocky, marked by chronic financial volatility and a widening economic divide.

- The global economy, overall, will return to the high levels of growth reached in the 1960s and early 1970s. Economic growth will be driven by political pressures for higher living standards, improved economic policies, rising foreign trade and investment, the diffusion of information technologies, and an increasingly dynamic private sector. Potential brakes on the global economy, such as a sustained financial crisis or prolonged disruption of energy supplies, could undo this optimistic projection.
- Regions, countries, and groups feeling left behind will face deepening economic stagnation, political instability, and cultural alienation. They will foster political, ethnic, ideological, and religious extremism, along with the violence that often accompanies it. They will force the United States and other developed countries to remain focused on "old-world" challenges while concentrating on the implications of "new-world" technologies at the same time.

5. *National and International Governance*

States will continue to be the dominant players on the world stage, but governments will have less and less control over flows of information, technology, diseases, migrants, arms, and financial transactions, whether licit or illicit, across their borders. Nonstate actors ranging from business firms to nonprofit organizations will play increasingly larger roles in both national and international affairs. The quality of governance, both nationally and internationally, will substantially determine how well states and societies cope with these global forces.

- States with competent governance, including the United States, will adapt government structures to a dramatically changed global environment, making them better able to engage with a more interconnected world. The responsibilities of once semiautonomous government agencies will intersect increasingly because of the transnational nature of national security priorities and because of the clear requirement for interdisciplinary policy responses. Shaping the complex, fast-moving world of 2015 will require reshaping traditional government structures.

- Effective governance will increasingly be determined by the ability and agility to form partnerships to exploit increased information flows, new technologies, migration, and the influence of nonstate actors. Most countries that succeed will be representative democracies.
- States with ineffective and incompetent governance not only will fail to benefit from globalization, but in some instances will spawn conflicts at home and abroad, ensuring an even wider gap between regional winners and losers than exists today.

Globalization will increase the transparency of government decision making, complicating the ability of authoritarian regimes to maintain control, but also complicating the traditional deliberative processes of democracies. Increasing migration will create influential diasporas, affecting policies, politics, and even national identity in many countries. Globalization also will create increasing demands for international cooperation on transnational issues, but the response of both states and international organizations will fall short in 2015.

6. *Future Conflict*

The United States will maintain a strong technological edge in IT-driven "battlefield awareness" and in precision-guided weaponry in 2015. The United States will face three types of threats:

- Asymmetric threats in which state and nonstate adversaries avoid direct engagements with the U.S. military but devise strategies, tactics, and weapons—some improved by "sidewise" technology—to minimize U.S. strengths and exploit perceived weaknesses.
- Strategic WMD threats, including nuclear missile threats, in which (barring significant political or economic changes) Russia, China, most likely North Korea, and probably Iran, have the capability to strike the United States, and the potential for unconventional delivery of WMD by both states or nonstate actors also will grow.
- Regional military threats in which a few countries maintain large military forces with a mix of cold war and post-cold war concepts and technologies.

The risk of war among developed countries will be low. The international community will continue, however, to face conflicts around the world, ranging from relatively frequent small-scale internal upheavals to less frequent regional interstate wars. The potential for conflict will arise from rivalries in Asia, ranging from India–Pakistan to China–Taiwan, as well as among the antagonists in the Middle East. Their potential lethality will grow, driven by the availability of WMD, longer-range missile delivery systems, and other technologies.

Internal conflicts stemming from religious, ethnic, economic, or political disputes will remain at current levels or even increase in number. The United Nations and regional organizations will be called upon to manage such conflicts because major states stressed by domestic concerns, perceived risk of failure, lack of political will, or tight resources will minimize their direct involvement.

Export control regimes and sanctions will be less effective because of the diffusion of technology, porous borders, defense industry consolidations, and reliance upon foreign markets to maintain profitability. Arms and weapons technology transfers will be more difficult to control.

- More sophisticated weaponry including weapons of mass destruction indigenously produced or externally acquired will get into the hands of state and nonstate belligerents, some hostile to the United States. The likelihood will increase over this period that WMDs will be used either against the United States or its forces, facilities, and interests overseas.

7. *The Role of the United States*

The United States will continue to be a major force in the world community. U.S. global, economic, technological, military, and diplomatic influence will be unparalleled among nations as well as regional and international organizations in 2015. This power not only will ensure America's pre-eminence, but also will cast the United States as a key driver of the international system.

The United States will continue to be identified throughout the world as the leading proponent and beneficiary of globalization. U.S. economic actions, even when pursued for such domestic goals as adjusting interest rates, will have a major global impact because of the tighter integration of global markets by 2015.

- The United States will remain in the vanguard of the technological revolution from information to biotechnology and beyond.
- Both allies and adversaries will factor continued U.S. military pre-eminence in their calculations of national security interests and ambitions.
- Some states, adversaries, and allies will try at times to check what they see as American hegemony. Although this posture will not translate into strategic, broad-based, and enduring anti-U.S. coalitions, it will lead to

tactical alignments on specific policies and demands for a greater role in international and economic institutions.

Diplomacy will be more complicated. Washington will have greater difficulty harnessing its power to achieve specific foreign policy goals; the U.S. government will exercise less powerful economic and cultural influences abroad.

- In the absence of a clear and overriding national security threat, the United States will have difficulty drawing on its economic prowess to advance its foreign policy agenda. The top priority of the American private sector, which will be central to maintaining the U.S. economic and technological lead, will be financial profitability, not foreign policy objectives.
- The United States also will have greater difficulty building coalitions to support its policy goals, although the international community will often turn to Washington, even if reluctantly, to lead multilateral efforts in real and potential conflicts.
- There will be increasing numbers of important actors on the world stage to challenge and check, as well as to reinforce, U.S. leadership: countries such as China, Russia, India, Mexico, and Brazil; regional organizations such as the European Union; and a vast array of increasingly powerful multinational corporations and nonprofit organizations with their own interests to defend in the world.[11]

B. World Community Challenges

Four very important areas that will challenge the world community by 2015 and impact security in many regions are health, water, energy, and space programs. With reference to health, the two biggest challenges are tuberculosis and AIDS, and both of these diseases will have destructive impacts on families and society primarily in Africa, where life span may be reduced by 30 to 40 years, generating more than 40 million orphans and contributing to increases in poverty, crime, and instability. Also facing severe AIDS problems are India, Southeast Asia, several countries formerly in the Soviet Union, Russia, and parts of China.

In addition to the health challenge, we can also anticipate developing crises and conflicts over the shortage of water. By 2015 nearly half the world's population or more than 3 billion people will live in water stressed areas located in Africa, the Middle East, South Asia, and China. Measures undertaken to increase water availability and to ease active water shortage by using water more efficiently, expanding use of desalination, and developing genetically modified crops that use less water will not be sufficient to substantially change the outlook of severe water shortages by 2015.

The world's continued reliance on energy from fossil fuel will also create new patterns of use and demands. It is estimated that total oil demand will increase from 75 million barrels per day in 2000 to more than 100 million barrels per day in 2015. Asia and particularly China will drive the expansion in energy demand, replacing North America as the leading energy consumer. By 2015 only one-tenth of the Persian Gulf product will be directed to Western markets, whereas three-fourths of the entire Middle East production of oil will be destined for Asia.

There will be greater international commercialization of space which will provide certain advantages to nation-states and nonstate adversaries to use high-resolution reconnaissance, global encrypted communications, and other navigation aids formerly available primarily to the United States, and which now may be available to terrorist groups who will be able to use this technology to target U.S. military force deployments. Because the U.S. military is noted for its use of electronic weapons and access to space-based programs, terrorist organizations will try to degrade our space assets and jam our electronic warfare capabilities.[12]

C. Implications for Terrorism in 2020

The report of the National Intelligence Council's 2020 Project identified new global players that will have an impact in shaping our new world. By 2020, China's gross national product is predicted to exceed all nations except the United States. China's and India's populations which are projected to be 1.4 billion and 1.3 billion people, respectively, by 2020 will have a profound impact upon shaping economic policies. In fact, as the world experiences expansion of the globalization process, the United States will see its relative economic power position eroded and will become more vulnerable to fluctuations as global commercial networking deepens. The U.S. dependence on foreign oil supplies also makes us more vulnerable as the competition for secure access grows, and the risks of supply-side disruptions increase.[13]

Although no country will be within striking distance of competing with the military power of the United States by 2020, the success of U.S.-led counterterrorism will depend upon our capabilities and the resolve of individual countries to fight terrorism on their own soil. Counterterrorism efforts in the years ahead, especially against a more diverse set of terrorists who are more connected by ideology than by geography, will be a more elusive challenge for our military and intelligence communities.[14] In fact, the report highlights the key factors that will be responsible for the spread of international terrorism as follows.

1. Transmitting International Terrorism

The key factors that spawned international terrorism show no signs of abating over the next 15 years. Experts assess that the majority of international terrorist groups will continue to identify with radical Islam. The revival of Muslim identity will create a framework for the spread of radical Islamic ideology both inside and outside the Middle East, including Western Europe, Southeast Asia and Central Asia.

> This revival has been accompanied by a deepening solidarity among Muslims caught up in national or regional separatist struggles, such as Palestine, Chechnya, Iraq, Kashmir, Mindanao, and Southern Thailand and has emerged in response to government repression, corruption, and ineffectiveness.
> A radical takeover in a Muslim country in the Middle East could spur the spread of terrorism in the region and give confidence to others that a new caliphate is not just a dream.
> Informal networks of charitable foundations, madrasas, hawalas, and other mechanisms will continue to proliferate and be exploited by radical elements.
> Alienation among unemployed youths will swell the ranks of those vulnerable to terrorist recruitment.

Our greatest concern is that (terrorist groups) might acquire biological agents, or less likely, a nuclear device, either of which could cause mass casualties.

There are indications that the Islamic radicals' professed desire to create a transnational insurgency, that is, a drive by Muslim extremists to overthrow a number of allegedly apostate secular governments with predominantly Muslim subjects, will have an appeal to many Muslims.

> Anti-globalization and opposition to US policies could cement a greater body of terrorist sympathizers, financiers, and collaborators.

We expect that by 2020 Al Qaeda will have been superseded by similarly inspired but more diffuse Islamic extremist groups.

Pressure from the global counterterrorism effort, together with the impact of advances in information technology, will cause the terrorist threat to become increasingly decentralized, evolving into an eclectic array of groups, cells, and individuals. While taking advantage of sanctuaries around the world to train, terrorists will not need a stationary headquarters to plan and carry out operations. Training materials, targeting guidance, weapons know-how, and fund-raising will increasingly become virtual (i.e., online).

The core of Al Qaeda membership probably will continue to dwindle, but other groups inspired by Al Qaeda, regionally based groups, and individuals labeled simply as Jihadists united by a common hatred of moderate regimes and the West are likely to conduct terrorist attacks. The Al Qaeda membership that was distinguished by having trained in Afghanistan will gradually dissipate, to be replaced in part by the dispersion of the experienced survivors of the conflict in Iraq. We expect that by 2020 Al Qaeda will have been superseded by similarly inspired but more diffuse Islamic extremist groups, all of which will oppose the spread of many aspects of globalization into traditional Islamic societies.

> Iraq and other possible conflicts in the future could provide recruitment, training grounds, technical skills and language proficiency for a new class of terrorists who are "professionalized" and for whom political violence becomes an end in itself.
> Foreign Jihadist individuals ready to fight anywhere they believe Muslim lands are under attack by what they see as "infidel invaders" enjoy a growing sense of support from Muslims who are not necessarily supporters of terrorism.

Even if the number of extremists dwindles, however, the terrorist threat is likely to remain. Through the Internet and other wireless communications technologies, individuals with ill intent will be able to rally adherents quickly on a broader, even global scale and do so obscurely. The rapid dispersion of bio and other lethal forms of technology increases the potential for an individual not affiliated with any terrorist group to be able to inflict widespread loss of life.

2. Weapons, Tactics, and Targets

In the past, terrorist organizations relied on state sponsors for training, weapons, logistical support, travel documents, and money in support of their operations. In a globalized world, groups such as Hezbollah are increasingly self-sufficient in meeting these needs and may act in a state-like manner to preserve a "plausible deniability" by supplying other groups, working through third parties to meet their objectives, and even engaging governments diplomatically.

Most terrorist attacks will continue to employ primarily conventional weapons, incorporating new twists to keep counterterrorist planners off balance. Terrorists probably will be most original not in the technologies or weapons they employ, but rather in their operational concept, i.e., the scope, design, or support arrangements for attacks.

> One such concept that is likely to continue is a large number of simultaneous attacks, possible in widely separated locations. While vehicle-borne improvised explosive devices will remain popular as asymmetric weapons, terrorists are likely to move up the technology ladder to employ advanced explosives and unmanned aerial vehicles.

Terrorist use of biological agents is therefore likely, and the range of options will grow.

The religious zeal of extremist Muslim terrorists increases their desire to perpetrate attacks resulting in high casualties. Historically, religiously inspired terrorism has been most destructive because such groups are bound by few constraints.

> Bioterrorism appears particularly suited to the smaller, better-informed groups. Indeed, the bioterrorist's laboratory could well be the size of a household kitchen, and the weapon built there could be smaller than a toaster. Terrorist use of biological agents is therefore likely, and the range of options will grow. Because the recognition of anthrax, smallpox or other diseases is typically delayed, under a "nightmare scenario" an attack could be well under way before authorities would be cognizant of it.
>
> The use of radiological dispersal devices can be effective in creating panic because of the public's misconception of the capacity of such attacks to kill large numbers of people.

With advances in the design of simplified nuclear weapons, terrorists will continue to seek to acquire fissile material in order to construct a nuclear weapon. Concurrently, they can be expected to continue attempting to purchase or steal a weapon, particularly in Russia or Pakistan. Given the possibility that terrorists could acquire nuclear weapons, the use of such weapons by extremists before 2020 cannot be ruled out. We expect that terrorists also will try to acquire and develop the capabilities to conduct cyber attacks to cause physical damage to computer systems and to disrupt critical information networks. The United States and its interests abroad will remain prime terrorist targets, but more terrorist attacks might be aimed at Middle East regimes and at Western Europe.[15]

4. 21st Century Nation-State Issues and Challenges

As we move into the 21st century, a number of challenging issues will confront the world community in general, and the United States in particular. Some of the issues have been languishing for as long as 60 years without successful closure or resolution. Great diplomacy will have to be demonstrated by the 12 nations identified below as providing the greatest challenges to a secure and peaceful world. Also, this is not to suggest other nations or regions are without substantial challenge, as clearly there is evidence of problem areas in Africa, Indonesia, and Latin America. However, these are the 12 nations in which misunderstanding could lead to conflict, which in turn could well escalate into violence and war, if not properly controlled and resolved. The 12 nation-states are:

1. India–Pakistan
2. Palestine–Israel
3. South Korea–North Korea
4. Syria
5. Saudi Arabia
6. Russia
7. China–Taiwan
8. Iran

A. India–Pakistan

India and Pakistan continue to have a serious dispute over the area of Kashmir, and in the past, their armies have skirmished around the disputed border areas. Because the attitudes of each nation have from time to time strained their diplomatic efforts, the world community must show great assistance in urging a peaceful and diplomatic approach to this serious problem. Another issue that complicates this dispute is the presence of Al Qaeda cells in Pakistan which offer opportunities for disruption of the current level of peace. Because both nations have nuclear weapons, great care must be consistently applied by all parties concerned. The presence of jihadist fundamentalists sympathetic to Al Qaeda terrorist activities also places a greater burden on U.S. intelligence agencies, as we must monitor the terrorist cell activities while also assuring that Pakistan properly secures its nuclear weapons. Should Al Qaeda obtain nuclear weapons from Pakistan via deception or terrorist activity, both India and the United States could become immediate targets. India would be targeted for substantial disruption while permitting the Al Qaeda program of creating a new world order to begin to take shape.

B. Palestine–Israel

The conflict between Palestine and Israel is a major source of the Middle East turmoil, and one of the world's most critical issues. This problem goes back directly to 1948 and the creation of the State of Israel. The involvement of the United States dates to 1967 and the shuttle diplomacy of Henry Kissinger, who sought to assist with the resolution of this disagreement over land. Until Palestine obtains statehood consistent with the mutual expectations of both Palestine and Israel, this turmoil will continue and Al Qaeda and other jihadist terrorist cells will continue to exploit this situation in an attempt to achieve disruption within the entire Middle East so that they can attain their own caliphate. The United States will forever be the target of terrorists until the Palestine–Israel problem is brought to some mutual resolution.

Based on the ideology supporting the jihadist terrorist and the potential for the group's acquiring weapons of mass destruction, we are at a juncture in which a settlement of this issue must occur, whether it is by mediation, arbitration, or simply a demand placed on both parties that the matter will be resolved through a phased-in solution monitored over a specified period by the United Nations, its Security Council, or some other constellation of nations. The potential danger for not resolving this matter is far too great, especially because weapons of mass destruction are within the range of use by various terrorist organizations.

C. South Korea–North Korea

The prospect for a reunification of South Korea and North Korea will require great diplomacy, as the financial needs of North Korea are substantial. When West Germany and East Germany were reunified, the economic cost to West Germany was substantial. The spirit of nationalism may enable South Korea to assume such an economic burden, but the fundamental question revolves around Kim Jung Il who expresses no interest in relinquishing his power base. Because North Korea does possess nuclear weapons and continues to develop ICBM missile capabilities, the situation is of great concern to Japan. Also, the economic distress of North Korea is so great that it is not out of the question that it may sell nuclear materials to a terrorist organization. Although the six party talks and negotiation with North Korea demonstrated some success, the problem is far from resolved. The possibility for a flareup is genuine and this situation requires careful diplomacy and monitoring.

D. Syria

Syria has been a major source of support for Hezbollah and has permitted jihadist terrorists to operate inside its borders. At some point the community of nations will have to insist and assure that Syria ceases to operate in its role of state-supported terrorism. Ultimately, the United States will have to confront Syria as any effort to end terrorism will by necessity have to address the support Syria provides Hezbollah and other terrorist groups. The clear message that this terrorist support must end must be conveyed to Syria in the strongest of terms. There is no room for supporting terrorist activities or other groups by proxy or as part of a national goal. Syrian activities will have to be addressed and resolved, as the opportunities for a terrorist organization to be shielded, armed, and supported is too great a problem to be ignored.

E. Saudi Arabia

The major issue with Saudi Arabia is whether the House of Saud will survive the activities of Al Qaeda and so many other disaffected jihadist terror cells. Clearly, Osama bin Laden has made it his goal to overthrow the royal family, and he has achieved success in creating a cell structure within the kingdom and has launched many attacks against the Saudi government. The royal family also must cease its funding of madrassa schools that preach violence to the students and anti-Israeli and anti-Western messages. Providing funds for fringe groups to spread their message outside of the kingdom and leaving the royal family alone is no longer tolerable or workable. The close relationship between the United States and Saudi Arabia will face many challenging issues in the next few years, particularly as the movement of Al Qaeda and the ideology that supports the jihadist terror groups continue to grow within the Middle East.

F. Russia

The principal concern centers on Russia's ability to secure the vast number of nuclear weapons developed under the Soviet Union. As the Soviet Union dissolved there was great international concern that the nuclear weapons and weapons-grade nuclear material might be stolen by terrorist groups. The United States has worked with Russia in developing plans to provide greater security of these materials, and the Sandia National Laboratory has provided excellent assistance in the securing of these materials.

Congress has authorized the Director of Central Intelligence (DCI) to submit to the congressional leadership and intelligence committees an annual unclassified report assessing the safety and security of the nuclear facilities and military forces in Russia. Congress has requested that each report include a discussion of the following.

- The ability of the Russian government to maintain its nuclear military forces
- The security arrangements at Russia's civilian and military nuclear facilities
- The reliability of controls and safety systems at Russia's civilian nuclear facilities
- The reliability of command and control systems and procedures of the nuclear military forces in Russia

In a report issued by the National Intelligence Council to the United States Congress on the safety and security of Russian nuclear facilities and military forces in 2004, the following points were noted.

- The United States continues to work cooperatively with Moscow to increase the safety and security of nuclear-related facilities, infrastructure, and personnel. Russia is upgrading its physical, procedural, and technical measures to secure its nuclear weapons against both external and internal threats. Russia's nuclear security has been slowly improving over the last several years, but risks remain. We remain concerned about vulnerabilities to an insider who attempts unauthorized actions as well as potential terrorist attacks.

- An unauthorized launch or accidental use of a Russian nuclear weapon is highly unlikely as long as current technical and procedural safeguards built into the command and control system are in place and are effectively enforced. Our concerns about possible circumvention of the system would rise if central political authority broke down.

Since the September 2001 terrorist attacks in the United States, President Putin and other Russian officials have conducted a public campaign to provide assurances that terrorists have not acquired Russian nuclear weapons. Russian officials have reported, however, that terrorists have targeted Russian nuclear weapon storage sites. Security was tightened in 2001 after Russian authorities twice thwarted terrorist efforts to reconnoiter nuclear weapon storage sites.

Russian facilities housing weapons-usable nuclear material vary from small research facilities and fuel cycle facilities to those involved with nuclear weapons research, development, and production. Small research facilities, although typically underfunded, usually have smaller static inventories of weapons-usable nuclear material and are easier to secure whereas large fuel fabrication facilities have larger varying inventories that are more difficult to account for and are much harder to secure.

We assess that progress on security enhancements is most advanced at civilian institutes and Russian navy sites. Progress is impeded at facilities within the Federal Agency for Atomic Energy nuclear weapons complex which contain most of the material of proliferation interest because Russian security concerns prevent direct U.S. access to sensitive materials. Russia's nuclear material protection, control, and accounting practices have been slowly improving over the last several years, but risks remain. We find it highly unlikely that Russian authorities would have been able to recover all the material reportedly stolen. We assess that undetected smuggling has occurred and we are concerned about the total amount of material that could have been diverted or stolen in the last 13 years.

As for security at nuclear power plants, the commander-in-chief of the Interior Ministry Force said in November 2003 that Russia would set up a special-purpose unit tasked to protect nuclear energy industry installations. The unit would be established to counter terrorists and augment existing security. Even with increased security, however, Russian nuclear power plants almost certainly will remain vulnerable to a well-planned and executed terrorist attack.

We are concerned that Russia may not be able to sustain U.S.-provided security upgrades of facilities over the long term given the cost and technical sophistication of at least some of the equipment involved.

Since the dissolution of the Soviet Union, Moscow has consolidated the former Soviet stockpile into storage sites in Russia. Russian officials have stated that thousands of nuclear warheads from the former Soviet stockpile have been dismantled since 1991; reportedly over 10,000 warheads have been eliminated. Moscow relies on nuclear weapons as its primary means of deterrence, however, and will continue to have thousands of nuclear warheads in its inventory for the foreseeable future.

Moscow maintains roughly 4000 operational strategic nuclear warheads in its strategic nuclear triad, which is composed of ICBMs, submarine-launched ballistic missiles, and heavy bombers carrying nuclear-tipped air-launched cruise missiles. Moscow has agreed under the Moscow Treaty to reduce its strategic forces so that on December 31, 2012 Russia would have no more than 1700 to 2200 warheads.

Detected Diversions—Russian institutes have lost weapons-grade and weapons-usable nuclear materials in thefts in amounts greater than a few milligrams, contrary to claims by Minatom officials. In each case that we know about, however, the diverted material eventually was seized by government authorities. For example,

- In 1992, 1.5 kilograms of 90-percent enriched weapons-grade uranium were stolen from the Luch Production Association.
- In 1994, approximately 3.0 kilograms of 90-percent enriched weapons-grade uranium were stolen in Moscow.
- In 1999, the U.S. government confirmed that a Bulgarian seizure of nuclear material was weapons-usable. The material, approximately four grams of HEU, probably originated in Russia.

Weapons-Usable Nuclear Material—Weapons-usable nuclear material is defined as uranium enriched to 20 percent or more 235 or 233 isotopes (highly enriched uranium, HEU) and any plutonium containing less than 80 percent of the 238 isotope.

Weapons-grade material is typically defined as uranium 233 or 235 enriched to about 90 percent or greater or plutonium containing about 90 percent or more 239 isotope.[16]

The United States continues to work with Russia to help secure the nuclear stockpile and to preclude terrorists from obtaining other nuclear weapons or the weapons-grade or weapons-usable nuclear material that Russia has in large quantity.

G. China–Taiwan

The transfer of economic power from the West to the East in this new era of globalization is translating China's economic wealth and power into a greater military and political power. There are many challenges for the United States as a result of this economic swing. First, China has now funded so much of the U.S. debt incurred as a result of the Iraq war that we are coming perilously close to being far too dependent on foreign investment and will sacrifice certain policy prerogatives by being so dependent upon foreign powers. What happens when this money spigot is turned off? This could be a new form of asynchronous warfare directed at our economic system.

Another challenge for the United States is creating and maintaining a relationship built upon trust, goodwill, and friendship with China, when we observe its astounding increase in its military defense spending. In fact, the Chinese military budget has been growing at double-digit rates for the past 15 years. Because China is not worried about a land invasion, it has been rebuilding its navy and air force. China is worried about a small nuclear force's ability to withstand a first strike and is enlarging this arsenal. Currently we estimate approximately 700–800 missiles are targeting and within the striking distance of Taiwan, and our Department of Defense estimates that China will have 60 intercontinental missiles by 2010.[17]

Taiwan is not the only international challenge but Taiwan is a greater risk despite more than 34 years of U.S. treaty obligations coupled with a recognition of "one" China and our insistence for a peaceful resolution of the Taiwan question.[18] Many observers believe that China wants to avoid a conflict with Taiwan, even offering Taiwan reunification that would grant Taiwan operational autonomy in domestic affairs. China expects in return that Taiwan would acknowledge a single shared sovereignty. At the same time, China refuses to renounce its use of force over Taiwan, and has also insisted that the United States stay out of this issue. China states that its main objective is not to assert direct territorial rule over Taiwan, but to avoid the permanent loss of Taiwan. Although China wants to avoid conflict it is clearly prepared to go to war over this issue.[19]

James F. Hoge, Jr. has observed that China is modernizing its military forces to win a conflict with Taiwan and also to deter the United States' participation in any conflict. In fact, the Chinese military doctrine is focusing on countering the U.S. high-tech capabilities which include stealth aircraft, cruise missiles, precision-guided bombs, and electronic warfare capabilities.[20] Henry A. Crumpton notes that China's PLA (Peoples Liberation Army) and its intelligence service, the Ministry of State Security, are adopting doctrines to launch cyber attacks against our infrastructure of computer systems, banking, and financial infrastructure. In fact, the "PLA Colonels on Unrestricted Warfare" was a 1999 document that stressed the need for

China to develop and deploy cyber weapons.[21] And after the plane collision of a Chinese fighter and one of our intelligence gathering aircraft in 2001, we did see evidence of substantial cyber attacks upon the FBI and Department of Defense and the White House.

In January 2006, the United States was startled when China destroyed one of its own weather satellites in space with a ballistic missile. The PLA's ability to successfully track and destroy a satellite with a direct kinetic impact demonstrates that the PLA's rebuilding effort is making advances well beyond our expectations. One other troubling feature of the antisatellite test was the fact that it created and placed into orbit more space debris than any other single event, putting at risk China's own satellites as well as satellites of other countries for decades to come. China has demonstrated its capability to threaten U.S. military assets, and because we depend on our military satellites for real-time communication, battlefield awareness, weapons targeting, intelligence gathering, and reconnaissance this was an important achievement of the PLA and cast doubt on China's reliability as a global partner and created concern within our diplomatic corps and State Department.[22]

There are three areas that will determine whether relations between China and the United States will continue to grow. First, China's role and its influence in helping to contain the nuclear ambition of North Korea will be a major factor in this deepening relationship. A second point will be China's assistance and cooperation in helping reduce proliferation of missile and dual-use technologies. Third, the United States supports the peaceful resolution of differences between the Peoples Republic of China and Taiwan.

In fact, the United States remains committed to its "one China" policy and to its obligations under the Taiwan Relations Act, but China's continuing deployment of missiles targeted against Taiwan generates tension and suspicion as to how meaningful our relationship is. Former Secretary of State Colin Powell captured the essence when he stated, "Whether China chooses peace or coercion to resolve its differences with Taiwan will tell us a great deal about the kind of role China seeks with its neighbors and seeks with us."[23]

H. Iran

Iran, of all nation-states, presents more problems to the United States and most of the world community as a result of its active support of terrorist groups such as Hamas, Palestine Islamic Jihad, Hezbollah, and the Islamic jihadist terrorists. In fact, the 1979 Iranian Revolution was a specific reason that the Middle East experienced a rise in terrorism from various Islamic groups. Another antecedent for the increase in Islamic terrorism was the Mujaheddin war against the Soviet Union in Afghanistan. Iran, during the 1990s, was the most active state sponsor of terrorism. Of course, terrorism is not the only concern we have with Iranian activities, as we are concerned about its nuclear program and acquisition of advanced weapons.[24] Iran has also created much opposition and unrest to the hope for a Middle East peace process. Finally, Iran's president, Mahmoud Ahmadinejad, in repeated public comments about the destruction of Israel, suggests the intolerance and commitment to terrorism that Iran's government holds to this day.

In analyzing current and future trends, Christopher Harmon notes that Iran's financial support for Hezbollah is approximately $100 million along with full diplomatic support. Iranian money and support also have been given to Hamas, Palestine Islamic Jihad, Abu Sayyaf, and Al Qaeda. In addition, Iran continues to develop its chemical and biological weapons programs, and it seeks to improve the capabilities it once used against Iraq in the Iraq–Iranian wars from 1985–1988.[25]

Former FBI Director Louis Freeh stated in no uncertain terms that the 1996 Khobar Towers bombing which killed 19 American soldiers and wounded 372 was sanctioned, funded, and directed by senior officials of the government of Iran. The Ministry of Intelligence and Security and the Iranian Revolutionary Guard had both been involved in the planning and the bombers were trained by Iranians in the Bekaa Valley of Lebanon, where the Iranian-supported Hezbollah is based. The bombers had passports issued by the Iranian Embassy in Damascus, Syria that permitted them to cross the border into Saudi Arabia. On June 21, 2001, a federal grand jury returned a 46-count indictment against 14 defendants charged in the Khobar Towers bombing.[26]

A more recent activity supported both by Iran and Syria occurred in July 2006 when Hezbollah crossed into Israel and kidnapped Israeli soldiers and began lobbing Katyusha rockets into Northern Israel. Part of the plan was to create situations that would force Israel into a confrontation with Lebanon.[27] In the battles between the Israeli military and Hezbollah, it was generally agreed that Israel lost the battle, the support of the Lebanese people and that of the world community for its destructive bombing of civilian homes and apartments in Lebanon.

Hezbollah has transformed itself and now is more than simply a terrorist group, and now has a strong guerilla and political army. Hezbollah also accepts more casualties than Israel. However, the fact that Hezbollah holds 23 seats in Lebanon's parliament of 128 and also has control of two government ministries, while operating hospitals and schools that are considered more efficient and effective than those operated by the Lebanese government provides Hezbollah with a very strong base of community and regional support. So the benefit for both Iran and Syria in their continuing support of Hezbollah is that they have what amounts to a proxy army that permits a degree of deniability, enabling them to strike at Israel or other targets with minimal risk for a confrontation directly. Syria also supports Hezbollah because as President Basher al-Asad has stated, Hezbollah is Syria's buffer against Israel.[28]

The transformation of Hezbollah from simply a terrorist organization to a guerilla organization that now supports and engages other terrorist groups is a new model of how terrorist groups are likely to emerge. Its active political wing which engenders support and to a degree some political legitimacy will make it more difficult for successful counterterrorist policies and operations. The proxy status it holds with Iran and Syria will some day have to be addressed by Israel, the United States, or the world community. At some point, Iran and Syria will have to be directly taken to task for their support and proxy use of Hezbollah.

Another worry is that if Iran obtains nuclear weapons and provides them to the proxy terrorist group it uses, namely Hezbollah, we will be confronted with a terrorist organization that has a full-fledged nuclear capability and no nation-state responsibility.

The United Nations International Atomic Energy Agency found evidence that Iran was secretly engaged in a nuclear weapons program.[29] The Iranian desire for nuclear capability is not a recent development, as the former shah signed a nuclear cooperation agreement with the United States in 1957 and sent students overseas for training. The civilian and military programs were shelved after the 1979 Iranian revolution, but the civilian program had been renewed by 1984 and the military program by 1987. In 2004, the International Atomic Energy Agency reported that Iran was not fully cooperating with inspections, and that Iran was going ahead with plans to produce enriched uranium, despite past assurance to the IAEA that it would freeze such activity.[30] In 2005, our Defense Intelligence Agency declared that Iran was devoting significant resources to its weapons of mass destruction and ballistic missiles programs.[31]

American and European intelligence agencies, as well as the International Atomic Energy Agency, all agree that Iran is intent on developing the capability to produce nuclear weapons, despite denials. The only item that the intelligence agencies are not able to agree on is when Iran will have this capability. Our intelligence community suggests sometime in the next three to five years, although some agencies feel it could range from three to ten years, and Israel's Mossad intelligence agency believes Iran is one to two years away from having enriched uranium. And Israel's government has warned for years that any attempt by Iran to begin enriching uranium will be a point of no return. An official of the war on terror stated that allowing Iran to have the nuclear bomb is not on the table. We cannot have nuclear weapons sent downstream to a terror network. It is too dangerous and the bottom line is that Iran cannot become a nuclear weapon state.[32]

The issues and challenges that Iran brings to the world community are serious and demand closely scrutinized attention. We simply cannot have a nation-state in the 21st century supporting terrorism, operating with a proxy army, and seeking nuclear weapons. The record of Iran and Hezbollah is quite clear, and has been documented for many years. The potential for weapons of mass destruction being provided to various terrorist organizations by Iran should not be tolerated by any civilized nation.

5. Summary

The alarming prospect of an ideology that encourages and calls for terrorism to overthrow civilized nation-states is a movement that continues to grow within the Middle East. The trends in global terrorism projected into the year 2020, along with the disturbing model of how some terrorist groups will transform themselves similar to Hezbollah, will create enormous counterterrorism problems for all countries attempting to eradicate this violence. The identification of some of the 21st century nation-state issues and challenges confronting the world community reveals dangerous choices that will have to be confronted and made. We can no longer permit some of these issues to linger for more than a half century as many of them have.

Although the present situation calls for wisdom of our leaders and diplomacy of and from all nations, we must nevertheless be realistic and we must take firm action to repel the ideology that permits terrorism to sustain itself.

Thus, as our nation uses and refines our instruments of statecraft to confront the global challenges of terrorism we will require more focus on how to prevent societies from collapsing and how best to manage and mitigate the risk that threatens the survivability of societies. The fine line that divides Islamic jihadism from becoming a religious war will require new dimensions of leadership from Islamic nations and the influential members of those communities. To prevent the "highjacking" of their religion and communities by the Islamic jihadist's brand of fundamentalism will require the emergence of Islamic leaders who will speak out against the medieval and militant beliefs that offer nothing more than chaos and destruction.

The challenge of protecting all societies that believe in law, justice, and the maintenance of civility will require a concerted and systematic approach to the protection and guardianship of the critical infrastructures that the Islamic jihadists seek to attack and destroy. The critical infrastructures of all nations provide a coupling mechanism that permits societies to trade together, to collaborate, and to sustain improved standards of living, all targets of these terrorists.

The availability of weapons of mass destruction selected from radiological, biological, chemical, or nuclear inventories now enable terrorists access to refine their attack strategies with a level of lethality never before attainable.

The existence of so many broken borders throughout the world only makes it more imperative that we systematically work to achieve greater cooperation and consensus among the community of nations confronting terrorism. The transformation of our intelligence community has resulted in our efforts to provide a 21st century capability with improved programs throughout all 16 of our intelligence agencies, all designed to provide our top leaders and policymakers with information they need to safeguard our nation.

Finally, the trends in global terrorism will continue to be mapped out to 2015, 2020, and 2025. The key drivers that will affect all nations and societies will require insights and research capabilities that will be guided by the most sophisticated and analytical research methodologies. The preparation of estimates, forecasts, and predictions will require the most advanced computational research methodologies fully reliant on statistical and modeling techniques that have not in the past been applied to the challenges of confronting, controlling, and defeating terrorists.

Endnotes

1. Thomas L. Friedman, *Longitudes and Attitudes: The World in the Age of Terrorism*, Anchor: New York, 2003, pp. 36, 78.
2. Thomas P. Barnett, *The Pentagon's New Map: War and Peace in the Twenty First Century*, G.P. Putnam's Sons: New York, 2004, pp. 50–51.
3. Barnett, loc.cit., p. 50.
4 Barnett, op.cit., p. 93.
5. Friedman, op. cit., p. 122.
6. Norman Podhoretz, *World War IV: The Long Struggle Against Islamic Fascism*, Doubleday: New York, 2007, pp. 27–31.
7. Barnett, op. cit., pp. 287–288.
8. Friedman, op. cit., pp. 34–35.
9. Barnett, Op. Cit., pp. 270–271.
10. National Intelligence Council, National Intelligence Estimate, *Trends in Global Terrorism: Implication for the United States*, Key Judgments, April 2006, Declassified, Director National Intelligence Office, 2006.
11. National Intelligence Council, *Global Trends 2015: A Dialogue About the Future with Non Government Experts*, NIC-2000-02, Approved for publication by the National Foreign Intelligence Board, under the authority of the Director of Central Intelligence Agency, December, 2000, pp. 5, 8–12.
12. National Intelligence Council, *Global Trends 2015*, ibid., pp. 25–28, 60.
13. National Intelligence Council, *Mapping the Global Future*, Report of the National Intelligence Councils 2020 Project, NIC-2004-13, National Intelligence Council, Washington, D.C., 2004, pp. 9–13.
14. National Intelligence Council, *Mapping the Global Future*, ibid., pp. 17–18.
15. National Intelligence Council, *Mapping the Global Future*, op.cit., pp. 93–95.

16. National Intelligence Council, *Annual Report to Congress on the Safety and Security of Russian Nuclear Facilities and Military Forces*, Prepared by the National Intelligence Officer for Weapons of Mass Destruction and Proliferation, Unclassified Report, December 2004, pp. 3, 5, 7.
17. David M. Lampton, The forces of Chinese power, *Foreign Affairs*, 86: 1, January–February, 2007, p. 118.
18. James F. Hoge, Jr., A global power shift in the making: Is the United States ready, *Foreign Affairs*, 83: 4, July–August, 2004, p. 4.
19. Michael D. Swaine, Trouble in Taiwan, *Foreign Affairs*, 83: 2, March–April, 2004, pp. 40–41.
20. James F. Hoge, Jr., op. cit., p. 5.
21. Henry A. Crumpton, Intelligence and homeland defense, in Jennifer E. Sims and Burton Gerber (Eds.), *Transforming U.S. Intelligence*, Georgetown University Press: Washington, DC, 2005, p. 201.
22. Bates Gill and Martin Kleiber, China's space odyssey: What the anti-satellite test reveals about decision making in Beijing, *Foreign Affairs*, 86: 3, May–June, 2007, p. 4.
23. Chuck Hagel, A Republican foreign policy, *Foreign Affairs*, 83: 4, July–August, 2004, p. 75.
24. Paul R. Pillar, *Terrorism and U.S. Foreign Policy*, Brookings Institution Press: Washington, DC, 2001, pp. 47, 159.
25. Christopher C. Harmon, *Terrorism Today*, Frank Cass: London, 2000, pp. 156–167.
26. Louis J. Freeh, *My FBI: Bringing Down the Mafia, Investigating Bill Clinton and Fighting the War on Terror*, St. Martins Press: New York, 2005, pp. 29, 32.
27. Mike Evans, *The Final Move Beyond Iraq: The Final Solution While the World Sleeps*, Front Line: Lake Mary, FL, 2007, p.72.
28. Daniel Byman, Israel and the Lebanese Hezbollah, in Robert J. Art and Louise Richardsen (Eds.), *Democracy and Counterterrorism: Lessons From the Past*, United States Institute of Peace: Washington, DC, 2007, pp. 306, 312, 314, 334.
29. Richard A. Clarke, *Against All Enemies: Inside America's War on Terror*, Free Press: New York, 2004, p. 284.
30. James Risen, *State of War: The Secret History of the CIA and the Bush Administration*, Free Press: New York, 2006, p. 218.
31. Abbas William Samii, The Iranian nuclear issue and informal networks, *Naval War College Review*, 59: 1, Winter 2006, pp. 73–74.
32. Seymour M. Hersh, Annals of national security: The Iran plans, *The New Yorker*, April 17, 2006, pp. 30, 34, 37.

Appendix A

National Strategy for Combating Terrorism: September 2006

Table of Contents

Overview of America's National Strategy for Combating Terrorism

America is at war with a transnational terrorist movement fueled by a radical ideology of hatred, oppression, and murder. Our National Strategy for Combating Terrorism, first published in February 2003, recognizes that we are at war and that protecting and defending the homeland, the American people, and their livelihoods remains our first and most solemn obligation.

Our strategy also recognizes that the War on Terror is a different kind of war. From the beginning, it has been both a battle of arms and a battle of ideas. Not only do we fight our terrorist enemies on the battlefield, we promote freedom and human dignity as alternatives to the terrorists' perverse vision of oppression and totalitarian rule. The paradigm for combating terrorism now involves the application of all elements of our national power and influence. Not only do we employ military power, we use diplomatic, financial, intelligence, and law enforcement activities to protect the homeland and extend our defenses, disrupt terrorist operations, and deprive our enemies of what they need to operate and survive. We have broken old orthodoxies that once confined our counterterrorism efforts primarily to the criminal justice domain.

This updated strategy sets the course for winning the War on Terror. It builds directly from the National Security Strategy issued in March 2006 as well as the February 2003 National Strategy for Combating Terrorism, and incorporates our increased understanding of the enemy. From the beginning, we understood that the War on Terror involved more than simply finding and bringing to justice those who had planned and executed the terrorist attacks on September 11, 2001. Our strategy involved destroying the larger al-Qaida network and also confronting the radical ideology that inspired others to join or support the terrorist movement. Since 9/11, we have made substantial progress in degrading the al-Qaida network, killing or capturing key lieutenants, eliminating safehavens, and disrupting existing lines of support. Through the freedom agenda, we also have promoted the best long-term answer to al-Qaida's agenda: the freedom and dignity that comes when human liberty is protected by effective democratic institutions.

In response to our efforts, the terrorists have adjusted, and so we must continue to refine our strategy to meet the evolving threat. Today, we face a global terrorist movement and must confront the radical ideology that justifies the use of violence against innocents in the name of religion. As laid out in this strategy, to win the War on Terror, we will:

- Advance effective democracies as the long-term antidote to the ideology of terrorism;
- Prevent attacks by terrorist networks;
- Deny weapons of mass destruction to rogue states and terrorist allies who seek to use them;
- Deny terrorists the support and sanctuary of rogue states;
- Deny terrorists control of any nation they would use as a base and launching pad for terror; and
- Lay the foundations and build the institutions and structures we need to carry the fight forward against terror and help ensure our ultimate success.

Today's Realities in the War on Terror

The terrorist attacks of September 11, 2001, were acts of war against the United States, peaceful people throughout the world, and the very principles of liberty and human dignity. The United States, together with our coalition partners, has fought back and will win this war. We will hold the perpetrators accountable and work to prevent the recurrence of similar atrocities on any scale—whether at home or abroad. The War on Terror extends beyond the current armed conflict that arose out of the attacks of September 11, 2001, and embraces all facets of continuing U.S. efforts to bring an end to the scourge of terrorism. Ultimately, we will win the long war to defeat the terrorists and their murderous ideology.

Successes

We have deprived al-Qaida of safehaven in Afghanistan and helped a democratic government to rise in its place. Once a terrorist sanctuary ruled by the repressive Taliban regime, Afghanistan is now a full partner in the War on Terror.

A multinational coalition joined by the Iraqis is aggressively prosecuting the war against the terrorists in Iraq. Together, we are working to secure a united, stable, and democratic Iraq, now a new War on Terror ally in the heart of the Middle East.

We have significantly degraded the al-Qaida network. Most of those in the al-Qaida network responsible for the September 11 attacks, including the plot's mastermind Khalid Shaykh Muhammad, have been captured or killed. We also have killed other key al-Qaida members, such as Abu Musab al-Zarqawi, the group's operational commander in Iraq who led a campaign of terror that took the lives of countless American forces and innocent Iraqis.

We have led an unprecedented international campaign to combat terrorist financing that has made it harder, costlier, and riskier for al-Qaida and related terrorist groups to raise and move money.

There is a broad and growing global consensus that the deliberate targeting of innocents is never justified by any calling or cause.

Many nations have rallied to fight terrorism, with unprecedented cooperation on law enforcement, intelligence, military, and diplomatic activity.

We have strengthened our ability to disrupt and help prevent future attacks in the Homeland by enhancing our counterterrorism architecture through the creation of the Department of Homeland Security, the Office of Director of National Intelligence, and the National Counterterrorism Center. Overall, the United States and our partners have disrupted several serious plots since September 11, including al-Qaida plots to attack inside the United States.

Numerous countries that were part of the problem before September 11 are now increasingly becoming part of the solution—and this transformation has occurred without destabilizing friendly regimes in key regions.

The Administration has worked with Congress to adopt, implement, and renew key reforms like the USA Patriot Act that promote our security while also protecting our fundamental liberties.

Yet while America is safer, we are not yet safe. The enemy remains determined, and we face serious challenges at home and abroad.

Challenges

Terrorist networks today are more dispersed and less centralized. They are more reliant on smaller cells inspired by a common ideology and less directed by a central command structure.

While the United States Government and its partners have thwarted many attacks, we have not been able to prevent them all. Terrorists have struck in many places throughout the world, from Bali to Beslan to Baghdad.

While we have substantially improved our air, land, sea, and border security, our Homeland is not immune from attack.

Terrorists have declared their intention to acquire and use weapons of mass destruction (WMD) to inflict even more catastrophic attacks against the United States, our allies, partners, and other interests around the world.

Some states, such as Syria and Iran, continue to harbor terrorists at home and sponsor terrorist activity abroad.

The ongoing fight for freedom in Iraq has been twisted by terrorist propaganda as a rallying cry.

Increasingly sophisticated use of the Internet and media has enabled our terrorist enemies to communicate, recruit, train, rally support, proselytize, and spread their propaganda without risking personal contact.

Today's Terrorist Enemy

The United States and our partners continue to pursue a significantly degraded but still dangerous al-Qaida network. Yet the enemy we face today in the War on Terror is not the same enemy we faced on September 11. Our effective counterterrorist efforts, in part, have forced the terrorists to evolve and modify their ways of doing business. Our understanding of the enemy has evolved as well. Today, the principal terrorist enemy confronting the United States is a transnational movement of extremist organizations, networks, and individuals—and their state and non-state supporters—which have in common that they exploit Islam and use terrorism for ideological ends.

This transnational movement is not monolithic. Although al-Qaida functions as the movement's vanguard and remains, along with its affiliate groups and those inspired by them, the most dangerous present manifestation of the enemy, the movement is not controlled by any single individual, group, or state. What unites the movement is a common vision, a common set of ideas about the nature and destiny of the world, and a common goal of ushering in totalitarian rule. What unites the movement is the ideology of oppression, violence, and hate.

Our terrorist enemies exploit Islam to serve a violent political vision. Fueled by a radical ideology and a false belief that the United States is the cause of most problems affecting Muslims today, our enemies seek to expel Western power and influence from the Muslim world and establish regimes that rule according to a violent and intolerant distortion of Islam. As illustrated by Taliban-ruled Afghanistan, such regimes would deny all political and religious freedoms and serve as sanctuaries for extremists to launch additional attacks against not only the United States, its allies and partners, but the Muslim world itself. Some among the enemy, particularly al-Qaida, harbor even greater territorial and geopolitical ambitions and aim to establish a single, pan-Islamic, totalitarian regime that stretches from Spain to Southeast Asia.

This enemy movement seeks to create and exploit a division between the Muslim and non-Muslim world and within the Muslim world itself. The terrorists distort the idea of jihad into a call for violence and murder against those they regard as apostates or unbelievers, including all those who disagree with them. Most of the terrorist attacks since September 11 have occurred in Muslim countries—and most of the victims have been Muslims.

In addition to this principal enemy, a host of other groups and individuals also use terror and violence against innocent civilians to pursue their political objectives. Though their motives and goals may be different, and often include secular and more narrow territorial aims, they threaten our interests and those of our partners as they attempt to overthrow civil order and replace freedom with conflict and intolerance. Their terrorist tactics ensure that they are enemies of humanity regardless of their goals and no matter where they operate.

For our terrorist enemies, violence is not only justified, it is necessary and even glorified—judged the only means to achieve a world vision darkened by hate, fear, and oppression. They use suicide bombings, beheadings, and other atrocities against innocent people as a means to promote their creed. Our enemy's demonstrated indifference to human life and desire to inflict catastrophic damage on the United States and its friends and allies around the world have fueled their desire for weapons of mass destruction. We cannot permit the world's most dangerous terrorists and their regime sponsors to threaten us with the world's most destructive weapons.

For the enemy, there is no peaceful coexistence with those who do not subscribe to their distorted and violent view of the world. They accept no dissent and tolerate no alternative points of view. Ultimately, the terrorist enemy we face threatens global peace, international security and prosperity, the rising tide of democracy, and the right of all people to live without fear of indiscriminant violence.

Strategic Vision for the War on Terror

From the beginning, the War on Terror has been both a battle of arms and a battle of ideas—a fight against the terrorists and their murderous ideology. In the short run, the fight involves the application of all instruments of national power and influence to kill or capture the terrorists; deny them safehaven and control of any nation; prevent them from gaining access to WMD; render potential terrorist targets less attractive by strengthening security; and cut off their sources of funding and other resources they need to operate and survive. In the long run, winning the War on Terror means winning the battle of ideas. Ideas can transform the embittered and disillusioned either into murderers willing to kill innocents, or into free peoples living harmoniously in a diverse society.

The battle of ideas helps to define the strategic intent of our National Strategy for Combating Terrorism. The United States will continue to lead an expansive international effort in pursuit of a two-pronged vision:

The defeat of violent extremism as a threat to our way of life as a free and open society; and

The creation of a global environment inhospitable to violent extremists and all who support them.

Strategy for Winning the War on Terror

Long-Term Approach: Advancing Effective Democracy

The long-term solution for winning the War on Terror is the advancement of freedom and human dignity through effective democracy. Elections are the most visible sign of a free society and can play a critical role in advancing effective democracy. But elections alone are not enough. Effective democracies honor and uphold basic human rights, including freedom of religion, conscience, speech, assembly, association, and press. They are responsive to their citizens, submitting to the will of the people. Effective democracies exercise effective sovereignty and maintain order within their own borders, address causes of conflict peacefully, protect independent and impartial systems of justice, punish crime, embrace the rule of law, and resist corruption. Effective democracies also limit the reach of government, protecting the institutions of civil society. In effective democracies, freedom is indivisible. They are the long-term antidote to the ideology of terrorism today. This is the battle of ideas.

To wage the battle of ideas effectively, we must recognize what does and does not give rise to terrorism:

Terrorism is not the inevitable by-product of poverty. Many of the September 11 hijackers were from middle-class backgrounds, and many terrorist leaders, like bin Laden, are from privileged upbringings.

Terrorism is not simply a result of hostility to U.S. policy in Iraq. The United States was attacked on September 11 and many years earlier, well before we toppled the Saddam Hussein regime. Moreover, countries that did not participate in Coalition efforts in Iraq have not been spared from terror attacks.

Terrorism is not simply a result of Israeli–Palestinian issues. Al-Qaida plotting for the September 11 attacks began in the 1990s, during an active period in the peace process.

Terrorism is not simply a response to our efforts to prevent terror attacks. The al-Qaida network targeted the United States long before the United States targeted al-Qaida. Indeed, the terrorists are emboldened more by perceptions of weakness than by demonstrations of resolve. Terrorists lure recruits by telling them that we are decadent, easily intimidated, and will retreat if attacked.

The terrorism we confront today springs from:

Political alienation. Transnational terrorists are recruited from populations with no voice in their own government and see no legitimate way to promote change in their own country. Without a stake in the existing order, they are vulnerable to manipulation by those who advocate a perverse political vision based on violence and destruction.

Grievances that can be blamed on others. The failures the terrorists feel and see are blamed both on others and on perceived injustices from the recent or sometimes distant past. The terrorists' rhetoric keeps wounds associated with this past fresh and raw, a potent motivation for revenge and terror.

Subcultures of conspiracy and misinformation. Terrorists recruit more effectively from populations whose information about the world is contaminated by falsehoods and corrupted by conspiracy theories. The distortions keep alive grievances and filter out facts that would challenge popular prejudices and self-serving propaganda.

An ideology that justifies murder. Terrorism ultimately depends upon the appeal of an ideology that excuses or even glorifies the deliberate killing of innocents. Islam has been twisted and made to serve an evil end, as in other times and places other religions have been similarly abused.

Defeating terrorism in the long run requires that each of these factors be addressed. Effective democracy provides a counter to each, diminishing the underlying conditions terrorists seek to exploit.

In place of alienation, democracy offers an ownership stake in society, a chance to shape one's own future.

In place of festering grievances, democracy offers the rule of law, the peaceful resolution of disputes, and the habits of advancing interests through compromise.

In place of a culture of conspiracy and misinformation, democracy offers freedom of speech, independent media, and the marketplace of ideas, which can expose and discredit falsehoods, prejudices, and dishonest propaganda.

In place of an ideology that justifies murder, democracy offers a respect for human dignity that abhors the deliberate targeting of innocent civilians.

Democracy is the antithesis of terrorist tyranny, which is why the terrorists denounce it and are willing to kill the innocent to stop it. Democracy is based on empowerment, while the terrorists' ideology is based on enslavement. Democracies expand the freedom of their citizens, while the terrorists seek to impose a single set of narrow beliefs. Democracy sees individuals as equal in worth and dignity, having an inherent potential to create, govern themselves, and exercise basic freedoms of speech and conscience. The terrorists see individuals as objects to be exploited, and then to be ruled and oppressed.

Democracies are not immune to terrorism. In some democracies, some ethnic or religious groups are unable or unwilling to grasp the benefits of freedom otherwise available in the society. Such groups can evidence the same alienation and despair that the transnational terrorists exploit in undemocratic states. This accounts for the emergence in democratic societies of homegrown terrorists—even among second- and third-generation citizens. Even in these cases, the long-term solution remains deepening the reach of democracy so that all citizens enjoy its benefits. We will continue to guard against the emergence of homegrown terrorists within our own Homeland as well.

The strategy to counter the lies behind the terrorists' ideology and deny them future recruits must empower the very people the terrorists most want to exploit: the faithful followers of Islam. We will continue to support political reforms that empower peaceful Muslims to practice and interpret their faith. We will work to undermine the ideological underpinnings of violent Islamic extremism and gain the support of non-violent Muslims around the world. The most vital work will be done within the Islamic world itself, and Jordan, Morocco, and Indonesia, among others, have begun to make important strides in this effort. Responsible Islamic leaders need to denounce an ideology that distorts and exploits Islam to justify the murder of innocent people and defiles a proud religion.

Many of the Muslim faith are already making this commitment at great personal risk. They realize they are a target of this ideology of terror. Everywhere we have joined in the fight against terrorism, Muslim allies have stood beside us, becoming partners in this vital cause. They know the stakes – the survival of their own liberty, the future of their own region, the justice and humanity of their own traditions—and the United States is proud to stand beside them. Not only will we continue to support the efforts of our Muslim partners overseas to reject violent extremism, we will continue to engage with and strengthen the efforts of Muslims within the United States as well. Through outreach programs and public diplomacy we will reveal the terrorists' violent extremist ideology for what it is—a form of totalitarianism following in the path of fascism and Nazism.

Over the Short Term: Four Priorities of Action

The advance of freedom, opportunity, and human dignity through democracy is the long-term solution to the transnational terror movement of today. To create the space and time for this long-term solution to take root, we are operating along four priorities of action in the short term.

Prevent attacks by terrorist networks. A government has no higher obligation than to protect the lives and livelihoods of its citizens. The hard core among our terrorist enemies cannot be reformed or deterred; they will be tracked down, captured, or killed. They will be cut off from the network of individuals, institutions, and other resources they depend on for support and that facilitate their activities. The network, in turn, will be deterred, disrupted, and disabled. Working with committed partners across the globe, we continue to use a broad range of tools at home and abroad to take the fight to the terrorists, deny them entry to the United States, hinder their movement across international borders, and establish protective measures to further reduce our vulnerability to attack.

- ***Attack terrorists and their capacity to operate.*** The United States and our partners continue to take active and effective measures against our primary terrorist enemies and certain other violent extremist groups that also pose a serious and continuing threat. We are attacking these terrorists and their capacity to operate effectively at home and abroad. Specifically, through the use of all elements of national power, we are denying or neutralizing what our terrorist enemies need to operate and survive:
    - *Leaders,* who provide the vision that followers strive to realize. They also offer the necessary direction, discipline, and motivation

for accomplishing a given goal or task. Most terrorist organizations have a central figure who embodies the cause, in addition to several operational leaders and managers who provide guidance on a functional, regional, or local basis. The loss of a leader can degrade a group's cohesiveness and in some cases may trigger its collapse. Other terrorist groups adapt by promoting experienced cadre or decentralizing their command structures, making our challenge in neutralizing terrorist leaders even greater.

- *Foot soldiers*, which include the operatives, facilitators, and trainers in a terrorist network. They are the lifeblood of a terrorist group; they make it run. Technology and globalization have enhanced the ability of groups to recruit foot soldiers to their cause, including well-educated recruits. We and our partners will not only continue to capture and kill foot soldiers, but will work to halt the influx of recruits into terrorist organizations as well. Without a continuing supply of personnel to facilitate and carry out attacks, these groups ultimately will cease to operate.
- *Weapons*, or the tools of terrorists and the means by which they murder to advance their cause. Terrorists exploit many avenues to develop and acquire weapons, including through state sponsors, theft or capture, and black market purchases. Our enemies employ existing technology—explosives, small arms, missiles and other devices—in both conventional and unconventional ways to terrorize and achieve mass effects. They also use non-weapon technologies such as the airplanes on September 11. Our greatest and gravest concern, however, is WMDs in the hands of terrorists. Preventing their acquisition and the dire consequences of their use is a key priority of this strategy.
- *Funds*, which provide the fungible, easily transportable means to secure all other forms of material support necessary to the survival and operation of terrorist organizations. Our enemies raise funds through a variety of means, including soliciting contributions from supporters; operating businesses, NGOs, and charitable fronts; and engaging in criminal activity such as fraud, extortion, and kidnapping for ransom. They transfer funds through several mechanisms, including the formal banking system, wire transfers, debit or "smart" cards, cash couriers, and *hawalas*, which are alternative remittance systems based on trust. Effective disruption of funding sources and interdiction of transfer mechanisms can help our partners and us to starve terrorist networks of the material support they require.
- *Communications*, which allow terrorists the ability to receive, store, manipulate, and exchange information. The methods by which ter-

rorists communicate are numerous and varied. Our enemies rely on couriers and face-to-face contacts with associates and tend to use what is accessible in their local areas as well as what they can afford. They also use today's technologies with increasing acumen and sophistication. This is especially true with the Internet, which they exploit to create and disseminate propaganda, recruit new members, raise funds and other material resources, provide instruction on weapons and tactics, and plan operations. Without a communications ability, terrorist groups cannot effectively organize operations, execute attacks, or spread their ideology. We and our partners will continue to target the communication nodes of our enemy.

- *Propaganda operations*, which are used by terrorists to justify violent action as well as inspire individuals to support or join the movement. The ability of terrorists to exploit the Internet and 24/7 worldwide media coverage allows them to bolster their prominence as well as feed a steady diet of radical ideology, twisted images, and conspiracy theories to potential recruits in all corners of the globe. Besides a global reach, these technologies allow terrorists to propagate their message quickly, often before an effective counter to terrorist messages can be coordinated and distributed. These are force multipliers for our enemy.

Deny terrorists entry to the United States and disrupt their travel internationally. Denying our enemies the tools to travel internationally and across and within our borders significantly impedes their mobility and can inhibit their effectiveness. They rely on illicit networks to facilitate travel and often obtain false identification documents through theft or in-house forgery operations. We will continue to enhance the security of the American people through a layered system of protections along our borders, at our ports, on our roadways and railways, in our skies, and with our international partners. We will continue to develop and enhance security practices and technologies to reduce vulnerabilities in the dynamic transportation network, inhibit terrorists from crossing U.S. borders, and detect and prevent terrorist travel within the United States. Our efforts will include improving all aspects of aviation security; promoting secure travel and identity documents; disrupting travel facilitation networks; improving border security and visa screening; and building international capacity and improving international information exchange to secure travel and combat terrorist travel. Our National Strategy to Combat Terrorist Travel and our National Strategy for Maritime Security will help guide our efforts.

Defend potential targets of attack. Our enemies are opportunistic, exploiting vulnerabilities and seeking alternatives to those targets with increased security measures. The targeting trend since at least September 11 has been away from hardened sites, such as official government facilities with formidable security, and toward softer targets—schools, restaurants, places of worship, and nodes of public transportation—where innocent civilians gather and which are not always well secured. Specific targets vary, but they tend to be symbolic and often selected because they will produce mass casualties, economic damage, or both.

While it is impossible to protect completely all potential targets all the time, we can deter and disrupt attacks, as well as mitigate the effects of those that do occur, through strategic security improvements at sites both at home and overseas. Among our most important defensive efforts is the protection of critical infrastructures and key resources—sectors such as energy, food and agriculture, water, telecommunications, public health, transportation, the defense industrial base, government facilities, postal and shipping, the chemical industry, emergency services, monuments and icons, information technology, dams, commercial facilities, banking and finance, and nuclear reactors, materials, and waste. These are systems and assets so vital that their destruction or incapacitation would have a debilitating effect on the security of our Nation. We will also continue to protect various assets such as historical attractions or certain high-profile events whose destruction or attack would not necessarily debilitate our national security but could damage the morale and confidence of the American people. Beyond the Homeland, we will continue to protect and defend U.S. citizens, diplomatic missions, and military facilities overseas, as well as work with our partners to strengthen their ability to protect their populations and critical infrastructures.

Deny WMD to rogue states and terrorist allies who seek to use them. Weapons of mass destruction in the hands of terrorists are some of the gravest threats we face. We have taken aggressive efforts to deny terrorists access to WMD-related materials, equipment, and expertise, but we will enhance these activities through an integrated effort at all levels of government and with the private sector and our foreign partners to stay ahead of this dynamic and evolving threat. In July 2006, the United States and Russia launched the Global Initiative to Combat Nuclear Terrorism to establish an international framework to enhance cooperation, build capacity, and act to combat the global threat of nuclear terrorism. This initiative will help drive international focus and action to ensure the international community is doing everything possible to prevent nuclear weapons, materials, and knowledge from reaching the hands of terrorists.

With regard to our own efforts, our comprehensive approach for addressing WMD terrorism hinges on six objectives, and we will work across all objectives simultaneously to maximize our ability to eliminate the threat.

Determine terrorists' intentions, capabilities, and plans to develop or acquire WMD. We need to understand and assess the credibility of threat reporting and provide technical assessments of terrorists' WMD capabilities.

Deny terrorists access to the materials, expertise, and other enabling capabilities required to develop WMD. We have an aggressive, global approach to deny our enemies access to WMD-related materials (with a particular focus on weapons-usable fissile materials), fabrication expertise, methods of transport, sources of funds, and other capabilities that facilitate the execution of a WMD attack. In addition to building upon existing initiatives to secure materials, we are developing innovative approaches that blend classic counterproliferation, nonproliferation, and counterterrorism efforts.

Deter terrorists from employing WMD. A new deterrence calculus combines the need to deter terrorists and supporters from contemplating a WMD attack and, failing that, to dissuade them from actually conducting an attack. Traditional threats may not work because terrorists show a wanton disregard for the lives of innocents and in some cases for their own lives. We require a range of deterrence strategies that are tailored to the situation and the adversary. We will make clear that terrorists and those who aid or sponsor a WMD attack would face the prospect of an overwhelming response to any use of such weapons. We will seek to dissuade attacks by improving our ability to mitigate the effects of a terrorist attack involving WMD – to limit or prevent large-scale casualties, economic disruption, or panic. Finally, we will ensure that our capacity to determine the source of any attack is well-known, and that our determination to respond overwhelmingly to any attack is never in doubt.

Detect and disrupt terrorists' attempted movement of WMD-related materials, weapons, and personnel. We will expand our global capability for detecting illicit materials, weapons, and personnel transiting abroad or heading for the United States or U.S. interests overseas. We will use our global partnerships, international agreements, and ongoing border security and interdiction efforts. We also will continue to work with countries to enact and enforce strict penalties for WMD trafficking and other suspect WMD-related activities.

- ***Prevent and respond to a WMD-related terrorist attack.*** Once the possibility of a WMD attack against the United States has been detected, we will seek to contain, interdict, and eliminate the threat. We will continue to develop requisite capabilities to eliminate the possibility of a WMD operation and to prevent a possible follow-on attack. We will prepare ourselves for possible WMD incidents by developing capabilities to manage the range of consequences that may result from such an attack against the United States or our interests around the world.

Define the nature and source of a terrorist-employed WMD device. Should a WMD terrorist attack occur, the rapid identification of the source and perpetrator of an attack will enable our response efforts and may be critical in disrupting follow-on attacks. We will develop the capability to assign responsibility for the intended or actual use of WMD via accurate attribution—the rapid fusion of technical forensic data with intelligence and law enforcement information.

Deny terrorists the support and sanctuary of rogue states. The United States and its allies and partners in the War on Terror make no distinction between those who commit acts of terror and those who support and harbor terrorists. Any government that chooses to be an ally of terror has chosen to be an enemy of freedom, justice, and peace. The world will hold those regimes to account. To break the bonds between rogue states and our terrorist enemies, we will work to disrupt the flow of resources from states to terrorists while simultaneously working to end state sponsorship of terrorism.

- ***End state sponsorship of terrorism.*** State sponsors are a critical resource for our terrorist enemies, often providing funds, weapons, training, safe passage, and sanctuary. Some of these countries have developed or have the capability to develop WMD and other destabilizing technologies that could fall into the hands of terrorists. The United States currently designates five state sponsors of terrorism: Iran, Syria, Sudan, North Korea, and Cuba. We will maintain sanctions against them and promote their international isolation until they end their support for terrorists, including the provision of sanctuary. To further isolate these regimes and persuade other states not to sponsor terror, we will use a range of tools and efforts to delegitimate terrorism as an instrument of statecraft. Any act of international terrorism, whether committed by a state or individual, is reprehensible, a threat to international peace and security, and should be unequivocally and uniformly rejected. Similarly, states that harbor and assist terrorists are as guilty as the terrorists, and they will be held to account.

Iran remains the most active state sponsor of international terrorism. Through its Islamic Revolutionary Guard Corps and Ministry of Intelligence and Security, the regime in Tehran plans terrorist operations and supports groups such as Lebanese Hizballah, Hamas, and Palestine Islamic Jihad (PIJ). Iran also remains unwilling to account for and bring to justice senior al-Qaida members it detained in 2003. Most troubling is the potential WMD-terrorism nexus that emanates from Tehran. Syria also is a significant state sponsor of terrorism and thus a priority for concern. The regime in Damascus supports and provides haven to Hizballah, Hamas, and PIJ. We will continue to stand with the people of Iran and Syria against the regimes that oppress them at home and sponsor terror abroad.

While Iranian and Syrian terrorist activities are especially worrisome, we are pressing all state sponsors to take the steps that are required to have state sponsorship designation rescinded. Each case is unique, and our approach to each will be tailored accordingly. Moreover, we never foreclose future membership in the coalition against tyranny and terror. The designation of Iraq as a state sponsor was rescinded in 2004 as it transitioned to democracy, ceased its terrorist support, and became an ally in the War on Terror. Similarly, the United States in June 2006 rescinded the designation of Libya, which has renounced terrorism and since September 11 has provided excellent cooperation to the United States and other members of the international community in response to the new global threats we face. Libya can serve as a model for states who wish to rejoin the community of nations by rejecting terror.

- ***Disrupt the flow of resources from rogue states to terrorists.*** Until we can eliminate state sponsorship of terror, we will disrupt and deny the flow of support from states to terrorists. We will continue to create and strengthen international will to interdict material support, akin to our efforts in the Proliferation Security Initiative—a global effort to stop shipments of WMD, their delivery systems, and related material. We will build international cooperation to financially isolate rogue states and their terrorist proxies. We also will continue to expose the vehicles and fronts that states use to support their terrorist surrogates.

Deny terrorists control of any nation they would use as a base and launching pad for terror. Our terrorist enemies are striving to claim a strategic country as a haven for terror. From this base, they could destabilize the Middle East and strike America and other free nations with ever-increasing violence. This we can never allow. Our enemies had established a sanctuary in Afghanistan prior to Operation Enduring Freedom, and today terrorists see Iraq as the central front of their fight against the United States. This is why success in helping the Afghan and Iraqi peoples forge effective democracies is vital. We will continue to prevent terrorists from exploiting ungoverned or under-governed areas as safehavens—secure spaces that allow our enemies to plan, organize, train, and prepare for operations. Ultimately, we will eliminate these havens altogether.

- ***Eliminate physical safehavens.*** Physical sanctuaries can stretch across an entire sovereign state, be limited to specific ungoverned or ill-governed areas in an otherwise functioning state, or cross national borders. In some cases the government wants to exercise greater effective sovereignty over its lands and maintain control within its borders but lacks the necessary capacity. We will strengthen the capacity of such War on Terror partners to reclaim full control of their territory

> through effective police, border, and other security forces as well as functioning systems of justice. To further counter terrorist exploitation of under-governed lands, we will promote effective economic development to help ensure long-term stability and prosperity. In failing states or states emerging from conflict, the risks are significant. Spoilers can take advantage of instability to create conditions terrorists can exploit. We will continue to work with foreign partners and international organizations to help prevent conflict and respond to state failure by building foreign capacity for peace operations, reconstruction, and stabilization so that countries in transition can reach a sustainable path to peace, democracy, and prosperity. Where physical havens cross national boundaries, we will continue to work with the affected countries to help establish effective cross-border control. Yet some countries will be reluctant to fulfill their sovereign responsibilities to combat terrorist-related activities within their borders. In addition to cooperation and sustained diplomacy, we will continue to partner with the international community to persuade states to meet their obligations to combat terrorism and deny safehaven under U.N. Security Council Resolution 1373.

Yet safehavens are not just limited to geographic territories. They also can be non-physical or virtual, existing within legal, cyber, and financial systems.

Legal safehavens. Some legal systems lack adequate procedural, substantive, and international assistance laws that enable effective investigation, prosecution, and extradition of terrorists. Such gaps offer a haven in which terrorists and their organizations can operate free from fear of prosecution. In the United States we have developed a domestic legal system that supports effective investigation and prosecution of terrorist activities while preserving individual privacy, the First Amendment rights of association, religious freedom, free speech, and other civil rights. We will continue to work with foreign partners to build their legal capacity to investigate, prosecute, and assist in the foreign prosecution of the full range of terrorist activities—from provision of material support to conspiracy to operational planning to a completed act of terrorism.

Cyber safehavens. The Internet provides an inexpensive, anonymous, geographically unbounded, and largely unregulated virtual haven for terrorists. Our enemies use the Internet to develop and disseminate propaganda, recruit new members, raise and transfer funds, train members on weapons use and tactics, and plan operations. Terrorist organizations can use virtual safehavens based anywhere in the world, regardless of where their members or operatives are located. Use of the Internet, however, creates opportunities for us to exploit. To counter terrorist use of the Internet as a virtual sanctuary, we will discredit terrorist propaganda by promoting truthful and peaceful messages. We will seek ultimately to deny the Internet to the terrorists as an effective safehaven for their propaganda, proselytizing, recruitment, fund-raising, training, and operational planning.

Financial safehavens. Financial systems are used by terrorist organizations as a fiscal sanctuary in which to store and transfer the funds that support their survival and operations. Terrorist organizations use a variety of financial systems, including formal banking, wire transfers, debit and other stored value cards, online value storage and value transfer systems, the informal *hawala* system, and cash couriers. Terrorist organizations may be able to take advantage of such financial systems either as the result of willful complicity by financial institutions or as the result of poor oversight and monitoring practices. Domestically, we have hardened our financial systems against terrorist abuse by promulgating effective regulations, requiring financial institutions to report suspicious transactions, and building effective public/private partnerships. We will continue to work with foreign partners to ensure they develop and implement similar regulations, requirements, and partnerships with their financial institutions. We also will continue to use the domestic and international designation and targeted sanctions regimes provided by, among other mechanisms, Executive Order 13224, USA Patriot Act Section 311, and United Nations Security Council Resolution 1267 and subsequent resolutions. These tools identify and isolate those actors who form part of terrorist networks or facilitate their activities.

Institutionalizing Our Strategy for Long-term Success

The War on Terror will be a long war. Yet we have mobilized to win other long wars, and we can and will win this one. During the Cold War we created an array of domestic and international institutions and enduring partnerships to defeat the threat of communism. Today, we require similar transformational structures to carry forward the fight against terror and to help ensure our ultimate success:

- ***Establish and maintain international standards of accountability.*** States that have sovereign rights also have sovereign responsibilities, including the responsibility to combat terrorism. The international community has developed a compelling body of international obligations relating to counterterrorism. Twelve universal conventions and protocols in force against terrorism have been developed under the auspices of the United Nations as well as various U.N. Security Council Resolutions related to combating terror. These include UNSCR 1373, which imposes binding obligations on all states to suppress and prevent terrorist financing, improve their border controls, enhance information sharing and law enforcement cooperation, suppress the recruitment of terrorists, and deny them sanctuary.

The Group of Eight (G-8) along with other multilateral and regional bodies also have been instrumental in developing landmark counterterrorism standards and best practices that have been adopted by international standard-setting organizations. But our obligations are not static. We will collaborate with our partners to update and tailor international obligations to meet the evolving nature of the terrorist enemies and threats we face. We also will work to ensure that each country is both willing and able to meet its counterterrorist responsibilities. Finally, we will not just continually monitor whether we and the community of nations are meeting these standards but will evaluate if we are achieving results both individually and collectively.

Strengthen coalitions and partnerships. Since September 11, most of our important successes against al-Qaida and other terrorist organizations have been made possible through effective partnerships. Continued success depends on the actions of a powerful coalition of nations maintaining a united front against terror. Multilateral groups such as the International Maritime Organization and the International Civil Aviation Organization, as well as regional organizations such as the Asia-Pacific Economic Cooperation, the Organization of American States, NATO, the European Union, the African Union, and the Association of South East Asia Nations, among others, are essential elements of this front.

- We will ensure that such international cooperation is an enduring feature of the long war we will fight. We will continue to leverage the comparative advantage of these institutions and organizations – drawing on what each does best in counterterrorism, from setting standards to developing regional strategies to providing forums for training and education. Indeed, a significant part of this effort includes expanding partnership capacity. We are building the capacity of foreign partners in all areas of counterterrorism activities, including strengthening their ability to conduct law enforcement, intelligence, and military counterterrorism operations. Through the provision of training, equipment, and other assistance, the United States, along with a coalition of willing and able states and organizations, will enhance the ability of partners across the globe to attack and defeat terrorists, deny them funding and freedom of movement, secure their critical infrastructures, and deny terrorists access to WMD and safehavens. Ultimately, it will be essential for our partners to come together to facilitate appropriate international, regional, and local solutions to the challenges of terrorism.

Enhance government architecture and interagency collaboration. In the aftermath of September 11, we have enhanced our counterterrorism architecture and interagency collaboration by setting clear national priorities and transforming the government to achieve those priorities. We have established the Department of Homeland Security, bringing under one authority 22 Federal entities with vital roles to play in preventing terrorist attacks within the Homeland, reducing America's vulnerability to terrorism, and minimizing the damage and facilitating the recovery from attacks that do occur. We have reorganized the Intelligence Community. The Director of National Intelligence (DNI) was created to better integrate the efforts of the Community into a more unified, coordinated, and effective whole. The DNI also launched a new Open Source Center to coordinate open source intelligence and ensure this information is integrated into Intelligence Community products.

In addition, a National Counterterrorism Center (NCTC) was established to serve as a multi-agency center analyzing and integrating all intelligence pertaining to terrorism, including threats to U.S. interests at home and abroad. NCTC also is responsible for developing, implementing, and assessing the effectiveness of strategic operational planning efforts to achieve counterterrorism objectives. We similarly established a National Counterproliferation Center to manage and coordinate planning and activities in those areas.

The transformation extends to the Federal Bureau of Investigation, which, with the help of legislation such as the USA Patriot Act, is now more fully integrated with the Intelligence Community, has refocused its efforts on preventing terrorism, and has been provided important tools to pursue this mission. CIA also has transformed to fulfill its role to provide overall direction for and coordination of overseas human intelligence operations of Intelligence Community elements. In addition, the Department of the Treasury created the Office of Terrorism and Financial Intelligence to arm ourselves for the long term with the intelligence and tools to undercut the financial underpinnings of terrorism around the world.

The Department of Defense also is preparing to meet a wider range of asymmetric challenges by restructuring its capabilities, rearranging its global posture, and adapting its forces to be better positioned to fight the War on Terror. This includes significantly expanding Special Operations Forces, increasing the capabilities of its general purpose forces to conduct irregular warfare operations, and initiating the largest rearrangement of its global force posture since the end of World War II.

The Department of State is implementing a new framework for foreign assistance to establish more integrated and coherent strategic direction and tactical plans to meet our current and long-term challenges, including terrorism. The State Department also is repositioning its domestic and overseas staff to better promote America's policies and interests and have more direct local and regional impact. This transformational diplomacy positions State to work with partners around the world to build and sustain democratic, well-governed states that will respond to the needs of their people and conduct themselves responsibly in the international system.

We will sustain the transformation already under way in these and other departments and agencies. Moreover, we will continue to build and strengthen a unified team across the counterterrorism community, and a key component of this effort will be fostering "jointness." Where practicable, we will increase interagency and intergovernmental assignments for personnel in counterterrorism-related positions. This will help to break down organizational stovepipes and advance the exchange of ideas and practices for more effective counterterrorism efforts.

Foster intellectual and human capital. To better prepare ourselves for a generational struggle against terrorism and the extremist ideologies fueling it, we will create an expert community of counterterrorism professionals. We will continue to establish more systematic programs for the development and education of current professionals in counterterrorism-related fields. We will substantively expand our existing programs with curricula that include not only training in counterterrorism policies, plans and planning, strategies, and legal authorities, but continuing education in appropriate area studies, religious philosophies, and languages. We also will ensure that personnel throughout all levels of government and in all fields related to combating terror are invited to participate.

Yet such development and education programs must not be restricted to current counterterrorism personnel. We will support multidisciplinary studies throughout our educational system to build a knowledgeable pool of counterterrorism recruits for the future. The recent National Security Language Initiative is an essential step forward. It will help to expand U.S. foreign language education beginning in early childhood and continuing throughout formal schooling and into the workforce. Our efforts to foster intellectual and human capital also will extend beyond our borders—to academic and nongovernmental forums with our international partners to discuss and enhance our knowledge about the critical counterterrorism challenges we confront.

In the War on Terror, there is also a need for all elements of our Nation —from Federal, State, and local governments to the private sector to local communities and individual citizens—to help create and share responsibilities in a Culture of Preparedness. This Culture of Preparedness, which applies to all catastrophes and all hazards, natural or man-made, rests on four principles: a shared acknowledgement of the certainty of future catastrophes and that creating a prepared Nation will be a continuing challenge; the importance of initiative and accountability at all levels of society; the role of citizen and community preparedness; and finally, the roles of each level of government and the private sector in creating a prepared Nation. Built upon a foundation of partnerships, common goals, and shared responsibility, the creation of a Culture of Preparedness will be among our most profound and enduring transformations in the broader effort to protect and defend the Homeland.

Conclusion

Since the September 11 attacks, America is safer, but we are not yet safe. We have done much to degrade al-Qaida and its affiliates and to undercut the perceived legitimacy of terrorism. Our Muslim partners are speaking out against those who seek to use their religion to justify violence and a totalitarian vision of the world. We have significantly expanded our counterterrorism coalition, transforming old adversaries into new and vital partners in the War on Terror. We have liberated more than 50 million Afghans and Iraqis from despotism, terrorism, and oppression, permitting the first free elections in recorded history for either nation. In addition, we have transformed our governmental institutions and framework to wage a generational struggle. There will continue to be challenges ahead, but along with our partners, we will attack terrorism and its ideology, and bring hope and freedom to the people of the world. This is how we will win the War on Terror.

Appendix B

The Commission on the Intelligence Capabilities of the United States Regarding Weapons of Mass Destruction: Overview of the Report to the President of the United States, March 31, 2005

Introduction

On the brink of war, and in front of the whole world, the United States government asserted that Saddam Hussein had reconstituted his nuclear weapons program, had biological weapons and mobile biological weapon production facilities, and had stockpiled and was producing chemical weapons. All of this was based on the assessments of the U.S. Intelligence Community. And not one bit of it could be confirmed when the war was over.

While the intelligence services of many other nations also thought that Iraq had weapons of mass destruction, in the end it was the United States that put its credibility on the line, making this one of the most public—and most damaging—intelligence failures in recent American history.

This failure was in large part the result of analytical shortcomings; intelligence analysts were too wedded to their assumptions about Saddam's intentions. But it was also a failure on the part of those who collect intelligence—CIA's and the Defense Intelligence Agency's (DIA) spies, the National Security Agency's (NSA) eavesdroppers, and the National Geospatial Intelligence Agency's (NGA) imagery experts.* In the end, those agencies collected precious little intelligence for the analysts to analyze, and much of what they did collect was either worthless or misleading. Finally, it was a failure to communicate effectively with policymakers; the Intelligence Community didn't adequately explain just how little good intelligence it had—or how much its assessments were driven by assumptions and inferences rather than concrete evidence.

Was the failure in Iraq typical of the Community's performance? Or was Iraq, as one senior intelligence official told the Commission, a sort of "perfect storm"—a one-time breakdown caused by a rare confluence of events that conspired to create a bad result? In our view, it was neither.

> [While we have attempted to write this report in a way that is accessible to those not acquainted with the world of intelligence, we have included a primer on the U.S. Intelligence Community at Appendix C of this report for readers who are new to the subject.]

The failures we found in Iraq are not repeated everywhere. The Intelligence Community played a key role, for example, in getting Libya to renounce weapons of mass destruction and in exposing the long-running A.Q. Khan nuclear proliferation network. It is engaged in imaginative, successful (and highly classified) operations in many parts of the world. Tactical support to counterterrorism efforts is excellent, and there are signs of a boldness that would have been unimaginable before September 11, 2001.

But neither was Iraq a "perfect storm." The flaws we found in the Intelligence Community's Iraq performance are still all too common. Across the board, the Intelligence Community knows disturbingly little about the nuclear programs of many of the world's most dangerous actors. In some cases, it knows less now than it did five or ten years ago. As for biological weapons, despite years of Presidential concern, the Intelligence Community has struggled to address this threat.

To be sure, the Intelligence Community is full of talented, dedicated people. But they seem to be working harder and harder just to maintain a *status quo* that is increasingly irrelevant to the new challenges presented by weapons of mass destruction. Our collection agencies are often unable to gather intelligence on the very things we care the most about. Too often, analysts simply accept these gaps; they do little to help collectors identify new opportunities, and they do not always tell decisionmakers just how limited their knowledge really is.

Taken together, these shortcomings reflect the Intelligence Community's struggle to confront an environment that has changed radically over the past decade. For almost 50 years after the passage of the National Security Act of 1947, the Intelligence Community's resources were overwhelmingly trained on a single threat—the Soviet Union, its nuclear arsenal, its massive conventional forces, and its activities around the world. By comparison, today's priority intelligence targets are greater in number (there are dozens of entities that could strike a devastating blow against the United States) and are often more diffuse in character (they include not only states but also nebulous transnational terror and proliferation networks). What's more, some of the weapons that would be most dangerous in the hands of terrorists or rogue nations are difficult to detect. Much of the technology, equipment, and materials necessary to develop biological and chemical weapons, for example, also has legitimate commercial applications. Biological weapons themselves can be built in small-scale facilities that are easy to conceal, and weapons-grade uranium can be effectively shielded from traditional detection techniques. At the same time, advances in technology have made the job of technical intelligence collection exceedingly difficult.

The demands of this new environment can only be met by broad and deep change in the Intelligence Community. The Intelligence Community we have today is buried beneath an avalanche of demands for "current intelligence"—the pressing need to meet the tactical requirements of the day. Current intelligence in support of military and other action is necessary, of course. But we also need an Intelligence Community with *strategic* capabilities: it must be equipped to develop long-term plans for penetrating today's difficult targets, and to identify political and social trends shaping the threats that lie over the horizon. We can imagine no threat that demands greater strategic focus from the Intelligence Community than that posed by nuclear, biological, and chemical weapons.

The Intelligence Community is also fragmented, loosely managed, and poorly coordinated; the 15 intelligence organizations are a "Community" in name only and rarely act with a unity of purpose. What we need is an Intelligence Community that is *integrated*: the Community's leadership must be capable of allocating and directing the Community's resources in a coordinated way. The strengths of our distinct collection agencies must be brought to bear together on the most difficult intelligence problems. At the same time we need a Community that preserves diversity of analysis, and that encourages structured debate among agencies and analysts over the interpretation of information.

Perhaps above all, the Intelligence Community is too slow to change the way it does business. It is reluctant to use new human and technical collection methods; it is behind the curve in applying cutting-edge technologies; and it has not adapted its personnel practices and incentives structures to fit the needs of a new job market. What we need is an Intelligence Community that is flexible—able to respond nimbly to an ever-shifting threat environment and to the rapid pace of today's technological changes.

In short, to succeed in confronting today's and tomorrow's threats, the Intelligence Community must be transformed—a goal that would be difficult to meet even in the best of all possible worlds. And we do not live in the best of worlds. The CIA and NSA may be sleek and omniscient in the movies, but in real life they and other intelligence agencies are vast government bureaucracies. They are bureaucracies filled with talented people and armed with sophisticated technological tools, but talent and tools do not suspend the iron laws of bureaucratic behavior. Like government bodies everywhere, intelligence agencies are prone to develop self-reinforcing, risk averse cultures that take outside advice badly. While laudable steps were taken to improve our intelligence agencies after September 11, 2001, the agencies have done less in response to the failures over Iraq, and we believe that many within those agencies do not accept the conclusion that we reached after our year of study: that the Community needs fundamental change if it is to successfully confront the threats of the 21st century.

We are not the first to say this. Indeed, commission after commission has identified some of the same fundamental failings we see in the Intelligence Community, usually to little effect. The Intelligence Community is a closed world, and many insiders admitted to us that *it has an almost perfect record of resisting external recommendations.*

But the present moment offers an unprecedented opportunity to overcome this resistance. About halfway through our inquiry, Congress passed the *Intelligence Reform and Terrorism Prevention Act of 2004*, which became a sort of a *deus ex machina* in our deliberations. The act created a Director of National Intelligence (DNI). The DNI's role could have been a purely coordinating position, with a limited staff and authority to match. Or it could have been something closer to a "Secretary of Intelligence," with full authority over the principal intelligence agencies and clear responsibility for their actions—which also might well have been consistent with a small bureaucratic superstructure. In the end, the DNI created by the intelligence reform legislation was neither of these things; the office is given broad responsibilities but only ambiguous authorities. While we might have chosen a different solution, we are not writing on a blank slate. So our focus has been in large part on how to make the new intelligence structure work, and in particular on giving the DNI tools (and support staff) to match his large responsibilities.

We are mindful, however, that there is a serious risk in creating too large a bureaucratic structure to serve the DNI: the risk that decisionmaking in the field, which sometimes requires quick action, will be improperly delayed. Balancing these two imperatives—necessary agility of operational execution and thoughtful coordination of intelligence activities—is, in our view, the DNI's greatest challenge.

In considering organizational issues, we did not delude ourselves that organizational structure alone can solve problems. More than many parts of government, the culture of the Intelligence Community is formed in the field, where organizational changes at headquarters are felt only lightly. We understand the limits of organizational change, and many of our recommendations go beyond organizational issues and would, if enacted, directly affect the way that intelligence is collected and analyzed. But we regret that we were not able to make such detailed proposals for some of the most important technical collection agencies, such as NSA and NGA. For those agencies, and for the many other issues that we could only touch upon, we must trust that our broader institutional recommendations will enable necessary reform. The DNI that we envision will have the budget and management tools to dig deep into the culture of each agency and to force changes where needed.

This Overview—and, in far more detail, the report that follows—offers our conclusions on what needs to be done. We begin by describing the results of our case studies—which include Iraq, Libya, Afghanistan, and others—and the lessons they teach about the Intelligence Community's current capabilities and weaknesses. We then offer our recommendations for reform based upon those lessons.

Three final notes before proceeding. First, our main tasks were to find out how the Intelligence Community erred in Iraq and to recommend changes to avoid such errors in the future. This is a task that often lends itself to hubris and to second-guessing, and we have been humbled by the difficult judgments that had to be made about Iraq and its weapons programs. We are humbled too by the complexity of the management and technical challenges intelligence professionals face today. We recommend substantial changes, and we believe deeply that such changes are necessary, but we recognize that other reasonable observers could come to a different view on some of these questions.

Second, no matter how much we improve the Intelligence Community, weapons of mass destruction will continue to pose an enormous threat. Intelligence will always be imperfect and, as history persuades us, surprise can never be completely prevented. Moreover, we cannot expect spies, satellites, and analysts to constitute our only defense. As our biological weapons recommendations make abundantly clear, all national capabilities—regulatory, military, and diplomatic—must be used to combat proliferation.

Finally, we emphasize two points about the scope of this Commission's charter, particularly with respect to the Iraq question. First, we were *not* asked to determine whether Saddam Hussein had weapons of mass destruction. That was the mandate of the Iraq Survey Group; our mission is to investigate the reasons why the Intelligence Community's pre-war assessments were so different from what the Iraq Survey Group found after the war. Second, we were not authorized to investigate how policymakers used the intelligence assessments they received from the Intelligence Community. Accordingly, while we interviewed a host of current and former policymakers during the course of our investigation, the purpose of those interviews was to learn about how the Intelligence Community reached and communicated its judgments about Iraq's weapons programs—not to review how policymakers subsequently used that information.

Looking Back: Case Studies in Failure and Success

Our first task was to evaluate the Intelligence Community's performance in assessing the nuclear, biological, and chemical weapons activities of three countries: Iraq, Afghanistan, and Libya. In addition, we studied U.S. capabilities against other pressing intelligence problems—including Iran, North Korea, Russia, China, and terrorism. We wanted a range of studies so we would not judge the Intelligence Community solely on its handling of Iraq, which was—however important—a single intelligence target. In all, the studies paint a representative picture. It is the picture of an Intelligence Community that urgently needs to be changed.

Iraq: An Overview

In October 2002, at the request of members of Congress, the National Intelligence Council produced a National Intelligence Estimate (NIE)—the most authoritative intelligence assessment produced by the Intelligence Community—which concluded that Iraq was reconstituting its nuclear weapons program and was actively pursuing a nuclear device. According to the exhaustive study of the Iraq Survey Group, this assessment was almost completely wrong. The NIE said that Iraq's biological weapons capability was larger and more advanced than before the Gulf War and that Iraq possessed mobile biological weapons production facilities. This was wrong. The NIE further stated that Iraq had renewed production of chemical weapons, including mustard, sarin, GF, and VX, and that it had accumulated chemical stockpiles of between 100 and 500 metric tons. All of this was also wrong. Finally, the NIE concluded that Iraq had unmanned aerial vehicles that were probably intended for the delivery of biological weapons, and ballistic missiles that had ranges greater than the United Nations' permitted 150 kilometer range. In truth, the aerial vehicles were not for biological weapons; some of Iraq's missiles were, however, capable of traveling more than 150 kilometers. The Intelligence Community's Iraq assessments were, in short, riddled with errors.

Contrary to what some defenders of the Intelligence Community have since asserted, these errors were *not* the result of a few harried months in 2002. Most of the fundamental errors were made and communicated to policymakers well before the now-infamous NIE of October 2002, and were not corrected in the months between the NIE and the start of the war. They were not isolated or random failings. Iraq had been an intelligence challenge at the forefront of U.S. attention for over a decade. It was a known adversary that had already fought one war with the United States and seemed increasingly likely to fight another. But, after ten years of effort, the Intelligence Community still had no good intelligence on the status of Iraq's weapons programs. Our full report examines these issues in detail. Here we limit our discussion to the central lessons to be learned from this episode.

The first lesson is that the Intelligence Community cannot analyze and disseminate information that it does not have. The Community's Iraq assessment was crippled by its inability to collect meaningful intelligence on Iraq's nuclear, biological, and chemical weapons programs. The second lesson follows from the first: lacking good intelligence, analysts and collectors fell back on old assumptions and inferences drawn from Iraq's past behavior and intentions.

The Intelligence Community had learned a hard lesson after the 1991 Gulf War, which revealed that the Intelligence Community's pre-war assessments had underestimated Iraq's nuclear program and had failed to identify all of its chemical weapons storage sites. Shaken by the magnitude of their errors, intelligence analysts were determined not to fall victim again to the same mistake. This tendency was only reinforced by later events. Saddam acted to the very end like a man with much to hide. And the dangers of underestimating our enemies were deeply underscored by the attacks of September 11, 2001.

Throughout the 1990s, therefore, the Intelligence Community assumed that Saddam's Iraq was up to no good—that Baghdad had maintained its nuclear, biological, and chemical technical expertise, had kept its biological and chemical weapons production capabilities, and possessed significant stockpiles of chemical agents and weapons precursors. Since Iraq's leadership had not changed since 1991, the Intelligence Community also believed that these capabilities would be further revved up as soon as inspectors left Iraq. Saddam's continuing cat-and-mouse parrying with international inspectors only hardened these assumptions.

These experiences contributed decisively to the Intelligence Community's erroneous National Intelligence Estimate of October 2002. That is not to say that its fears and assumptions were foolish or even unreasonable. At some point, however, these premises stopped being working hypotheses and became more or less unrebuttable conclusions; worse, the intelligence system became too willing to find confirmations of them in evidence that should have been recognized at the time to be of dubious reliability. Collectors and analysts too readily accepted any evidence that supported their theory that Iraq had stockpiles and was developing weapons programs, and they explained away or simply disregarded evidence that pointed in the other direction.

Even in hindsight, those assumptions have a powerful air of common sense. If the Intelligence Community's estimate and other pre-war intelligence had relied principally and explicitly on inferences the Community drew from

Iraq's past conduct, the estimate would still have been wrong, but it would have been far more defensible. For good reason, it was hard to conclude that Saddam Hussein had indeed abandoned his weapons programs. But a central flaw of the NIE is that it took these defensible assumptions and swathed them in the mystique of intelligence, providing secret information that seemed to support them but was in fact nearly worthless, if not misleading. The NIE simply didn't communicate how weak the underlying intelligence was.

This was, moreover, a problem that was not limited to the NIE. Our review found that *after* the publication of the October 2002 NIE but *before* Secretary of State Colin Powell's February 2003 address to the United Nations, intelligence officials within the CIA failed to convey to policymakers new information casting serious doubt on the reliability of a human intelligence source known as "Curveball." This occurred despite the pivotal role Curveball's information played in the Intelligence Community's assessment of Iraq's biological weapons programs, and in spite of Secretary Powell's efforts to strip every dubious piece of information out of his proposed speech. In this instance, once again, the Intelligence Community failed to give policymakers a full understanding of the frailties of the intelligence on which they were relying.

Finally, we closely examined the possibility that intelligence analysts were pressured by policymakers to change their judgments about Iraq's nuclear, biological, and chemical weapons programs. The analysts who worked Iraqi weapons issues universally agreed that in no instance did political pressure cause them to skew or alter any of their analytical judgments. That said, it is hard to deny the conclusion that intelligence analysts worked in an environment that did not encourage skepticism about the conventional wisdom.

Other Case Studies: An Overview

Our remaining case studies present a more mixed picture. On the positive side, Libya is fundamentally a success story. The Intelligence Community assessed correctly the state of Libya's nuclear and chemical weapons programs, and the Intelligence Community's use of new techniques to penetrate the A.Q. Khan network allowed the U.S. government to pressure Libya into dismantling those programs. In counterterrorism, the Intelligence Community has made great strides since September 11, in particular with respect to tactical operations overseas. These successes stemmed from isolated efforts that need to be replicated in other areas of intelligence; in the case of Libya, from innovative collection techniques and, in the case of terrorism, from an impressive fusion of interagency intelligence capabilities.

But we also reviewed the state of the Intelligence Community's knowledge about the unconventional weapons programs of several countries that pose current proliferation threats, including Iran, North Korea, China, and

Russia. We cannot discuss many of our findings from these studies in our unclassified report, but we can say here that we found that we have only limited access to critical information about several of these high-priority intelligence targets.

Lessons Learned from the Case Studies

Our case studies revealed failures and successes that ran the gamut of the intelligence process. Although each of these studies is covered in far greater detail in the report itself, we include here a summary of the central lessons we drew from them.

Poor target development: not getting intelligence on the issues we care about most. You can't analyze intelligence that you don't have—and our case studies resoundingly demonstrate how little we know about some of our highest priority intelligence targets. It is clear that in today's context the traditional collection techniques employed by individual collection agencies have lost much of their power to surprise our adversaries. The successful penetrations of "hard targets" that we did find were usually the result either of an innovative collection technique or of a creative integration of collection capabilities across agencies. In general, however, the Intelligence Community has not developed the long-term, coordinated collection strategies that are necessary to penetrate today's intelligence targets.

Lack of rigorous analysis. Long after the Community's assessment of Iraq had begun to fall apart, one of the main drafters of the NIE told us that, if he had to grade it, he would still give the NIE an "A." By that, he presumably meant that the NIE fully met the standards for analysis that the Community had set for itself. That is the problem. The scope and quality of analysis has eroded badly in the Intelligence Community and it must be restored. In part, this is a matter of tradecraft and training; in part, too, it is a matter of expertise.

Analytic "tradecraft"—the way analysts think, research, evaluate evidence, write, and communicate—must be strengthened. In many instances, we found finished intelligence that was loosely reasoned, ill-supported, and poorly communicated. Perhaps most worrisome, we found too many analytic products that obscured how little the Intelligence Community actually *knew* about an issue and how much their conclusions rested on inference and assumptions. We believe these tendencies must be reversed if decision-makers are to have confidence in the intelligence they receive. And equally important, analysts must be willing to admit what they don't know in order to focus future collection efforts. Conversely, policymakers must be prepared to accept uncertainties and qualifications in intelligence judgments and not expect greater precision than the evaluated data permits.

Good "tradecraft" without expertise, however, will only get you so far. Our case studies identified areas in which the Community's level of expertise was far below what it should be. In several instances, the Iraq assessments rested on failures of technical analysis that should have been obvious at the time—failure to understand facts about weapons technology, for example, or failures to detect obvious forgeries. Technical expertise, particularly relating to weapons systems, has fallen sharply in the past ten years. And in other areas, such as biotechnology, the Intelligence Community is well behind the private sector.

But the problem of expertise goes well beyond technical knowledge. During the Cold War, the Intelligence Community built up an impressive body of expertise on Soviet society, organization, and ideology, as well as on the Soviet threat. Regrettably, no equivalent talent pool exists today for the study of Islamic extremism. In some cases, the security clearance process limits the Intelligence Community's ability to recruit analysts with contacts among relevant groups and with experience living overseas. Similarly, some security rules limit the ways in which analysts can develop substantive expertise. Finally, poor training or bad habits lead analysts to rely too much on secret information and to use non-clandestine and public information too little. Non-clandestine sources of information are critical to understanding societal, cultural, and political trends, but they are insufficiently utilized.

Lack of political context—and imagination. The October 2002 NIE contained an extensive technical analysis of Iraq's suspected weapons programs but little serious analysis of the socio-political situation in Iraq, or the motives and intentions of Iraqi leadership—which, in a dictatorship like Iraq, really meant understanding Saddam. It seems unlikely to us that weapons experts used to combing reports for tidbits on technical programs would ever have asked: "Is Saddam bluffing?" or "Could he have decided to suspend his weapons programs until sanctions are lifted?" But an analyst steeped in Iraq's politics and culture at least *might* have asked those questions, and, of course, those turn out to be the questions that could have led the Intelligence Community closer to the truth. In that respect, the analysts displayed a lack of imagination. The Iraq example also reflects the Intelligence Community's increasing tendency to separate regional, technical, and (now) terrorism analysis—a trend that is being exacerbated by the gravitational pull toward centers like the National Counterterrorism Center (NCTC).

Overemphasis on and underperformance in daily intelligence products. As problematic as the October 2002 NIE was, it was not the Community's biggest analytic failure on Iraq. Even more misleading was the river of intelligence that flowed from the CIA to top policymakers over long periods of time—in the President's Daily Brief (PDB) and in its more widely distributed companion, the Senior Executive Intelligence Brief (SEIB). These daily reports were, if anything, more alarmist and less nuanced than the NIE. It was not that the intelligence was markedly different. Rather, it was that the PDBs and SEIBs, with their attention-grabbing headlines and drumbeat of repetition, left an impression of many corroborating reports where in fact there were very few sources. And in other instances, intelligence suggesting the existence of weapons programs was conveyed to senior policy-makers, but later information casting doubt upon the validity of that intelligence was not. In ways both subtle and not so subtle, the daily reports seemed to be "selling" intelligence—in order to keep its customers, or at least the First Customer, interested.

Inadequate information sharing. There is little doubt that, at least in the context of counterterrorism, information sharing has improved substantially since September 11. This is in no small part due to the creation of the Terrorist Threat Integration Center (now NCTC) and the increased practice of housing collectors and analysts together, which provides a real-world solution to some of the bureaucratic and institutional barriers that exist between the big intelligence-collecting agencies. But in the three and a half years since September 11, this push to share information has not spread to other areas, including counterproliferation, where sharing is also badly needed. Furthermore, even in the counterterrorism context, information sharing still depends too much on physical co-location and personal relationships as opposed to integrated, Community-wide information networks. Equally problematic, individual departments and agencies continue to act as though they own the information they collect, forcing other agencies to pry information from them. Similarly, much information deemed "operational" by the CIA and FBI isn't routinely shared, even though analysts have repeatedly stressed its importance. All of this reveals that extensive work remains yet to be done.

Poor human intelligence. When the October 2002 NIE was written the United States had little human intelligence on Iraq's nuclear, biological, and chemical weapons programs and virtually no human intelligence on leadership intentions. While classification prevents us from getting into the details, the picture is much the same with respect to other dangerous threats. We recognize that espionage is always chancy at best; 50 years of pounding away at the Soviet Union resulted in only a handful of truly important human sources. Still, we have no choice but to do better. Old approaches to human intelligence alone are not the answer. Countries that threaten us are well aware of our human intelligence services' *modus operandi* and they know how to counter it. More of the same is unlikely to work. Innovation is needed. The CIA deserves credit for its efforts to discover and penetrate the A.Q. Khan network, and it needs to put more emphasis on other innovative human intelligence methods.

Worse than having no human sources is being seduced by a human source who is telling lies. In fact, the Community's position on Iraq's biological weapons program was largely determined by sources who were telling lies—most notably a source provided by a foreign intelligence service through the Defense Intelligence Agency. Why DIA and the rest of the Community didn't find out that the source was lying is a story of poor asset validation practices and the problems inherent in relying on semi-cooperative liaison services. That the NIE (and other reporting) didn't make clear to policymakers how heavily it relied on a single source that no American intelligence officer had ever met, and about whose reliability several intelligence professionals had expressed serious concern, is a damning comment on the Intelligence Community's practices.

The challenge to traditional signals intelligence. Signals intelligence—the interception of radio, telephone, and computer communications—has historically been a primary source of good intelligence. But changes in telecommunications technology have brought new challenges. This was the case in Iraq, where the Intelligence Community lost access to important aspects of Iraqi communications, and it remains the case elsewhere. We offer a brief additional discussion of some of the modern challenges facing signals intelligence in our classified report, but we cannot discuss this information in an unclassified format.

Regaining signals intelligence access must be a top priority. The collection agencies are working hard to restore some of the access that they have lost; and they've had some successes. And again, many of these recent steps in the right direction are the result of innovative examples of cross-agency cooperation. In addition, successful signals intelligence will require a sustained research and development effort to bring cutting-edge technology to operators and analysts. Success on this front will require greater willingness to accept financial costs, political risks, and even human casualties.

Declining utility of traditional imagery intelligence against unconventional weapons programs. The imagery collection systems that were designed largely to work against the Soviet Union's military didn't work very well against Iraq's unconventional weapons program, and our review found that they aren't working very well against other priority targets, either. That's because our adversaries are getting better at denial and deception, and because the threat is changing. Again, we offer details about the challenges to imagery intelligence in our classified report that we cannot provide here.

Making the problem even more difficult, there is little that traditional imagery can tell us about chemical and biological facilities. Biological and chemical weapons programs for the most part can exist inside commercial buildings with no suspicious signatures. This means that we can get piles of incredibly sharp photos of an adversary's chemical factories, and we still will not know much about its chemical weapons programs. We can still see a lot—and imagery intelligence remains valuable in many contexts, including support to military operations and when used in conjunction with other collection disciplines—but too often what we can see doesn't tell us what we need to know about nuclear, biological, and chemical weapons.

Measurement and signature intelligence (MASINT) is not sufficiently developed. The collection of technologies known as MASINT, which includes a virtual grab bag of advanced collection and analytic methods, is not yet making a significant contribution to our intelligence efforts. In Iraq, MASINT played a negligible role. As in other contexts, we believe that the Intelligence Community should continue to pursue new technology aggressively—whether it is called MASINT, imagery, or signals intelligence. Innovation will be necessary to defeat our adversaries' denial and deception.

An absence of strong leadership. For over a year, despite unambiguous presidential direction, a turf battle raged between CIA's Counterterrorist Center (CTC) and the Terrorist Threat Integration Center (now NCTC). The two organizations fought over roles, responsibilities, and resources, and the Intelligence Community's leadership was unable to solve the problem. The intelligence reform act may put an end to this particular conflict, but we believe that the story reflects a larger, more pervasive problem within the Intelligence Community: the difficulty of making a decision and imposing the consequences on all agencies throughout the Community. Time and time again we have uncovered instances like this, where powerful agencies fight to a debilitating stalemate masked as consensus, because no one in the Community has been able to make a decision and then make it stick. The best hope for filling this gap is an empowered DNI.

Looking Forward: Our Recommendations for Change

Our case studies collectively paint a picture of an Intelligence Community with serious deficiencies that span the intelligence process. Stated succinctly, it has too little *integration* and too little *innovation* to succeed in the 21st century. It rarely adopts integrated strategies for penetrating high-priority targets; decisionmakers lack authority to resolve agency disputes; and it develops too few innovative ways of gathering intelligence.

This section summarizes our major recommendations on how to change this state of affairs so that full value can be derived from the many bright, dedicated, and deeply committed professionals within the Intelligence Community. We begin at the top, and suggest how to use the opportunity presented by the new intelligence reform legislation to bring better integration and management to the Intelligence Community. Our management recommendations are developed in greater detail in Chapter 6 of our report. We next offer recommendations that would improve intelligence collection (Chapter 7) and analysis (Chapter 8). Then we examine several specific and important intelligence challenges—improving information sharing (Chapter

9); integrating domestic and foreign intelligence in a way that both satisfies national security imperatives and safeguards civil liberties (Chapter 10); organizing the Community's counterintelligence mission (Chapter 11); and a largely classified chapter on managing covert action (Chapter 12). We then devote a stand-alone chapter to examining the most dangerous unconventional weapons challenges the Intelligence Community faces today and offer specific prescriptions for improving our intelligence capabilities against these threats (Chapter 13).

Leadership and Management: Forging an Integrated Intelligence Community

A former senior Defense Department official described today's Intelligence Community as "not so much poorly managed as unmanaged." We agree. Everywhere we looked, we found important (and obvious) issues of interagency coordination that went unattended, sensible Community-wide proposals blocked by pockets of resistance, and critical disputes left to fester. Strong interagency cooperation was more likely to result from bilateral "treaties" between big agencies than from Community-level management. This ground was well-plowed by the 9/11 Commission and by several other important assessments of the Intelligence Community over the past decade.

In the chapter of our report devoted to management (Chapter 6), we offer detailed recommendations that we believe will equip the new Director of National Intelligence to forge today's loose confederation of 15 separate intelligence operations into a real, integrated Intelligence Community. A short summary of our more important management recommendations follows:

Strong leadership and management of the Intelligence Community are indispensable. Virtually every senior intelligence official acknowledged the difficulty of leading and managing the Intelligence Community. Along with acting as the President's principal intelligence advisor, this will be the DNI's main job. His success in that job will determine the fate of many other necessary reforms. We thus recommend ways in which the DNI can use his limited, but not insignificant, authorities over money and people. No matter what, the DNI will not be able to run the Intelligence Community alone. He will need to create a management structure that allows him to see deep into the Intelligence Community's component agencies, and he will need to work closely with the other cabinet secretaries—especially the Secretary of Defense—for whom several Intelligence Community agencies also work. New procedures are particularly needed in the budget area, where today's Intelligence Community has a wholly inadequate Planning, Programming, and Budgeting System.

Organize around missions. One of the most significant problems we identified in today's Intelligence Community is a lack of cross-Community focus on priority intelligence missions. By this, we mean that in most cases there is not one office, or one individual, who is responsible for making sure the Intelligence Community is doing all it can to collect and analyze intelligence on a subject like proliferation, or a country like Iran. Instead, intelligence agencies allocate their scarce resources among intelligence priorities in ways that seem sensible to them but are not optimal from a Community-wide perspective. The DNI needs management structures and processes that ensure a strategic, Community-level focus on priority intelligence missions. The specific device we propose is the creation of several "Mission Managers" on the DNI staff who are responsible for developing strategies for all aspects of intelligence relating to a priority intelligence target: the Mission Manager for China, for instance, would be responsible for driving collection on the China target, watching over China analysis, and serving as a clearinghouse for senior policymakers seeking China expertise.

Establish a National Counter Proliferation Center. The new intelligence legislation creates one "national center"—the National Counterterrorism Center (NCTC)—and suggests the creation of a second, similar center devoted to counterproliferation issues. We agree that a National Counter Proliferation Center (NCPC) should be established but believe that it should be fundamentally different in character from the NCTC. The NCTC is practically a separate agency; its large staff is responsible not only for conducting counterterrorism analysis and intelligence gathering but also for "strategic operational planning" in support of counterterrorism policy. In contrast, we believe that the NCPC should be a relatively small center (*i.e.*, fewer than 100 people); it should primarily play a *management and coordination* function by overseeing analysis and collection on nuclear, biological, and chemical weapons across the Intelligence Community. In addition, although we agree that government-wide strategic planning is required to confront proliferation threats, we believe that entities other than the NCPC— such as a Joint Interagency Task Force we propose to coordinate interdiction efforts—should perform this function.

Build a modern workforce. The intelligence reform legislation grants the DNI substantial personnel authorities. In our view, these authorities come none too soon. The Intelligence Community has difficulty recruiting and retaining individuals with critically important skill sets—such as technical and scientific expertise, and facility with foreign languages—and has not adapted well to the diverse cultures and settings in which today's intelligence experts must operate. We propose the creation of a new human resources authority in the Office of the DNI to develop Community-wide personnel policies and overcome these systemic shortcomings. We also offer specific proposals aimed at encouraging "joint" assignments between intelligence agencies, improving job training at all stages of an intelligence professional's career, and building a better personnel incentive structure.

Create mechanisms for sustained oversight from outside the Intelligence Community—and for self-examination from the inside. Many sound past proposals for intelligence reform have withered on the vine. Either the Intelligence Community is inherently resistant to outside recommendations, or it lacks the institutional capacity to implement them. In either case, sustained external oversight is necessary. We recommend using the new Joint Intelligence Community Council—which comprises the DNI and the cabinet secretaries with intelligence responsibilities— as a high-level "consumer council." We also recommend the President's Foreign Intelligence Advisory Board play a more substantial advisory role. Like others before us, we suggest that the President urge Congress to reform its own procedures to provide better oversight. In particular, we recommend that the House and Senate intelligence committees create focused oversight subcommittees, that the Congress create an intelligence appropriations subcommittee and reduce the Intelligence Community's reliance on supplemental funding, and that the Senate intelligence committee be given the same authority over joint military intelligence programs and tactical intelligence programs that the House intelligence committee now exercises. Finally—and perhaps most importantly—we recommend that the DNI create mechanisms to ensure that the Intelligence Community conducts "lessons learned" and after-action studies so that it will be better equipped to identify its *own* strengths and weaknesses.

Additional Leadership and Management Recommendations

In addition to those described above, Chapter 6 of our report offers recommendations concerning:

- How to build a coordinated process for "target development"—that is, the directing of collection resources toward priority intelligence subjects;
- How to spur innovation outside individual collection agencies;
- How the DNI might handle the difficult challenges of integrating intelligence from at home and abroad, and of coordinating activities and procedures with the Department of Defense; and
- How the DNI might organize the office of the DNI to fit needed leadership and management functions into the framework created by the intelligence reform legislation.

Integrated and Innovative Collection

The intelligence failure in Iraq did not begin with faulty analysis. It began with a sweeping collection failure. The Intelligence Community simply couldn't collect good information about Iraq's nuclear, biological, or chemical programs. Regrettably, the same can be said today about other important targets, none of which will ever be easy targets—but we can and should do better.

Urging each individual collection agency to do a better job is not the answer. Where progress has been made against such targets, the key has usually been more integration and more innovation in collecting intelligence. As a result, we recommend the following:

Create a new Intelligence Community process for managing collection as an "integrated enterprise." In order to gather intelligence effectively, the Intelligence Community must develop and buy sophisticated technical collection systems, create strategies for focusing those systems on priority targets, process and exploit the data that these systems collect, and plan for the acquisition of future systems. Today, each of these functions is performed primarily within individual collection agencies, often with little or no Community-level direction or interagency coordination. We propose that the DNI create what we call an "integrated collection enterprise" for the Intelligence Community—that is, a management structure in which the Community's decentralized collection capabilities are harmonized with intelligence priorities and deployed in a coordinated way.

Create a new Human Intelligence Directorate. Both the Defense Department and the FBI are substantially increasing their human intelligence activities abroad, which heightens the risk that intelligence operations will not be properly coordinated with the CIA's human espionage operations, run by its Directorate of Operations (DO). The human intelligence activities of the Defense Department and the FBI should continue, but in the world of foreign espionage, a lack of coordination can have dangerous, even fatal, consequences. To address this pressing problem, we suggest the creation of a new Human Intelligence Directorate within the CIA, to which the present DO would be subordinate, to ensure the coordination of all U.S. agencies conducting human intelligence operations overseas. In addition to this coordination role, the Human Intelligence Directorate would serve as the focal point for Community-wide human intelligence issues, including helping to develop a national human intelligence strategy, broadening the scope of human intelligence activities, integrating (where appropriate) collection and reporting systems, and establishing Community-wide standards for training and tradecraft.

Develop innovative human intelligence techniques. The CIA's Directorate of Operations is one of the Intelligence Community's elite and storied organizations. However, the DO has remained largely wedded to the traditional model—a model that does not meet the challenges posed by terrorist organizations and nations that are "denied areas" for U.S. personnel. Accordingly, we recommend the establishment of an "Innovation Center" within the CIA's new Human Intelligence Directorate— but not within the DO. This center would spur the use of new and nontraditional methods of collecting human intelligence. In the collection chapter of our report, we also detail several new methods for collecting human intelligence that in our judgment should either be explored or used more extensively.

Create an Open Source Directorate within the CIA. We are convinced that analysts who use open source information can be more effective than those who don't. Regrettably, however, the Intelligence Community does not have an entity that collects, processes, and makes available to analysts the mass of open source information that is available in the world today. We therefore recommend the creation of an Open Source Directorate at the CIA. The directorate's mission would be to deploy sophisticated information technology to make open source information available across the Community. This would, at a minimum, mean gathering and storing digital newspapers and periodicals that are available only temporarily on the Internet and giving Intelligence Community staff easy (and secure) access to Internet materials. In addition, because we believe that part of the problem is analyst resistance, not lack of collection, we recommend that some of the new analysts allocated to CIA be specially trained to use open sources and then to act as open source "evange-analysts" who can jumpstart the open source initiative by showing its value in addressing particular analytic problems. All of this, we believe, will help improve the Intelligence Community's surprisingly poor "feel" for cultural and political issues in the countries that concern policymakers most. The Open Source Directorate should also be the primary test bed for new information technology because the security constraints—while substantial—are lower for open source than for classified material.

Reconsider MASINT. Measurements and signatures can offer important intelligence about nuclear, biological, and chemical weapons. But the tools we use to collect these measurements and signatures—tools collectively referred to within the intelligence community as MASINT—do not obviously constitute a single discipline. In a world of specialized collection agencies, there is reason to suspect that these orphaned technologies may have been underfunded and under-utilized. We recommend that the DNI take responsibility for developing and coordinating new intelligence technologies, including those that now go under the title MASINT. This could be done by a special coordinator, or as part of the DNI's Office of Science and Technology. The DNI's office does not need to directly control MASINT collection. Rather, we recommend that individual collection agencies assume responsibility for aspects of MASINT that fall naturally into their bailiwicks. At the same time, the DNI's designated representative would promote and monitor the status of new technical intelligence programs throughout the Intelligence Community to ensure that they are fully implemented and given the necessary attention.

Additional Collection Recommendations

In addition to those described above, Chapter 7 of our report offers recommendations concerning:

- Developing new human and technical collection methods;
- Professionalizing human intelligence across the Intelligence Community;
- Creating a larger and better-trained human intelligence officer cadre;
- Amending the Foreign Intelligence Surveillance Act to extend the duration of certain forms of electronic surveillance against non-U.S. persons, to ease administrative burdens on NSA and the Department of Justice; and
- Improving the protection of sources and methods by reducing authorized and unauthorized disclosures.

Transforming Analysis

Integrated, innovative collection is just the beginning of what the Intelligence Community needs. Some of the reforms already discussed, particularly the DNI-level "Mission Managers," will improve analysis. But much more is needed. In particular, analytic expertise must be deepened, intelligence gaps reduced, and existing information made more usable—all of which would improve the quality of intelligence.

As an overarching point, however, the Intelligence Community must recognize the central role of analysts in the intelligence process. Needless to say, analysts are the people who analyze intelligence, put it in context, and communicate the intelligence to the people who need it. But in addition, analysts are the repositories for what the Intelligence Community doesn't know, and they must clearly convey these gaps to decisionmakers—as well as to collectors so that the Intelligence Community does everything it can to fill the holes. (Analysts will also play an increasingly prominent role in information security, as they "translate" intelligence from the most sensitive of sources to a variety of consumers, ranging from state and local first responders to senior policymakers.) To enable analysts to fulfill these roles, we recommend the following:

Empower Mission Managers to coordinate analytic efforts on a given topic. The Mission Managers we propose would serve as the focal point for all aspects of the intelligence effort on a particular issue. They would be aware of the analytic expertise in various intelligence agencies, assess the quality of analytic products, identify strategic questions receiving inadequate attention, encourage alternative analysis, and ensure that dissenting views are expressed to intelligence users. When necessary, they would recommend that the DNI use his personnel authorities to move analysts to priority intelligence topics. At the same time, Mission Managers should not be responsible for providing a single, homogenized analytic product to decisionmakers; rather, Mission Managers should be responsible for encouraging alternative analysis and for ensuring that dissenting views are expressed to intelligence customers. In sum, Mission Managers should be able to find the right people and expertise and make sure that the right analysis, including alternative analysis, is getting done.

Strengthen long-term and strategic analysis. The most common complaint we heard from analysts in the Intelligence Community was that the pressing demand for current intelligence "eats up everything else." Analysts cannot maintain their expertise if they cannot conduct long-term and strategic analysis. Because this malady is so pervasive and has proven so resistant to conventional solutions, we recommend establishing an organization to perform only long-term and strategic analysis under the National Intelligence Council, the Community's existing focal point for interagency long-term analytic efforts. The new unit could serve as a focal point for Community-wide alternative analysis, thereby complementing agency-specific efforts at independent analysis. And although some analysts in this organization would be permanently assigned, at least half would serve only temporarily and would come from all intelligence agencies, including NGA and NSA, as well as from outside the government. Such rotations would reinforce good tradecraft habits, as well as foster a greater sense of Community among analysts and spur collaboration on other projects.

Encourage diverse and independent analysis. We believe that diverse and independent analysis—often referred to as "competitive analysis"—should come from many sources. As we have just noted, we recommend that our proposed long-term research and analysis unit, as well as the National Intelligence Council, conduct extensive independent analysis. In some circumstances there is also a place for a "devil's advocate"—someone appointed to challenge the consensus view. We also think it important that a not-for-profit "sponsored research institute" be created outside the Intelligence Community; such an institute would serve as a critical window into outside expertise, conduct its own research, and reach out to specialists, including academics and technical experts, business and industry leaders, and representatives from the nonprofit sector. Finally, the Intelligence Community should encourage independent analysis throughout its analytic ranks. In our view, this can best be accomplished through the preservation of dispersed analytic resources (as opposed to consolidation in large "centers"), active efforts by Mission Managers to promote independent analysis, and Community-wide training that instills the importance of such analysis.

Improve the rigor and "tradecraft" of analysis. Our studies, and many observers, point to a decline in analytic rigor within the Intelligence Community. Analysts have suffered from weak leadership, insufficient training, and budget cutbacks that led to the loss of our best, most senior analysts. There is no quick fix for tradecraft problems. However, we recommend several steps: increasing analyst training; ensuring that managers and budget writers allot time and resources for analysts to actually get trained; standardizing good tradecraft practices through the use of a National Intelligence University; creating structures and practices that increase competitive analysis; increasing managerial training for Intelligence Community supervisors; enabling joint and rotational assignment opportunities; ensuring that finished intelligence products are sufficiently transparent so that an analyst's reasoning is visible to intelligence customers; and implementing other changes in human resource policies—such as merit-based-pay—so that the best analysts are encouraged to stay in government service.

Communicating intelligence to policymakers. The best intelligence in the world is worthless unless it is effectively and accurately communicated to those who need it. The Iraq weapons of mass destruction case is a stark example. The daily reports sent to the President and senior policymakers discussing Iraq over many months proved to be disastrously one-sided. We thus offer recommendations on ways in which intelligence products can be enhanced, including how the President's Daily Brief (PDB) might be improved. In this regard, we suggest the elimination of the inherently misleading "headline" summaries in PDBs and other senior policymaker briefs, and that the DNI oversee production of the PDB. To accomplish this, we recommend the DNI create an analytic staff too small to routinely undertake drafting itself, but large enough to have background on many of the issues that are covered by the PDB. The goal would be to enable the DNI to coordinate and oversee the process, without requiring him to take on the heavy—and almost overwhelming—mantle of daily intelligence support to the President. Critically, the DNI's staff would also ensure that the PDB reflects alternative views from the Community to the greatest extent feasible.

We also recommend that the DNI take responsibility, with the President's concurrence, for the three primary sources of intelligence that now reach the President: the PDB, the President's Terrorism Threat Report—a companion publication produced by the NCTC and focused solely on terrorism-related issues—and the briefing by the Director of the FBI. We suggest that the DNI coordinate this intelligence in a manner that eliminates redundancies and ensures that only material that is necessary for the President be included. We think this last point is especially important because we have observed a disturbing trend whereby intelligence is passed to the President (as well as other senior policymakers) not because it requires high-level attention, but because passing the information "up the chain" provides individuals and organizations with bureaucratic cover.

Demand more from analysts. We urge that policymakers actively probe and question analysts. In our view, such interaction is not "politicization." Analysts should expect such demanding and aggressive testing without—as a matter of principle and professionalism—allowing it to subvert their judgment.

Additional Analysis Recommendations

In addition to those described above, Chapter 8 of our report offers recommendations concerning:

- Developing technologies capable of exploiting large volumes of foreign language data without the need for human translations;
- Improving career-long analytical and managerial training;
- Creating a database for all finished intelligence, as well as adopting technology to update analysts and decisionmakers when intelligence judgments change;
- Improving the Intelligence Community's science, technology, and weapons expertise;
- Changing the way analysts are hired, promoted, and rewarded; and
- Institutionalizing "lessons learned" procedures to learn from past analytical successes and failures.

Reorient the Department of Justice. Every agency that has major responsibility for terrorism and intelligence has been overhauled in the past four years. With one exception: at the Department of Justice, the famous "wall" between intelligence and criminal law still lingers, at least on the organization charts. On one side is the Office of Intelligence Policy and Review, which handles Foreign Intelligence Surveillance Court orders—those court orders that permit wiretaps and physical searches for national security reasons. On the other side are two separate sections of the Criminal Division (Counterterrorism and Counterespionage), reporting to two separate Deputy Assistant Attorneys General. This organizational throwback to the 1990s scatters intelligence expertise throughout the Department and in some cases has contributed to errors that hampered intelligence gathering. A single office with responsibility for counterterrorism, counterintelligence, and intelligence investigations would ensure better communication and reduce the tendency to rebuild the wall along bureaucratic lines.

We recommend that these three components (perhaps joined by a fourth Justice Department component that coordinates issues related to transnational crimes) be placed together under the authority of an Assistant Attorney General for National Security who would, like the Assistant Attorney General for the Criminal Division, report either directly to the Deputy Attorney General, or to a newly created Associate Attorney General responsible for both the National Security and Criminal Divisions.

Strengthen the Department of Homeland Security's relationship with the Intelligence Community. The Department of Homeland Security is the primary repository of information about what passes in and out of the country—a critical participant in safeguarding the United States from nuclear, biological, or chemical attack. Yet, since its inception, Homeland Security has faced immense challenges in collecting information effectively, making it available to analysts and users both inside and outside the Department, and bringing intelligence support to law enforcement and first responders who seek to act on such information. We did not conduct a detailed study of Homeland Security's capabilities, but it is clear to us that the department faces challenges in all four roles it plays in the intelligence community—as collector, analyst, disseminator, and customer.

Among the obstacles confronting Homeland Security, we found during the course of our study that the Department's Immigration and Customs Enforcement still operates under an order inherited from the Treasury Department in the 1980s. The order requires high-level approval for virtually all information sharing and assistance to the Intelligence Community. We think this order should be rescinded, and we believe the DNI should carefully examine how Homeland Security works with the rest of the Intelligence Community.

Counterintelligence

Every intelligence service on the planet wants to steal secrets from the last remaining superpower. But as other nations increase their intelligence operations against the United States, U.S. counterintelligence has been in a defensive crouch—fractured, narrowly focused, and lacking national direction. This may change as a result of the President's newly announced counterintelligence strategy. The good ideas in the strategy must, however, still be put into practice.

CIA does counterintelligence abroad, but its capabilities are limited. The FBI's counterintelligence efforts within the United States are well-staffed, but hardly strategic in their nature. Finally, the Defense Department's counterintelligence capabilities lack effective cross-department integration and direction. To address these concerns, we recommend four steps to strengthen counterintelligence: the empowerment of the nation's chief counterintelligence officer, the National Counterintelligence Executive (NCIX); the development of a new CIA capability for enhancing counterintelligence abroad; the centralization of the Defense Department's counterintelligence functions; and, as suggested earlier, bringing the FBI into the Intelligence Community to ensure that its robust counterintelligence capabilities are employed in line with the DNI's priorities. Moreover, all of these efforts must focus greater attention on the technical aspects of counterintelligence, as our adversaries shift from human spying to attempting to penetrate our information infrastructure.

Covert Action

If used in a careful and limited way, covert action can serve as a more subtle and surgical tool than forms of acknowledged employment of U.S. power and influence. As part of our overall review of the Intelligence Community, we conducted a careful study of U.S. covert action capabilities. Our findings were included in a short, separate chapter of our classified report. Regrettably, this area is so heavily classified that we could not include a chapter on the subject in our unclassified report.

We will, however, state here—at a necessarily high level of generality—some of our overall conclusions on covert action. At the outset, we note that we found current covert action programs in the counterproliferation and counterterrorism areas to be energetic, innovative, and well-executed within the limits of their authority and funding. Yet some critically important programs are hobbled by lack of sustained strategic planning, insufficient commitment of resources on a long-term basis, and a disjointed management structure. In our classified report we suggest organizational changes that we believe would consolidate support functions for covert action and improve the management of covert action programs within the Intelligence Community; we are unable to provide further details on these recommendations, however, in this unclassified format.

Addressing Proliferation

So far, we have focused on improving the Intelligence Community writ large—on the theory that only a redesigned Community can substantially improve its performance in assessing the threat posed by weapons of mass destruction. But quite apart from the structural changes we have already recommended, the Intelligence Community also needs to change the way it approaches two of the greatest threats—biological weapons and new forms of nuclear proliferation.

Biological Weapons

The 2001 anthrax attacks on the United States killed five people, crippled mail delivery in several cities for a year, and imposed more than a billion dollars in decontamination costs. For all that, we were lucky. Biological weapons are cheaper and easier to acquire than nuclear weapons—and they could be more deadly. The threat is deeply troubling today; it will be more so tomorrow, when genetic modification techniques will allow the creation of even worse biological weapons. Most of the traditional Intelligence Community collection tools are of little or no use in tackling biological weapons. In our classified report, we discuss some of the specific challenges that confront our intelligence effort against the biological threat—but regrettably we cannot discuss them here.

Faced with a high-priority problem that does not yield to traditional methods, large parts of the Intelligence Community seem to have lowered their expectations and focused on other priorities. This is unacceptable. The Intelligence Community, and the government as a whole, needs to approach the problem with a new urgency and new strategies:

Work with the biological sciences community. The Intelligence Community simply does not have the in-depth technical knowledge about biological weapons that it has about nuclear weapons. To close the expertise gap, the Community cannot rely on hiring biologists, whose knowledge and skills are extremely important, but whose depth and timeliness of expertise begins eroding as soon as they move from the laboratory to the intelligence profession. Instead, the DNI should create a Community Biodefense Initiative to institutionalize outreach to technical experts inside and outside of government. We describe specific components of this initiative in the body of our report.

Make targeted collection of biological weapons intelligence a priority within the Intelligence Community. The Intelligence Community's collection woes starkly illustrate the need for more aggressive, targeted approaches to collection on biological threats. We recommend that the DNI create a deputy within the National Counter Proliferation Center who is specifically responsible for biological weapons; this deputy would ensure the implementation of a comprehensive biological weapons targeting strategy, which would entail gaining real-time access to non-traditional sources of information, filtering open source data, and devising specific collection initiatives directed at the resulting targets.

Leverage regulation for biological weapons intelligence. The United States should look outside of intelligence channels for enforcement mechanisms that can provide new avenues of international cooperation and resulting opportunities for intelligence collection on biological threats. In the corresponding chapter of our report, we recommend encouraging foreign criminalization of biological weapons development and establishing biosafety and biosecurity regulations under United Nations Security Council Resolution 1540. We also propose extending biosecurity and biosafety regulations to foreign institutions with commercial ties to the United States.

Nuclear Weapons

The intelligence challenge posed by nuclear weapons continues to evolve. The Intelligence Community must continue to monitor established nuclear states such as Russia and China, and at the same time face newer and potentially more daunting challenges like terrorist use of a nuclear weapon. But the focus of the U.S. Intelligence Community has historically been on the capabilities of large nation states. When applied to the problem of terrorist organizations and smaller states, many of our intelligence capabilities are inadequate.

The challenges posed by the new environment are well-illustrated by two aspects of nuclear proliferation. The first is the continuing challenge of monitoring insecure nuclear weapons and materials, or "loose nukes"—mainly in the former Soviet Union but also potentially in other nations. The second aspect is the appearance of non-state nuclear "brokers," such as the private proliferation network run by the Pakistani scientist A.Q. Khan. In Khan's case, innovative human intelligence efforts gave the United States access to this proliferation web. However, not only does the full scope of Khan's work remain unknown, but senior officials readily acknowledge that the Intelligence Community must know more about the private networks that support proliferation. The Intelligence Community must adapt to the changing threat.

Intelligence Support to Interdiction

So far, the Intelligence Community has enjoyed a number of successes intercepting materials related to nuclear, biological, and chemical weapons (and their related delivery systems)—the process commonly referred to as "interdiction." But success has come at a cost. The Intelligence Community has focused so much energy on its own efforts that the Community shows less ambition and imagination in supporting other agencies that should play a large role in interdiction. Many other federal agencies could do more to interdict precursors, weapons components, and dangerous agents if they had effective intelligence support. We recommend several mechanisms to improve intelligence support to these agencies, most particularly the creation of a counterproliferation Joint Interagency Task Force modeled on similar entities that have proved successful in the counternarcotics context.

Moreover, since it may not be possible in all cases to identify proliferation shipments before they reach the United States, our last line of defense is detecting and stopping these shipments before they reach our border. Yet new sensor technologies have faced challenges. In the corresponding chapter of this report, we suggest how the Intelligence Community and Department of Homeland Security can work together on this issue.

Leveraging Legal and Regulatory Mechanisms

Intelligence alone cannot solve the proliferation threat. But it may not have to. Information that spies and eavesdroppers would spend millions for and risk their lives to steal can sometimes be easily obtained by the right Customs, Treasury, or export control officials. The industries that support proliferation are subject to a host of regulatory regimes. But the agencies that regulate industry in these areas—Treasury, State, Homeland Security, and Commerce—do not think of themselves as engaged in the collection of intelligence, and the Intelligence Community only rarely appreciates the authorities and opportunities presented by regulatory regimes.

Given the challenges presented by quasi-governmental proliferation, the United States must leverage all of its capabilities to flag potential proliferators, gain insight into their activities, and interdict them, where appropriate. We therefore recommend a series of possible changes to existing regulatory regimes, all designed to improve insight into nuclear, biological, or chemical proliferation and enhance our ability to take action. These changes include negotiating ship boarding agreements that include tagging and tracking provisions to facilitate the surveillance of suspect vessels, taking steps to facilitate greater coordination between the Commerce Department (and Immigrations and Customs Enforcement) and the Intelligence Community, using Commerce Department and Customs and Border Protection regulations to facilitate information sharing about suspect cargo and persons and to justify related interdictions, and expanding the Treasury Department's authority to block assets of proliferators.

Conclusion

The harm done to American credibility by our all too public intelligence failings in Iraq will take years to undo. If there is good news it is this: without actually suffering a massive nuclear or biological attack, we have learned how badly the Intelligence Community can fail in struggling to understand the most important threats we face. We must use the lessons from those failings, and from our successes as well, to improve our intelligence for the future, and do so with a sense of urgency. We already have thousands of dedicated officers and many of the tools needed to do the job. With that in mind, we now turn first to what went wrong in Iraq, then to other intelligence cases, and finally to our detailed recommendations for action.

Appendix C

Address to the House of Commons: Review of Intelligence on Weapons of Mass Destruction: Report of a Committee of Privy Counsellors

July 14, 2004

Introduction

Our Terms of Reference

1. On 3 February 2004, the Foreign and Commonwealth Secretary announced in the House of Commons:

My right hon. friend the Prime Minister has decided to establish a committee to review intelligence on weapons of mass destruction. This committee will be composed of Privy Counsellors. It will have the following terms of reference: to investigate the intelligence coverage available in respect of WMD programmes in countries of concern and on the global trade in WMD, taking into account what is now known about these programmes; as part of this work, to investigate the accuracy of intelligence on Iraqi WMD up to March 2003, and to examine any discrepancies between the intelligence gathered, evaluated and used by the Government before the conflict, and between that intelligence and what has been discovered by the Iraq survey group since the end of the conflict; and to make recommendations to the Prime Minister for the future on the gathering, evaluation and use of intelligence on WMD, in the light of the difficulties of operating in countries of concern.

My right hon. friend the Prime Minister has asked the committee to report before the summer recess. The committee will follow the precedent in terms of procedures of the Franks committee. It will have access to all intelligence reports and assessments and other relevant Government papers, and will be able to call witnesses to give oral evidence in private. The committee will work closely with the US inquiry and the Iraq survey group.

The committee will submit its final conclusions to my right hon. friend the Prime Minister in a form for publication, along with any classified recommendations and material. The Government will, of course, co-operate fully with the committee.

Our Work

2. The Committee met for the first time on Thursday 5 February and four of us were sworn in as Members of the Privy Council on Wednesday 11 February. Mrs Taylor was already a Privy Counsellor.

3. In view of the very tight timetable for our Review, it was essential to make a rapid start. We are therefore especially grateful for the speed with which the Security and Intelligence Coordinator, Sir David Omand, supplied us with accommodation and an excellent team of support staff in the Cabinet Office. We are also grateful to the Intelligence and Security Committee and their staff for enabling us to use the Committee's room in the Cabinet Office for our hearings, and for the forbearance and co-operation they extended to us.

4. Since 5 February, we have met 36 times. We have visited Washington, where we met the co-Chairs of the President's Commission on the Intelligence Capabilities of the United States Regarding Weapons of Mass Destruction, Governor Charles S. Robb and Judge Laurence H. Silberman and members of their Commission; General Brent Scowcroft, Chairman of the President's Foreign Intelligence Advisory Board; and senior members of the Administration and the Congress, including Senator Pat Roberts and Senator John Rockefeller, Chairman and Ranking Member of the Senate Intelligence Committee; Congressman Porter Goss and Congresswoman Jane Harman, Chairman and Ranking Member of the House Intelligence Committee; Dr Condoleezza Rice, National Security Adviser; General Colin Powell and Mr Richard Armitage, State Department; Mr George Tenet, Director, and staff of the Central Intelligence Agency; and Vice Admiral Lowell Jacoby and staff of the Defense Intelligence Agency. We are grateful to Sir David Manning, HM Ambassador at Washington, and his team for making the arrangements for this visit. We also visited Baghdad and we express our particular appreciation to Major General Keith Dayton, Brigadier Graeme Morrison and Mr Charles Duelfer and their staffs for being willing to receive and brief us at a very

difficult and busy time, and to staff of the Ministry of Defence and the Royal Air Force for organising the visit and arranging our safe journey there and back. We also had useful discussions with representatives of a number of other countries.

5. The tight timetable for our Report has caused some difficulties for us. The main one is that the Iraq Survey Group, with whose findings our terms of reference require us to compare the intelligence received by the British Government, have not yet produced any publicly available report. They produced an interim report in September 2003 and a status report in March 2004. We have had access to these. We were very grateful to General Dayton and Mr Duelfer for also briefing us about their progress. We have undertaken not to anticipate their findings but, on the basis of the information they gave us, we believe that our conclusions are not inconsistent with what they have discovered so far. The much longer timetable given to the US Presidential Commission has had the result that, while we had useful initial discussions with them, we have not been able to fulfil the Foreign Secretary's statement that we would work closely with them.

6. On the other hand, we were greatly helped by the evidence given to Lord Hutton's Inquiry, by the report of the House of Commons Foreign Affairs Committee on "The Decision to go to War in Iraq" (HC 813) and above all by the report of the Intelligence and Security Committee entitled "Iraqi Weapons of Mass Destruction—Intelligence and Assessments" (Cm 5972). We should like to express particular thanks to the Intelligence and Security Committee for giving us access to the classified evidence which underlay their report. This saved us much spadework.

7. It may be asked what further we could add by going over such heavily traversed ground. One answer is perhaps that, as in the search for weapons in Iraq, one can never do too much digging. But others are that we have had the considerable advantage of the further passage of time which has allowed us to consider the evidence that has emerged since the war on Iraqi nuclear, biological, chemical and ballistic missile programmes and the results of post-war validation by the Secret Intelligence Service of their relevant human intelligence sources. More importantly, we have had much wider access to the Government's intelligence and policy papers. Even so, we do not pretend that ours can be the last word on every aspect of the issues we cover.

Our Approach

8. Our approach has been to start with the intelligence assessments of the Joint Intelligence Committee (JIC) and then to get from the intelligence agencies a full list of the underlying intelligence, both accepted and rejected, which was available to inform those assessments. We have then compared

that intelligence with the JIC's assessments and considered whether it appears to have been properly evaluated. In the other direction, we, like the Franks Committee, have obtained from Government departments those policy papers which their Permanent Secretaries have certified as containing all the material relevant to our Review, to allow us to establish the use which was made of the intelligence. Finally, where outcomes are known, we have compared the prior intelligence and the assessments made of it with those outcomes.

9. We have received 68 written submissions from members of the public and have taken oral evidence from 47 witnesses, some of whom gave evidence more than once. Except where witnesses asked for their identity to be protected, we list our witnesses at Annex A.

10. We have focussed on the intelligence available to the British Government and the use made of it by our Government. Although that inevitably has led us to areas of UK/US cooperation, we have deliberately not commented in this Report on the actions of the US intelligence agencies, ground that is being covered by the Presidential Commission.

11. We have been conscious of the Foreign Secretary's statement that our report should be submitted to the Prime Minister in a form fit for publication. We have also been conscious of the overriding need not to prejudice continuing or future intelligence operations or to endanger sources and have shaped our report accordingly. We are confident that what is published here gives Parliament and the public a fair representation of our conclusions and views.

12. In furtherance of this, we have exceptionally included in our Report extensive quotations from assessments of the Joint Intelligence Committee. We have ensured that in all cases our quoting these will not have implications for national security. The Government has made clear that our action in doing so will not be accepted as a precedent for putting those assessments into the public domain in the future.

Definitions and Usage

13. The Intelligence and Security Committee started their report with definitions of the terminology they used. We repeat their definitions in our 'Terminology and Glossary' and have tried to follow them. But we believe that there are problems with the term 'weapons of mass destruction' and with the shorthand 'chemical and biological weapons' (CBW) and 'chemical, biological, radiological and nuclear' (CBRN) weapons.

WMD

14. There is a considerable and long-standing academic debate about the proper interpretation of the phrase 'weapons of mass destruction'. We have some sympathy with the view that, whatever its origin, the phrase and its accompanying abbreviation are now used so variously as to confuse rather than enlighten readers. Rather than adding to this debate and this confusion, we have in our Report chosen to spell out what we mean in full. In cases where it is used by others, most notably in JIC assessments, we have had in mind in interpreting those assessments the definition at paragraphs 8 and 9 of United Nations Security Council Resolution 687 of 3 April 1991, which defined the systems which Iraq was required to abandon:

Nuclear weapons or nuclear weapons-usable material or any sub-systems or components or any research, development, support or manufacturing facilities relating to [nuclear weapons].

Chemical and biological weapons and all stocks of agents and all related subsystems and components and all research, development, support and manufacturing facilities.

Ballistic missiles with a range greater than 150 kilometres and related major parts, and repair and production facilities.

CBW

15. The abbreviation 'CBW' (often expressed as 'BCW') occurs regularly both in intelligence reporting and in related analysis and assessment. At a certain level of generality, 'CBW' can be a useful term to embody the concept of chemical and biological warfare. Thus, for example, in the face of a 'CBW' attack the tempo of military operations is significantly impeded by soldiers having to don cumbersome clothing whether facing chemical weapons or biological weapons. But for detailed technical intelligence assessments, the distinction is important. Chemical weapons and biological weapons involve very different technologies, and are usually developed by different people at different facilities. Delivery requirements, and hence doctrine, training, storage and handling, are different, as are the troops involved. One of our witnesses said that any report in which the terms 'CW' and 'BW' were interwoven or combined through the use of the single acronym 'CBW':... always makes me slightly suspicious.

16. We agree that such use is confusing. Thus, although the term may have some value in some contexts, we have sought to avoid it altogether, although it does feature in some of the extracts from JIC assessments which we have taken in to our Report.

CBRN

17. As well as nuclear, biological and chemical weapons, JIC assessments and intelligence reports, especially those on terrorism, also consider radiological weapons, which employ conventional, typically high-explosive means to distribute radioactive material. As a result, our Report includes where relevant the phrase 'chemical, biological, radiological and nuclear weapons', and its abbreviation 'CBRN'.

Our Thanks

18. Notwithstanding our short timetable, a massive amount of paper has been relevant to our Review. Sorting out and providing these papers has been a huge task for the intelligence agencies and departments at a time when they have also had their vital day-to-day work to undertake. As noted above, we have relied on certificates from Permanent Secretaries that all papers relevant to our interpretation of our terms of reference have been supplied to us. While we have on some occasions been critical of the slow rate at which these have been supplied and by the coverage of those originally offered, we are now reasonably confident that we have obtained the papers relevant to our work. We are grateful to all those who have had the task of identifying them and providing them. We have also been greatly helped by the fact that the intelligence community co-operated in providing a coordinated service so that we did not receive separate streams of papers from each agency which we would subsequently have had to relate to each other.

19. We would like to express our particular thanks to Mr Daniel Thornton and his team who were our link with the Government for the supply of intelligence material, departmental papers and other evidence. The documents they provided and the other evidence have of course all come to rest on the desks of our Secretary, Mr Bruce Mann, and his team, Mr Michael Ryder, Mr Peter Freeman, Mr Nigel Pearce, Mr Patrick Sprunt, Ms Carol Hook, Ms Judith Freeman and an additional team of transcribers. They have been indefatigable and we cannot find words to praise their skill and commitment adequately. We thank and commend them above all.

Chapter 1
The Nature and Use of Intelligence

"Much of the intelligence that we receive in war is contradictory, even more of it is plain wrong, and most of it is fairly dubious. What one can require of an officer, under these circumstances, is a certain degree of discrimination, which can only be gained from knowledge of men and affairs and from good judgement. The law of probability must be his guide." [Clausewitz, On War, Vol I, Bk I, Ch VI]

1.1 Introduction

20. In view of the subject matter of our Review, and of what we have found in the course of it, we think that it may be helpful to the general reader to describe the nature of intelligence; the successive processes of validation, analysis and assessment which are necessary for using it properly; its limitations; and the risks which nevertheless remain.

21. Governmental decisions and actions, at home and abroad, are based on many types of information. Most is openly available or compiled, much is published, and some is consciously provided by individuals, organisations or other governments in confidence. A great deal of such information may be accurate, or accurate enough in its own terms. But equally much is at best uninformed, while some is positively intended to mislead. To supplement their knowledge in areas of concern where information is for one reason or another inadequate, governments turn to secret sources. Information acquired against the wishes and (generally) without the knowledge of its originators or possessors is processed by collation with other material, validation, analysis and assessment and finally disseminated as 'intelligence'. To emphasise the point, the term 'secret intelligence' is often used (as, for instance, enshrined in the title of the Secret Intelligence Service), but in this Review we shall use the simple word 'intelligence'.

22. The protective security barriers which intelligence collectors have to penetrate are usually formidable, and particularly so in the case of programmes which are the subject of this Review. Nuclear, biological and chemical programmes are amongst the ultimate state secrets, controlled by layers of security protection going beyond those applied to conventional weapons. Those of the greatest concern to governments are usually embedded within a strong apparatus of state control. Few of the many people who are necessarily involved in such programmes have a view of more than their own immediate working environment, and very few have comprehensive knowledge of the arrangements for the control, storage, release and use of the resulting weapons. At every stage from initial research and development to deployed forces, nuclear, biological and chemical weapons and their delivery systems are treated as being of particular sensitivity, often to the extent of the establishment of special command and control arrangements in parallel with, but separate from, normal state or military channels.

1.2 Collection

23. The UK has three intelligence and security agencies ('the agencies') responsible for the collection of intelligence:[1] the Secret Intelligence Service (SIS), the Security Service and Government Communications Headquarters (GCHQ). The Defence Intelligence Staff (DIS), part of the Ministry of Defence (MOD), also manages some intelligence collection, notably that of imagery, but its main function is all-source analysis and assessment and the production of collated results, primarily to serve MOD requirements.

24. There is a panoply of collection techniques to acquire intelligence which do not exactly correspond to inter-departmental organisational boundaries. The three main ones are signals intelligence (the product of interception, generally abbreviated to 'Sigint'); information from human sources such as classical espionage agents (which is conveniently described, by extension from the previous category, as 'Humint'): and photography, or more generally imagery ('Imint'). Signals intelligence and human intelligence are of widespread and general applicability. They can produce intelligence on any topic (for example, the intentions, plans, negotiations, activities and achievements of people involved in the development, acquisition, deployment and use of unconventional weapons), since ultimately the data they acquire stem from the human beings involved. Imagery is more confined to the study of objects (buildings, aircraft, roads, topography), though modern techniques have extended its abilities (for example, infra-red photography can in some circumstances show where an object was, even though it may have gone by the time the photograph is taken).

25. There are also other, more specialised intelligence techniques, some of particular relevance to this Review.[2] For example, the development of nuclear explosives inevitably involves highly radioactive materials, radiation from which may be detected. Leakage from facilities concerned with the development of chemical and biological agents, and deposits in testing areas, can provide characteristic indicators. Missile testing may involve the generation of considerable heat, which can be detected, and missiles may be tracked by radar.

26. In the case of the weapons covered by this Review, there is additionally another category of information which is frequently mentioned by the Joint Intelligence Committee (JIC) in its assessments. International inspection and enforcement bodies have been established, on a permanent basis (e.g., the International Atomic Energy Agency), or temporary basis (e.g., the United Nations Special Commission), to ensure compliance with

[1] They also have other functions not relevant here.

[2] The term 'Masint' (Measurement and Signature Intelligence) has been coined for at least some of these techniques, though they lack the unifying themes which characterise Sigint and Humint.

international treaties or United Nations resolutions.[3] Some of the findings and reports of these bodies are published on an official basis to United Nations members and are of considerable importance. In Iraq between 1991 and 1998, in many ways they surpassed anything that national intelligence agencies could do, but since their work is carried out on behalf of the United Nations it can hardly be considered 'intelligence' by the definitions to which we are working. Data obtained in the course of work on export licensing can also be important.

1.3 Validation

27. Intelligence, though it may not differ in type or, often, reliability from other forms of information used by governments, operates in a field of particular difficulty. By definition the data it is trying to provide have been deliberately concealed. Before the actual content of an intelligence report can be considered, the validity of the process which has led to its production must be confirmed. For imagery and signals intelligence this is not usually an issue, although even here the danger of deception must be considered. But for human intelligence the validation process is vital.

28. Human intelligence reports are usually available only at second-hand (for example, when the original informant talks to a case officer[4] who interprets—often literally—his words to construct an intelligence report), and maybe third- or fourth-hand (the original informant talks to a friend, who more or less indirectly talks to a case officer). Documentary or other physical evidence is often more compelling than the best oral report,[5] and has the advantage of being more accessible to specialised examination, but is usually more difficult to acquire. Conventional oral reporting can be difficult enough if all in the chain understand the subject under discussion. When the topic is unfamiliar to one or more of the people involved, as can be the case when details of (say) nuclear weapons design are at issue, there is always the chance of misunderstanding. There is in such cases a considerable load on the case officer to be familiar with the subject matter and sufficiently expert in explaining it. It need only be added that often those involved in providing intelligence may for one reason or another have deliberately misrepresented (or at least concealed) their true identities, their country of origin or their

[3] Such bodies often also have a wider operational role in the implementation of treaties or Security Council Resolutions.

[4] An official responsible for handling and receiving reports from human intelligence sources.

[5] Such evidence is no more immune to deception or fabrication than is oral testimony, though of a different type.

employment to their interlocutors,[6] to show how great is the need for careful evaluation of the validity of any information which eventually arrives.

29. The validation of a reporting chain requires both care and time, and can generally only be conducted by the agency responsible for collection. The process is informed by the operational side of the agency, but must include a separate auditing element, which can consider cases objectively and quite apart from their apparent intelligence value. Has the informant been properly quoted, all the way along the chain? Does he have credible access to the facts he claims to know? Does he have the right knowledge to understand what he claims to be reporting? Could he be under opposition control, or be being fed information? Is he fabricating? Can the bona fides, activities, movements or locations attributed to those involved in acquiring or transmitting a report be checked? Do we understand the motivations of those involved, their private agenda,[7] and hence the way in which their reports may be influenced by a desire to please or impress? How powerful is a wish for (in particular) financial reward? What, if any, distorting effect might such factors exert? Is there—at any stage—a deliberate intention to deceive? Generally speaking, the extent and depth of validation required will depend on the counter-intelligence sophistication of the target, although the complexity of the operational situation will affect the possibility of confusion, misrepresentation or deception.

1.4 Analysis

30. The validation process will often have involved consideration of the coherence and consistency of intelligence being provided by an informant, as one of the ways in which that source's reliability can be tested. But at the next stage, analysis, the factual material inside the intelligence report is examined in its own right. This stage may not be required where the material is self-explanatory, or it may be readily subsumed into assessment and conducted by the same people. But much intelligence is fragmentary or specialised and needs at least a conscious analytic stage. Analysis assembles individual intelligence reports into meaningful strands, whether weapons programmes, military operations or diplomatic policies. Intelligence reports take on meaning as they are put into context. Analysis is also the process required to convert complex technical evidence into descriptions of real-world objects or events.

[6] The ultimate in such deceptions is the classic 'double agent', who is infiltrated into an espionage network to discover, misinform, expose or pervert it.

[7] We have been assured that SIS has for half a century been viscerally wary of emigre organisations. We return to this below in the context of Iraq.

31. The department which receives the largest quantity of intelligence is the MOD, where analysis is carried out by the DIS[8] whose reports are distributed not only internally in the MOD but also to other relevant departments. Although the DIS is a component of the MOD, funded from the Defence Account and managed in accordance with defence priorities, it is a vital component of and contributor to the national intelligence machinery, and its priorities and work programme are linked with those of the Cabinet Office.

32. Analysis can be conducted only by people expert in the subject matter —a severe limitation when the topic is as specialised as biological warfare or uranium enrichment, or the internal dynamics of terrorist cells or networks. A special danger here can be the failure to recognise just what particular expertise is required. The British intelligence assessment of the German V-2 rocket during the Second World War was hindered by the involvement of the main British rocket expert, who opined that the object visible on test-stands could not possibly be a rocket. The unrecognised problem was that he was an expert only on solid powder rockets, of the type that the UK had developed for short-range artillery. It was true that a solid firework of the size of the V-2 was, with the technology then available, impracticable. But the Germans had developed liquid-propellant rocket engines, with the combustion chamber fed by powerful turbo-pumps. On that subject, there were no British experts.

1.5 Assessment

33. Assessment may be conducted separately from analysis or as an almost parallel process in the mind of the analyst. Intelligence reports often do not immediately fit into an established pattern, or extend a picture in the expected way. Assessment has to make choices, but in so doing runs the risk of selection that reinforces earlier conclusions. The risk is that uneven standards of proof may be applied; reports that fit the previous model are readily accepted, while contrary reports have to reach a higher threshold. This is not only perfectly understandable, it is the way perception normally operates. But in the intelligence world in which data are scanty, may be deliberately intended to confuse and may sometimes be more inadequate than can be appreciated, normal rules do not apply.

34. In the UK, assessment is usually explicitly described as 'all-source'. Given the imperfections of intelligence, it is vital that every scrap of evidence be examined, from the most secret sources through confidential diplomatic reports to openly published data. Intelligence cannot be checked too often.

[8] The DIS also has other management and intelligence collection responsibilities.

Corroboration is always important but seldom simple, particularly in the case of intelligence on 'hard targets'[9] such as nuclear, biological or chemical weapons programmes or proliferation networks. The simple fact of having apparently coincident reports from multiple types of intelligence sources is not in itself enough. Although reports from different sources may say the same thing, they may not necessarily confirm one another. Is a human intelligence report that a factory has been put into operation confirmed by imagery showing trucks moving around it? Or are both merely based on the same thing—observation of physical external activity? Reporting of different but mutually consistent activities can be complementary. This can build up knowledge to produce a picture which is more than the simple sum of the parts. But it may be false, if there is no link between the pieces other than the attractiveness of the resulting picture. Complementary information is not necessarily confirmatory information.

35. Multiple sources may conflict, and common sense has to be used in evaluation. A dozen captured soldiers may have provided mutually consistent and supportive reports about the availability of chemical weapons to their neighbouring battalion. But if these were flatly contradicted by a single report from a senior member of that battalion, which should be believed?

36. It is incorrect to say, as some commentators have done, that 'single source' intelligence is always suspect. A single photograph showing missiles on launchers, supporting a division deployed in the field, trumps any number of agent reports that missiles are not part of a division's order of battle. During the Second World War, innumerable Allied command decisions were taken on the basis of intelligence reports from a single type of source (signals intelligence, providing decrypts of high-level German and Japanese military plans and orders), and quite often (e.g. re-routing convoys in the middle of the Atlantic) important decisions had to be taken on the basis of a single report. As before, common sense and experience are the key.

37. Assessment must always be aware that there may be a deeper level of reality at which apparently independent sources have a common origin. Multiple sources may have been marshalled in a deception campaign, as the Allies did in Operation Fortitude before D-Day to mislead the German High Command about the location of the landings. Although deception on so grand a scale is rare, the chance of being deceived is in inverse proportion to the number of independent sources—which, for 'hard targets', are few.

[9] In a sense, almost all intelligence is conducted against 'hard targets'. If the information were readily available, it would not be necessary to call on intelligence resources to acquire it. But within the hierarchy of intelligence activities it is inevitable, given the protection afforded to nuclear, biological and chemical weapons programmes, that they are among the hardest targets.

38. Many of the manifestations of nuclear, biological or chemical weapons programmes can have innocuous, or at least non-proscribed, explanations—the 'dual-use' problem. Nuclear developments can be for peaceful purposes. Technologies for the production of chemical and biological agents seldom diverge from those employed in normal civilian chemical or biochemical industries. And, in the case of missile development, some procurement and development activities may be permissible.

39. Thus, the recipients of intelligence have normally to make decisions on the basis of the balance of probabilities. That requires, first, the most effective deployment of all possible sources and, secondly, the most objective assessment possible, as unaffected as may be by motives and pressures which may distort judgement.

40. In the UK, central intelligence assessment is the responsibility of the Assessments Staff. This comprises some 30 senior and middle-ranking officials on secondment from other departments, within the Cabinet Office, together with secretarial and administrative support.

1.6 The Joint Intelligence Committee

41. The agencies and the DIS are brought together with important policy departments in the JIC.[10] The JIC was established in 1936 as a sub-committee of the Committee of Imperial Defence. During the Second World War, it comprised the heads of the agencies and the three Services' Directors of Intelligence, under the chairmanship of a senior member of the Foreign Office and was joined by other relevant departments such as the Ministry of Economic Warfare, responsible for the Special Operations Executive.

42. The JIC has evolved since 1945. It became part of the Cabinet Office rather than of the Chiefs of Staff organisation in 1957. To the original membership of the JIC (intelligence producers, with users from MOD and the FCO) were added the Intelligence Co-ordinator when that post was established in 1968, the Treasury (1968), the Department of Trade and Industry (1997) and the Home Office (2000). Other departments attend when papers of relevance to them are taken. Representatives of the Australian, Canadian and United States intelligence communities also attend as appropriate. In 1993, the post of Chairman of the JIC and that of the Head of the Cabinet Office's Defence and Overseas Secretariat[11] were combined, the two posts remaining so until 1999. From 1992 to 2002, the chairmanship was combined

[10] For a fuller description see National Intelligence Machinery, HMSO 2001, which puts the JIC into context within the structures of Parliamentary and Cabinet government.

[11] From 1984 to the end of 1993 the Chairman of the JIC was also the Prime Minister's Foreign Policy Adviser. This title was revived in September 2001 and assumed by the Head of the Defence and Overseas Secretariat.

with the post of Intelligence Co-ordinator. A new post of Security and Intelligence Co-ordinator was created in 2002, taking on the responsibilities of the previous Intelligence Co-ordinator together with wider responsibilities in the field of counter-terrorism and crisis management. The holder became a member of the JIC.

43. The JIC's main function[12] on which its regular weekly meetings are centred, is to provide ministers and senior officials with co-ordinated intelligence assessments on a range of issues of immediate and long-term importance to national interests, primarily in the fields of security, defence and foreign affairs.

The Assessments Staff are central to this role, and the Chief of the Assessments Staff is a member of the JIC in his own right. With the assistance of other departments, the Assessments Staff draft the JIC assessments, which are usually debated at Current Intelligence Groups (CIGs) including experts in the subject before being submitted to the JIC. The JIC can itself ask the Assessments Staff to draft an assessment, but the process is usually triggered by a request from a policy department. The forward programme of assessments to be produced is issued three times a year, but is revised and, when necessary, overridden by matters of more immediate concern. The JIC thus brings together in regular meetings the most senior people responsible for intelligence collection, for intelligence assessment and for the use of intelligence in the main departments for which it is collected, in order to construct and issue assessments on the subjects of greatest current concern. The process is robust, and the assessments that result are respected and used at all levels of government.

44. Intelligence is disseminated at various levels and in different forms. The agencies send reports direct to users in departments and military commands; these reports are used by civil and military officials in their daily business, and some of them are selected and brought to ministers' attention. The JIC's co-ordinated intelligence assessments, formally agreed at their weekly meetings, are sent to ministers and senior officials. In addition the JIC produces Intelligence Updates and Immediate Assessments whenever required, which are sent to a standard distribution throughout government.

45. A feature of JIC assessments is that they contain single statements of position; unlike the practice in the US, there are no minority reports or noted dissents. When the intelligence is unclear or otherwise inadequate and the JIC at the end of its debate is still uncertain, it may report alternative interpretations of the facts before it such as they are; but in such cases all the membership agrees that the interpretations they are proposing are viable alternatives. The JIC does not (and this is borne out by our examination of

[12]The JIC also has other responsibilities, for the establishment of intelligence collection priorities and monitoring of agency performance.

several hundred JIC assessments in the course of our Review) characterise such alternatives as championed by individual members who disagree with colleagues' points of view. While the JIC has at times been criticised for its choice of language and the subtlety of the linguistic nuances and caveats it applies,[13] it has responded that when the intelligence is ambiguous it should not be artificially simplified.

46. In the sometimes lengthy line that leads to the production of the JIC's output, all the components of the system—from collection through analysis and assessment to a well briefed and educated readership—must function successfully. Problems can arise if the JIC has to make bricks without (enough) straw. Collection agencies may produce too little intelligence, or too much intelligence about the wrong subjects, or the right intelligence but too late to be of value. Although assessments generated under such circumstances may have proper caveats, with attention drawn to important gaps in knowledge and with the dubious steps in an argument clearly identified, they may reach misleading conclusions. Or—which is equally destructive of their purpose—even if they are correct they may be mistrusted. In either case, the reputation of the JIC product is at risk, and the Committee has on occasion refused to issue drafted papers which it has felt are not sufficiently supported by new intelligence or add nothing to the information already publicly available.

1.7 The Limitations of Intelligence

47. Intelligence merely provides techniques for improving the basis of knowledge. As with other techniques, it can be a dangerous tool if its limitations are not recognised by those who seek to use it.

48. The intelligence processes described above (validation, analysis, assessment) are designed to transform the raw material of intelligence so that it can be assimilated in the same way as other information provided to decision-makers at all levels of government. Validation should remove information which is unreliable (including reporting which has been deliberately inserted to mislead). Analysis should assemble fragmentary intelligence into coherent meaningful accounts. Assessment should put intelligence into a sensible real-world context and identify how it can affect policy making. But there are limitations, some inherent and some practical on the scope of intelligence, which have to be recognised by its ultimate recipients if it is to be used wisely.

[13]We have been told that some readers believe that important distinctions are intended between such phrases as "intelligence indicates...", "intelligence demonstrates..." and "intelligence shows...", or between "we assess that...", "we judge that..." and "we believe that...". We have also been told that there is in reality no established glossary, and that drafters and JIC members actually employ their natural language.

49. The most important limitation on intelligence is its incompleteness. Much ingenuity and effort is spent on making secret information difficult to acquire and hard to analyse. Although the intelligence process may overcome such barriers, intelligence seldom acquires the full story. In fact, it is often, when first acquired, sporadic and patchy, and even after analysis may still be at best inferential.

50. The very way that intelligence is presented can contribute to this misperception. The necessary protective security procedures with which intelligence is handled can reinforce a mystique of omniscience. Intelligence is not only—like many other sources—incomplete, it can be incomplete in undetectable ways. There is always pressure, at the assessment stage if not before, to create an internally consistent and intellectually satisfying picture. When intelligence becomes the dominant, or even the only, source of government information, it can become very difficult for the assessment process to establish a context and to recognise that there may be gaps in that picture.

51. A hidden limitation of intelligence is its inability to transform a mystery into a secret. In principle, intelligence can be expected to uncover secrets. The enemy's order of battle may not be known, but it is knowable. The enemy's intentions may not be known, but they too are knowable. But mysteries are essentially unknowable: what a leader truly believes, or what his reaction would be in certain circumstances, cannot be known, but can only be judged. JIC judgements have to cover both secrets and mysteries. Judgement must still be informed by the best available information, which often means a contribution from intelligence. But it cannot import certainty.

52. These limitations are best offset by ensuring that the ultimate users of intelligence, the decision makers at all levels, properly understand its strengths and limitations and have the opportunity to acquire experience in handling it. It is not easy to do this while preserving the security of sensitive sources and methods. But unless intelligence is properly handled at this final stage, all preceding effort and expenditure are wasted.

1.8 Risks to Good Assessment

53. It is a well-known phenomenon within intelligence communities that memory of past failures can cause over-estimation next time around. It is equally possible to be misled by past success. For 45 years of Cold War, the intelligence community's major task was to assess the intentions and capabilities of the Soviet Union and its satellite states.[14] As the details which had been sought became more accessible, first through glasnost' and explicit

[14]The intelligence community did, of course, have many other tasks during this period ranging from the consequences of the withdrawal from empire through the many facets of the conflicts and confrontations in the Middle East to the Falklands War.

exchanges of data under international agreements and then fairly readily through open sources after the dissolution of the Soviet empire, most of the intelligence community's conclusions were vindicated—at least in the areas in which it had spent the largest part of its efforts, the Soviet bloc's military equipment, capabilities and order of battle.

54. But it is risky to transfer one model to cases where that model will only partially apply. Against dictatorships, dependent upon personal or tribal loyalties and insensitive to international politics, an approach that worked well for a highly structured, relatively cohesive state target is not necessarily applicable even though many aspects of the work may appear to be identical. The targets which the UK intelligence community needs to study most carefully today are those that structurally and culturally look least like the Government and society it serves. We return to this when we consider terrorism, at Chapter 3.

55. Risks in intelligence assessment will arise if this limitation is not readily recognised. There may be no choice but to apply the same intelligence processes, methods and resources to one target as were developed for and applied to others. But it is important to recognize that the resulting intelligence may need to be analysed and assessed in different ways.

56. A further risk is that of 'mirror-imaging'—the belief that can permeate some intelligence analysts that the practices and values of their own cultures are universal. The more diffuse range of security challenges of the 21st century means that it will not be possible to accumulate the breadth and depth of understanding which intelligence collectors, analysts and users built up over the years about the single subject of the Soviet Union. But the more alien the target, the more important is the ability of intelligence analysts to appreciate that their own assumptions do not necessarily apply everywhere. The motives and methods of non-state organisations built on a special interest (whether criminal, religious or political) can be particularly hard for members of a stable society to assess.

57. There is also the risk of 'group think'—the development of a 'prevailing wisdom'. Well developed imagination at all stages of the intelligence process is required to overcome preconceptions. There is a case for encouraging it by providing for structured challenge, with established methods and procedures, often described as a 'devil's advocate' or a 'red teaming' approach. This may also assist in countering another danger: when problems are many and diverse, on any one of them the number of experts can be dangerously small, and individual, possibly idiosyncratic, views may pass unchallenged.

58. One final point should be mentioned here, to which we return in our Conclusions. The assessment process must be informed by an understanding of policy makers' requirements for information, but must avoid being so captured by policy objectives that it reports the world as policy makers would wish it to be rather than as it is. The JIC is part (and an important part) of

the UK's governmental machinery or it is nothing; but to have any value its product must be objective. The JIC has always been very conscious of this.

1.9 The Use of Intelligence

59. In addition to the use of intelligence to inform government policy, which we describe in Chapters 2 and 3, there are important applications in the enforcement of compliance with national law or international treaties and other obligations, in warning of untoward events, in the support of military and law enforcement operations, and in long-term planning for future national security capabilities. The British Government's machinery for the areas covered by our Review is described at Chapter 4.

Members of the Committee

The Rt Hon The Lord Butler of Brockwell KG GCB CVO (Chairman)
The Rt Hon Sir John Chilcot GCB
The Rt Hon Field Marshal The Lord Inge KG GCB DL
The Rt Hon Michael Mates MP
The Rt Hon Ann Taylor MP

Appendix D

Iraq's Weapons of Mass Destruction: The Assessment of the British Government

Foreword by the Prime Minister, The Right Honourable Tony Blair, MP

The document published today is based, in large part, on the work of the Joint Intelligence Committee (JIC). The JIC is at the heart of the British intelligence machinery. It is chaired by the Cabinet Office and made up of the heads of the UK's three Intelligence and Security Agencies, the Chief of Defence Intelligence, and senior officials from key government departments. For over 60 years the JIC has provided regular assessments to successive Prime Ministers and senior colleagues on a wide range of foreign policy and international security issues.

Its work, like the material it analyses, is largely secret. It is unprecedented for the Government to publish this kind of document. But in light of the debate about Iraq and Weapons of Mass Destruction (WMD), I wanted to share with the British public the reasons why I believe this issue to be a current and serious threat to the UK national interest.

In recent months, I have been increasingly alarmed by the evidence from inside Iraq that despite sanctions, despite the damage done to his capability in the past, despite the UN Security Council Resolutions expressly outlawing it, and despite his denials, Saddam Hussein is continuing to develop WMD, and with them the ability to inflict real damage upon the region, and the stability of the world.

Gathering intelligence inside Iraq is not easy. Saddam's is one of the most secretive and dictatorial regimes in the world. So I believe people will understand why the Agencies cannot be specific about the sources, which have formed the judgements in this document, and why we cannot publish everything we know. We cannot, of course, publish the detailed raw intelligence. I and other Ministers have been briefed in detail on the intelligence and are satisfied as to its authority. I also want to pay tribute to our Intelligence and Security Services for the often extraordinary work that they do.

What I believe the assessed intelligence has established beyond doubt is that Saddam has continued to produce chemical and biological weapons, that he continues in his efforts to develop nuclear weapons, and that he has been able to extend the range of his ballistic missile programme. I also believe that, as stated in the document, Saddam will now do his utmost to try to conceal his weapons from UN inspectors.

The picture presented to me by the JIC in recent months has become more not less worrying. It is clear that, despite sanctions, the policy of containment has not worked sufficiently well to prevent Saddam from developing these weapons.

I am in no doubt that the threat is serious and current, that he has made progress on WMD, and that he has to be stopped.

Saddam has used chemical weapons, not only against an enemy state, but against his own people. Intelligence reports make clear that he sees the building up of his WMD capability, and the belief overseas that he would use these weapons, as vital to his strategic interests, and in particular his goal of regional domination. And the document discloses that his military planning allows for some of the WMD to be ready within 45 minutes of an order to use them.

I am quite clear that Saddam will go to extreme lengths, indeed has already done so, to hide these weapons and avoid giving them up.

In today's inter-dependent world, a major regional conflict does not stay confined to the region in question. Faced with someone who has shown himself capable of using WMD, I believe the international community has to stand up for itself and ensure its authority is upheld.

The threat posed to international peace and security, when WMD are in the hands of a brutal and aggressive regime like Saddam's, is real. Unless we face up to the threat, not only do we risk undermining the authority of the UN, whose resolutions he defies, but more importantly and in the longer term, we place at risk the lives and prosperity of our own people.

The case I make is that the UN Resolutions demanding he stops his WMD programme are being flouted; that since the inspectors left four years ago he has continued with this programme; that the inspectors must be allowed back in to do their job properly; and that if he refuses, or if he makes it impossible for them to do their job, as he has done in the past, the international community will have to act.

I believe that faced with the information available to me, the UK Government has been right to support the demands that this issue be confronted and dealt with. We must ensure that he does not get to use the weapons he has, or get hold of the weapons he wants.

Executive Summary

1. Under Saddam Hussein Iraq developed chemical and biological weapons, acquired missiles allowing it to attack neighbouring countries with these weapons and persistently tried to develop a nuclear bomb. Saddam has used chemical weapons, both against Iran and against his own people. Following the Gulf War, Iraq had to admit to all this. And in the ceasefire of 1991 Saddam agreed unconditionally to give up his weapons of mass destruction.
2. Much information about Iraq's weapons of mass destruction is already in the public domain from UN reports and from Iraqi defectors. This points clearly to Iraq's continuing possession, after 1991, of chemical and biological agents and weapons produced before the Gulf War. It shows that Iraq has refurbished sites formerly associated with the production of chemical and biological agents. And it indicates that Iraq remains able to manufacture these agents, and to use bombs, shells, artillery rockets and ballistic missiles to deliver them.
3. An independent and well-researched overview of this public evidence was provided by the International Institute for Strategic Studies (IISS) on 9 September. The IISS report also suggested that Iraq could assemble nuclear weapons within months of obtaining fissile material from foreign sources.
4. As well as the public evidence, however, significant additional information is available to the Government from secret intelligence sources, described in more detail in this paper. This intelligence cannot tell us about everything. However, it provides a fuller picture of Iraqi plans and capabilities. It shows that Saddam Hussein attaches great importance to possessing weapons of mass destruction which he regards as the basis for Iraq's regional power. It shows that he does not regard them only as weapons of last resort. He is ready to use them, including against his own population, and is determined to retain them, in breach of United Nations Security Council Resolutions (UNSCR).
5. Intelligence also shows that Iraq is preparing plans to conceal evidence of these weapons, including incriminating documents, from renewed inspections. And it confirms that despite sanctions and the policy of containment, Saddam has continued to make progress with his illicit weapons programmes.
6. As a result of the intelligence we judge that Iraq has:
 -continued to produce chemical and biological agents;

-military plans for the use of chemical and biological weapons, including against its own Shia population. Some of these weapons are deployable within 45 minutes of an order to use them;
-command and control arrangements in place to use chemical and biological weapons. Authority ultimately resides with Saddam Hussein. (There is intelligence that he may have delegated this authority to his son Qusai);
-developed mobile laboratories for military use, corroborating earlier reports about the mobile production of biological warfare agents;
-pursued illegal programmes to procure controlled materials of potential use in the production of chemical and biological weapons programmes;
-tried covertly to acquire technology and materials which could be used in the production of nuclear weapons;
-sought significant quantities of uranium from Africa, despite having no active civil nuclear power programme that could require it;
-recalled specialists to work on its nuclear programme;
-illegally retained up to 20 al-Hussein missiles, with a range of 650 km, capable of carrying chemical or biological warheads;
-started deploying its al-Samoud liquid propellant missile, and has used the absence of weapons inspectors to work on extending its range to at least 200 km, which is beyond the limit of 150 km imposed by the United Nations;
-started producing the solid-propellant Ababil-100, and is making efforts to extend its range to at least 200 km, which is beyond the limit of 150 km imposed by the United Nations;
-constructed a new engine test stand for the development of missiles capable of reaching the UK Sovereign Base Areas in Cyprus and NATO members (Greece and Turkey), as well as all Iraq's Gulf neighbours and Israel;
-pursued illegal programmes to procure materials for use in its illegal development of long range missiles;
-learnt lessons from previous UN weapons inspections and has already begun to conceal sensitive equipment and documentation in advance of the return of inspectors.

7. These judgements reflect the views of the Joint Intelligence Committee (JIC). More details on the judgements and on the development of the JIC's assessments since 1998 are set out in Part 1 of this paper.
8. Iraq's weapons of mass destruction are in breach of international law. Under a series of UN Security Council Resolutions Iraq is obliged to destroy its holdings of these weapons under the supervision of UN inspectors. Part 2 of the paper sets out the key UN Security Council Resolutions. It also summarises the history of the UN inspection

regime and Iraq's history of deception, intimidation and concealment in its dealings with the UN inspectors.

9. But the threat from Iraq does not depend solely on the capabilities we have described. It arises also because of the violent and aggressive nature of Saddam Hussein's regime. His record of internal repression and external aggression gives rise to unique concerns about the threat he poses. The paper briefly outlines in Part 3 Saddam's rise to power, the nature of his regime and his history of regional aggression. Saddam's human rights abuses are also catalogued, including his record of torture, mass arrests and summary executions.
10. The paper briefly sets out how Iraq is able to finance its weapons programme. Drawing on illicit earnings generated outside UN control, Iraq generated illegal income of some $3 billion in 2001.

Appendix E

National Security Strategy of the United States of America, March 2006

I. Overview of America's National Security Strategy

It is the policy of the United States to seek and support democratic movements and institutions in every nation and culture, with the ultimate goal of ending tyranny in our world. In the world today, the fundamental character of regimes matters as much as the distribution of power among them. The goal of our statecraft is to help create a world of democratic, well-governed states that can meet the needs of their citizens and conduct themselves responsibly in the international system. This is the best way to provide enduring security for the American people.

Achieving this goal is the work of generations. The United States is in the early years of a long struggle, similar to what our country faced in the early years of the Cold War. The 20th century witnessed the triumph of freedom over the threats of fascism and communism. Yet a new totalitarian ideology now threatens, an ideology grounded not in secular philosophy but in the perversion of a proud religion. Its content may be different from the ideologies of the last century, but its means are similar: intolerance, murder, terror, enslavement, and repression.

Like those who came before us, we must lay the foundations and build the institutions that our country needs to meet the challenges we face. The chapters that follow will focus on several essential tasks. The United States must:

- Champion aspirations for human dignity;
- Strengthen alliances to defeat global terrorism and work to prevent attacks against us and our friends;
- Work with others to defuse regional conflicts;

- Prevent our enemies from threatening us, our allies, and our friends with weapons of mass destruction (WMD);
- Ignite a new era of global economic growth through free markets and free trade;
- Expand the circle of development by opening societies and building the infrastructure of democracy;
- Develop agendas for cooperative action with other main centers of global power;
- Transform America's national security institutions to meet the challenges and opportunities of the 21st century; and
- Engage the opportunities and confront the challenges of globalization.

II. Champion Aspirations for Human Dignity

A. Summary of National Security Strategy 2002

The United States must defend liberty and justice because these principles are right and true for all people everywhere. These nonnegotiable demands of human dignity are protected most securely in democracies. The United States Government will work to advance human dignity in word and deed, speaking out for freedom and against violations of human rights and allocating appropriate resources to advance these ideals.

B. Successes and Challenges Since 2002

Since 2002, the world has seen extraordinary progress in the expansion of freedom, democracy, and human dignity:

- The peoples of Afghanistan and Iraq have replaced tyrannies with democracies.
- In Afghanistan, the tyranny of the Taliban has been replaced by a freely elected government; Afghans have written and ratified a constitution guaranteeing rights and freedoms unprecedented in their history; and an elected legislature gives the people a regular voice in their government.
- In Iraq, a tyrant has been toppled; over 8 million Iraqis voted in the nation's first free and fair election; a freely negotiated constitution was passed by a referendum in which almost 10 million Iraqis participated; and, for the first time in their history, nearly 12 million Iraqis have elected a permanent government under a popularly determined constitution.

- The people of Lebanon have rejected the heavy hand of foreign rule. The people of Egypt have experienced more open but still flawed elections. Saudi Arabia has taken some preliminary steps to give its citizens more of a voice in their government. Jordan has made progress in opening its political process. Kuwait and Morocco are pursuing agendas of political reform.
- The "color revolutions" in Georgia, Ukraine, and Kyrgyzstan have brought new hope for freedom across the Eurasian landmass.
- Democracy has made further advances in Africa, Latin America, and Asia, with peaceful transfers of power; growth in independent judiciaries and the rule of law; improved election practices; and expanding political and economic rights.

The human desire for freedom is universal, but the growth of freedom is not inevitable. Without support from free nations, freedom's spread could be hampered by the challenges we face:

- Many governments are at fragile stages of political development and need to consolidate democratic institutions—and leaders that have won democratic elections need to uphold the principles of democracy;
- Some governments have regressed, eroding the democratic freedoms their peoples enjoy;
- Some governments have not delivered the benefits of effective democracy and prosperity to their citizens, leaving them susceptible to or taken over by demagogues peddling an anti-free market authoritarianism;
- Some regimes seek to separate economic liberty from political liberty, pursuing prosperity while denying their people basic rights and freedoms; and
- Tyranny persists in its harshest form in a number of nations.

C. The Way Ahead

The United States has long championed freedom because doing so reflects our values and advances our interests. It reflects our values because we believe the desire for freedom lives in every human heart and the imperative of human dignity transcends all nations and cultures.

Championing freedom advances our interests because the survival of liberty at home increasingly depends on the success of liberty abroad. Governments that honor their citizens' dignity and desire for freedom tend to uphold responsible conduct toward other nations, while governments that brutalize their people also threaten the peace and stability of other nations. Because democracies are the most responsible members of the international system, promoting democracy is the most effective long-term measure for strengthening international stability; reducing regional conflicts; countering terrorism and terror-supporting extremism; and extending peace and prosperity.

To protect our Nation and honor our values, the United States seeks to extend freedom across the globe by leading an international effort to end tyranny and to promote effective democracy.

1. *Explaining the Goal: Ending Tyranny*

Tyranny is the combination of brutality, poverty, instability, corruption, and suffering, forged under the rule of despots and despotic systems. People living in nations such as the Democratic People's Republic of Korea (DPRK), Iran, Syria, Cuba, Belarus, Burma, and Zimbabwe know firsthand the meaning of tyranny; it is the bleak reality they endure every day. And the nations they border know the consequences of tyranny as well, for the misrule of tyrants at home leads to instability abroad. All tyrannies threaten the world's interest in freedom's expansion, and some tyrannies, in their pursuit of WMD or sponsorship of terrorism, threaten our immediate security interests as well.

Tyranny is not inevitable, and recent history reveals the arc of the tyrant's fate. The 20th century has been called the "Democracy Century," as tyrannies fell one by one and democracies rose in their stead. At mid-century about two dozen of the world's governments were democratic; 50 years later this number was over 120. The democratic revolution has embraced all cultures and all continents.

Though tyranny has few advocates, it needs more adversaries. In today's world, no tyrant's rule can survive without the support or at least the tolerance of other nations. To end tyranny we must summon the collective outrage of the free world against the oppression, abuse, and impoverishment that tyrannical regimes inflict on their people and summon their collective action against the dangers tyrants pose to the security of the world.

An end to tyranny will not mark an end to all global ills. Disputes, disease, disorder, poverty, and injustice will outlast tyranny, confronting democracies long after the last tyrant has fallen. Yet tyranny must not be tolerated—it is a crime of man, not a fact of nature.

2. *Explaining the Goal: Promoting Effective Democracies*

As tyrannies give way, we must help newly free nations build effective democracies: states that are respectful of human dignity, accountable to their citizens, and responsible towards their neighbors. Effective democracies:

- Honor and uphold basic human rights, including freedom of religion, conscience, speech, assembly, association, and press;
- Are responsive to their citizens, submitting to the will of the people, especially when people vote to change their government;

- Exercise effective sovereignty and maintain order within their own borders, protect independent and impartial systems of justice, punish crime, embrace the rule of law, and resist corruption; and
- Limit the reach of government, protecting the institutions of civil society, including the family, religious communities, voluntary associations, private property, independent business, and a market economy.

In effective democracies, freedom is indivisible. Political, religious, and economic liberty advance together and reinforce each other. Some regimes have opened their economies while trying to restrict political or religious freedoms. This will not work.

Over time, as people gain control over their economic lives, they will insist on more control over their political and personal lives as well. Yet political progress can be jeopardized if economic progress does not keep pace. We will harness the tools of economic assistance, development aid, trade, and good governance to help ensure that new democracies are not burdened with economic stagnation or endemic corruption.

Elections are the most visible sign of a free society and can play a critical role in advancing effective democracy. But elections alone are not enough—they must be reinforced by other values, rights, and institutions to bring about lasting freedom. Our goal is human liberty protected by democratic institutions.

Participation in elections by individuals or parties must include their commitment to the equality of all citizens; minority rights; civil liberties; voluntary and peaceful transfer of power; and the peaceful resolution of differences. Effective democracy also requires institutions that can protect individual liberty and ensure that the government is responsive and accountable to its citizens. There must be an independent media to inform the public and facilitate the free exchange of ideas. There must be political associations and political parties that can freely compete. Rule of law must be reinforced by an independent judiciary, a professional legal establishment, and an honest and competent police force.

These principles are tested by the victory of Hamas candidates in the recent elections in the Palestinian territories. The Palestinian people voted in a process that was free, fair, and inclusive.

The Palestinian people having made their choice at the polls, the burden now shifts to those whom they have elected to take the steps necessary to advance peace, prosperity, and statehood for the Palestinian people. Hamas has been designated as a terrorist organization by the United States and European Union (EU) because it has embraced terrorism and deliberately killed innocent civilians. The international community has made clear that there is a fundamental contradiction between armed group and militia activities and the building of a democratic state. The international community has also made clear that a two-state solution to the conflict requires all participants in the democratic process to renounce violence and terror, accept Israel's right to exist, and disarm as outlined in the Roadmap. These requirements are clear, firm, and of long standing. The opportunity for peace and statehood —a consistent goal of this Administration—is open if Hamas will abandon its terrorist roots and change its relationship with Israel.

The elected Hamas representatives also have an opportunity and a responsibility to uphold the principles of democratic government, including protection of minority rights and basic freedoms and a commitment to a recurring, free, and fair electoral process. By respecting these principles, the new Palestinian leaders can demonstrate their own commitment to freedom and help bring a lasting democracy to the Palestinian territories. But any elected government that refuses to honor these principles cannot be considered fully democratic, however it may have taken office.

3. *How We Will Advance Freedom: Principled in Goals and Pragmatic in Means*

We have a responsibility to promote human freedom. Yet freedom cannot be imposed; it must be chosen. The form that freedom and democracy take in any land will reflect the history, culture, and habits unique to its people.

The United States will stand with and support advocates of freedom in every land. Though our principles are consistent, our tactics will vary. They will reflect, in part, where each government is on the path from tyranny to democracy. In some cases, we will take vocal and visible steps on behalf of immediate change. In other cases, we will lend more quiet support to lay the foundation for future reforms. As we consider which approaches to take, we will be guided by what will most effectively advance freedom's cause while we balance other interests that are also vital to the security and well-being of the American people.

In the cause of ending tyranny and promoting effective democracy, we will employ the full array of political, economic, diplomatic, and other tools at our disposal, including:

- Speaking out against abuses of human rights;
- Supporting publicly democratic reformers in repressive nations, including by holding high-level meetings with them at the White House, Department of State, and U.S. Embassies;
- Using foreign assistance to support the development of free and fair elections, rule of law, civil society, human rights, women's rights, free media, and religious freedom;
- Tailoring assistance and training of military forces to support civilian control of the military and military respect for human rights in a democratic society;

- Applying sanctions that designed to target those who rule oppressive regimes while sparing the people;
- Encouraging other nations not to support oppressive regimes;
- Partnering with other democratic nations to promote freedom, democracy, and human rights in specific countries and regions;
- Strengthening and building new initiatives such as the Broader Middle East and North Africa Initiative's Foundation for the Future, the Community of Democracies, and the United Nations Democracy Fund;
- Forming creative partnerships with nongovernmental organizations and other civil society voices to support and reinforce their work;
- Working with existing international institutions such as the United Nations and regional organizations such as the Organization for Security and Cooperation in Europe, the African Union (AU), and the Organization of American States (OAS) to help implement their democratic commitments, and helping establish democracy charters in regions that lack them;
- Supporting condemnation in multilateral institutions of egregious violations of human rights and freedoms;
- Encouraging foreign direct investment in and foreign assistance to countries where there is a commitment to the rule of law, fighting corruption, and democratic accountability; and
- Concluding free trade agreements (FTAs) that encourage countries to enhance the rule of law, fight corruption, and further democratic accountability. These tools must be used vigorously to protect the freedoms that face particular peril around the world: religious freedom, women's rights, and freedom for men, women, and children caught in the cruel network of human trafficking.
- Against a terrorist enemy that is defined by religious intolerance, we defend the First Freedom: the right of people to believe and worship according to the dictates of their own conscience, free from the coercion of the state, the coercion of the majority, or the coercion of a minority that wants to dictate what others must believe.
- No nation can be free if half its population is oppressed and denied fundamental rights. We affirm the inherent dignity and worth of women, and support vigorously their full participation in all aspects of society.
- Trafficking in persons is a form of modern-day slavery, and we strive for its total abolition. Future generations will not excuse those who turn a blind eye to it.

Our commitment to the promotion of freedom is a commitment to walk alongside governments and their people as they make the difficult transition to effective democracies. We will not abandon them before the transition is secure because immature democracies can be prone to conflict and vulnerable to exploitation by terrorists. We will not let the challenges of democratic transitions frighten us into clinging to the illusory stability of the authoritarian.

America's closest alliances and friendships are with countries with whom we share common values and principles. The more countries demonstrate that they treat their own citizens with respect and are committed to democratic principles, the closer and stronger their relationship with America is likely to be.

The United States will lead and calls on other nations to join us in a common international effort. All free nations have a responsibility to stand together for freedom because all free nations share an interest in freedom's advance.

III. Strengthen Alliances to Defeat Global Terrorism and Work to Prevent Attacks Against Us and Our Friends

A. Summary of National Security Strategy, 2002

Defeating terrorism requires a long-term strategy and a break with old patterns. We are fighting a new enemy with global reach. The United States can no longer simply rely on deterrence to keep the terrorists at bay or defensive measures to thwart them at the last moment. The fight must be taken to the enemy, to keep them on the run. To succeed in our own efforts, we need the support and concerted action of friends and allies. We must join with others to deny the terrorists what they need to survive: safe haven, financial support, and the support and protection that certain nation-states historically have given them.

B. Current Context: Successes and Challenges

The war against terror is not over. America is safer, but not yet safe. As the enemy adjusts to our successes, so too must we adjust. The successes are many:

- Al-Qaida has lost its safe haven in Afghanistan.
- A multinational coalition joined by the Iraqis is aggressively prosecuting the war against the terrorists in Iraq.
- The al-Qaida network has been significantly degraded. Most of those in the al-Qaida network responsible for the September 11 attacks, including the plot's mastermind Khalid Shaykh Muhammad, have been captured or killed.
- There is a broad and growing global consensus that the deliberate killing of innocents is never justified by any calling or cause.

- Many nations have rallied to fight terrorism, with unprecedented cooperation on law enforcement, intelligence, military, and diplomatic activity.
- Numerous countries that were part of the problem before September 11 are now increasingly becoming part of the solution—and this transformation has occurred without destabilizing friendly regimes in key regions.
- The Administration has worked with Congress to adopt and implement key reforms like the Patriot Act which promote our security while also protecting our fundamental liberties.

The enemy is determined, however, and we face some old and new challenges:

- Terrorist networks today are more dispersed and less centralized. They are more reliant on smaller cells inspired by a common ideology and less directed by a central command structure.
- While the United States Government and its allies have thwarted many attacks, we have not been able to stop them all. The terrorists have struck in many places, including Afghanistan, Egypt, Indonesia, Iraq, Israel, Jordan, Morocco, Pakistan, Russia, Saudi Arabia, Spain, and the United Kingdom. And they continue to seek WMD in order to inflict even more catastrophic attacks on us and our friends and allies.
- The ongoing fight in Iraq has been twisted by terrorist propaganda as a rallying cry.
- Some states, such as Syria and Iran, continue to harbor terrorists at home and sponsor terrorist activity abroad.

C. The Way Ahead

From the beginning, the War on Terror has been both a battle of arms and a battle of ideas—a fight against the terrorists and against their murderous ideology. In the short run, the fight involves using military force and other instruments of national power to kill or capture the terrorists, deny them safe haven or control of any nation; prevent them from gaining access to WMD; and cut off their sources of support. In the long run, winning the war on terror means winning the battle of ideas, for it is ideas that can turn the disenchanted into murderers willing to kill innocent victims.

While the War on Terror is a battle of ideas, it is not a battle of religions. The transnational terrorists confronting us today exploit the proud religion of Islam to serve a violent political vision: the establishment, by terrorism and subversion, of a totalitarian empire that denies all political and religious freedom. These terrorists distort the idea of jihad into a call for murder against those they regard as apostates or unbelievers—including Christians, Jews, Hindus, other religious traditions, and all Muslims who disagree with them. Indeed, most of the terrorist attacks since September 11 have occurred in Muslim countries and most of the victims have been Muslims.

To wage this battle of ideas effectively, we must be clear-eyed about what does and does not give rise to terrorism:

- Terrorism is not the inevitable by-product of poverty. Many of the September 11 hijackers were from middle-class backgrounds, and many terrorist leaders, like bin Laden, are from privileged upbringings.
- Terrorism is not simply a result of hostility to U.S. policy in Iraq. The United States was attacked on September 11 and earlier, well before we toppled the Saddam Hussein regime. Moreover, countries that stayed out of the Iraq war have not been spared from terror attack.
- Terrorism is not simply a result of Israeli–Palestinian issues. Al-Qaida plotting for the September 11 attacks began in the 1990s, during an active period in the peace process.
- Terrorism is not simply a response to our efforts to prevent terror attacks. The al- Qaida network targeted the United States long before the United States targeted al- Qaida. Indeed, the terrorists are emboldened more by perceptions of weakness than by demonstrations of resolve. Terrorists lure recruits by telling them that we are decadent and easily intimidated and will retreat if attacked.

The terrorism we confront today springs from:

- Political alienation. Transnational terrorists are recruited from people who have no voice in their own government and see no legitimate way to promote change in their own country. Without a stake in the existing order, they are vulnerable to manipulation by those who advocate a perverse vision based on violence and destruction.
- Grievances that can be blamed on others. The failures the terrorists feel and see are blamed on others, and on perceived injustices from the recent or sometimes distant past. The terrorists' rhetoric keeps wounds associated with this past fresh and raw, a potent motivation for revenge and terror.
- Sub-cultures of conspiracy and misinformation. Terrorists recruit more effectively from populations whose information about the world is contaminated by falsehoods and corrupted by conspiracy theories. The distortions keep alive grievances and filter out facts that would challenge popular prejudices and self-serving propaganda.
- An ideology that justifies murder. Terrorism ultimately depends upon the appeal of an ideology that excuses or even glorifies the deliberate killing of innocents. A proud religion—the religion of Islam—has been

twisted and made to serve an evil end, as in other times and places other religions have been similarly abused.

Defeating terrorism in the long run requires that each of these factors be addressed. The genius of democracy is that it provides a counter to each.

- In place of alienation, democracy offers an ownership stake in society, a chance to shape one's own future.
- In place of festering grievances, democracy offers the rule of law, the peaceful resolution of disputes, and the habits of advancing interests through compromise.
- In place of a culture of conspiracy and misinformation, democracy offers freedom of speech, independent media, and the marketplace of ideas, which can expose and discredit falsehoods, prejudices, and dishonest propaganda.
- In place of an ideology that justifies murder, democracy offers a respect for human dignity that abhors the deliberate targeting of innocent civilians.

Democracy is the opposite of terrorist tyranny, which is why the terrorists denounce it and are willing to kill the innocent to stop it. Democracy is based on empowerment, while the terrorists' ideology is based on enslavement. Democracies expand the freedom of their citizens, while the terrorists seek to impose a single set of narrow beliefs. Democracy sees individuals as equal in worth and dignity, having an inherent potential to create and to govern themselves. The terrorists see individuals as objects to be exploited, and then to be ruled and oppressed.

Democracies are not immune to terrorism. In some democracies, some ethnic or religious groups are unable or unwilling to grasp the benefits of freedom otherwise available in the society. Such groups can evidence the same alienation and despair that the transnational terrorists exploit in undemocratic states. This accounts for the emergence in democratic societies of homegrown terrorists such as were responsible for the bombings in London in July 2005 and for the violence in some other nations. Even in these cases, the long-term solution remains deepening the reach of democracy so that all citizens enjoy its benefits.

The strategy to counter the lies behind the terrorists' ideology is to empower the very people the terrorists most want to exploit: the faithful followers of Islam. We will continue to support political reforms that empower peaceful Muslims to practice and interpret their faith. The most vital work will be done within the Islamic world itself, and Jordan, Morocco, and Indonesia have begun to make important strides in this effort. Responsible

Islamic leaders need to denounce an ideology that distorts and exploits Islam for destructive ends and defiles a proud religion.

Many of the Muslim faith are already making this commitment at great personal risk. They realize they are a target of this ideology of terror. Everywhere we have joined in the fight against terrorism, Muslim allies have stood beside us, becoming partners in this vital cause. Pakistan and Saudi Arabia have launched effective efforts to capture or kill the leadership of the al-Qaida network. Afghan troops are in combat against Taliban remnants. Iraqi soldiers are sacrificing to defeat al-Qaida in their own country. These brave citizens know the stakes—the survival of their own liberty, the future of their own region, the justice and humanity of their own traditions—and the United States is proud to stand beside them.

The advance of freedom and human dignity through democracy is the long-term solution to the transnational terrorism of today. To create the space and time for that long-term solution to take root, there are four steps we will take in the short term.

- **Prevent attacks by terrorist networks before they occur.** A government has no higher obligation than to protect the lives and livelihoods of its citizens. The hard core of the terrorists cannot be deterred or reformed; they must be tracked down, killed, or captured. They must be cut off from the network of individuals and institutions on which they depend for support. That network must in turn be deterred, disrupted, and disabled by using a broad range of tools.
- **Deny WMD to rogue states and to terrorist allies who would use them without hesitation**. Terrorists have a perverse moral code that glorifies deliberately targeting innocent civilians. Terrorists try to inflict as many casualties as possible and seek WMD to this end. Denying terrorists WMD will require new tools and new international approaches. We are working with partner nations to improve security at vulnerable nuclear sites worldwide and bolster the ability of states to detect, disrupt, and respond to terrorist activity involving WMD.
- **Deny terrorist groups the support and sanctuary of rogue states.** The United States and its allies in the War on Terror make no distinction between those who commit acts of terror and those who support and harbor them, because they are equally guilty of murder. Any government that chooses to be an ally of terror, such as Syria or Iran, has chosen to be an enemy of freedom, justice, and peace. The world must hold those regimes to account.
- **Deny the terrorists control of any nation that they would use as a base and launching pad for terror.** The terrorists' goal is to overthrow a rising democracy; claim a strategic country as a haven for terror; destabilize the Middle East; and strike America and other free nations with

> ever-increasing violence. This we can never allow. This is why success in Afghanistan and Iraq is vital, and why we must prevent terrorists from exploiting ungoverned areas.

America will lead in this fight, and we will continue to partner with allies and will recruit new friends to join the battle.

Afghanistan and Iraq: The Front Lines in the War on Terror

Winning the War on Terror requires winning the battles in Afghanistan and Iraq. In Afghanistan, the successes already won must be consolidated. A few years ago, Afghanistan was condemned to a pre-modern nightmare. Now it has held two successful free elections and is a staunch ally in the war on terror. Much work remains, however, and the Afghan people deserve the support of the United States and the entire international community.

The terrorists today see Iraq as the central front of their fight against the United States. They want to defeat America in Iraq and force us to abandon our allies before a stable democratic government has been established that can provide for its own security. The terrorists believe they would then have proven that the United States is a waning power and an unreliable friend.

In the chaos of a broken Iraq the terrorists believe they would be able to establish a safe haven like they had in Afghanistan, only this time in the heart of a geopolitically vital region.

Surrendering to the terrorists would likewise hand them a powerful recruiting tool: the perception that they are the vanguard of history.

When the Iraqi Government, supported by the Coalition, defeats the terrorists, terrorism will be dealt a critical blow. We will have broken one of al-Qaida's most formidable factions—the network headed by Zarqawi—and denied him the safe haven he seeks in Iraq. And the success of democracy in Iraq will be a launching pad for freedom's success throughout a region that for decades has been a source of instability and stagnation.

The Administration has explained in some detail the strategy for helping the Iraqi people defeat the terrorists and neutralize the insurgency in Iraq. This requires supporting the Iraqi people in integrating activity along three broad tracks:

Political: Work with Iraqis to:

- **Isolate** hardened enemy elements who are unwilling to accept a peaceful political process;
- **Engage** those outside the political process who are willing to turn away from violence and invite them into that process; and
- **Build** stable, pluralistic, and effective national institutions that can protect the interests of all Iraqis.

Security: Work with Iraqi Security Forces to:

- **Clear** areas of enemy control by remaining on the offensive, killing and capturing enemy fighters, and denying them safe haven;
- **Hold** areas freed from enemy control with an adequate Iraqi security force presence that ensures these areas remain under the control of a peaceful Iraqi Government; and
- **Build** Iraqi Security Forces and the capacity of local institutions to deliver services, advance the rule of law, and nurture civil society.

Economic: Work with the Iraqi Government to:

- **Restore** Iraq's neglected infrastructure so that Iraqis can meet increasing demand and the needs of a growing economy;
- **Reform** Iraq's economy so that it can be self-sustaining based on market principles; and
- **Build** the capacity of Iraqi institutions to maintain their infrastructure, rejoin the international economic community, and improve the general welfare and prosperity of all Iraqis.

IV. Work with Others to Defuse Regional Conflicts

A. Summary of National Security Strategy 2002

Regional conflicts are a bitter legacy from previous decades that continue to affect our national security interests today. Regional conflicts do not stay isolated for long and often spread or devolve into humanitarian tragedy or anarchy. Outside parties can exploit them to further other ends, much as al-Qaida exploited the civil war in Afghanistan. This means that even if the United States does not have a direct stake in a particular conflict, our interests are likely to be affected over time. Outsiders generally cannot impose solutions on parties that are not ready to embrace them, but outsiders can sometimes help create the conditions under which the parties themselves can take effective action.

B. Current Context: Successes and Challenges

The world has seen remarkable progress on a number of the most difficult regional conflicts that destroyed millions of lives over decades.

- In Sudan, the United States led international negotiations that peacefully resolved the 20-year conflict between the Government of Sudan and the Sudanese Peoples Liberation Movement.

- In Liberia, the United States led international efforts to restore peace and bolster stability after vicious internal conflict.
- Israeli forces have withdrawn from the Gaza Strip and the northern West Bank, creating the prospect for transforming Israeli-Palestinian relations and underscoring the need for the Palestinian Authority to stand up an effective, responsible government.
- Relations between India and Pakistan have improved, with an exchange of high-level visits and a new spirit of cooperation in the dispute over Kashmir—a cooperation made more tangible by humanitarian actions undertaken following a destructive earthquake.
- The cooperative approach to the relief effort following the tsunami that hit Indonesia resulted in political shifts that helped make possible a peaceful settlement in the bitter separatist conflict in Aceh.
- In Northern Ireland, the implementation of key parts of the Good Friday Agreement, including the decommissioning of weapons, marked a substantial milestone in ending that long-standing civil conflict.

Numerous remaining regional challenges demand the world's attention:

- In Darfur, the people of an impoverished region are the victims of genocide arising from a civil war that pits a murderous militia, backed by the Sudanese Government, against a collection of rebel groups.
- In Colombia, a democratic ally is fighting the persistent assaults of Marxist terrorists and drug-traffickers.
- In Venezuela, a demagogue awash in oil money is undermining democracy and seeking to destabilize the region.
- In Cuba, an anti-American dictator continues to oppress his people and seeks to subvert freedom in the region.
- In Uganda, a barbaric rebel cult—the Lord's Resistance Army—is exploiting a regional conflict and terrorizing a vulnerable population.
- In Ethiopia and Eritrea, a festering border dispute threatens to erupt yet again into open war.
- In Nepal, a vicious Maoist insurgency continues to terrorize the population while the government retreats from democracy.

C. The Way Ahead

Regional conflicts can arise from a wide variety of causes, including poor governance, external aggression, competing claims, internal revolt, tribal rivalries, and ethnic or religious hatreds. If left unaddressed, however, these different causes lead to the same ends: failed states, humanitarian disasters, and ungoverned areas that can become safe havens for terrorists.

The Administration's strategy for addressing regional conflicts includes three levels of engagement: conflict prevention and resolution; conflict intervention; and post-conflict stabilization and reconstruction.

Effective international cooperation on these efforts is dependent on capable partners. To this end, Congress has enacted new authorities that will permit the United States to train and equip our foreign partners in a more timely and effective manner. Working with Congress, we will continue to pursue foreign assistance reforms that allow the President to draw on the skills of agencies across the United States Government.

1. *Conflict Prevention and Resolution*

The most effective long-term measure for conflict prevention and resolution is the promotion of democracy. Effective democracies may still have disputes, but they are equipped to resolve their differences peacefully, either bilaterally or by working with other regional states or international institutions.

In the short term, however, a timely offer by free nations of "good offices" or outside assistance can sometimes prevent conflict or help resolve conflict once started. Such early measures can prevent problems from becoming crises and crises from becoming wars. The United States is ready to play this role when appropriate. Even with outside help, however, there is no substitute for bold and effective local leadership.

Progress in the short term may also depend upon the stances of key regional actors. The most effective way to address a problem within one country may be by addressing the wider regional context. This regional approach has particular application to Israeli–Palestinian issues, the conflicts in the Great Lakes region of Africa, and the conflict within Nepal.

2. *Conflict Intervention*

Some conflicts pose such a grave threat to our broader interests and values that conflict intervention may be needed to restore peace and stability. Recent experience has underscored that the international community does not have enough high-quality military forces trained and capable of performing these peace operations. The Administration has recognized this need and is working with the North Atlantic Treaty Organization (NATO) to improve the capacity of states to intervene in conflict situations. We launched the Global Peace Operations Initiative at the 2004 G-8 Summit to train peacekeepers for duty in Africa. We are also supporting United Nations (U.N.) reform to improve its ability to carry out peacekeeping missions with enhanced accountability, oversight, and results based management practices.

3. *Post-Conflict Stabilization and Reconstruction*

Once peace has been restored, the hard work of post-conflict stabilization and reconstruction must begin. Military involvement may be necessary to stop a bloody conflict, but peace and stability will last only if follow-on efforts to restore order and rebuild are successful. The world has found through bitter experience that success often depends on the early establishment of strong local institutions such as effective police forces and a functioning justice and penal system. This governance capacity is critical to establishing the rule of law and a free market economy, which provide long-term stability and prosperity.

To develop these capabilities, the Administration established a new office in the Department of State, the Office of the Coordinator for Reconstruction and Stabilization, to plan and execute civilian stabilization and reconstruction efforts. The office draws on all agencies of the government and integrates its activities with our military's efforts. The office will also coordinate United States Government efforts with other governments building similar capabilities (such as the United Kingdom, Canada, the EU, and others), as well as with new international efforts such as the U.N. Peacebuilding Commission.

4. *Genocide*

Patient efforts to end conflicts should not be mistaken for tolerance of the intolerable. Genocide is the intent to destroy in whole or in part a national, ethnic, racial, or religious group. The world needs to start honoring a principle that many believe has lost its force in parts of the international community in recent years: genocide must not be tolerated. It is a moral imperative that states take action to prevent and punish genocide. History teaches that sometimes other states will not act unless America does its part. We must refine United States Government efforts—economic, diplomatic, and law-enforcement—so that they target those individuals responsible for genocide and not the innocent citizens they rule. Where perpetrators of mass killing defy all attempts at peaceful intervention, armed intervention may be required, preferably by the forces of several nations working together under appropriate regional or international auspices.

We must not allow the legal debate over the technical definition of "genocide" to excuse inaction. The world must act in cases of mass atrocities and mass killing that will eventually lead to genocide even if the local parties are not prepared for peace.

V. Prevent Our Enemies from Threatening Us, Our Allies, and Our Friends with Weapons of Mass Destruction

A. Summary of National Security Strategy, 2002

The security environment confronting the United States today is radically different from what we have faced before. Yet the first duty of the United States Government remains what it always has been: to protect the American people and American interests. It is an enduring American principle that this duty obligates the government to anticipate and counter threats, using all elements of national power, before the threats can do grave damage. The greater the threat, the greater is the risk of inaction—and the more compelling the case for taking anticipatory action to defend ourselves, even if uncertainty remains as to the time and place of the enemy's attack. There are few greater threats than a terrorist attack with WMD.

To forestall or prevent such hostile acts by our adversaries, the United States will, if necessary, act preemptively in exercising our inherent right of self-defense. The United States will not resort to force in all cases to preempt emerging threats. Our preference is that nonmilitary actions succeed. And no country should ever use preemption as a pretext for aggression.

Countering proliferation of WMD requires a comprehensive strategy involving strengthened nonproliferation efforts to deny these weapons of terror and related expertise to those and defeat WMD and missile threats before they are unleashed; and *improved protection* seeking them; *proactive counterproliferation efforts* to defend against to mitigate the consequences of WMD use. We aim to convince our adversaries that they cannot achieve their goals with WMD, and thus deter and dissuade them from attempting to use or even acquire these weapons in the first place.

B. Current Context: Successes and Challenges

We have worked hard to protect our citizens and our security. The United States has worked extensively with the international community and key partners to achieve common objectives.

- The United States has begun fielding ballistic missile defenses to deter and protect the United States from missile attacks by rogue states armed with WMD. The fielding of such missile defenses was made possible by the United States' withdrawal from the 1972 Anti-Ballistic Missile Treaty, which was done in accordance with the treaty's provisions.
- In May 2003, the Administration launched the Proliferation Security Initiative (PSI), a global effort that aims to stop shipments of WMD, their delivery systems, and related material. More than 70 countries

have expressed support for this initiative, and it has enjoyed several successes in impeding WMD trafficking.

- United States leadership in extensive law enforcement and intelligence cooperation involving several countries led to the roll-up of the A.Q. Khan nuclear network.
- Libya voluntarily agreed to eliminate its WMD programs shortly after a PSI interdiction of a shipment of nuclear-related material from the A.Q. Khan network to Libya.
- The United States led in securing passage in April 2004 of United Nations Security Council (UNSC) Resolution 1540, requiring nations to criminalize WMD proliferation and institute effective export and financial controls.
- We have led the effort to strengthen the ability of the International Atomic Energy Agency (IAEA) to detect and respond to nuclear proliferation.
- The Administration has established a new comprehensive framework, *Biodefense for the 21st Century*, incorporating innovative initiatives to protect the United States against bioterrorism. Nevertheless, serious challenges remain.
- Iran has violated its non-proliferation treaty safeguards obligations and refuses to provide objective guarantees that its nuclear program is solely for peaceful purposes.
- The DPRK continues to destabilize its region and defy the international community, now boasting a small nuclear arsenal and an illicit nuclear program in violation of its international obligations.
- Terrorists, including those associated with the al-Qaida network, continue to pursue WMD.
- Some of the world's supply of weapons-grade fissile material—the necessary ingredient for making nuclear weapons—is not properly protected.
- Advances in biotechnology provide greater opportunities for state and non-state actors to obtain dangerous pathogens and equipment.

C. The Way Ahead

We are committed to keeping the world's most dangerous weapons out of the hands of the world's most dangerous people.

1. Nuclear Proliferation

The proliferation of nuclear weapons poses the greatest threat to our national security. Nuclear weapons are unique in their capacity to inflict instant loss of life on a massive scale. For this reason, nuclear weapons hold special appeal to rogue states and terrorists. The best way to block aspiring nuclear states or nuclear terrorists is to deny them access to the essential ingredient of fissile material. It is much harder to deny states or terrorists other key components, for nuclear weapons represent a 60-year old technology and the knowledge is widespread. Therefore, our strategy focuses on controlling fissile material with two priority objectives: first, to keep states from acquiring the capability to produce fissile material suitable for making nuclear weapons; and second, to deter, interdict, or prevent any transfer of that material from states that have this capability to rogue states or to terrorists.

The first objective requires closing a loophole in the Non-Proliferation Treaty that permits regimes to produce fissile material that can be used to make nuclear weapons under cover of a civilian nuclear power program. To close this loophole, we have proposed that the world's leading nuclear exporters create a safe, orderly system that spreads nuclear energy without spreading nuclear weapons. Under this system, all states would have reliable access at reasonable cost to fuel for civilian nuclear power reactors. In return, those states would remain transparent and renounce the enrichment and reprocessing capabilities that can produce fissile material for nuclear weapons. In this way, enrichment and reprocessing will not be necessary for nations seeking to harness nuclear energy for strictly peaceful purposes.

The Administration has worked with the international community in confronting nuclear proliferation.

We may face no greater challenge from a single country than from Iran. For almost 20 years, the Iranian regime hid many of its key nuclear efforts from the international community. Yet the regime continues to claim that it does not seek to develop nuclear weapons. The Iranian regime's true intentions are clearly revealed by the regime's refusal to negotiate in good faith; its refusal to come into compliance with its international obligations by providing the IAEA access to nuclear sites and resolving troubling questions; and the aggressive statements of its President calling for Israel to "be wiped off the face of the earth." The United States has joined with our EU partners and Russia to pressure Iran to meet its international obligations and provide objective guarantees that its nuclear program is only for peaceful purposes. This diplomatic effort must succeed if confrontation is to be avoided.

As important as are these nuclear issues, the United States has broader concerns regarding Iran. The Iranian regime sponsors terrorism; threatens Israel; seeks to thwart Middle East peace; disrupts democracy in Iraq; and denies the aspirations of its people for freedom. The nuclear issue and our other concerns can ultimately be resolved only if the Iranian regime makes the strategic decision to change these policies, open up itspolitical system, and afford freedom to its people. This is the ultimate goal of U.S. policy. In the interim, we will continue to take all necessary measures to protect our national and economic security against the adverse effects of their bad conduct. The problems lie with the illicit behavior and dangerous ambition of the Iranian regime, not the legitimate aspirations and interests of the Iranian people. Our strategy is to block the threats posed by the regime while expanding our engagement and outreach to the people the regime is oppressing.

The North Korean regime also poses a serious nuclear proliferation challenge. It presents a long and bleak record of duplicity and bad-faith negotiations. In the past, the regime has attempted to split the United States from its allies. This time, the United States has successfully forged a consensus among key regional partners—China, Japan, Russia, and the Republic of Korea (ROK)—that the DPRK must give up all of its existing nuclear programs. Regional cooperation offers the best hope for a peaceful, diplomatic resolution of this problem. In a joint statement signed on September 19, 2005, in the Six-Party Talks among these participants, the DPRK agreed to abandon its nuclear weapons and all existing nuclear programs. The joint statement also declared that the relevant parties would negotiate a permanent peace for the Korean peninsula and explore ways to promote security cooperation in Asia. Along with our partners in the Six-Party Talks, the United States will continue to press the DPRK to implement these commitments. The United States has broader concerns regarding the DPRK as well. The DPRK counterfeits our currency; traffics in narcotics and engages in other illicit activities; threatens the ROK with its army and its neighbors with its missiles; and brutalizes and starves its people. The DPRK regime needs to change these policies, open up its political system, and afford freedom to its people. In the interim, we will continue to take all necessary measures to protect our national and economic security against the adverse effects of their bad conduct.

The second nuclear proliferation objective is to keep fissile material out of the hands of rogue states and terrorists. To do this we must address the danger posed by inadequately safeguarded nuclear and radiological materials worldwide. The Administration is leading a global effort to reduce and secure such materials as quickly as possible through several initiatives including the Global Threat Reduction Initiative (GTRI). The GTRI locates, tracks, and reduces existing stockpiles of nuclear material This new initiative also discourages trafficking in nuclear material by emplacing detection equipment at key transport nodes.

Building on the success of the PSI, the United States is also leading international efforts to shut down WMD trafficking by targeting key maritime and air transportation and transshipment routes, and by cutting off proliferators from financial resources that support their activities.

2. *Biological Weapons*

Biological weapons also pose a grave WMD threat because of the risks of contagion that would spread disease across large populations and around the globe. Unlike nuclear weapons, biological weapons do not require hard-to-acquire infrastructure or materials. This makes the challenge of controlling their spread even greater.

Countering the spread of biological weapons requires a strategy focused on improving our capacity to detect and respond to biological attacks, securing dangerous pathogens, and limiting the spread of materials useful for biological weapons. The United States is working with partner nations and institutions to strengthen global biosurveillance capabilities for early detection of suspicious outbreaks of disease. We have launched new initiatives at home to modernize our public health infrastructure and to encourage industry to speed the development of new classes of vaccines and medical countermeasures. This will also enhance our Nation's ability to respond to pandemic public health threats, such as avian influenza.

3. *Chemical Weapons*

Chemical weapons are a serious proliferation concern and are actively sought by terrorists, including al-Qaida. Much like biological weapons, the threat from chemical weapons increases with advances in technology, improvements in agent development, and ease in acquisition of materials and equipment.

To deter and defend against such threats, we work to identify and disrupt terrorist networks that seek chemical weapons capabilities, and seek to deny them access to materials needed to make these weapons. We are improving our detection and other chemical defense capabilities at home and abroad, including ensuring that U.S. military forces and emergency responders are trained and equipped to manage the consequences of a chemical weapons attack.

4. *The Need for Action*

The new strategic environment requires new approaches to deterrence and defense. Our deterrence strategy no longer rests primarily on the grim premise of inflicting devastating consequences on potential foes. Both offenses and defenses are necessary to deter state and non-state actors, through denial of the objectives of their attacks and, if necessary, responding with overwhelming force.

Safe, credible, and reliable nuclear forces continue to play a critical role. We are strengthening deterrence by developing a new triad composed of offensive strike systems (both nuclear and improved conventional capabilities); active and passive defenses, including missile defenses; and a responsive infrastructure, all bound together by enhanced command and control, planning, and intelligence systems. These capabilities will better deter some of the new threats we face, while also bolstering our security commitments to allies. Such security commitments have played a crucial role in convincing some countries to forgo their own nuclear weapons programs, thereby aiding our nonproliferation objectives.

Deterring potential foes and assuring friends and allies, however, is only part of a broader approach. Meeting WMD proliferation challenges also requires effective international action—and the international community is most engaged in such action when the United States leads.

Taking action need not involve military force. Our strong preference and common practice is to address proliferation concerns through international diplomacy, in concert with key allies and regional partners. If necessary, however, under long-standing principles of self defense, we do not rule out the use of force before attacks occur, even if uncertainty remains as to the time and place of the enemy's attack. When the consequences of an attack with WMD are potentially so devastating, we cannot afford to stand idly by as grave dangers materialize. This is the principle and logic of preemption.

The place of preemption in our national security strategy remains the same. We will always proceed deliberately, weighing the consequences of our actions. The reasons for our actions will be clear, the force measured, and the cause just.

Iraq and Weapons of Mass Destruction

This Administration inherited an Iraq threat that was unresolved. In early 2001, the international support for U.N. sanctions and continued limits on the Iraqi regime's weapons-related activity was eroding, and key UNSC members were asking that they be lifted. For America, the September 11 attacks underscored the danger of allowing threats to linger unresolved. Saddam Hussein's continued defiance of 16 UNSC resolutions over 12 years, combined with his record of invading neighboring countries, supporting terrorists, tyrannizing his own people, and using chemical weapons, presented a threat we could no longer ignore. The UNSC unanimously passed Resolution 1441 on November 8, 2002, calling for full and immediate compliance by the Iraqi regime with its disarmament obligations. Once again, Saddam defied the international community. According to the Iraq Survey Group, the team of inspectors that went into Iraq after Saddam Hussein was toppled and whose report provides the fullest accounting of the Iraqi regime's illicit activities:

> Saddam continued to see the utility of WMD. He explained that he purposely gave an ambiguous impression about possession as a deterrent to Iran. He gave explicit direction to maintain the intellectual capabilities. As U.N. sanctions eroded there was a concomitant expansion of activities that could support full WMD reactivation. He directed that ballistic missile work continue that would support long-range missile development. Virtually no senior Iraqi believed that Saddam had forsaken WMD forever. Evidence suggests that, as resources became available and the constraints of sanctions decayed, there was a direct expansion of activity that would have the effect of supporting future WMD reconstitution.

With the elimination of Saddam's regime, this threat has been addressed, once and for all. The Iraq Survey Group also found that pre-war intelligence estimates of Iraqi WMD stockpiles were wrong—a conclusion that has been confirmed by a bipartisan commission and congressional investigations. We must learn from this experience if we are to counter successfully the very real threat of proliferation.

First, our intelligence must improve. The President and the Congress have taken steps to reorganize and strengthen the U.S. intelligence community. A single, accountable leader of the intelligence community with authorities to match his responsibilities, and increased sharing of information and increased resources, are helping realize this objective.

Second, there will always be some uncertainty about the status of hidden programs since proliferators are often brutal regimes that go to great lengths to conceal their activities. Indeed, prior to the 1991 Gulf War, many intelligence analysts underestimated the WMD threat posed by the Iraqi regime. After that conflict, they were surprised to learn how far Iraq had progressed along various pathways to try to produce fissile material.

Third, Saddam's strategy of bluff, denial, and deception is a dangerous game that dictators play at their peril. The world offered Saddam a clear choice: effect full and immediate compliance with his disarmament obligations or face serious consequences. Saddam chose the latter course and is now facing judgment in an Iraqi court. It was Saddam's reckless behavior that demanded the world's attention, and it was his refusal to remove the ambiguity that he created that forced the United States and its allies to act. We have no doubt that the world is a better place for the removal of this dangerous and unpredictable tyrant, and we have no doubt that the world is better off if tyrants know that they pursue WMD at their own peril.

VI. Ignite a New Era of Global Economic Growth through Free Markets and Free Trade

A. Summary of National Security Strategy, 2002

Promoting free and fair trade has long been a bedrock tenet of American foreign policy. Greater economic freedom is ultimately inseparable from political liberty. Economic freedom empowers individuals, and empowered individuals increasingly demand greater political freedom. Greater economic freedom also leads to greater economic opportunity and prosperity for everyone. History has judged the market economy as the single most effective economic system and the greatest antidote to poverty. To expand economic liberty and prosperity, the United States promotes free and fair trade, open markets, a stable financial system, the integration of the global economy, and secure, clean energy development.

B. Current Context: Successes and Challenges

The global economy is more open and free, and many people around the world have seen their lives improve as prosperity and economic integration have increased. The Administration has accomplished much of the economic freedom agenda it set out in 2002:

Seizing the global initiative. We have worked to open markets and integrate the global economy through launching the Doha Development Agenda negotiations of the World Trade Organization (WTO). The United States put forward bold and historic proposals to reform global agricultural trade, to eliminate farm export subsidies and reduce trade distorting support programs, to eliminate all tariffs on consumer and industrial goods, and to open global services markets. When negotiations stalled in 2003, the United States took the initiative to put Doha back on track, culminating in a successful framework agreement reached in Geneva in 2004. As talks proceed, the United States continues to lead the world in advancing bold proposals for economic freedom through open markets.

We also have led the way in helping the accessions of new WTO members such as Armenia, Cambodia, Macedonia, and Saudi Arabia.

Pressing regional and bilateral trade initiatives. We have used FTAs to open markets, support economic reform and the rule of law, and create new opportunities for American farmers and workers. Since 2001, we have:

- Implemented or completed negotiations for FTAs with **14** countries on **5** continents, and are negotiating agreements with **11** additional countries;
- Partnered with Congress to pass the Central America Free Trade Agreement–Dominican Republic (CAFTA-DR), long sought by the leaders of El Salvador, Honduras, Guatemala, Nicaragua, Costa Rica, and Dominican Republic;
- Called in 2003 for the creation of a Middle East Free Trade Area (MEFTA) by 2013 to bring the Middle East into an expanding circle of opportunity;
- Negotiated FTAs with Bahrain, Jordan, Morocco, and Oman to provide a foundation for the MEFTA initiative;
- Launched in 2002 the Enterprise for ASEAN Initiative, which led to the completion of a free trade agreement with Singapore, and the launch of negotiations with Thailand and Malaysia;
- Concluded an FTA with Australia, one of America's strongest allies in the Asia-Pacific region and a major trading partner of the United States; and

- Continued to promote the opportunities of increased trade to sub-Saharan Africa through the African Growth and Opportunity Act (AGOA), and extended opportunity to many other developing countries through the Generalized System of Preferences.

Pressing for open markets, financial stability, and deeper integration of the world economy. We have partnered with Europe, Japan, and other major economies to promote structural reforms that encourage growth, stability, and opportunity across the globe. The United States has:

- Gained agreement in the G-7 on the Agenda for Growth, which commits member states to take concrete steps to reform domestic economic systems;
- Worked with other nations that serve as regional and global engines of growth—such as India, China, the ROK, Brazil, and Russia—on reforms to open markets and ensure financial stability;
- Urged China to move to a market-based, flexible exchange rate regime—a step that would help both China and the global economy; and
- Pressed for reform of the International Financial Institutions to focus on results, fostering good governance and sound policies, and freeing poor countries from unpayable debts.

Enhancing energy security and clean development. The Administration has worked with trading partners and energy producers to expand the types and sources of energy, to open markets and strengthen the rule of law, and to foster private investment that can help develop the energy needed to meet global demand. In addition, we have:

- Worked with industrialized and emerging nations on hydrogen, clean coal, and advanced nuclear technologies; and
- Joined with Australia, China, India, Japan, and the ROK in forming the Asia-Pacific Partnership for Clean Development and Climate to accelerate deployment of clean technologies to enhance energy security, reduce poverty, and reduce pollution.

Several challenges remain:

- Protectionist impulses in many countries put at risk the benefits of open markets and impede the expansion of free and fair trade and economic growth.
- Nations that lack the rule of law are prone to corruption, lack of transparency, and poor governance. These nations frustrate the economic aspirations of their people by failing to promote entrepreneurship, pro-

tect intellectual property, or allow their citizens access to vital investment capital.

- Many countries are too dependent upon foreign oil, which is often imported from unstable parts of the world.
- Economic integration spreads wealth across the globe, but also makes local economies more subject to global market conditions.
- Some governments restrict the free flow of capital, subverting the vital role that wise investment can play in promoting economic growth. This denies investments, economic opportunity, and new jobs to the people who need them most.

C. The Way Ahead

Economic freedom is a moral imperative. The liberty to create and build or to buy, sell, and own property is fundamental to human nature and foundational to a free society. Economic freedom also reinforces political freedom. It creates diversified centers of power and authority that limit the reach of government. It expands the free flow of ideas; with increased trade and foreign investment comes exposure to new ways of thinking and living which give citizens more control over their own lives. To continue extending liberty and prosperity, and to meet the challenges that remain, our strategy going forward involves:

1. Opening Markets and Integrating Developing Countries

While most of the world affirms in principle the appeal of economic liberty, in practice too many nations hold fast to the false comforts of subsidies and trade barriers. Such distortions of the market stifle growth in developed countries, and slow the escape from poverty in developing countries. Against these short-sighted impulses, the United States promotes the enduring vision of a global economy that welcomes all participants and encourages the voluntary exchange of goods and services based on mutual benefit, not favoritism.

We will continue to advance this agenda through the WTO and through bilateral and regional FTAs.

- The United States will seek completion of the Doha Development Agenda negotiations. A successful Doha agreement will expand opportunities for Americans and for others around the world. Trade and open markets will empower citizens in developing countries to improve their lives, while reducing the opportunities for corruption that afflict state-controlled economies.
- We will continue to work with countries such as Russia, Ukraine, Kazakhstan, and Vietnam on the market reforms needed to join the

WTO. Participation in the WTO brings opportunities as well as obligations— to strengthen the rule of law and honor the intellectual property rights that sustain the modern knowledge economy, and to remove tariffs, subsidies, and other trade barriers that distort global markets and harm the world's poor.

- We will advance MEFTA by completing and bringing into force FTAs for Bahrain, Oman, and the United Arab Emirates and through other initiatives to expand open trade with and among countries in the region.
- In Africa, we are pursuing an FTA with the countries of the Southern African Customs Union: Botswana, Lesotho, Namibia, South Africa, and Swaziland.
- In Asia, we are pursuing FTAs with Thailand, the ROK, and Malaysia. We will also continue to work closely with China to ensure it honors its WTO commitments and protects intellectual property.
- In our own hemisphere, we will advance the vision of a free trade area of the Americas by building on North American Free Trade Agreement, CAFTA-DR, and the FTA with Chile. We will complete and bring into force FTAs with Colombia, Peru, Ecuador, and Panama.

2. *Opening, Integrating, and Diversifying Energy Markets to Ensure Energy Independence*

Most of the energy that drives the global economy comes from fossil fuels, especially petroleum. The United States is the world's third largest oil producer, but we rely on international sources to supply more than 50 percent of our needs. Only a small number of countries make major contributions to the world's oil supply.

The world's dependence on these few suppliers is neither responsible nor sustainable over the long term. The key to ensuring our energy security is ***diversity*** in the regions from which energy resources come and in the types of energy resources on which we rely.

- The Administration will work with resource-rich countries to increase their openness, transparency, and rule of law. This will promote effective democratic governance and attract the investment essential to developing their resources and expanding the range of energy suppliers.
- We will build the Global Nuclear Energy Partnership to work with other nations to develop and deploy advanced nuclear recycling and reactor technologies. This initiative will help provide reliable, emission-free energy with less of the waste burden of older technologies and without making available separated plutonium that could be used by rogue states

or terrorists for nuclear weapons. These new technologies will make possible a dramatic expansion of safe, clean nuclear energy to help meet the growing global energy demand.

- We will work with international partners to develop other transformational technologies such as clean coal and hydrogen. Through projects like our FutureGen initiative, we seek to turn our abundant domestic coal into emissions-free sources of electricity and hydrogen, providing our economies increased power with decreased emissions.
- On the domestic front, we are investing in zero-emission coal-fired plants; revolutionary solar and wind technologies; clean, safe nuclear energy; and cutting-edge methods of producing ethanol.

Our comprehensive energy strategy puts a priority on reducing our reliance on foreign energy sources. Diversification of energy sources also will help alleviate the "petroleum curse"—the tendency for oil revenues to foster corruption and prevent economic growth and political reform in some oil-producing states. In too many such nations, ruling elites enrich themselves while denying the people the benefits of their countries' natural wealth. In the worst cases, oil revenues fund activities that destabilize their regions or advance violent ideologies. Diversifying the suppliers within and across regions reduces opportunities for corruption and diminishes the leverage of irresponsible rulers.

3. *Reforming the International Financial System to Ensure Stability and Growth*

In our interconnected world, stable and open financial markets are an essential feature of a prosperous global economy. We will work to improve the stability and openness of markets by:

- Promoting Growth-Oriented Economic Policies Worldwide. Sound policies in the United States have helped drive much international growth. We cannot be the only source of strength, however. We will work with the world's other major economies, including the EU and Japan, to promote structural reforms that open their markets and increase productivity in their nations and across the world.
- Encouraging Adoption of Flexible Exchange Rates and Open Markets for Financial Services. The United States will help emerging economies make the transition to the flexible exchange rates appropriate for major economies. In particular, we will continue to urge China to meet its own commitment to a market-based, flexible exchange rate regime. We will also promote more open financial service markets, which encourage stable and sound financial practices.

- Strengthening International Financial Institutions. At the dawn of a previous era six decades ago, the United States championed the creation of the World Bank and the International Monetary Fund (IMF). These institutions were instrumental in the development of the global economy and an expansion of prosperity unprecedented in world history. They remain vital today, but must adapt to new realities:
  - For the World Bank and regional development banks, we will encourage greater emphasis on investments in the private sector. We will urge more consideration of economic freedom, governance, and measurable results in allocating funds. We will promote an increased use of grants to relieve the burden of unsustainable debt.
  - For the IMF, we will seek to refocus it on its core mission: international financial stability. This means strengthening the IMF's ability to monitor the financial system to prevent crises before they happen. If crises occur, the IMF's response must reinforce each country's responsibility for its own economic choices. A refocused IMF will strengthen market institutions and market discipline over financial decisions, helping to promote a stable and prosperous global economy. By doing so, over time markets and the private sector can supplant the need for the IMF to perform in its current role.
- Building Local Capital Markets and the Formal Economy in the Developing World. The first place that small businesses in developing countries turn to for resources is their own domestic markets. Unfortunately, in too many countries these resources are unavailable due to weak financial systems, a lack of property rights, and the diversion of economic activity away from the formal economy into the black market. The United States will work with these countries to develop and strengthen local capital markets and reduce the black market. This will provide more resources to helping the public sector govern effectively and the private sector grow and prosper.
- Creating a More Transparent, Accountable, and Secure International Financial System. The United States has worked with public and private partners to help secure the international financial system against abuse by criminals, terrorists, money launderers, and corrupt political leaders. We will continue to use international venues like the Financial Action Task Force to ensure that this global system is transparent and protected from abuse by tainted capital. We must also develop new tools that allow us to detect, disrupt, and isolate rogue financial players and gatekeepers.

VII. Expand the Circle of Development by Opening Societies and Building the Infrastructure of Democracy

A. Summary of National Security Strategy, 2002

Helping the world's poor is a strategic priority and a moral imperative. Economic development, responsible governance, and individual liberty are intimately connected. Past foreign assistance to corrupt and ineffective governments failed to help the populations in greatest need. Instead, it often impeded democratic reform and encouraged corruption. The United States must promote development programs that achieve measurable results—rewarding reforms, encouraging transparency, and improving people's lives. Led by the United States, the international community has endorsed this approach in the Monterrey Consensus.

B. Current Context: Successes and Challenges

The United States has improved the lives of millions of people and transformed the practice of development by adopting more effective policies and programs.

- Advancing Development and Reinforcing Reform. The Administration pioneered a revolution in development strategy with the Millennium Challenge Account program, rewarding countries that govern justly, invest in their people, and foster economic freedom. The program is based on the principle that each nation bears the responsibility for its own development. It offers governments the opportunity and the means to undertake transformational change by designing their own reform and development programs, which are then funded through the Millennium Challenge Corporation (MCC). The MCC has approved over $1.5 billion for compacts in eight countries, is working with over a dozen other countries on compacts, and has committed many smaller grants to other partner countries.
- Turning the Tide Against AIDS and Other Infectious Diseases. The President's Emergency Plan for AIDS Relief is an unprecedented, 5-year, $15 billion effort. Building on the success of pioneering programs in Africa, we have launched a major initiative that will prevent 7 million new infections, provide treatment to 2 million infected individuals, and care for 10 million AIDS orphans and others affected by the disease. We have launched a $1.2 billion, 5-year initiative to reduce malaria deaths by 50 percent in at least 15 targeted countries. To mobilize other nations and the private sector, the United States pioneered the creation

of the Global Fund to Fight HIV/AIDS, Tuberculosis, and Malaria. We are the largest donor to the Fund and have already contributed over $1.4 billion.

- Promoting Debt Sustainability and a Path Toward Private Capital Markets. The Administration has sought to break the burden of debt that traps many poor countries by encouraging international financial institutions to provide grants instead of loans to low-income nations. With the United Kingdom, we spearheaded the G-8 initiative to provide 100 percent multilateral debt relief to qualifying Heavily Indebted Poor Countries. Reducing debt to sustainable levels allows countries to focus on immediate development challenges. In the long run, reducing debt also opens access to private capital markets which foster sound policies and long-term growth.
- Addressing Urgent Needs and Investing in People. The United States leads the world in providing food relief. We launched the Initiative to End Hunger in Africa, using science, technology, and market incentives to increase the productivity of African farmers. We launched a 3-year, $900 million initiative to provide clean water to the poor. We have tripled basic education assistance through programs such as the Africa Education Initiative, which will train teachers and administrators, build schools, buy textbooks, and expand opportunities inside and outside the classroom.
- Unleashing the Power of the Private Sector. The Administration has sought to multiply the impact of our development assistance through initiatives such as the Global Development Alliance, which forges partnerships with the private sector to advance development goals, and Volunteers for Prosperity, which enlists some of our Nation's most capable professionals to serve strategically in developing nations.
- Fighting Corruption and Promoting Transparency. Through multilateral efforts like the G-8 Transparency Initiative and our policy of denying corrupt foreign officials entry into the United States, we are helping ensure that organized crime and parasitic rulers do not choke off the benefits of economic assistance and growth. We have increased our overall development assistance spending by 97 percent since 2000. In all of these efforts, the United States has sought concrete measures of success. Funding is a means, not the end. We are giving more money to help the world's poor, and giving it more effectively.

Many challenges remain, including:

- Helping millions of people in the world who continue to suffer from poverty and disease;

- Ensuring that the delivery of assistance reinforces good governance and sound economic policies; and
- Building the capacity of poor countries to take ownership of their own development strategies.

C. The Way Ahead

America's national interests and moral values drive us in the same direction: to assist the world's poor citizens and least developed nations and help integrate them into the global economy. We have accomplished many of the goals laid out in the 2002 National Security Strategy. Many of the new initiatives we launched in the last 4 years are now fully operating to help the plight of the world's least fortunate. We will persevere on this path.

Development reinforces diplomacy and defense, reducing long-term threats to our national security by helping to build stable, prosperous, and peaceful societies. Improving the way we use foreign assistance will make it more effective in strengthening responsible governments, responding to suffering, and improving people's lives.

1. *Transformational Diplomacy and Effective Democracy*

Transformational diplomacy means working with our many international partners to build and sustain democratic, well-governed states that will respond to the needs of their citizens and conduct themselves responsibly in the international system. Long-term development must include encouraging governments to make wise choices and assisting them in implementing those choices. We will encourage and reward good behavior rather than reinforce negative behavior. Ultimately it is the countries themselves that must decide to take the necessary steps toward development, yet we will help advance this process by creating external incentives for governments to reform themselves. Effective economic development advances our national security by helping promote responsible sovereignty, not permanent dependency. Weak and impoverished states and ungoverned areas are not only a threat to their people and a burden on regional economies, but are also susceptible to exploitation by terrorists, tyrants, and international criminals. We will work to bolster threatened states, provide relief in times of crisis, and build capacity in developing states to increase their progress.

2. *Making Foreign Assistance More Effective*

The Administration has created the new position of Director of Foreign Assistance (DFA) in the State Department. The DFA will serve concurrently as Administrator of U.S. Agency for International Development (USAID), a position that will continue to be at the level of Deputy Secretary, and will have, consistent with existing legal requirements, authority over all State

Department and USAID foreign assistance. This reorganization will create a more unified and rational structure that will more fully align assistance programs in State and USAID, increase the effectiveness of these programs for recipient countries, and ensure that we are being the best possible stewards of taxpayer dollars. And it will focus our foreign assistance on promoting greater ownership and responsibility on the part of host nations and their citizens.

With this new authority, the DFA/Administrator will develop a coordinated foreign assistance strategy, including 5-year, country-specific assistance strategies and annual country-specific assistance operational plans. The DFA/Administrator also will provide guidance for the assistance delivered through other entities of the United States Government, including the MCC and the Office of the Global AIDS Coordinator.

To ensure the best stewardship of our foreign assistance, the United States will:

- Distinguish among the different challenges facing different nations and address those challenges with tools appropriate for each country's stage of development;
- Encourage and reward good government and economic reform, both bilaterally and through the multilateral institutions such as international financial institutions, the G-8, and the Asia-Pacific Economic Cooperation (APEC);
- Engage the private sector to help solve development problems;
- Promote graduation from economic aid dependency with the ultimate goal of ending assistance;
- Build trade capacity to enable the poorest countries to enter into the global trade system; and
- Empower local leaders to take responsibility for their country's development. Our assistance efforts will also highlight and build on the lessons learned from successful examples of wise development and economic policy choices, such as the ROK, Taiwan, Ireland, Poland, Slovakia, Chile, and Botswana.

VIII. Develop Agendas for Cooperative Action with the Other Main Centers of Global Power

A. Summary of National Security Strategy, 2002

Relations with the most powerful countries in the world are central to our national security strategy. Our priority is pursuing American interests within cooperative relationships, particularly with our oldest and closest friends and allies. At the same time, we must seize the opportunity—unusual in historical terms—of an absence of fundamental conflict between the great powers. Another priority, therefore, is preventing the reemergence of the great power rivalries that divided the world in previous eras. New times demand new approaches, flexible enough to permit effective action even when there are reasonable differences of opinions among friends, yet strong enough to confront the challenges the world faces.

B. Current Context: Successes and Challenges

The United States has enjoyed unprecedented levels of cooperation on many of its highest national security priorities:

- The global coalition against terror has grown and deepened, with extensive cooperation and common resolve. The nations that have partnered with us in Afghanistan and Iraq have developed capabilities that can be applied to other challenges.
- We have joined with other nations around the world as well as numerous multilateral organizations to improve the capability of all nations to defend their homelands against terrorists and transnational criminals.
- We have achieved extraordinary coordination among historic rivals in pressing the DPRK to abandon its nuclear program.
- We have partnered with European allies and international institutions to pressure Iran to honor its non-proliferation commitments.
- The North Atlantic Treaty Organization (NATO) is transforming itself to meet current threats and is playing a leading role in stabilizing the Balkans and Afghanistan, as well as training the Iraqi military leadership to address its security challenges.
- We have set aside decades of mistrust and put relations with India, the world's most populous democracy, on a new and fruitful path. At the same time, America's relations with other nations have been strong enough to withstand differences and candid exchanges of views.
- Some of our oldest and closest friends disagreed with U.S. policy in Iraq. There are ongoing and serious debates with our allies about how best to address the unique and evolving nature of the global terrorist threat.
- We have disagreed on the steps to reduce agricultural subsidies and achieve success in the WTO Doha round of trade negotiations. We have also faced challenges in forging consensus with other major nations on the most effective measures to protect the environment.

C. The Way Ahead

The struggle against militant Islamic radicalism is the great ideological conflict of the early years of the 21st century and finds the great powers all on the same side—opposing the terrorists. This circumstance differs profoundly from the ideological struggles of the 20th century, which saw the great powers divided by ideology as well as by national interest.

The potential for great power consensus presents the United States with an extraordinary opportunity. Yet certain challenges must be overcome. Some nations differ with us on the appropriate pace of change. Other nations provide rhetorical support for free markets and effective democracy but little action on freedom's behalf.

Five principles undergird our strategy for relations with the main centers of global power.

- First, these relations must be set in their proper context. Bilateral policies that ignore regional and global realities are unlikely to succeed.
- Second, these relations must be supported by appropriate institutions, regional and global, to make cooperation more permanent, effective, and wide-reaching. Where existing institutions can be reformed to meet new challenges, we, along with our partners, must reform them. Where appropriate institutions do not exist, we, along with our partners, must create them.
- Third, we cannot pretend that our interests are unaffected by states' treatment of their own citizens. America's interest in promoting effective democracies rests on an historical fact: states that are governed well are most inclined to behave well. We will encourage all our partners to expand liberty, and to respect the rule of law and the dignity of the individual, as the surest way to advance the welfare of their people and to cement close relations with the United States.
- Fourth, while we do not seek to dictate to other states the choices they make, we do seek to influence the calculations on which these choices are based. We also must hedge appropriately in case states choose unwisely.
- Fifth, we must be prepared to act alone if necessary, while recognizing that there is little of lasting consequence that we can accomplish in the world without the sustained cooperation of our allies and partners.

1. The Western Hemisphere

These principles guide our relations within our own Hemisphere, the frontline of defense of American national security. Our goal remains a hemisphere fully democratic, bound together by good will, security cooperation, and the opportunity for all our citizens to prosper. Tyrants and those who would follow them belong to a different era and must not be allowed to reverse the progress of the last two decades. Countries in the Hemisphere must be helped to the path of sustained political and economic development. The deceptive appeal of anti-free market populism must not be allowed to erode political freedoms and trap the Hemisphere's poorest in cycles of poverty. If America's nearest neighbors are not secure and stable, then Americans will be less secure.

Our strategy for the Hemisphere begins with deepening key relationships with Canada and Mexico, a foundation of shared values and cooperative policies that can be extended throughout the region. We must continue to work with our neighbors in the Hemisphere to reduce illegal immigration and promote expanded economic opportunity for marginalized populations. We must also solidify strategic relationships with regional leaders in Central and South America and the Caribbean who are deepening their commitment to democratic values. And we must continue to work with regional partners to make multilateral institutions like the OAS and the Inter-American Development Bank more effective and better able to foster concerted action to address threats that may arise to the region's stability, security, prosperity, or democratic progress. Together, these partnerships can advance our four strategic priorities for the region: bolstering security, strengthening democratic institutions, promoting prosperity, and investing in people.

2. *Africa*

Africa holds growing geo-strategic importance and is a high priority of this Administration. It is a place of promise and opportunity, linked to the United States by history, culture, commerce, and strategic significance. Our goal is an African continent that knows liberty, peace, stability, and increasing prosperity.

Africa's potential has in the past been held hostage by the bitter legacy of colonial misrule and bad choices by some African leaders. The United States recognizes that our security depends upon partnering with Africans to strengthen fragile and failing states and bring ungoverned areas under the control of effective democracies.

Overcoming the challenges Africa faces requires partnership, not paternalism. Our strategy is to promote economic development and the expansion of effective, democratic governance so that African states can take the lead in addressing African challenges. Through improved governance, reduced corruption, and market reforms, African nations can lift themselves toward a better future. We are committed to working with African nations to strengthen their domestic capabilities and the regional capacity of the AU to support post-conflict transformations, consolidate democratic transitions, and improve peacekeeping and disaster responses.

3. *Middle East*

The Broader Middle East continues to command the world's attention. For too long, too many nations of the Middle East have suffered from a freedom deficit. Repression has fostered corruption, imbalanced or stagnant economies, political resentments, regional conflicts, and religious extremism. These maladies were all cloaked by an illusion of stability. Yet the peoples of the Middle East share the same desires as people in the rest of the world: liberty, opportunity, justice, order, and peace. These desires are now being expressed in movements for reform. The United States is committed to supporting the efforts of reformers to realize a better life for themselves and their region.

We seek a Middle East of independent states, at peace with each other, and fully participating in an open global market of goods, services, and ideas. We are seeking to build a framework that will allow Israel and the Palestinian territories to live side by side in peace and security as two democratic states. In the wider region, we will continue to support efforts for reform and freedom in traditional allies such as Egypt and Saudi Arabia. Tyrannical regimes such as Iran and Syria that oppress at home and sponsor terrorism abroad know that we will continue to stand with their people against their misrule. And in Iraq, we will continue to support the Iraqi people and their historic march from tyranny to effective democracy. We will work with the freely elected, democratic government of Iraq—our new partner in the War on Terror—to consolidate and expand freedom, and to build security and lasting stability.

4. *Europe*

The North Atlantic Treaty Organization remains a vital pillar of U.S. foreign policy. The Alliance has been strengthened by expanding its membership and now acts beyond its borders as an instrument for peace and stability in many parts of the world. It has also established partnerships with other key European states, including Russia, Ukraine, and others, further extending NATO's historic transformation. The internal reform of NATO structures, capabilities, and procedures must be accelerated to ensure that NATO is able to carry out its missions effectively. The Alliance's door will also remain open to those countries that aspire for membership and meet NATO standards. Further, NATO must deepen working relationships between and across institutions, as it is doing with the EU, and as it also could do with new institutions. Such relationships offer opportunities for enhancing the distinctive strengths and missions of each organization.

Europe is home to some of our oldest and closest allies. Our cooperative relations are built on a sure foundation of shared values and interests. This foundation is expanding and deepening with the ongoing spread of effective democracies in Europe, and must expand and deepen still further if we are to reach the goal of a Europe whole, free, and at peace. These democracies are effective partners, joining with us to promote global freedom and prosperity. Just as in the special relationship that binds us to the United Kingdom, these cooperative relationships forge deeper ties between our nations.

5. *Russia*

The United States seeks to work closely with Russia on strategic issues of common interest and to manage issues on which we have differing interests. By reason of geography and power, Russia has great influence not only in Europe and its own immediate neighborhood, but also in many other regions of vital interest to us: the broader Middle East, South and Central Asia, and East Asia. We must encourage Russia to respect the values of freedom and democracy at home and not to impede the cause of freedom and democracy in these regions. Strengthening our relationship will depend on the policies, foreign and domestic, that Russia adopts. Recent trends regrettably point toward a diminishing commitment to democratic freedoms and institutions. We will work to try to persuade the Russian government to move forward, not backward, along freedom's path.

Stability and prosperity in Russia's neighborhood will help deepen our relations with Russia; but that stability will remain elusive as long as this region is not governed by effective democracies. We will seek to persuade Russia's government that democratic progress in Russia and its region benefits the peoples who live there and improves relationships with us, with other Western governments, and among themselves. Conversely, efforts to prevent democratic development at home and abroad will hamper the development of Russia's relations with the United States, Europe, and its neighbors.

6. *South and Central Asia*

South and Central Asia is a region of great strategic importance where American interests and values are engaged as never before. India is a great democracy, and our shared values are the foundation of our good relations. We are eager to see Pakistan move along a stable, secure, and democratic path. Our goal is for the entire region of South and Central Asia to be democratic, prosperous, and at peace.

We have made great strides in transforming America's relationship with India, a major power that shares our commitment to freedom, democracy, and rule of law. In July 2005, we signed a bold agreement—a roadmap to realize the meaningful cooperation that had eluded our two nations for decades. India now is poised to shoulder global obligations in cooperation with the United States in a way befitting a major power.

Progress with India has been achieved even as the United States has improved its strategic relationship with Pakistan. For decades, outsiders acted as if good relations with India and Pakistan were mutually exclusive. This Administration has shown that improved relations with both are possible and can help India and Pakistan make strides toward a lasting peace between themselves. America's relationship with Pakistan will not be a mirror image of our relationship with India. Together, our relations with the nations of South Asia can serve as a foundation for deeper engagement throughout Central Asia. Increasingly, Afghanistan will assume its historical role as a land bridge between South and Central Asia, connecting these two vital regions.

Central Asia is an enduring priority for our foreign policy. The five countries of Central Asia are distinct from one another and our relations with each, while important, will differ. In the region as a whole, the elements of our larger strategy meet, and we must pursue those elements simultaneously: promoting effective democracies and the expansion of free-market reforms, diversifying global sources of energy, and enhancing security and winning the War on Terror.

7. *East Asia*

East Asia is a region of great opportunities and lingering tensions. Over the past decade, it has been a source of extraordinary economic dynamism and also of economic turbulence. Few regional economies have more effectively harnessed the engines of future prosperity: technology and globalized trade. Yet few regions have had greater difficulty overcoming the suspicions of the past.

The United States is a Pacific nation, with extensive interests throughout East and Southeast Asia. The region's stability and prosperity depend on our sustained engagement: maintaining robust partnerships supported by a forward defense posture supporting economic integration through expanded trade and investment and promoting democracy and human rights.

Forging new international initiatives and institutions can assist in the spread of freedom, prosperity, and regional security. Existing institutions like the APEC forum and the Association of Southeast Asian Nations (ASEAN) Regional Forum, can play a vital role. New arrangements, such as the U.S.-ASEAN Enhanced Partnership, or others that are focused on problem-solving and action, like the Six-Party Talks and the PSI, can likewise bring together Asian nations to address common challenges. And Asian nations that share our values can join us in partnership to strengthen new democracies and promote democratic reforms throughout the region. This institutional framework, however, must be built upon a foundation of sound bilateral relations with key states in the region.

With Japan, the United States enjoys the closest relations in a generation. As the world's two largest economies and aid donors, acting in concert multiplies each of our strengths and magnifies our combined contributions to global progress. Our shared commitment to democracy at home offers a sure foundation for cooperation abroad.

With Australia, our alliance is global in scope. From Iraq and Afghanistan to our historic FTA, we are working jointly to ensure security, prosperity, and expanded liberty. With the ROK, we share a vision of a prosperous, democratic, and united Korean peninsula. We also share a commitment to democracy at home and progress abroad and are translating that common vision into joint action to sustain our alliance into the 21st century.

With Southeast Asia, we celebrate the dynamism of increased economic freedom and look to further extend political freedom to all the people in the region, including those suffering under the repressive regime in Myanmar. In promoting greater economic and political liberty, we will work closely with our allies and key friends, including Indonesia, Malaysia, the Philippines, Singapore, and Thailand.

China encapsulates Asia's dramatic economic successes, but China's transition remains incomplete. In one generation, China has gone from poverty and isolation to growing integration into the international economic system. China once opposed global institutions; today it is a permanent member of the UNSC and the WTO. As China becomes a global player, it must act as a responsible stakeholder that fulfills its obligations and works with the United States and others to advance the international system that has enabled its success: enforcing the international rules that have helped China lift itself out of a century of economic deprivation, embracing the economic and political standards that go along with that system of rules, and contributing to international stability and security by working with the United States and other major powers.

China's leaders proclaim that they have made a decision to walk the transformative path of peaceful development. If China keeps this commitment, the United States will welcome the emergence of a China that is peaceful and prosperous and that cooperates with us to address common challenges and mutual interests. China can make an important contribution to global prosperity and ensure its own prosperity for the longer term if it will rely more on domestic demand and less on global trade imbalances to drive its economic growth. China shares our exposure to the challenges of globalization and other transnational concerns. Mutual interests can guide our cooperation on issues such as terrorism, proliferation, and energy security. We will work to increase our cooperation to combat disease pandemics and reverse environmental degradation.

The United States encourages China to continue down the road of reform and openness, because in this way China's leaders can meet the legitimate needs and aspirations of the Chinese people for liberty, stability, and prosperity. As economic growth continues, China will face a growing demand from its own people to follow the path of East Asia's many modern democracies, adding political freedom to economic freedom. Continuing along this path will contribute to regional and international security.

China's leaders must realize, however, that they cannot stay on this peaceful path while holding on to old ways of thinking and acting that exacerbate concerns throughout the region and the world. These old ways include:

- Continuing China's military expansion in a non-transparent way;
- Expanding trade, but acting as if they can somehow "lock up" energy supplies around the world or seek to direct markets rather than opening them up—as if they can follow a mercantilism borrowed from a discredited era; and
- Supporting resource-rich countries without regard to the misrule at home or misbehavior abroad of those regimes.

China and Taiwan must also resolve their differences peacefully, without coercion and without unilateral action by either China or Taiwan.

Ultimately, China's leaders must see that they cannot let their population increasingly experience the freedoms to buy, sell, and produce, while denying them the rights to assemble, speak, and worship. Only by allowing the Chinese people to enjoy these basic freedoms and universal rights can China honor its own constitution and international commitments and reach its full potential. Our strategy seeks to encourage China to make the right strategic choices for its people, while we hedge against other possibilities.

IX. Transform America's National Security Institutions to Meet the Challenges and Opportunities of the 21st Century

A. Summary of National Security Strategy, 2002

The major institutions of American national security were designed in a different era to meet different challenges. They must be transformed.

B. Current Context: Successes and Challenges

In the last four years, we have made substantial progress in transforming key national security institutions.

- The establishment of the Department of Homeland Security brought under one authority 22 federal entities with vital roles to play in protecting our Nation and preventing terrorist attacks within the United States. The Department is focused on three national security priorities:

preventing terrorist attacks within the United States; reducing America's vulnerability to terrorism; and minimizing the damage and facilitating the recovery from attacks that do occur.

- In 2004, the Intelligence Community launched its most significant reorganization since the 1947 National Security Act. The centerpiece is a new position, the Director of National Intelligence, endowed with expanded budgetary, acquisition, tasking, and personnel authorities to integrate more effectively the efforts of the Community into a more unified, coordinated, and effective whole. The transformation also includes a new National Counterterrorism Center and a new National Counterproliferation Center to manage and coordinate planning and activities in those critical areas. The transformation extends to the FBI, which has augmented its intelligence capabilities and is now more fully and effectively integrated with the Intelligence Community.
- The Department of Defense has completed the 2006 Quadrennial Defense Review, which details how the Department will continue to adapt and build to meet new challenges.
- We are pursuing a future force that will provide tailored deterrence of both state and non-state threats (including WMD employment, terrorist attacks in the physical and information domains, and opportunistic aggression) while assuring allies and dissuading potential competitors. The Department of Defense also is expanding Special Operations Forces and investing in advanced conventional capabilities to help win the long war against terrorist extremists and to help dissuade any hostile military competitor from challenging the United States, its allies, and partners.
- The Department is transforming itself to better balance its capabilities across four categories of challenges:
  - **Traditional** challenges posed by states employing conventional armies, navies, and air forces in well-established forms of military competition.
  - **Irregular** challenges from state and non-state actors employing methods such as terrorism and insurgency to counter our traditional military advantages, or engaging in criminal activity such as piracy and drug trafficking that threaten regional security.
  - **Catastrophic** challenges involving the acquisition, possession, and use of WMD by state and non-state actors; and deadly pandemics and other natural disasters that produce WMD-like effects.
  - **Disruptive** challenges from state and non-state actors who employ technologies and capabilities (such as biotechnology, cyber and space operations, or directed energy weapons) in new ways to counter military advantages the United States currently enjoys.

C. The Way Ahead

We must extend and enhance the transformation of key institutions, both domestically and abroad. At home, we will pursue three priorities:

- Sustaining the transformation already under way in the Departments of Defense, Homeland Security, and Justice; the Federal Bureau of Investigation; and the Intelligence Community.
- Continuing to reorient the Department of State towards transformational diplomacy, which promotes effective democracy and responsible sovereignty. Our diplomats must be able to step outside their traditional role to become more involved with the challenges within other societies, helping them directly, channeling assistance, and learning from their experience. This effort will include:
    - Promoting the efforts of the new Director for Foreign Assistance/Administrator to ensure that foreign assistance is used as effectively as possible to meet our broad foreign policy objectives. This new office will align more fully the foreign assistance activities carried out by the Department of State and USAID, demonstrating that we are responsible stewards of taxpayer dollars.
    - Improving our capability to plan for and respond to post-conflict and failedstate situations. The Office of Reconstruction and Stabilization will integrate all relevant United States Government resources and assets in conducting reconstruction and stabilization operations. This effort must focus on building the security and law enforcement structures that are often the prerequisite for restoring order and ensuring success.
    - Developing a civilian reserve corps, analogous to the military reserves. The civilian reserve corps would utilize, in a flexible and timely manner, the human resources of the American people for skills and capacities needed for international disaster relief and post-conflict reconstruction.
    - Strengthening our public diplomacy, so that we advocate the policies and values of the United States in a clear, accurate, and persuasive way to a watching and listening world. This includes actively engaging foreign audiences, expanding educational opportunities for Americans to learn about foreign languages and cultures and for foreign students and scholars to study in the United States; empowering the voices of our citizen ambassadors as well as those foreigners who share our commitment to a safer, more compassionate world; enlisting the support of the private sector; increasing our channels for dialogue with Muslim leaders and citizens; and confronting

propaganda quickly, before myths and distortions have time to take root in the hearts and minds of people across the world.

- ***Improving the capacity of agencies to plan, prepare, coordinate, integrate and execute responses*** covering the full range of crisis contingencies and long-term challenges. We need to strengthen the capacity of departments and agencies to do comprehensive, results-oriented planning. Agencies that traditionally played only a domestic role increasingly have a role to play in our foreign and security policies. This requires us to better integrate interagency activity both at home and abroad.

Abroad, we will work with our allies on three priorities:

- Promoting meaningful reform of the U.N., including:
  - Creating structures to ensure financial accountability and administrative and organizational efficiency.
  - Enshrining the principle that membership and participation privileges are earned by responsible behavior and by reasonable burden-sharing of security and stability challenges.
  - Enhancing the capacity of the U.N. and associated regional organizations to stand up well-trained, rapidly deployable, sustainable military and gendarme units for peace operations.
  - Ensuring that the U.N. reflects today's geopolitical realities and is not shackled by obsolete structures.
  - Reinvigorating the U.N.'s commitment, reflected in the U.N. Charter, to the promotion of democracy and human rights.
- Enhancing the role of democracies and democracy promotion throughout international and multilateral institutions, including:
  - Strengthening and institutionalizing the Community of Democracies.
  - Fostering the creation of regional democracy-based institutions in Asia, the Middle East, Africa, and elsewhere.
  - Improving the capacity of the U.N. and other multilateral institutions to advance the freedom agenda through tools like the U.N. Democracy Fund.
  - Coordinating more effectively the unique contributions of international financial institutions and regional development banks.
- Establishing results-oriented partnerships on the model of the PSI to meet new challenges and opportunities. These partnerships emphasize international cooperation, not international bureaucracy. They rely on voluntary adherence rather than binding treaties. They are oriented towards action and results rather than legislation or rule-making.

X. Engage the Opportunities and Confront the Challenges of Globalization

In recent years, the world has witnessed the growing importance of a set of opportunities and challenges that were addressed indirectly in National Security Strategy, 2002: the national security implications of globalization.

Globalization presents many opportunities. Much of the world's prosperity and improved living standards in recent years derive from the expansion of global trade, investment, information, and technology. The United States has been a leader in promoting these developments, and we believe they have improved significantly the quality of life of the American people and people the world over. Other nations have embraced these opportunities and have likewise benefited. Globalization has also helped the advance of democracy by extending the marketplace of ideas and the ideals of liberty.

These new flows of trade, investment, information, and technology are transforming national security. Globalization has exposed us to new challenges and changed the way old challenges touch our interests and values, while also greatly enhancing our capacity to respond. Examples include:

- Public health challenges like pandemics (HIV/AIDS, avian influenza) that recognize no borders. The risks to social order are so great that traditional public health approaches may be inadequate, necessitating new strategies and responses.
- Illicit trade, whether in drugs, human beings, or sex, that exploits the modern era's greater ease of transport and exchange. Such traffic corrodes social order; bolsters crime and corruption; undermines effective governance; facilitates the illicit transfer of WMD and advanced conventional weapons technology; and compromises traditional security and law enforcement.
- Environmental destruction, whether caused by human behavior or cataclysmic mega-disasters such as floods, hurricanes, earthquakes, or tsunamis. Problems of this scope may overwhelm the capacity of local authorities to respond, and may even overtax national militaries, requiring a larger international response.

These challenges are not traditional national security concerns, such as the conflict of arms or ideologies. But if left unaddressed they can threaten national security. We have learned that:

- Preparing for and managing these challenges requires the full exercise of national power, up to and including traditional security instruments. For example, the U.S. military provided critical logistical support in the response to the Southeast Asian tsunami and the South Asian earthquake until U.N. and civilian humanitarian responders could relieve the military of these vital duties.

- Technology can help, but the key to rapid and effective response lies in achieving unity of effort across a range of agencies. For example, our response to the Katrina and Rita hurricanes underscored the need for communications systems that remain operational and integrated during times of crisis. Even more vital, however, is improved coordination within the Federal government, with state and local partners, and with the private sector.
- Existing international institutions have a role to play, but in many cases coalitions of the willing may be able to respond more quickly and creatively, at least in the short term. For example, U.S. leadership in mobilizing the Regional Core Group to respond to the tsunami of 2004 galvanized the follow-on international response.
- The response and the new partnerships it creates can sometimes serve as a catalyst for changing existing political conditions to address other problems. For example, the response to the tsunami in Southeast Asia and the earthquake in Pakistan developed new lines of communication and cooperation at a local level, which opened the door to progress in reconciling long-standing regional conflicts in Aceh and the Kashmir.

Effective democracies are better able to deal with these challenges than are repressive or poorly governed states. Pandemics require robust and fully transparent public health systems, which weak governments and those that fear freedom are unable or unwilling to provide. Yet these challenges require effective democracies to come together in innovative ways.

The United States must lead the effort to reform existing institutions and create new ones—including forging new partnerships between governmental and nongovernmental actors, and with transnational and international organizations.

To confront illicit trade, for example, the Administration launched the Proliferation Security Initiative and the APEC Secure Trade in the APEC Region Initiative, both of which focus on tangible steps governments can take to combat illegal trade.

To combat the cultivation and trafficking of narcotics, the Administration devotes over $1 billion annually to comprehensive counternarcotics efforts, working with governments, particularly in Latin America and Asia, to eradicate crops, destroy production facilities, interdict shipments, and support developing alternative livelihoods.

To confront the threat of a possible pandemic, the Administration took the lead in creating the International Partnership on Avian and Pandemic Influenza, a new global partnership of states committed to effective surveillance and preparedness that will help to detect and respond quickly to any outbreaks of the disease.

XI. Conclusion

The challenges America faces are great, yet we have enormous power and influence to address those challenges. The times require an ambitious national security strategy, yet one recognizing the limits to what even a nation as powerful as the United States can achieve by itself. Our national security strategy is idealistic about goals, and realistic about means.

There was a time when two oceans seemed to provide protection from problems in other lands, leaving America to lead by example alone. That time has long since passed. America cannot know peace, security, and prosperity by retreating from the world. America must lead by deed as well as by example. This is how we plan to lead, and this is the legacy we will leave to those who follow.

Appendix F

National Intelligence Strategy of the United States of America

Our Vision—What We Will Become

A unified enterprise of innovative intelligence professionals whose common purpose in defending American lives and interests, and advancing American values, draws strength from our democratic institutions, diversity, and intellectual and technological prowess.

Our Mission—What We Must Do

- Collect, analyze, and disseminate accurate, timely, and objective intelligence, independent of political considerations, to the President and all who make and implement US national security policy, fight our wars, protect our nation, and enforce our laws.
- Conduct the US government's national intelligence program and special activities as directed by the President.
- Transform our capabilities in order to stay ahead of evolving threats to the United States, exploiting risk while recognizing the impossibility of eliminating it.
- Deploy effective counterintelligence measures that enhance and protect our activities to ensure the integrity of the intelligence system, our technology, our armed forces, and our government's decision processes.
- Perform our duties under law in a manner that respects the civil liberties and privacy of all Americans.

Our Strategy—How We Will Succeed

The stakes for America in the 21st century demand that we be more agile and resourceful than our adversaries. Our strategy is to integrate, through intelligence policy, doctrine, and technology, the different enterprises of the Intelligence Community. It encompasses current intelligence activities as well as future capabilities to ensure that we are more effective in the years ahead than we are today. The fifteen strategic objectives outlined in this strategy can be differentiated as mission objectives and enterprise objectives.

Mission objectives relate to our efforts to predict, penetrate, and preempt threats to our national security and to assist all who make and implement US national security policy, fight our wars, protect our nation, and enforce our laws in the implementation of national policy goals.

Enterprise objectives relate to our capacity to maintain competitive advantages over states and forces that threaten the security of our nation.

Transformation of the Intelligence Community will be driven by the doctrinal principle of integration. Our transformation will be centered on a high-performing intelligence workforce that is:

- Results-focused
- Collaborative
- Bold
- Future-oriented
- Self-evaluating
- Innovative

These six characteristics are interdependent and mutually reinforcing. They will shape our internal policies, programs, institutions, and technologies.

Strategic Objectives

Mission Objectives: To provide accurate and timely intelligence and conduct intelligence programs and activities directed by the President, we must support the following objectives drawn from the *National Security Strategy*:

1. Defeat terrorists at home and abroad by disarming their operational capabilities and seizing the initiative from them by promoting the growth of freedom and democracy.
2. Prevent and counter the spread of weapons of mass destruction.
3. Bolster the growth of democracy and sustain peaceful democratic states.

4. Develop innovative ways to penetrate and analyze the most difficult targets.
5. Anticipate developments of strategic concern and identify opportunities as well as vulnerabilities for decision makers.

Enterprise Objectives: To transform our capabilities faster than threats emerge, protect what needs to be protected, and perform our duties according to the law, we must:

1. Build an integrated intelligence capability to address threats to the homeland, consistent with US laws and the protection of privacy and civil liberties.
2. Strengthen analytic expertise, methods, and practices; tap expertise wherever it resides; and explore alternative analytic views.
3. Rebalance, integrate, and optimize collection capabilities to meet current and future customer and analytic priorities.
4. Attract, engage, and unify an innovative and results-focused Intelligence Community workforce.
5. Ensure that Intelligence Community members and customers can access the intelligence they need when they need it.
6. Establish new and strengthen existing foreign intelligence relationships to help us meet global security challenges.
7. Create clear, uniform security practices and rules that allow us to work together, protect our nation's secrets, and enable aggressive counterintelligence activities.
8. Exploit path-breaking scientific and research advances that will enable us to maintain and extend intelligence advantages against emerging threats.
9. Learn from our successes and mistakes to anticipate and be ready for new challenges.
10. Eliminate redundancy and programs that add little or no value and redirect savings to existing and emerging national security priorities.

Strategy Guidance

Mission Objectives

1. **Defeat terrorists at home and abroad by disarming their operational capabilities and seizing the initiative from them by promoting the growth of freedom and democracy.**

The United States is fighting a war against terror in which our first priority is to identify, disrupt, and destroy terrorist organizations of global reach and attack their leadership, their command, control, and communications, and their material support and finances. Intelligence Community efforts therefore must:

- Integrate and invigorate all US intelligence efforts to identify and disrupt terrorist organizations abroad and within US borders.
- Uncover terrorist plans and intentions, especially those that may involve obtaining or using weapons of mass destruction.
- Deny terrorists operational haven, sanctuary, and political legitimacy by supporting democratization and the rule of law in vulnerable areas.
- Enable those outside the Intelligence Community with valuable counterterrorism information (such as police, corrections officers, and border patrol officers) to contribute to the national counterterrorism effort.
- Create an information sharing environment in which access to terrorism information is matched to the roles, responsibilities, and missions of all organizations engaged in countering terrorism, and is timely, accessible, and relevant to their needs.

The Director of the National Counterterrorism Center will develop a comprehensive national intelligence plan for supporting the nation's war on terror. The plan will identify the roles and responsibilities of each member of the Intelligence Community involved in supporting our national counterterrorism efforts, including their relationships with law enforcement and homeland security authorities. The Program Manager, Information Sharing Environment, will ensure the information needs of federal, state, local, and tribal governments and the private sector are identified and satisfied.

2. Prevent and counter the spread of weapons of mass destruction.

The comprehensive strategy of the US government to combat weapons of mass destruction includes proactive counterproliferation efforts, strengthened nonproliferation efforts to prevent rogue states and terrorists from acquiring these technologies, and effective consequence management to respond to the effects of their use—whether by terrorists or hostile states.

As the WMD Commission stated in its March 2005 report, "There is no single strategy the Intelligence Community can pursue to counter the 'proliferation' menace." Rather, each destructive capability—biological, nuclear, chemical, radiological, or otherwise—will require unique and focused approaches to combating their use. To this end, Intelligence Community efforts must:

- Focus aggressive and innovative collection techniques to close knowledge gaps related to these technologies and associated weapons

programs, particularly in the area of bioterrorism, to identify the methods of conveyance, and to prevent them from reaching our shores.
- Reach outside the Intelligence Community for information and expertise relevant to these technologies.
- Integrate the analytic effort within the Intelligence Community, under the leadership of the National Counterproliferation Center, by drawing upon the unique expertise and comparative advantages of each Intelligence Community organization.
- Work closely with foreign intelligence services to form a common assessment of threats and develop effective options in response.
- Ensure that weapons of mass destruction intelligence information is coupled with protective countermeasures information and disseminated to all who fight our wars, protect our nation, and enforce our laws.

The Director of the National Counterproliferation Center will develop a comprehensive national intelligence plan for supporting the nation's efforts to prevent and counter the development and proliferation of weapons of mass destruction. The plan will identify the roles and responsibilities of each member of the Intelligence Community, including their relationships with law enforcement and homeland security authorities.

3. Bolster the growth of democracy and sustain peaceful democratic states.

We have learned to our peril that the lack of freedom in one state endangers the peace and freedom of others and that failed states are a refuge and breeding ground of extremism. Self-sustaining democratic states are essential to world peace and development.

The Intelligence Community—its collectors, analysts, and operators—therefore must:

- Support diplomatic and military efforts (including pre- and post-conflict) when intervention is necessary.
- Forge relationships with new and incipient democracies that can help them strengthen the rule of law and ward off threats to representative government.
- Provide policymakers with an enhanced analytic framework for identifying both the threats to and opportunities for promoting democracy (including free markets and economic development), as well as warning of state failure.

The Deputy Director of National Intelligence for Customer Outcomes will develop a plan to accomplish these objectives. The Deputy Director of

National Intelligence for Analysis will contribute to that plan by surveying the analytic expertise and production on democratization and state failure, and the level of Community support now provided to policymakers, identifying knowledge gaps and ways to address them, and improving support to those responsible for monitoring and assisting political and economic development and reducing the danger of state failure. The Deputy Director of National Intelligence for Collection will draft a collection plan, including the use of open sources, responsive to the information needs of this integrated plan.

4. Develop innovative ways to penetrate and analyze the most difficult targets.

America's toughest adversaries know a great deal about our intelligence system and are becoming better at hiding their intentions and capabilities. Some are ruled by closed leadership cadres, and protected by disciplined security and intelligence services. Others are amorphous groups or networks that may share common goals, training, and methods, but which operate independently. The Intelligence Community needs capabilities to penetrate the thinking of both sets of leaders by:

- Making the best use of all-source intelligence, including from open sources, on the most difficult targets.
- Developing new methodologies, including specialized training and career development, for analyzing the capabilities and intentions of hard targets.
- Improving human intelligence and corresponding technical intelligence capabilities.
- Assessing the intelligence capabilities and actions of our adversaries to ensure that an insightful counterintelligence analytic capability helps to penetrate hard targets and understand their leadership cadres.

The Deputy Director of National Intelligence for Collection will develop a plan for improving penetration of hard targets. The Deputy Director of National Intelligence for Analysis will develop a plan to assess the current state of knowledge, identify and close gaps, bolster expertise and research on these targets, and develop new methodologies against them. The National Counterterrorism Center and the National Counterintelligence Executive will devise plans to enhance analysis of terror networks and foreign intelligence establishments and activities. The latter plan will include a means to integrate counterintelligence with other sources to capitalize on opportunities for strategic offensive activities.

5. **Anticipate developments of strategic concern and identify opportunities as well as vulnerabilities for decision-makers.**

In a world in which developments anywhere can quickly affect American citizens and interests at home and abroad, the Intelligence Community must alert policymakers to problems before they escalate, and provide insights into their causes and effects. Analysis must do more than just describe what is happening and why; it must identify a range of opportunities for (and likely consequences of) diplomatic, military, law enforcement, or homeland security action.

To support policymakers, the Intelligence Community should develop, sustain, and have access to expertise on every region, every transnational security issue, and every threat to the American people. The Intelligence Community will:

- Identify and analyze possible opportunities as well as warn of potential problems.
- Promote deeper cultural understanding, better language proficiency, and scientific and technological knowledge among personnel at all levels.
- Identify gaps in coverage and work to close them through recruitment, training, and consultation with outside expertise.
- Make attention to long-term and strategic analysis a part of every analyst's assigned responsibilities, train analysts to anticipate developments likely to affect US interests, and ensure they are alert to possibilities for timely action.

The Deputy Director of National Intelligence for Analysis will establish a strategic research and analysis unit in the National Intelligence Council; develop procedures to inventory Intelligence Community analytic capabilities on all regions, specified threats, and transnational issues; develop a plan to improve the language skills, scientific and technological skills, and cultural insight of analysts; and work with the analytic components of all Intelligence Community agencies to close gaps, facilitate collaboration, and achieve appropriate balances between long-term and current analysis.

Enterprise Objectives

1. **Build an integrated intelligence capability to address threats to the homeland, consistent with US laws and the protection of privacy and civil liberties.**

Ubiquitous communications technology, easy international travel, and extremists with the resources and the intent to harm Americans wherever they may reside force us to re-think the way we conduct intelligence collection at home and its relationship with traditional intelligence gathering methods abroad. Consistent with applicable laws and the protection of civil liberties and privacy, US intelligence elements must focus their capabilities to ensure that:

- Intelligence elements in the Departments of Justice and Homeland Security are properly resourced and closely integrated within the larger Intelligence Community.
- All Intelligence Community components assist in facilitating the integration of collection and analysis against terrorists, weapons of mass destruction, and other threats to the homeland.
- State, local, and tribal entities and the private sector are connected to our homeland security and intelligence efforts.

The Deputy Director of National Intelligence for Management will develop a financial, information, and human resource plan for our intelligence capabilities to deal with threats at home that ensures the full and lawful integration of the Intelligence Community elements of the Departments of Justice and Homeland Security with the other Community elements. The Program Manager, Information Sharing Environment, in conjunction with the Chief Information Officer, will develop a plan to facilitate the means for sharing terrorism information among all appropriate federal, state, local, and tribal entities, and the private sector. The Civil Liberties Protection Officer will develop a plan to ensure that improvements to these capabilities are achieved with due regard for the privacy and civil liberties of Americans.

2. Strengthen analytic expertise, methods, and practices; tap expertise wherever it resides; and explore alternative analytic views.

To avoid intelligence failures, the analytic judgments presented to policy makers must be the product of an enterprise that values differing perspectives, nurtures and rewards expertise, and is agile and innovative in the way it deploys and utilizes that expertise.

To strengthen and sustain Intelligence Community analytic capabilities and to ensure that appropriate expertise is brought to bear efficiently and constructively, the Intelligence Community must:

- Build and sustain the expertise and capacity of the Intelligence Community's analyst "corps," leveraging the unique capabilities of each component, and fostering cross-agency collaboration at all levels.

- Utilize expertise from outside the Intelligence Community to inform judgments and to bolster areas where knowledge is lacking in the Community.
- Improve analytic methods and practices across the Community, ensuring rigor and the exploration of alternative analysis.

The Deputy Director of National Intelligence for Analysis will develop a plan to identify expertise inside and outside government, establish virtual teams of experts and interested analysts from across the Intelligence Community and US government, improve cooperation between analysis and collection, improve analytic methods and practices, and ensure analytic integrity. The plan will also address new processes to allow the Office of the Director of National Intelligence to manage key intelligence issues, including inventorying analytic leads and activities for high priority issues, identifying knowledge gaps, and working with collection managers to close them.

3. Rebalance, integrate, and optimize collection capabilities to meet current and future customer and analytic priorities.

Our technical means of collecting information must remain unmatched. They allow us to avert conflict, expand peace, and win wars. The nation gains when our technical systems are developed for multiple purposes, but long development schedules and changing requirements undermine our agility and resources. Accordingly, the Intelligence Community must:

- Expand collection and analysis from open sources, and manage them as integrated intelligence activities.
- Establish a national clandestine service to integrate all the elements of human source collection in accord with the highest traditions of professionalism and intellectual prowess.
- Rebalance the technical collection architecture to improve responsiveness to user requirements; enhance flexibility and survivability; and provide new sources and methods for current and emerging targets.
- Expand the reporting of information of intelligence value from state, local, and tribal law enforcement entities and private sector stakeholders.

The Deputy Director of National Intelligence for Collection will develop a comprehensive plan for achieving a new balance among our various collection methods—open, human, and technical sources—while taking account of the differing legal and policy framework for collection within the United States. The plan will reflect the changed nature of the threats we face, the vast opportunities of the information age, and new non-traditional sources of information now available. The Foreign Denial and Deception Committee will complete a plan for countering denial and deception practices deployed against us.

4. Attract, engage, and unify an innovative and results-focused Intelligence Community workforce.

The complexity of the challenges the United States faces in the 21st century will require those who serve in the Intelligence Community, both military and civilian, to apply expertise against a wide range of threats, and to become more adept and innovative in acquiring, analyzing, and communicating the knowledge that policymakers need.

In order to ensure the Intelligence Community is able to meet these expectations, it must:

- Recruit exceptional individuals from a diverse talent pool, train and develop them to meet the challenges they will face, and then deploy them in ways that maximize their talents and potential.
- Reward expertise, excellence, and commitment to service; provide opportunities for professional growth and leadership development, and encourage initiative, innovation, resourcefulness, and resilience among the civilian and military members of the Intelligence Community and those who lead them.
- Build an Intelligence Community-wide culture that values the abilities of each of its members and provides them developmental opportunities across the Intelligence Community in accord with their aptitudes and aspirations.

The Chief Human Capital Officer, in partnership with the Chief Training and Education Officer, will develop an Intelligence Community Strategic Human Capital Plan that will enable Community elements to: identify mission-critical human resource requirements; train, develop, and promote Community professionals according to rigorous, competency-based standards; select a senior leadership cadre that promotes high performance, employee engagement, information sharing, and collaboration; and develop evaluation and reward systems that reinforce excellence among professionals and those who lead them.

5. Ensure that Intelligence Community members and customers can access the intelligence they need when they need it.

The Intelligence Reform and Terrorism Prevention Act of 2004 directed the Director of National Intelligence to "ensure maximum availability of and access to intelligence information." We must ensure maximum interoperability inside the Community while creating effective, flexible links to customers. Intelligence Community efforts must:

- Remove impediments to information sharing within the Community, and establish policies that reflect need-to-share (versus need-to-know) for all data, removing the "ownership" by agency of intelligence information.
- Build a user-friendly system that allows customers to find needed intelligence and access it immediately.
- Develop flexible and secure networks adaptable to a rapidly changing environment and capable of getting intelligence in an unclassified form to non-traditional customers such as state, local, and tribal governments and the private sector.
- Create an intelligence "cyber community" where analysts, collectors, and customers can interact swiftly and easily in considering classified information.

The Deputy Director of National Intelligence for Customer Outcomes will oversee the development of plans to provide maximum access to intelligence information among Intelligence Community customers, consistent with applicable laws and the protection of civil liberties and privacy. The Program Manager, Information Sharing Environment, will create a plan to ensure that the Information Sharing Environment provides the functional equivalent of, or otherwise supports, a decentralized, distributed, and coordinated environment as described in Section 1016(b)(2) of the Intelligence Reform and Terrorism Prevention Act of 2004. The Chief Information Officer will develop a plan to ensure that activities and procurements relating to the information technology infrastructure and enterprise architecture of the Intelligence Community meet the need to share information more broadly.

6. Establish new and strengthen existing foreign intelligence relationships to help us meet global security challenges.

Since our most serious national security challenges are transnational, the Community must enlist like-minded nations to extend our reach. As the *National Security Strategy* states, "no nation can build a safer, better world alone." To this end, we must:

- Engage and invigorate friendly foreign intelligence services' efforts that could aid in the identification and disruption of terrorist organizations abroad and within US borders.
- Coordinate closely with foreign intelligence services to inform a common assessment of threats and options in response.

- Ensure that insights gained from our foreign intelligence relationships inform intelligence judgments and develop effective options in response.

The Deputy Director of National Intelligence for Customer Outcomes will direct the development of a strategic plan on foreign intelligence relationships to ensure that the relationships are being adequately coordinated and employed to meet national security threats. This plan will include a process to identify existing gaps as well as to determine if new foreign intelligence relationships need to be established or existing relationships strengthened.

7. Create clear, uniform security practices and rules that allow us to work together, protect our nation's secrets, and enable aggressive counterintelligence activities.

The Intelligence Community must dramatically change the basis of its security and counterintelligence policies in order to remain effective. We must rigorously assess threat, vulnerability, and protection requirements to further overall Community objectives. Intelligence Community efforts must:

- Redefine classification guidelines to allow for a large body of "sensitive" information with flexible use and sharing arrangements, and a smaller body of "restricted" information available to fewer personnel.
- Establish uniform and reciprocal Intelligence Community guidance on security issues of common concern, including access to facilities, and electronic access to systems and databases.
- Institute new procedures, including innovative security assessment and reliability monitoring, permitting agencies to expeditiously assess personnel with potential vulnerabilities.
- Ensure the various Intelligence Community elements conducting counterintelligence activities act as a cohesive whole to undertake aggressive, unified counterintelligence operations.

The Deputy Director of National Intelligence for Management will develop a plan for changing physical, information, and personnel security policies impeding the Intelligence Community's ability to achieve its mission and enterprise objectives. The National Counterintelligence Executive, in the plan for implementing the National Counterintelligence Strategy, will describe how the Community will undertake aggressive counterintelligence operations with greater unity of effort. The Chief Information Officer will develop a plan for new security policies that promote information sharing across the Intelligence Community.

8. Exploit path-breaking scientific and research advances that will enable us to maintain and extend intelligence advantages against emerging threats.

Globalization and accelerating scientific and technological progress threaten to erode the Intelligence Community's technical collection means, to undermine our ability to identify/access world-class scientific expertise, and to degrade our ability to exploit emerging technological advances.

The Intelligence Community's ability to identify and leverage cutting-edge scientific and technological research depends on our capacity to forecast technological trends, interact with leading researchers, and gain early access to innovative concepts and designs. To this end, Intelligence Community efforts must:

- Establish a centrally led, but de-centrally executed, process for Intelligence Community scientific and technological activities.
- Deepen technical expertise and strengthen advanced research and development programs within the agencies.
- Identify high risk, high reward research for special emphasis by the Office of the Director of National Intelligence, particularly in the "white spaces" between various agency efforts.
- Foster joint development among agency research efforts, where appropriate.

The Associate Director of National Intelligence for Science and Technology will develop a plan for leading the Intelligence Community's science and technology resources and activities. The plan will identify the roles and responsibilities for each member of the Intelligence Community engaged in scientific and technological activities.

9. Learn from our successes and mistakes to anticipate and be ready for new challenges.

The Intelligence Community must continuously improve its ability to record, assess, and learn from its performance, in part by establishing metrics to measure its performance. The process of conducting performance reviews and learning from both successes and failures should help identify systemic shortcomings. In addition to assimilating lessons, the Community must also assess its readiness. Intelligence Community efforts must:

- Create a lessons-learned function to assess the effectiveness of the Community's activities as a "system of systems" in supporting national policy goals.

- Establish a rigorous evaluation process that determines how well individual strategic plans meet their stated goals and how effectively they support the relevant mission and enterprise objectives.
- Incorporate into each agency's strategic plan a readiness component addressing crises and contingencies.
- Create a robust command and control system for the Director of National Intelligence.

The Deputy Director of National Intelligence for Management will develop plans to assess the Community's performance against mission and enterprise objectives, establish a Community-wide lessons-learned function, and guide the improvement of readiness within the agencies. The Chief Information Officer will develop a plan to ensure the functioning of the Director of National Intelligence's command and control system in all contingencies.

10. Eliminate redundancy and programs that add little or no value and re-direct savings to existing and emerging national security priorities.

The Intelligence Community is a vast enterprise, with areas of overlapping missions and expertise. In some instances, the overlap adds value; in others it consumes resources more appropriately directed to the Intelligence Community member having the mission at its core, or to emerging national security threats.

The Intelligence Community must manage its resources by examining national security priorities, both short and long term, and quickly adapt to changes in them. The Community must also revise its financial procedures and processes; existing budget reports are not providing the level of consistency required for appropriate oversight. To this end, the Intelligence Community must:

- Standardize, synchronize, and coordinate financial reporting in order to provide a comprehensive and auditable record of Community expenditures.
- Assess the current program development process with emphasis on evaluating how program submissions are aligned against objectives.
- Eliminate mission and program redundancy that adds little or no value.
- End programs/projects that no longer meet national security priorities or that do not deliver as promised.
- Consolidate similar programs and missions under one Community lead.
- Redirect resources saved through consolidation and terminated programs to existing and emerging threats.

- Ensure that new systems are developed in compliance with an Intelligence Community Enterprise Architecture.

The Deputy Director of National Intelligence for Management will develop a plan to identify and eliminate unnecessary redundancy and low value programs within the Intelligence Community. The plan will also address how to identify missions and programs where resources should be redirected to meet new and emerging national security threats and to enhance secure intelligence capabilities for organizations that function primarily in the United States. The plan will specify the roles and responsibilities of Intelligence Community members engaged in resource management and program development to continually examine their programs and missions and to collaborate with one another in arriving at recommendations for mission adjustments, program consolidations or terminations, and areas ripe for redirection of resources. It will also describe how to strengthen the Community's financial management systems with the goal of achieving comprehensive audits of the major intelligence programs.

Next Steps

These strategic objectives will guide Intelligence Community policy, planning, collection, analysis, operations, programming, acquisition, budgeting, and execution. They will be overseen by senior officials of the Office of the Director of National Intelligence, but will be implemented through an integrated Intelligence Community effort to capitalize on the comparative advantages of constituent organizations.

- The Deputy Director of National Intelligence for Management will develop a strategic planning and evaluation process for the Intelligence Community.
- The Fiscal Year 2008 planning, programming, and performance guidance will reflect these mission and enterprise objectives. Ongoing program and budget activities for Fiscal Years 2006 and 2007 will adjust to these objectives to the maximum extent possible.

Bibliography

Allison, Graham. *Nuclear Terrorism: The Ultimate Preventable Catastrophe*, Owl Books, Henry Holt: New York, 2004.

Anonymous. *Imperial Hubris: Why the West is Losing the War on Terror*, Brassey's: Washington, DC, 2004.

Baer, Robert, *See No Evil: The True Story of a Ground Soldier in the CIA's War on Terrorism*, Random House: New York, 2002.

Barnett, Thomas P.M. *The Pentagon's New Map: Blueprint for Action: A Future Worth Creating*, Penguin: New York, 2005.

Barnett, Thomas P., *The Pentagons New Map: War and Peace in the Twenty-First Century*. G.P. Putnam's Sons: New York, 2004.

Benjamin, Daniel and Simon, Steven. *The Next Attack: The Failure of the War on Terror and a Strategy for Getting it Right*, Henry Holt: New York, 2005.

Bernstein, Peter L. *Against the Gods: The Remarkable Story of Risk*. John Wiley & Sons: New York, 1998.

Best, Richard A. and Bazan, Elizabeth, *Intelligence Spending: Public Disclosure Issues*, CRS Report for Congress, Congressional Research Service: The Library of Congress: Washington, DC, February 15, 2007.

Blair, Tony, A battle for global values, *Foreign Affairs*, **86**: 1, January–February 2007.

Bodansky, Yossef. *Bin Laden: The Man Who Declared War on America*, Prima: Roseville, CA, 2001.

Byman, Daniel. Israel and the Lebanese Hezbollah, in Art, Robert J. and Richardson, Louise (Eds.), *Democracy and Counterterrorism: Lessons From the Past*, United States Institute of Peace: Washington, DC, 2007.

Clarke, Richard A., *Against All Enemies: Inside America's War on Terror*, The Free Press: New York, 2004.

Commission on the Intelligence Capabilities of the United States Regarding Weapons of Mass Destruction, The, Report to the President of the United States, March 31, 2005.

Cooper, Jeffrey, R., *Curing Analytic Pathologies: Pathways to Improved Intelligence*, Center for the Study of Intelligence, Central Intelligence Agency, Government Printing Office: Pittsburgh, PA, December, 2005.

Cordesman, Anthony E., *Terrorism, Asymmetric Warfare, and Weapons of Mass Destruction: Defending the U.S. Homeland*, Praeger: Westport, CT, 2002.

Crumpton, Henry A., Intelligence and homeland defense, in Sims, Jennifer E. and Gerber, Burton (Eds.), *Transforming U.S. Intelligence*, Georgetown University Press: Washington, DC, 2005.

Diamond, Jared, *Collapse: How Societies Choose to Fail or Succeed*. Penguin: New York, 2005.

Dupont, Daniel G., Nuclear explosions in orbit, *Scientific American*, **290**: 6, June, 2004.

Ervin, Clark Kent, *Open Target: Where America Is Vulnerable to Attack*, Macmillan: New York, 2006.

Evans, Mike, *The Final Move Beyond Iraq: The Final Solution While the World Sleeps*, Front Line: Lake Mary, FL, 2007.

Evolution of the U.S. Intelligence Community: An Historical Overview, July 2004, HTTP://www.gpo.gov/int/int022.html.

Executive Office of the President, Office of Science and Technology Policy, Department of Homeland Security, Science and Technology Directorate, *The National Plan for Research and Development in Support of Critical Infrastructure Protection*, White House, Washington, DC, 2004.

Flynn, Stephen, *The Edge of Disaster: Rebuilding a Resilient Nation*, Random House: New York, in cooperation with the Council on Foreign Relations, 2007.

Flynn, Stephen, *America the Vulnerable: How Our Government Is Failing to Protect Us from Terrorism*. HarperCollins: New York, in cooperation with the Council on Foreign Relations, 2004.

Freeh, Louis J., *My FBI: Bringing Down the Mafia, Investigating Bill Clinton, and Fighting the War on Terror*, St. Martins Press: New York, 2005.

Friedman, Thomas L., *The World is Flat: A Brief History of the Twenty First Century*. Farrar, Straus and Giroux: New York, 2005.

Friedman, Thomas L., *Longitudes and Attitudes: The World in the Age of Terrorism*. Anchor Books: New York, 2003.

Gerges, Fawaz A., *Journey of the Jihadist: Inside Muslim Militancy*, Harcourt: Orlando, FL, 2007.

Gill, Bates and Kleiber, Martin, China's space odyssey: What the anti-satellite test reveals about decision making in Beijing, *Foreign Affairs*, **86**: 3, May–June, 2007.

Gordon, Philip H., Can the war on terror be won?: How to fight the right war, *Foreign Affairs*, **86**: 6, November–December 2007.

Greenwood, M.R.C. Research Universities in the Post-September 11 Era, *Science and Technology in a Vulnerable World*, Supplement to the *AAAS Science and Technology Policy Yearbook 2003*, Washington, DC: 2002.

Hagel, Chuck, A Republican foreign policy, *Foreign Affairs*, **83**: 4, July–August 2004.

Harmon, Christopher C., *Terrorism Today*, Frank Cass: London, 2000.

Hersh, Seymour M., Annals of national security: The Iran plans, *The New Yorker*, April 17, 2006.

Hoge, James F., Jr., A global power shift in the making: Is the United States ready? *Foreign Affairs*, **83**: 4, July–August, 2004.

Huntington, Samuel P., The clash of civilizations? *Foreign Affairs*, **72**: 3, Summer 1993.

Inderfuth, Karl F. and Johnson, Lock K., *Fateful Decisions: Inside the National Security Council*, Oxford University Press: New York, 2004.

Johnson, Thomas A., National security issues in science, law and technology, in Simon Kenyon (Ed.) *Agroterrorism*, Taylor & Francis: Boca Raton, FL, 2007a.

Johnson, Thomas A., National security issues in science, law and technology, in Michael Allswede, *Medical Response to Chemical and Biological Terrorism*, Taylor & Francis: Boca Raton, FL, 2007b.

Johnson, Thomas A., An introduction to the intelligence process for addressing national security threats and vulnerabilities, in *National Security Issues in Science, Law and Technology*, Taylor & Francis: Boca Raton, FL, 2007c.

Kaiser, Frederick M., Congressional oversight of intelligence: Current structure and alternatives, *CRS Report for Congress*, Congressional Research Service, February 15, 2007.

Kenyon, Simon, Agroterrorism, in Thomas A. Johnson (Ed.), *National Security Issues in Science, Law and Technology*, Taylor & Francis: Boca Raton, FL, 2007.

Kotkin, Joel, *The City: A Global History*, Random House: New York, 2005.

Lampton, David M., The faces of Chinese power, *Foreign Affairs*, **86**: 1, January–February, 2007.

Leacacos, John, P., Kissinger's apparat, in Inderfurth, Karl F. and Johnson, Loch, K. (Eds.), *Fateful Decisions: Inside the National Security Council*, Oxford University Press: New York, 2004.

Lowenthal, Mark M., *Intelligence: From Secrets to Policy*, 3rd ed., Congressional Quarterly Press: Washington, DC, 2006.

MacIver, Robert M., *Power Transformed: The Age-Slow Deliverance of the Folk and Now the Potential Deliverance of the Nations from the Rule of Force*. MacMillan: New York, 1964.

McAuliffe, Mary S. (Ed.), *CIA Documents on the Cuban Missile Crisis 1962*, These documents have been declassified and approved for release through the Historical Review Program of the Central Intelligence Agency, September 16, 1992, HRP: 92-9; *National Intelligence Estimate Number 85-2-62, The Situation and Prospects in Cuba*, August 1, 1962, excerpts pp. 9–12; Central Intelligence Agency, 1992. Also included, *National Intelligence Estimate Number 85-3-62, The Military Buildup in Cuba*, September 19, 1962; *Joint Evaluation of Soviet Missile Threat in Cuba*, October 19, 1962; and President's Foreign Intelligence Advisory Board, Memorandum for the President and Report, February 4, 1963; Central Intelligence Agency, 1992.

McConnell, Mike, Overhauling Intelligence, *Foreign Affairs*, **86**: 4, July–August, 2007.

Miller, Judith, Engelberg, Stephen, and Broad, William, *Germs: Biological Weapons and America's Secret War*, Simon & Schuster: New York, 2002.

National Commission on Terrorist Attacks Upon the United States, *The 9/11 Commission Report: Authorized Editor*, W.W. Norton: New York, 2004.

National Intelligence Council, *National Intelligence Estimate on Iran: Nuclear Intentions and Capabilities*, unclassified portions of report, November 2007.

National Intelligence Council, *National Intelligence Estimate, Trends in Global Terrorism: Implications for the United States*, Key Judgments, April 2006, declassified, Director National Intelligence Office, 2006.

National Intelligence Council, *Mapping the Global Future*, Report of the National Intelligence Council 2020 Project, NIC 2004-13, National Intelligence Council: Washington, DC, 2004a.

National Intelligence Council, *Annual Report to Congress on the Safety and Security of Russian Nuclear Facilities and Military Forces*, Prepared by the National Intelligence Officer for Weapons of Mass Destruction and Proliferation, unclassified report, December 2004b.

National Intelligence Council, *Global Trends 2015: A Dialogue About the Future with Non-Government Experts*, NIC 2000-02, Approved for publication by the National Intelligence Board, under the authority of the Director of Central Intelligence, December 2000.

National Research Council, *Making the Nation Safer: The Role of Science and Technology in Countering Terrorism*, National Academy Press: Washington, DC, 2002.

National Research Council of the National Academies, *Making the Nation Safer: The Role of Science and Technology in Countering Terrorism*, National Academy Press: Washington, DC, 2003.

National Strategy for the Physical Protection of Critical Infrastructure and Key Assets, White House, Washington, DC, 2003.

Neuman, Peter R., Negotiating with terrorists, *Foreign Affairs*, **86**: 1, January–February, 2007.

Office of the Director of National Intelligence, *An Overview of the United States Intelligence Community: A Report*, U.S. Government, January 2007.

Perrow, Charles, *The Next Catastrophe: Reducing Our Vulnerabilities to Natural, Industrial and Terrorist Disasters.* Princeton University Press: Princeton, NJ, 2007.

Pillar, Paul R., *Terrorism and U.S. Foreign Policy*, Brookings Institution Press: Washington, DC, 2001.

Podhoretz, Norman, *World War IV: The Long Struggle Against Islamic Fascism*, Doubleday: New York, 2007.

Posner, Richard A., *Uncertain Shield: The U.S. Intelligence System in the Throes of Reform*, Rowman & Littlefield, in cooperation with Hoover Institution, Stanford University: New York, 2006.

Rees, Martin, *Our Final Hour: A Scientists Warning: How Terror, Error and Environmental Disaster Threaten Humankinds Future in this Century—On Earth and Beyond.* Basic Books: New York, 2003.

Report of a Committee of Privy Counsellors, Lord Butler, Chairman, *Review of Intelligence on Weapons of Mass Destruction*, House of Commons, London: The Stationery Office, 2004.

Richardson, Louise, *Understanding the Enemy: What Terrorists Want: Containing the Threat*, Random House: New York, 2006.

Risen, James, *State of War: The Secret History of the CIA and the Bush Administration*, Free Press: New York, 2006.

Sageman, Marc, *Understanding Terror Networks*, University of Pennsylvania Press: Philadelphia, 2004.

Samii, Abbas William, The Iranian nuclear issue and informal networks, *Naval War College Review*, **59**: 1, Winter 2006.

Sims, Jennifer, E., Understanding friends and enemies: The context for American intelligence reform, in Jennifer E. Sims and Burton Gerber (Eds.), *Transforming U.S. Intelligence*, Georgetown University Press: Washington, DC, 2005.

Skolnikoff, Eugene B., Research universities and national security, *Science and Technology in a Vulnerable World*, Supplement to the AAAS Science and Technology Policy Yearbook 2003, Washington, DC: 2002.

Snider, L. Brett, Congressional oversight of intelligence after September 11, in Jennifer E. Sims and Burton Gerber (Eds.), *Transforming U.S. Intelligence*, Georgetown University Press: Washington, DC, 2005.

Stern, Jessica, *Terror in the Name of God: Why Religious Militants Kill*, HarperCollins: New York, 2003.

Stern, Jessica, *The Ultimate Terrorists*, Harvard University Press: Cambridge, MA, 1999.

Suskind, Ron, *The One Percent Doctrine: Deep Inside America's Pursuit of its Enemies Since 9/11*, Simon & Schuster: New York, 2006.

Swaine, Michael D., Trouble in Taiwan, *Foreign Affairs*, **83**: 2, March–April, 2004.

Tenet, George with Harlow, Bill, *At the Center of the Storm: My Years at the CIA*. HarperCollins: New York, 2007.

Treverton, Gregory F., Balancing security and liberty in the war on terror, in Campbell Public Affairs Institute and the Institute for National Security and Counterterrorism, *Information Sharing and Homeland Security*, Syracuse University: New York, 2004.

Tucker, Robert W., and Hendrickson, David C., The sources of American legitimacy, *Foreign Affairs*, **83**: 6, November–December 2004.

United States Intelligence Community, *Deputy Secretary of Defense Memorandum on Implementation Guidance on Restructuring Defense Intelligence and Related Matters (Excerpt)*, May 8, 2003.

Wright, Lawrence, *The Looming Tower: Al Qaeda and the Road to 9/11*, Alfred A. Knopf: New York, 2006.

York, David, Illicit trafficking in nuclear and radiological materials, in Thomas A. Johnson (Ed.), *National Security Issues in Science, Law and Technology*, Taylor & Francis: Boca Raton, FL, 2007.

Index

C

E

F

G

H

I

J

K

O

P

Q

R

S

T

U

V

W

Y

Z